Music Management, Marketing and PR

Sara Miller McCune founded SAGE Publishing in 1965 to support the dissemination of usable knowledge and educate a global community. SAGE publishes more than 1000 journals and over 800 new books each year, spanning a wide range of subject areas. Our growing selection of library products includes archives, data, case studies and video. SAGE remains majority owned by our founder and after her lifetime will become owned by a charitable trust that secures the company's continued independence.

Los Angeles | London | New Delhi | Singapore | Washington DC | Melbourne

Music Management, Marketing and PR

Chris Anderton, James Hannam
and Johnny Hopkins

Los Angeles | London | New Delhi
Singapore | Washington DC | Melbourne

Los Angeles I London I New Delhi
Singapore I Washington DC I Melbourne

SAGE Publications Ltd
1 Oliver's Yard
55 City Road
London EC1Y 1SP

SAGE Publications Inc.
2455 Teller Road
Thousand Oaks, California 91320

SAGE Publications India Pvt Ltd
B 1/I 1 Mohan Cooperative Industrial Area
Mathura Road
New Delhi 110 044

SAGE Publications Asia-Pacific Pte Ltd
3 Church Street
#10-04 Samsung Hub
Singapore 049483

Editor: Michael Ainsley
Production editor: Rachel Burrows
Cover design: Jennifer Crisp
Typeset by: KnowledgeWorks Global Ltd.
Printed in the UK

Library of Congress Control Number: 2021944612

British Library Cataloguing in Publication data

A catalogue record for this book is available from the British Library

ISBN 978-1-5264-9739-0
ISBN 978-1-5264-9738-3 (pbk)

At SAGE we take sustainability seriously. Most of our products are printed in the UK using responsibly sourced papers and boards. When we print overseas we ensure sustainable papers are used as measured by the PREPS grading system. We undertake an annual audit to monitor our sustainability.

CONTENTS

LIST OF BOXES, TABLES AND FIGURES

LIST OF BOXES

LIST OF TABLES

LIST OF FIGURES

ABOUT THE AUTHORS

Chris Anderton

Dr Chris Anderton is Associate Professor in Cultural Economy at Solent University, Southampton, UK. His research interests focus on the music industries, music culture, and music history. He is author or co-editor of several books including *Understanding the Music Industries* (2013), *Music Festivals in the UK: Beyond the Carnivalesque* (2019), *Media Narratives in Popular Music* (2022) and *Researching Live Music: Gigs, Tours, Concerts and Festivals* (2022). He has also guest edited issues of the academic journals *Rock Music Studies* and *Arts & the Market*, and published in numerous other edited collections and journals.

James Hannam

James Hannam is a Senior Lecturer at Solent University, Southampton, UK, where he is also Course Leader for the Music Business degree. His research interests within music include funding, publishing and education. James was previously a Senior Manager at PRS Foundation, an organisation that supports emerging artists and music companies. James also achieved success as a musician, providing official remixes for several Top 40 singles. His music has been broadcast on BBC Radio 1, Classic FM, BBC 1 and Channel 4. James has worked on partnership projects with the BBC Performing Arts Fund, British Council, Glastonbury Festival, MOBO and several other UK universities. His contribution to the music industry has been recognised by the Royal Society of the Arts, who invited him to become a fellow in 2014.

Johnny Hopkins

Johnny Hopkins is a Senior Lecturer in Music & Media Industries at Solent University and a PR director. The focus of his PhD (Cultural Studies at University of Sussex) is national identity, nationalism and the uses of the Union Jack in pop music. He has published research on: Elvis Presley; William Eggleston; The Who, Swinging London and the rebranding of post-colonial Britain; and Velvet Underground (with Martin James). Other research interests include: John and Alice Coltrane; music photography; representation of Native Americans in popular music; and popular music and the fight for Native American civil rights. With over 30 years' music industry experience as a PR, live promoter and DJ, he was Head of Press at Creation Records and has worked with Oasis, Sinead O'Connor, Kasabian, Lee 'Scratch' Perry, Graham Coxon, Billy Childish, Adrian Sherwood, Primal Scream and The Jesus & Mary Chain.

ACKNOWLEDGEMENTS

The authors would like to thank the music industries personnel interviewed and consulted for this book: Natalie Wade, Ellie Giles, Marc Brown, Chloe Walsh, Tom Sheehan, Lois Wilson, Sophie Labrey, Jamie Woolgar, Cerne Canning, Murray Curnow, Bill Acharjee and Jo Howarth. We would also like to thank the Music Business degree students and staff at Solent University, Michael Ainsley and the team at SAGE, and all of our families for their encouragement and support.

1

INDUSTRY OVERVIEW AND THEORETICAL APPROACHES

SUMMARY

This chapter provides an overview of the music industries in terms of its key sectors and institutions. We discuss key theories that are used for studying the music industries and introduce our own relationship approach to their study. This approach is rooted in theories of the cultural economy and highlights the importance of connectivity and conversation. The chapter concludes with an overview of the structure of the book.

Chapter objectives

- To provide an overview of the key sectors and institutions of the contemporary music industries.
- To discuss theories of political economy, music ecologies and cultural economy.
- To introduce our relationship approach to studying the music industries.

This chapter introduces the book and provides an overview of the music industries and key businesses which operate at a global level, followed by discussion of various theoretical approaches to their study. We then present our relationship approach to the study of the music industries – one that is rooted in notions of connectivity and conversation. Finally, we conclude with a brief overview of the content and structure of the book as a whole. The book is intended for musicians, students and others who are interested in pursuing a career within a creative, exciting and often high-paced industry, but it is not presented as a 'how-to' guide. Such guides are commonly available on the internet, yet rarely allow readers to gain a deeper understanding of the complexity of the business or its issues. They often act as marketing materials for companies offering music-related services, or are told from very specific points of view. Instead, our aim is to provide readers with an understanding of that complexity and to encourage them to think for themselves about how the industries work.

This book was largely written during the Covid-19 coronavirus pandemic that swept the world during 2020–21. This had profound consequences for the live music sector, shuttering most venues for months on end and creating financial hardship not only for venues and performers, but for the network of support personnel reliant upon it. At the same time, there was a boom in online streaming that was highly beneficial to record companies and streaming platforms. There was also an acceleration in other online trends, such as livestreaming, virtual reality apps and new ways to engage directly with fans and audiences. We address such developments in this book, yet we do not dwell specifically on them. Instead, our main focus is on the structures, relationships and strategies that underpin the various elements of the music industries and which will continue to be present as the lockdowns and restrictions are eased. Furthermore, we examine more broadly how the political, economic, social and cultural landscapes of the twenty-first-century music industries have fundamentally altered (above and beyond Covid) and how key institutions have responded to such changes. Examples include adaptations related to copyright law and digital services, to DIY artists and label services, to the survival of grassroots venues, and to the growth and use of data and algorithms in the online music market.

OVERVIEW OF THE MUSIC INDUSTRIES

In this section we briefly examine the macro-level structure of the music industries in relation to three main sectors: recording, publishing and live music. More detailed discussion of various music industry functions, from artist development through to revenue collection and funding, will be covered in later chapters. Each of the three main sectors discussed below – recording, publishing and live music – can be referred to as oligopolistic markets, which means that a small core of large companies dominates global market share. The same is also true of online streaming where, according to MIDiA Research, the top four companies accounted for nearly three-quarters of the subscription market in the first three months of 2021: Spotify (32 percent), Apple Music (16 percent), Amazon Music (13 percent) and Tencent Music (13 percent). In fifth place was Google's YouTube Music, whose subscriber figures grew by 60 percent in 2020 (cited in Mulligan, 2021a). These companies, like those operating in the radio, television and film sectors, are not typically deemed to be a core part of the music industries. Nevertheless, they play a significant role in the promotion and distribution of music and will, therefore, be discussed throughout this book.

In the recorded music and music publishing sectors the dominant companies are referred to as the 'majors'. According to the music industry research blog *Music & Copyright* (2021), Universal Music Group held a 32.1 percent market share for recorded music in 2020, followed by Sony Music Entertainment (20.6 percent) and Warner Music Group (15.9 percent). On a global level, the overall revenue achieved by the recorded music sector fell from 2001 to 2014, but consistent year on year growth has been seen since that time as online streaming has become mainstream (IFPI, 2021). Revenues from physical products continue to fall, yet the vinyl format has seen modest growth, representing perhaps a perception of authenticity and value that is lost in digital formats. *Music & Copyright* (2021) further reported that, in 2020, the principal companies in music publishing were Sony Music Publishing (24.5 percent), Universal Music Publishing Group (23 percent) and Warner Chappell Music (11.2 percent). Each of these major publishing companies is directly linked to their namesake companies in the recorded music sector, with Sony achieving first position because of its 2018 acquisition of a majority share in EMI Music Publishing. It is notable that a significant share of the market in recorded music and music publishing is comprised of 'independents': companies that have no direct financial relationships to a major company or who are not majority-owned by one (though they may in some cases be financially supported by them or make use of their services).

In both recording and publishing, the independent sector collectively achieves a greater market share than the largest of the majors – 31.4 percent in 2020 for recording and 41.3 percent for publishing (Music & Copyright, 2021). However, the sector comprises thousands of individual companies and artists, hence their revenues and market power are considerably weaker. Within the independent sector we can distinguish between companies that sign artists to recording contracts, artists who trade directly with the public or through online distributors without a recording contract, and artists who are signed to 'label services' deals. Label services deals allow artists to retain ownership of their own copyrights (unlike a traditional recording contract), while paying for the marketing, promotion, distribution and other services and expertise provided by a record label or label services specialist. This means that the artist continues to be classified as independent, despite the support that they may be receiving from a major record company. Such deals have become increasingly common, especially for artists who were formerly signed to record companies and for those artists who can afford the initial expenses involved in recording their music themselves. In turn, this may mean that the balance of power is tilting more towards artists, with the artist–record company relationship becoming more akin to a joint venture or collaboration in some circumstances. Furthermore, it is now easier than ever before for an artist to independently record, release and distribute their music to the public, but a downside of this reduction to the barriers of entry is that there is now an overabundance of new (and old) music being distributed through online streaming sites, with tens of thousands of tracks being added each week.

Making a meaningful connection with potential listeners, and a sustainable financial return on releases, is increasingly difficult in such a crowded market, with many artists choosing to focus on live performance as, prior to the coronavirus pandemic, it provided a more reliable source of income (Mortimer et al., 2012). One of the key drivers in live music has been the growth of the music festival sector, with the overall number of outdoor events doubling in the UK between 2005 and 2011 (Anderton, 2019a: 38), and continued growth in global terms since that time. In the US, European-style multi-day camping festivals made a return in the 2000s (having largely died out after their late 1960s/early 1970s heyday), with Coachella inspiring the creation of many more such events (Waksman, 2010: 9). According to a report by the ticketing agency StubHub, the world's top 50 events saw significant expansion in their attendance figures during the 2000s, with electronic dance music (EDM) events having the fastest growth rates (StubHub, 2019). The so-called 'boutique festival' sector also grew during this time – smaller-scale events that are less reliant on headliners to drive ticket sales, and which may be seen as cost-effective family holidays (Robinson, 2015a, 2015b; Anderton, 2019a). Indeed, the traditional headliner-driven camping festival became a much more difficult business proposition during the 2010s, with several large-scale British events closing down, including V Festival, Wakestock, Sonisphere, T in the Park and Bestival (AIF, 2018; Anderton, 2019b). A countertrend has offset these losses: the growth in city centre-based outdoor events presented in the format of day-long concerts without camping. Examples from the UK include the BST Hyde Park festival in London and the TRNSMT Festival in Glasgow. Beyond the UK, music festivals also grew in popularity and numbers during the 2000s, with events held on every continent, and proving significant in terms of incoming tourist revenues (Cormany, 2015; Festival Insights, 2018).

The total revenues attributed to the live music sector in the UK were first reported to exceed those of the recorded music sector in 2008 (Page and Carey, 2009), with the gap continuing to grow since that time (UK Music, 2015, 2018a). A similar pattern has also been seen in the US, while various studies have shown how ticket price rises for arena shows worldwide have consistently exceeded inflation levels since the 1980s (Brennan and Webster, 2010; Holt, 2010; Westgate, 2019), thus driving significant revenue growth for arena-level artists. In 2019, Pollstar reported that the global live music market was dominated by just two companies: Live Nation and AEG Presents. Live Nation was the market leader, selling 46.6 million tickets valued at $3.8 billion. In comparison AEG Presents sold 14.8 million tickets valued at $1.4 billion. No other promoters came close to achieving such sales figures, though the launch of a new company, Eventim Live, in March 2019 may lead to future competition. It was created by the German company CTS Eventim, which brought together 26 European promoters (including 27 festivals) into a single company structure. The venture forges a promoter network that allows booking agents to deal with a single contact at Eventim Live, and to route entire tours throughout Europe without needing to negotiate with multiple companies (Chapple, 2019). 2020 figures from Pollstar are skewed by the coronavirus lockdown, but showed that Eventim Live sold more tickets than AEG Presents that year. The shuttering of live music venues and festivals for much of 2020–21 led to severe hardship for artists, promoters and venue owners (Anderton, 2022), with accountancy firm PricewaterhouseCoopers (PwC) reporting lost ticket and sponsorship revenue of $18 billion (cited by *IQ-Mag*, 2020). However, the same report suggested that once the disruption of the pandemic was over, the live sector would continue to grow year on year above its pre-pandemic levels.

POLITICAL ECONOMY

Music businesses and institutions exist within political and economic frameworks at a local, national and international level. Such frameworks guide how those businesses and institutions operate on a day-to-day basis. Academic work in political economy focuses on how government policies and market forces affect individuals, societies and companies. For instance, the global music industries typically operate within a capitalist free-market framework, but Western companies seeking to work in China must adapt their models to meet

Chinese regulations. As a result, the major record labels licensed their catalogues to Tencent which previously held an exclusive right to sub-license to the many music and social networks within China. As a result, Western companies lost an element of control over their catalogues in the country. However, the situation changed in 2021 when the Chinese State Administration for Market Regulation ordered Tencent to relinquish its exclusive rights as part of a crackdown on the power of its domestic technology firms (Tan, 2021). Academic work within the political economy tradition tends to focus not only on how these broad frameworks influence developments and structures within the music industries, but also on how music industry companies and trade bodies have sought to exert their influence over state policies to enhance their own economic interests. Moreover, by examining how different businesses operate within these frameworks, we are able to reveal more clearly the inequalities present within existing systems. This process shows how unequal power relations affect the opportunities available to artists, and how revenues are managed and split between different companies. An example of the latter is the introduction of the Music Modernization Act, signed into US law in 2018. The aim of this legislation was to update US copyright law in line with changes in digital distribution. One major outcome was the creation of the Mechanical Licensing Collective (MLC) to help songwriters and publishers receive revenue from streaming and download services in a more accurate and timely fashion than in the past. In early 2021 the streaming services paid over $424 million in historical unmatched royalties to the MLC, including $163 million from Apple Inc. and $152 million from Spotify. The MLC will now work with the usage data provided by the services to pay copyright owners (MLC, 2021). However, another element of the legislation, the Fair Play Fair Pay Act, failed to become law. If passed, it would have allowed recorded music artists to receive performance royalties when their songs were played on terrestrial radio in the US. It would appear that US radio representatives successfully lobbied to remove this legislation and to retain the past arrangement whereby radio broadcasters would only pay songwriters and publishers. In justification they argued, as they had in the past, that radio play is essentially a promotional activity, with radio play driving sales of an artist's music.

The fate of the Fair Play Fair Pay Act raises an important point: that narratives are created to help convince policy makers that certain actions need to be taken, and that those organisations in positions of power and influence are best placed to guide the narratives that benefit them the most. A further example relates to how the recorded music industry seeks to justify the strengthening and lengthening of copyright protection by invoking ideas about success ratios, music piracy and the 'value gap'. Success ratios are invoked to describe the risk-taking position of record companies: that in the process of pushing boundaries and supporting new artists, there is a high likelihood of failure, therefore record companies need to protect their assets in order to be viable in the long term. Success rates quoted in music industry literature vary somewhat, with Willard Ahdritz of AWAL suggesting in 2018 that 'record labels were always like *The Hunger Games*: 20 artists go in but only one star comes out' (quoted in Ingham, 2018). His ratio is especially low, and reflects his own narrative of the time in encouraging artists to sign with what was then an independent company rather than with a major label. Richard Osborne's (2021) comprehensive review of the literature suggests that a ratio of one in 10 is common, and that music industry personnel employ it to justify why so few artists achieve long-term success. He also notes (as does Marshall, 2013) that it helps to reinforce the notion of a star system in which high investment is given to a handful of artists at the expense of others on a record label's roster. The justification here is that the star artists make so much money that they offset the losses made by the rest. Success ratios are also used in this rhetorical fashion to lobby governments to strengthen copyright law and address music piracy, yet there is typically no evidence to fully support the claims made, nor much discussion of how these success ratios were calculated. At what point is an artist declared to be a success? Is it when they fully recoup their advances from their royalty income (perhaps 12–20 percent of revenue attributable to their releases)? When the debt incurred by the record label is repaid from the record company's share of the revenue (typically more than 80 percent)? Or when they have achieved a number 1 album or a gold certification for sales?

The one in 10 statistic has become industry lore in much the same way that music piracy statistics have been used to explain the rapid fall in global revenues seen in the recorded music sector during the 2000s. By blaming music piracy, record industry bodies were able to push governments to take stronger action, and the narrative that every download or illegal stream represented a lost sale allowed the industry to argue they had lost millions of dollars of potential revenue – a strong lobbying position. By focusing on piracy, other factors that led to the decline could be ignored, such as the saturation of the re-release CD market, increased competition from other leisure sectors, such as DVD and computer gaming, and the failure of the industry to successfully adapt to the introduction of the mp3 format. Instead, high-profile legal cases were brought in the US against peer-to-peer (P2P) networks and users, followed by lobbying to enhance domestic legislation and propose international treaties to tackle internet piracy sites based outside the US. By the mid-2000s, the major record companies realised that they had to embrace digital downloads, leading to licensing deals with Apple's iTunes and then many hundreds of other platforms. Attention has now turned to streaming platforms, arguing that they do not pay fairly for the music content that they use, and that YouTube in particular is underpaying in comparison to the others. This new narrative has had some success in Europe, but has yet to have effect in the US, where the lobbying activities of the major technology companies, such as Apple, Amazon and Google, are much stronger (see Chapter 7).

THE ECOLOGICAL APPROACH

In 2007, Williamson and Cloonan argued that the term 'the music industry' was often confused with the term 'recording industry' – a rhetorical device employed by record industry organisations to help in their lobbying efforts with governments. In so doing, other parts of the music industries were side-lined, including music publishing and the live sector. More recently, recognition of the variety of businesses involved in making and distributing music has led organisations such as UK Music to redefine their approach. For instance, UK Music's *Music By Numbers* report (UK Music, 2020a) not only refers to recording, publishing and live music (as in prior reports), but to three other 'core' sectors: 'music creators' (songwriters, performers, producers and engineers), 'music representatives' (artist managers, lawyers, accountants, trade bodies and copyright administration) and 'music retail' (physical and digital sales of recorded music, including streaming subscriptions, and the manufacture and sale of musical instruments). In justifying these six sectors, they refer to first- and second-order activities that create 'commercial assets' in music: i.e. those which generate revenue. Primary activities include the creative process of composing, performing and recording music, while secondary activities relate to bringing 'these assets to a position where they are able to be distributed and transacted with consumers and businesses in one way or another' (UK Music, 2020a: 8). Interestingly, retailers of equipment used for recording and for live performance (such as DAWs (Digital Audio Workstations), amplifiers, microphones, effects pedals and so on) are excluded from 'music retail', as are aspects related to marketing and public relations (including campaign planning, playlisting and plugging) and media production (such as website design, social media content and music video production). Yet, these areas are often crucial to the success of an artist beyond simply the quality of the music itself, as shown in later chapters of this book.

It has now become commonplace in academia, business and state policy to refer to the music industries as an 'ecology' (Behr et al., 2016): to explicitly acknowledge the various organisations and people involved in making music available to the public. Behr et al.'s (2016) work examined live music venues in Glasgow to explore the usefulness of the ecological framework, and found that it was useful for recognising the interdependence of the various organisations and people involved. It also allowed them to examine the physical properties and meanings of music venues and to think about issues of market sustainability – how the ecology had changed over time, and how it might continue to exist and thrive in the future. Similar findings have also been found in relation to music festivals. Here, the interaction between particular spaces/places, audiences, promoters, the media and various other stakeholders helps to create and annually recreate festivals, and to foster the special festival 'atmosphere' that is so prized by festivalgoers (Anderton, 2019a). We would argue that such ecological thinking can be applied in many more ways across the music industries as a whole – that there are multiple and interlocking ecologies at play. The distinctions between recorded music, music publishing and live music are, for example, somewhat artificial, and the interconnectedness of these sectors needs to be considered, as well as those people within the music industries that operate across them. This is, in part, why we have focused on the management, marketing and public relations functions within this book, alongside broader issues related to funding, copyright, online platforms, and health and well-being.

CULTURAL ECONOMY AND A RELATIONSHIP APPROACH TO STUDYING THE MUSIC INDUSTRIES

For us, what lies at the heart of an ecological approach to understanding the various sectors of the music industries is the importance of connectivity and conversation – of a relationship approach to the music industries that acknowledges that businesses thrive when different people and organisations work effectively with each other. This is as true of the business-to-business (B2B) relationships found between the different sectors as it is of business-to-fan (B2F) relationships that need to foster direct engagement in order to achieve success.

A relationship approach therefore expands on a cultural economy framework by bringing together the political economy approach discussed earlier with the 'production of culture' perspective associated with Richard A. Peterson (1976) and the 'cultures of production' perspective proposed by Keith Negus (1996, 1999). In each case, 'culture' is conceptualised as the shared beliefs and preferences of particular social groups, though this may be applied to both societies as a whole and to particular genres, industry sectors and workplaces. In the production of culture perspective, researchers focus on the effects of legal and regulatory frameworks (including copyright) and changes to organisational structures and technologies (such as the disruptions caused by peer-to-peer music piracy or the introduction of music streaming). They also examine how cultural producers seek to control the consumption of symbolic goods: in other words, those, such as music and music-related merchandising, that embody cultural meanings over and above their utilitarian use. The notion of control is particularly important as it involves a filtering process through which consumers are grouped together into 'markets' around which a company can focus production, marketing and sales. In the process they help to shape the market they have conceptualised. Good examples include the emergence of 'world music' as a sales category in the 1980s (Frith, 1996: 84–85) and the media's creation of the term 'Britpop' in the 1990s (Hopkins, 2022). In contrast, the 'cultures of production' perspective suggests that the music industries do not necessarily create music cultures, but instead exploit cultural practices and musical scenes that have emerged organically (whether locally based or through online means) by organising business activities around them. Furthermore, this perspective suggests that we should focus on how the internal culture of a business shapes the decisions and strategies of that business. In other words, that the cultural backgrounds, understandings and preferences of workers are also important (Negus, 1999). Moreover, culture isn't just produced by cultural businesses, but cultural businesses are themselves a product of internal work-based cultures that are influenced by broader cultural trends and beliefs.

There is, therefore, a cultural economy at play, with music companies changing over time and responding to both macro-level influences such as legislation, business trends, technological change, audience tastes and so on (which can be analysed through a production of culture or political economy approach), and micro-level influences drawn from local scenes and from the cultural beliefs and tastes of music industry personnel (the cultures of production approach). The cultural economy approach allows us to examine the different sides, and to recognise that music is produced and consumed within interconnected industries of businesses, personnel and ideas ranging from the local to the global level. By examining the institutions and practices of the music industries as cultural entities in this manner, we can contextualise how they operate rather than seeing them simply as economic producers and exploiters of culture.

In the cultural economy and relationship approach we are proposing, we see connectivity and conversation as key drivers for understanding how the music industries work, and for how artists, managers and others can best forge a career path through them – with the music manager as a central nexus around whom different parts of the music industries connect. Our notion of connectivity extends on that of Malcolm Gladwell (2000) to apply in a number of ways – from building a team around an artist, campaign or business to making connections between artists/businesses and audiences – and is broadly analogous with the concept of business networking. We argue that these B2B and business-to-consumer (B2C) networks need to be built and sustained in an active manner, forging long-term relationships that are mutually beneficial to all parties and allow new ideas and new connections to be fostered and pursued. A good example of this connectivity is how artists and managers dealt with the coronavirus pandemic by creating livestreaming opportunities and by launching companies that adapted to the new promotional and revenue routes that livestreaming generated. Artist managers were in the ideal position to do this because they regularly work with the different sectors involved (booking, venues, video production, streaming and so on).

The rise of social media applications and other platforms in the online economy has allowed artists and their teams to connect more directly with their fans and audiences than ever before, and to drive active and interactive conversations with them. This can help to develop casual listeners into engaged fans that actively seek updates about an artist, and then perhaps into 'superfans' who want to consume everything about an artist. Such superfans may themselves be important nodes of connectivity and conversation, creating personal networks that are of promotional benefit to the artist, and establishing a respected (and seemingly independent) reputation within particular scenes or fan communities as sources of insider or in-depth knowledge. They may run social media groups, blogs and websites that maintain conversation about an artist during times when that artist is relatively inactive, but can also be brought into grassroots marketing campaigns around new releases and tours, thus raising profile within the fan community that they have access to. In this sense they are, in Gladwell's (2000) terms, both 'connectors' and 'mavens', which are analogous to social media content creators and influencers. Yet superfans are also super-consumers, thus they can be an important and reliable source of revenue (a modern form of patronage) that can help niche artists fund their activities. Online platforms such as Bandcamp, SoundCloud, Patreon and FanCircles are good examples of sites where this form of activity has become commercialised, and where interaction between artists and fans is actively fostered.

The enhanced connectivity afforded by online platforms produces rich datasets of information. For example, the UK Music Managers Forum (MMF) published a report in 2019 detailing 10 different sources of data gathered both actively and passively from a range of online platforms that may be available to artists and their managers. However, it also noted that while some data is easily accessible (such as artist-controlled websites and social media accounts), it may be more difficult to access other sources (such as ticketing data and email information) due to data protection laws and the wording of contracts. The report suggests that artist managers should audit the platforms and partners they currently use to better understand the data they have access to, and it encourages future contract negotiations to include consideration of data access (MMF, 2019a: 20). Where available, this data can be used, among other things, to plan tours, target advertising, adapt marketing campaigns, and attract lucrative sponsorship and endorsement deals. Data from streaming services can also yield valuable information about the performance of tracks. Such data can include not only the total number of plays per track, but the total number of listeners, the source of the plays (playlists, artist pages), whether the track has been added to user playlists and libraries, and information about skips (how often a track is skipped and at what point within a track) (2019a: 11). Such information is valuable for future playlist plugging and for understanding whether and how particular tracks are being responded to by audiences on the streaming site – data that can inform ongoing artist development and release strategies. However, specific detail about listeners is often not available, making it difficult for artists and managers to target those listeners and convert them into fans who will engage with the artist across other platforms.

In tandem with such connectivity, we also stress the importance of the mutually beneficial conversations that permeate and drive forward the cultural industries on a daily basis. Since at least the 1500s, artistic and scientific societies have met to discuss noteworthy developments in informal settings, sometimes known as 'conversaziones' or 'salons'. The music world of today remains inherently social, with connections made, deals struck and jobs offered during conference events or nights out. The coronavirus lockdowns strongly demonstrated the human need for regular face-to-face conversation, as populations around the globe reported high levels of loneliness and isolation. But, as the pandemic was financially beneficial to many technology and record companies, so too did digital conversation platforms prosper amid an otherwise gloomy outlook for public health and the economy. Zoom, Clubhouse, Facetime and Teams became indispensable online tools for many, allowing regular online interactions with family, friends, educators and businesses. Homeworking also became the norm for many music industry personnel, offering both benefits (such as the opportunity to be based outside major cities) and challenges (a lack of human contact and camaraderie). Music companies must consider which innovations to retain and which to slowly discard. But the pandemic has demonstrated, above all else, a clear and deep human desire for connections and conversations – fires that will never be extinguished.

STRUCTURE OF THE BOOK

In this book, we focus particularly on the roles undertaken by artist and business managers (including self-managing artists) and those working in marketing and public relations (PR), though our scope is much broader, since these roles cross-cut different parts of the music industries ecology. As noted earlier, it is easier than ever before to make and distribute music through the internet, and most artists have an online presence of some variety; however, this does not guarantee that anyone is paying attention, listening or buying. It can also make it hard to navigate and understand the different organisations and structures that we find in the music industries, and the issues that they raise. Our aim is to cast light on these and to help readers make sense of them, while also encouraging an enquiring mindset that can help readers to keep up to date with future developments and identify opportunities for their own careers. Throughout the book we draw on a range of examples and sources from across the academic and industry literature together with insights from industry personnel.

In Chapter 2 we discuss how artist managers and self-managing artists need to build their contacts and assemble a team that can support their ongoing development, including lawyers, producers, accountants and so on. With so many individuals responsible for an artist's success, the chapter focuses on the essential interpersonal skills that a manager must develop, such as networking and delegation: the key ingredients of connectivity and conversation that lie at the heart of this book. Chapter 3 builds on this starting point by examining artist development strategies and the setting of career goals that may vary considerably from artist to artist. These will depend, for example, on their personal ambition, genre, career stage, commercial viability and attitude regarding intellectual property ownership. Do they ultimately seek an exclusive recording contract with an established company? Or would they be more comfortable with the DIY or label services route favoured by artists such as Chance the Rapper, Stormzy and others? The chapter also considers the often-challenging balancing act between creativity and commerce, in addition to an overview of the many individuals and organisations that influence A&R (artists and repertoire) and artist development processes.

Chapters 4, 5 and 6 then focus on how connections and engagement are forged between artists and their (potential) audiences. Chapter 4 looks at the early stages of the process when the artist's verbal and visual identity are becoming established. Consideration is given to how the artist can be presented to a potential audience and where that artist fits within current and emerging market trends. The roles of fans and audiences are also explored, as industry personnel must take their needs and expectations into account when developing their strategic plans. Chapter 5 focuses on marketing. In music, the marketing role treads the line between detailed planning, analytics and structure on the one hand, and instinct and creativity on the other, with the most effective campaigns incorporating all of these elements in a consistent manner across all platforms. New marketing models are discussed, and the importance of market research, planning and strategy asserted. In Chapter 6, attention turns to the public relations (PR) sector, including promotional roles such as plugging. Here we focus on how PR personnel instigate conversations with the media and the public, and how they shape opinions about music, musicians and events. The knowledge and contacts provided by PR staff are invaluable in the contemporary digital landscape. Hence, while artists will initially connect directly with their fans through social media, many will later employ a PR representative or company. These offer the expert skills required to develop meaningful strategies, to manage artist-to-fan and business-to-business relationships, and to craft stories, messages, and content that will be impactful.

The growth of media platforms, including crowdsourcing sites and streaming music services, is discussed in Chapter 7, together with the issues that these platforms raise in terms of revenue generation and promotion. We examine how Spotify, YouTube and the other major streaming platforms generate and distribute revenues to record companies and publishers, and discuss alternatives to their methods. We also discuss the role and operations of curated and automated music recommendation systems.

Chapter 8 turns attention to the live music sector, extending and exploring the metaphor of the live music ecology. We look at the value of the sector for artists, locations and audiences, explore the work of promoters, bookers and tour managers, and show how live music has been the subject of lobbying action by industry organisations in relation to grassroots venues and secondary ticketing. We also show how festivals have become important sites for raising socio-cultural issues such as drug use and environmental sustainability. Brand sponsorships have become increasingly important for both the live music sector and for artists and records labels. They form the focus of Chapter 9, which investigates the many and varied forms of sponsorship that are found within the music industries, from basic endorsement deals for individual artists and musicians through to brand-centric experiential areas created within festival sites. In the chapter we also introduce a cultural economy approach to thinking about artists as brands formed around the 'artist–brand matrix', and consider the issues that brand partnerships raise in terms of authenticity and 'brand fit'.

The next two chapters focus on two important aspects of the music industries that have yet to be discussed: (1) how revenue streams and funding are developed and maintained for artists, and (2) how artist managers and teams deal not only with financial matters, but with the well-being of the artists they work with. Chapter 10 discusses long-established sources of revenue, such as record sales, streaming, and performance and broadcast royalties, alongside other sources of income, such as merchandising, synchronisation, ticketing, product endorsements, VIP fan interactions, and other forms of entertainment or culture. We provide essential information about intellectual property and the royalty collection process, and consider the many options available for accessing music funding. Chapter 11 acknowledges the considerable pressures placed upon musicians by touring, recording schedules and media interviews, which are often exacerbated by the need to be creative in challenging and sometimes hectic circumstances. We look at some of the initiatives introduced by music industry organisations to help foster the well-being of both artists and their management teams, and discuss concepts designed to enhance time management and project implementation. Furthermore, we consider how networks of support are required to help music professionals and artists achieve a good working balance and a sustainable career. The chapter also reflects on how the music industries can be more diverse, inclusive and equitable for the benefit of all, with a particular focus on gender and ethnicity. It provides an in-depth discussion of current barriers to success and of initiatives established to help address them. The book then concludes (Chapter 12) by giving advice on how readers can extend their knowledge and keep up to date with music industry news and emerging trends. They may then continue to learn, to ask questions and to reflect on how the different parts of the music industries are developing and what it means for them in their own careers.

Key discussion points

- How will the relationship between the major and independent companies develop in the coming years?
- What issues are music industry organisations currently lobbying governments about, and how are they justifying their requests for action?
- At the local level of your own town or city, how is the music ecology structured, and what issues need to be addressed to make it healthier?
- Consider your own music industry networks. How can you enhance them through the notions of connectivity and conversation?

2

GETTING STARTED: BUILDING TEAMS AND UNDERSTANDING MANAGEMENT FUNCTIONS

SUMMARY

This chapter draws on social network theory to explore the music manager's pivotal role in creating working relationships and deals between the artists they manage and the many other sectors of the music and media industries. It also discusses the first steps towards a career in music management, building an understanding of company structures, artist management contracts, regulation and the likely participants of an artist's wider team.

Chapter objectives

- To explore how artists and managers can develop their careers through building interpersonal skills, a broad industry knowledge, and connections with others.
- To explore the many management styles and structures available to support artists during their careers.
- To consider the importance of building and managing a successful team around an artist.
- To analyse key contractual clauses in artist management contracts.

THE ARTIST MANAGER

The artist manager is a key figure who negotiates with individuals and companies in the music and media industries. Therefore, finding the right manager can significantly help both with industry relations and in obtaining funding. UK music funder PRS Foundation (PRSF, n.d.) notes that managers make a 'significant contribution' to the development and implementation of projects. Thus, from an industry perspective, a professional figurehead with a strong reputation is likely to be more appealing than corresponding with a band of five members with different email addresses. Indeed, music lawyer Andrew Thompson (2012: 12) states that record labels usually prefer to work with managers, as this setup provides further legitimacy to a music project: something which is also the case for live booking agencies (see Chapter 8). Working with a manager also relieves the administrative burden placed on an artist, allowing them to spend more of their time creating and performing music: few artists want to spend their time completing financial spreadsheets or arranging travel.

Managers develop and represent artists by finding, creating and developing strategic goals and opportunities, and by providing day-to-day support to ensure that things run smoothly and to plan (Anderton et al., 2013: 184–185). They must maintain an artist's confidence through any difficult periods and manage a variety of often highly pressured and stressful situations. A good manager therefore offers a sense of reassurance and stability for the artist, with music lawyer Donald Passman (2019: 33) describing the role as a 'buffer'. This involves taking enquiries on behalf of the artist from a variety of interested parties, representing and protecting the artist if things do not run smoothly, and providing mental health support to both artists and team members (MMF, 2019b: 21–23; see also Chapter 11). The UK Music Managers Forum (MMF) suggests that a contemporary music manager's role comprises six key areas: representation, strategic thinking, leadership, decision-making, organisation and implementation (MMF, 2017). As Michael Jones (2012: 91) suggests, artist management is the 'only position in the music industry which interacts with all other areas of activity' – a point reinforced by MMF chair Paul Craig, who argues that managers need to comprehend 'all facets of [an artist's] creative and commercial life' (MMF, 2019b: 2; see also Morrow, 2009). The role has become increasingly important in the twenty-first-century music business, since the role of artist development in particular (as discussed in more detail in Chapter 3) has shifted away from record companies to lie more directly with artist managers (Hracs, 2012; Hesmondhalgh, 2019).

Managers may be regarded as occupying the centre of a network of relationships. In social network theory they would be termed 'hubs' or 'connectors' (Barabási, 2002: 64) as they have numerous ties to other music and media industries personnel and organisations. The concept of connectivity within the music industries has previously been discussed by music industries scholar Patrik Wikström (2019: 6; see also Hracs, 2015; Lizé, 2016), who used it to measure 'how well the members of a network' were linked together, noting that highly-connected systems provide an ease of flow for finance, trends, ideas and information. It has also been used by the journalist Malcolm Gladwell (2000), who defined two types of social influencer: mavens and connectors. Mavens are tastemakers and opinion-leaders who have a respected knowledge of a field, while connectors are those who have access to a wide range of contacts. Artist managers may combine these into one, thus having 'more influence, access to information or prestige' (Borgatti et al., 2013: 166) within a network than other industry personnel. As a result, new opportunities and relationships may come more easily to established and successful managers. They are not just hubs or connectors, but what we might term 'attractors' within a network: people that others actively wish to work with. Expectations are therefore high; music managers are often expected, somewhat unreasonably, to know almost everything (and everyone) within the music industries. Yet this is highly dependent on their pre-existing experience and the depth and breadth of their ties within music and media industry networks.

Music lawyer Ann Harrison (2021: 46) lists the personal qualities for the manager role as diplomacy, business acumen, contractual knowledge, motivation, sales ability and patience, in addition to strong organisational and strategic abilities. A music manager's skillset should also ideally include networking, negotiation, delegation, time management and digital capabilities (such as data analysis and social media management). As the music industries consistently present subjective grey areas and challenging situations, managers are required to think on their feet while considering multiple potential solutions to issues and opportunities that arise. Thus, lateral thinking and creativity in decision-making are also important skills to develop, both in terms of business and of artistic endeavour. Such a demanding role requires additional support from fellow creatives, given the wide range of skills required. Therefore, music managers often build teams that provide the requisite expertise across all aspects of an artist's career.

This chapter examines management structures and typologies, before focusing on how managers and artists get started in creating the connections needed to find success. This is followed by a discussion of the roles and responsibilities of the team members that managers will typically work with. The final section explores the contractual terms that are commonly found in management contracts.

STRUCTURES, ROLES AND REGULATION

Sociologist Chris Rojek (2011: 152) builds on the work of Burns (1978) in proposing a general distinction between transactional and transformational management. Transactional managers plan strategically for the future, advise on contractual decisions and manage the day-to-day running of an artist's ongoing career, yet remain largely unknown to the general public. Transformational managers, on the other hand, may seek to share the limelight and present themselves as celebrities. Examples include Allen Klein (The Beatles), Peter Grant (Led Zeppelin) and Simon Napier-Bell (Wham!) (Rojek, 2011: 162–163). However, Rojek's binary and personality-based conceptualisation of the role obscures the many and varied ways in which current music managers operate.

Creative industries scholar Olivia Gable's (2019: 182) research in the UK (influenced by Hracs, 2015; Lizé, 2016) suggested a typology of managerial work that identifies four broad types: focused, comprehensive, combined and as-needed. 'Focused' refers to management companies which work with artists on the basis of standardised management contracts and are not, unlike the other three types, involved in broader activities. 'Comprehensive' refers to managers or management companies who also own record labels and release their clients' music, while 'combined' refers to companies that act as both record labels and artist managers, but who additionally release music from artists they do not themselves manage. Finally, 'as-needed' refers to independent record label owners who may undertake an *ad hoc* management role with the unsigned artists with whom they work, but who do not request a formal management contract with them. In this chapter, we propose a further type – the artist-as-manager – and distinguish between management companies on the basis of their management structure: something that depends in part on their size, ambition and roster (see Table 2.1). We also extend our understanding of artist management by defining different management types on the basis of the roles that they typically undertake (see Table 2.2).

Income for each team member within an artist management company (whether a small or a large firm) will take the form either of a salary, a commission percentage or a profit share, depending on each team member's position within the company and what they have negotiated in their employment contract. Some companies offer their managers office space and administrative support, though the individual remains officially self-employed: essentially each operates as a separate business under the 'umbrella' company. Management structures are highly dynamic and flexible, with the MMF stating that while individual manager duties have developed over recent years, 'this is not yet reflected in the organisational structure at [companies]' and 'that there is an ongoing evolution towards creating clear departments and responsibilities' (MMF, 2019b: 24). The MMF also notes that expertise from other businesses or individuals may be 'bought in' for specific short-term campaigns where the management company is required to scale-up for certain projects (2019b: 24–25). Some management companies will charge the artist an additional fee for any extra services or consultants that are bought in (known as the 'service on top' model), though this depends on the specific agreements or contracts that have been made with the artist (2019b: 25). We will return to artist contracts and commissions later in the chapter. The list of manager types and roles we have proposed in Table 2.2 is by no means exhaustive due to the continuing development of the sector, but it reflects the many roles that may currently be identified within management companies.

Anyone can be an artist manager – a situation which is in equal parts inspiring and concerning. The artist management sector lacks regulation, with managers voluntarily signing up to professional organisations as opposed to the compulsory certification demanded in many other professions. As a result, competence varies significantly and disagreements between artists and managers are common (particularly for younger or emerging artists who may be represented by inexperienced friends or family). In the UK, a manager's membership of the MMF, while not guaranteeing their influence or effectiveness, demonstrates an engagement with a trade body and a willingness to connect with others in the industry. The MMF also requires its members to agree to a code of practice (MMF, 2020), which outlines the essentials of professional behaviour and respectful conduct for the profession (also discouraging other unfair or ethically questionable practices). The overall intention is for managers to develop their clients' careers to their highest potential, though the code also helps to enhance the reputation of artist management as a sector – to counter the stereotypical presentation of music managers in film and television shows as 'unprincipled opportunists' (Anderton et al., 2013: 184). Such professional initiatives also provide a counterpoint to the historic examples of raucous behaviour, violence and intimidation that can be found in the biographies of some former managers (2013: 184).

Nevertheless, the lack of formal regulation means that questionable practices continue in some cases, with financial scams presenting the most noteworthy current risk to aspiring artists in the music industries. Research by the Musicians' Union (MU) in the UK found that

Table 2.1 Artist management company structures and their potential advantages and disadvantages

Management structure	Potential advantages	Potential disadvantages
Artist-as-manager	Retain creative and financial control If a band, roles can be shared between members	Time-consuming and stressful May not be taken as seriously by label or wider industries Contacts limited to artist's own network
Individual manager/sole trader	Close working relationship Manager may dedicate more time to the artist Fairly simple to manage own finances and tax A quicker decision-making process	High workload for an individual May lack the wide skillset which a larger company could provide Contacts limited to one person's network Potentially limited funds Held personally liable for debt, unlike a limited company
Small management company	Access to a greater number of specialist staff and skills Access to a wider range of contacts Benefit from links to other artists on the roster May offer other related music services If set up as limited company, restricted financial liability for the individuals involved	Less money available than larger management companies Potential for disagreements between partners Key person at the company may leave
Large management company	Established contacts across the music and media industries May offer other related music services Global reach and influence If set up as limited company, restricted financial liability for the individuals involved	A larger roster means that artists must ensure that they are prioritised Company may change ownership Potential for disagreements between partners Key person at the company may leave

such scams included promises of record deals, requests to play unpaid gigs (with claims that A&R personnel would be in attendance) and assurances of working with well-known artists (cited in Lynn and Greenwood, 2018). Other issues that aspiring artists need to be aware of are 'battle of the band'-style events where a fee is demanded for participation (Harrison, 2021: 15), and similar competition-based opportunities where the manager or promoter earns from entry fees rather than the value and revenue they produce for the artist. Furthermore, artist manager Steve Rennie (2016) warns that musicians should avoid anyone calling themselves a 'manager' who requests money upfront or a monthly fee that is unrelated to commission earned. If in doubt, artists should consult a specialist legal professional.

Table 2.2 Manager types and roles

Manager type	Role
Management assistant	Assists senior members of team. May link or overlap with a personal assistant role, occasionally supporting artists with issues outside their music careers.
Day-to-day artist manager	Adopts a more strategic overview of an artist's career development. May share some administrative tasks with management assistant.
Personal or senior artist manager	Takes strategic responsibility for an artist's development, maintaining relationships with key members of the artist's team.
Business manager	A role more common in the US, working alongside a personal manager to assist with financial planning. Outside the US, personal managers may take the role themselves or work with an accountant.
Co-management	Two management companies combining their strengths to develop an artist's career. Alternatively, two managers within a company may collaborate to ensure a wide skillset and larger contact base.
Salaried manager	Works on behalf of a well-known artist, being paid an agreed salary rather than taking a percentage of earnings. This option may not appeal to all managers, many of whom would prefer a percentage. Nevertheless, Rys (2016) reports that artists, including Bruno Mars, Taylor Swift and Beyoncé, have adopted this approach at some point during their careers.

GETTING STARTED: CREATING CONNECTIONS

Contacts are a hugely important resource in the music industries, and it may take several years for a manager to build a strong network; to become a 'hub' or 'connector' within the musical and/or geographical field in which they are active. This raises the question of how an aspiring manager might start to build such a network. Being courteous, efficient and knowledgeable will play a large part in developing a credible and reliable reputation. But there is far more an aspiring music business professional can do in terms of actively seeking contacts. An effective starting point is for them to become immersed in their local music scene (as an artist themselves or as a promoter or fan). This may involve attending shows, assisting at music venues or offering to help local artists with an aspect of their career development. An aspiring manager should get to know their local concert promoters, photographers, recording studios, radio DJs, journalists, videographers and any others whose work intersects with music. Participation in the local music scene means that a network will begin to develop organically, allowing relationships of trust to emerge.

Networking with music and media industries personnel can be somewhat daunting at first, but business consultant Simon Phillips (2014: 4) suggests that it is better considered as simply making new friends. As a network develops, stronger connections will begin to be made both in person and online. The music business is highly sociable, but this does not mean that success is limited to extroverts: despite media portrayals to the contrary, aggression and intensity are not prerequisite personality traits for artist managers. While assertiveness is undoubtedly important, it is worth considering the words of Ed Sheeran's manager

Stuart Camp: 'I don't do screaming and shouting – be nice, be fair and people will work hard for you' (Roberts, 2017). Such polite persistence is a key element to consider when building contacts. When sending emails or social media messages, it is good practice to wait for at least a few days before following up. Communication is not necessarily being ignored, it is simply that the industries are fast-moving and the people working within them are often busy. Receiving a response to every communication is unlikely, but respectfully keeping in touch with contacts on a regular basis with relevant communication will gradually help to establish a reputation as a pleasant, knowledgeable and reliable individual. Conversely, industry personnel are likely to be deterred by relentless messaging or approaches that are overtly self-interested, irrelevant or aggressive.

Managers seeking artists

Managers discover artists in a variety of ways: at live shows, online through social media platforms such as Soundcloud, YouTube, Instagram and TikTok, or through personal introductions from friends, acquaintances, other musicians and music industry contacts at both the local and the national level. Where managers believe that an artist shows strong potential for development, they may approach the artist directly. In such cases, they should ensure that they are ready to answer an artist's questions by researching the artist thoroughly and having a solid understanding of how they might be able to help them. If the manager is new and has little prior experience, they may have to persuade the artist to work with them, rather than vice versa. In this instance, managers could apply the 'ABC' strategy suggested (in a different context) by Daniel H. Pink (2013: 4): attunement, buoyancy and clarity. In a music management context, attunement, familiarity and close attention to an artist's career demonstrates dedication and support. Managers should also be buoyant and positive when discussing the artist's potential and later when promoting the artist. Clarity, meanwhile, is essential for good communication, both within and beyond the artist's team. These factors remain important for more experienced managers, though they will also have examples of past achievements and successes that they can draw from, which makes their 'pitch' to the artist more compelling.

Managers may consider multiple artistic and commercial elements when deciding whether to work with an artist, including musical quality, genre, image, style, level of commitment, attitude and personality. They may also consider the artist's level of originality or, in some cases, notable similarity to successful artists. Emerging managers are likely to actively search for new acts to represent, whereas more established ones will typically receive recommendations from their contacts or be approached directly by artists themselves. Paul Allen (2018: 50–51) suggests that a manager is likely to want to know about the musician's level of experience, their organisational capabilities and their career aspirations (gauging how realistic these may be).

Artists seeking managers

Artists may be approached by managers as discussed above, but they may also seek them through a management directory, such as that provided by the trade publication *Music Week*.

In the UK, the MMF offers an online tool for artists seeking a manager, where they can upload information and musical examples to raise awareness with a manager who has relevant genre expertise; artists should, where possible, support their submission with recommendations from other sources. Music industry networking events and conferences are also useful to attend, such as those provided by the MMF, PRS for Music, the Music Publishers Association and Young Guns in the UK, as well as industry showcases such as The Great Escape (UK), Eurosonic Noorderslag (the Netherlands) or SXSW (US). At these showcases, many hundreds of industry professionals will meet over several days to discover new artists and attend conference presentations. Artists and their managers are encouraged to have specific goals in mind when attending these events – to seek contacts and conversations with specific booking agents, record company personnel and so on who can help to develop their careers. It is not enough to simply gain a performance slot (Galuszka, in press).

Artists may also seek managers by approaching those who are already managing artists of a similar style, or those who are known to work with artists in specific genres (Harrison, 2021: 33). This is an important piece of research for artists themselves to undertake, to ensure that they are approaching established managers who are likely to have an interest in their work. As trusted personal contacts are more likely to gain a response, artists may find it most useful to approach a local acquaintance of a manager working elsewhere in the music industries, such as a regional promoter, radio DJ, lawyer, producer or journalist. These contacts can then pass on the artist's details and music to the manager directly, which is likely to at least result in the manager listening to the music and potentially sending a response. Artists can of course approach managers at gigs or networking events, but should again consider their approach in advance to avoid appearing desperate or impolite. If managed well, personal approaches via an intermediary are far more effective than cold-calling or sending emails directly to an established artist manager, both of which are likely to be ignored.

Finding a manager is one of the most important decisions that an artist will make in their early career. The MMF suggests that an ideal time to start the process is when it becomes difficult to juggle all the required tasks that need to be done, and when it becomes financially worthwhile to pay someone a percentage to undertake them (cited in AWAL, 2017). But before approaching a manager, Bobby Borg (2014: 82) suggests that artists should first carefully consider their career plan, current set of songs, their fan base and their potential to generate income. Andrew Thompson (2012: 12–13) notes that an artist's considerations before taking on a manager would include: the manager's track record of success and their level of experience; their reputation, personality, time commitment and international experience; and their contacts and attention to detail. Other relevant questions include the manager's current roster and team members and an initial financial discussion regarding likely income, expenditure and commission (Allen, 2018: 52). Passman (2019: 45) suggests that choosing a manager is essentially a compromise 'between power and clout on the one hand, and time and attention on the other'. This refers to the conundrum faced by artists seeking representation, who must weigh up the influence of an established (but possibly very busy) manager against the dedication and enthusiasm of an aspiring executive.

It is often tempting for artists to self-manage their career by promoting their releases, booking gigs and undertaking the networking tasks themselves in order to maximise their income. But self-managed artists may find it difficult to progress beyond the emerging level, because large music companies prefer a separate manager to be in place when negotiating financial and other terms. In addition, difficulties may arise when one member of a band takes on a management role within the group (Thompson, 2012: 14), potentially leading to interpersonal arguments, power imbalances and differing levels of income (due to commission being paid to the one band member acting as the manager). Alternative options are for the band to split managerial duties or for an individual to take a more administrative role and receive a small fee instead of commission.

Passman (2019: 48) suggests that artists should be similarly cautious if family or friends are part of the team, noting that they may not be appropriately qualified, or may not take a suitably objective view of the artist's career. It would also be very difficult to end the working relationship. While well-meaning managers such as family and friends can work well initially, problems may arise during a period of growing success, when a more nuanced understanding of the music industries may be required. It is at this turning point that more established professional management is often helpful in bringing expertise and contacts that can further boost the artist's career. For instance, Beyoncé and Charlotte Church were both initially managed by parents but moved to more experienced managers as their careers developed (Anderton et al., 2013: 186). As noted above, there is still a clear preference for artists to work with an established manager, one who may ultimately offer a smoother and more professional process for all involved. Once established, it is not uncommon for artists to move from one manager to another as their career needs and target audiences develop over time. But Harrison (2021: 45–46) provides encouragement for emerging managers by suggesting that someone new to the role may have a natural talent for it. She remarks that those who have some familiarity with the music industries (such as musicians, tour managers or label staff) may be well suited to the task, while some marketing experience would also prove helpful. Indeed, it is not unusual to find music industry personnel working full-time in one role while also acting as artist managers on the side, thus building their own careers and keeping their options open for the future.

BUILDING A SUCCESSFUL TEAM

Music managers are indispensable connectors, skilfully balancing the needs of an artist, their wider team, industry personnel and fans. They are 'curators' and 'coordinators' who bring together a range of collaborators to translate the artist's creative vision and career goals into action (Hracs, 2015: 470). In more general terms, a successful team requires an inspiring, optimistic and positive leadership culture (driven by the manager) where new ideas can be 'shared and integrated' (West, 2012: 4; see also Gilson, 2015). David Hesmondhalgh (2019: 93) builds on the earlier work of Ryan (1992) in discussing cultural production as carried out by project teams. His ideas may be applied and extended to the music industry as follows:

- 'Primary creative personnel' (e.g. musicians, performers and songwriters).
- 'Technical workers' (e.g. sound engineers and stage crew).
- 'Creative managers' (e.g. artist managers and tour managers).
- 'Marketing personnel' (e.g. pluggers, merchandisers and music PRs who promote and publicise work).
- 'Owners and executives' (e.g. record labels, publishers and concert promoters).

We can add to this list several other areas including, for example, booking agents, lawyers, accountants, and other stakeholders such as technology companies and brand sponsors. It is typically the artist manager's role to coordinate these different personnel while retaining a strong focus on the strategic planning objectives of an artist's career. The roles and responsibilities of key team members will be discussed in the following section, but it is important to note here that teams are constituted in different ways depending on an artist's specific goals and immediate needs. Therefore, the process of building a team should be seen as both cumulative and flexible.

It is possible that some team members may work on a *pro bono* (i.e. voluntary) basis initially, on the condition that they will be rewarded with a paid contract when the artist begins to generate income. However, this is entirely up to the individual and should never be assumed. Team members should be selected with care and attention, as the relationship must be mutually trustworthy, reliable and effective. Each relationship has the potential to either help or hinder an artist's development, which is why trial periods may be considered to ensure a mutually beneficial fit. Therefore, when building a team, artists and managers should consider the potential partner's ability and track record alongside the ever-important interpersonal traits, such as reliability, communication skills, approachability and negotiation abilities. Payment structures and rates should also be discussed in advance.

As with any recruitment process, managers should seek references and reassurance from others who have previously worked with the potential team member. Team members should also share a strong passion about the artist's musical and aesthetic vision, and there should be a high degree of trust between all parties involved. Such trust enables a team to work freely, creatively and effectively. Harrison (2021) highlights high-profile cases where such trust has been broken to the detriment of artists such as Elton John and Joan Armatrading. Managers should therefore be aware of using their 'undue influence' in contractual negotiations (i.e. taking advantage of a power imbalance or an artist's lack of industry expertise). This is particularly important when working with minors (under-18s), where different legal rules will apply regarding both working hours and safeguarding.

Both artists and managers should be aware of conflicts of interest when a team is being assembled. Such issues occur when one part of the team may be acting for another, such as an accountant or lawyer advising both the artist and their record company. Conflicts of interest can also arise if a manager is taking on a dual role, such as acting as the artist's label and publisher. This ambition may be understandable on the manager's part (it will boost their overall income), but all parties should proceed with caution to ensure transparency between the various income streams. The clearest route for managers is simply to take a standard commission rate on all music-related income, as this will avoid what some in the industry informally refer to as 'double-dipping', where the manager receives multiple commission payments or fees from an artist. For example, if an artist is signed to a publishing company owned by their manager, that manager may receive commission on the artist's share of the songwriting income, and also from the publishing company (Anderton et al., 2013: 186). Managers may also represent multiple artists, so conflicts can occur if there is a touring, collaborative or branding opportunity that may be suitable for several artists on the roster. Similarly, when working with a band, what is best for one member may not necessarily be the best for another. Situations such as these often leave the manager in an awkward position, from which they will aim to negotiate a compromise option to satisfy all parties involved. Therefore, artists and managers should be aware of how conflicts can arise and how they can be mitigated via contractual negotiations in advance.

Team members: roles and responsibilities

This section introduces some of the roles and responsibilities of key team members. The roles may overlap or combine with others in a variety of ways, and many may be fulfilled by an artist or manager during the early stages of an artist's career development. However, as the artist's career grows so, typically, does the number of specialised personnel. Key live music roles, including booking agent, tour manager and promoter, are covered in detail in Chapter 8, while promotional roles, such as publicist, public relations/press officer, photographer, videographer and plugger, are discussed across Chapters 4, 5 and 6. Brand sponsorship is addressed in Chapter 9, while the roles of record companies and music publishers are explored in Chapter 3 and Chapter 10, respectively. Some other important parts of an artist's broad team are outlined below: business managers, accountants, lawyers and record producers.

A notable aspect of the US music industry is that artists are likely to work with a business manager in addition to their personal manager. Elsewhere, an artist manager is likely either to take on both roles or to work with an accountant (Harrison, 2021: 47). The business manager role is similar to that of an accountant, but business managers will usually play a more significant role in developing artist development strategies. For instance, they may create financial plans, suggest investment strategies, and advise on touring. Accountancy firms offer different industry specialisms, but one working with an artist or manager would be expected to have knowledge of tour accounting, company structures, investments, royalty statements, auditing, bookkeeping, tax regulations and overseas activities. Artists and managers can find an accountant through chartered institutes and associations. They should be qualified as either a certified or chartered accountant, regulated and authorised to provide such services (Harrison, 2021: 27–31). For more information on business and financial planning, see Chapter 10.

Lawyers, known as attorneys in the US, are an influential and well-connected group within the music industries, due to their legal expertise and the wide overview of the business that their role provides. A lawyer is an essential part of a music team, utilising both specialist knowledge and contacts to assist an artist's career development. It is common for some lawyers to act in an A&R role, attending concerts and introducing artists to managers, publishers and record companies. By building a relationship of trust at this early stage, the lawyer hopes to be retained for future contractual negotiations. Considerations for selecting a lawyer could include their level of influence both internally (their position in the law firm) and externally (their contact base and reputation). Many lawyers often have a genre knowledge or legal specialism which may make them ideal for specific negotiations. Trade bodies such as the MMF and Musicians' Union can recommend lawyers to their members. Lawyers may receive an hourly rate or a one-off fee for negotiating deals, but established artists may employ a law firm on a retainer basis. High-profile lawyers, particularly in the US, may request a percentage of royalties from the project that they have negotiated (normally 5 percent). Many music businesses, including royalty collection societies and record labels, will employ their own salaried lawyers (known as in-house counsels), who may launch or defend legal actions on behalf of the company. Such actions may include instances of copyright infringement, defamation or breaches of contract.

Finally, a record producer works with an artist both before and during recording sessions to ensure that songs are arranged, recorded, engineered and mixed to their highest potential. The role also involves the delicate negotiation of tension, ego and musical disagreements. The right choice of producer can significantly enhance an artist's recordings, so they are an essential part of the creative team (Anderton et al., 2013: 79). Producers may be focused on successfully capturing a band's live sound, or more actively involved in creative choices related to the music itself. A famous example of the latter is George Martin's contribution to the recordings of The Beatles, which helped the band to develop its sound and style in the mid- to late-1960s. Artists and managers may discover a producer through online sites, through recommendations from fellow musicians and industry personnel, or by approaching producers who have worked on influential albums within particular genres. Producers often work on a freelance basis, but some may be employed directly by a recording studio.

ARTIST MANAGEMENT CONTRACTS

Guy Morrow (2018a: 86) describes the artist–manager relationship 'as a form of group creativity' yet one which is ultimately 'subordinate to the artist'. This power balance is also reflected in management contracts, which are based on the legal concept of principal (artist) and agent (manager). However, in the early stages of an artist's and manager's working relationship, it is unlikely that either side would request the immediate signing of a contract. Instead, there is typically a period of several months during which initial developments are being made and trust established. A difficult decision for both artists and managers, therefore, is *when* to formalise their working relationship. Andrew Thompson (2012: 14) suggests that managers may not be fully confident in dedicating their full attention, effort and financial investment to an artist unless there is an element of security in the relationship (a contract), and notes that any uncertainty or reluctance to discuss terms will present difficulties and disputes in the future. As a result, it is a good idea to discuss potential terms at a relatively early stage in order to outline how the artist, manager and other members of the team will work together.

One option is to use a trial period, most commonly of six months (though they can last up to a year). Such trial periods may also be applied to other team relationships to ensure that the partnerships are mutually beneficial before longer-term commitments are secured. Thompson (2012: 21) presents two options for formalising trial periods. The first is for the trial period to run for its agreed duration, followed by negotiation of a lengthier and more detailed contract. The second is that a full contract can be negotiated at an early stage, but with an option to terminate at the end of the initial trial period. An additional option is for both parties to use a short-term, non-binding arrangement known as a Memorandum of Understanding or Heads of Agreement (usually one or two pages), where duties and objectives are briefly outlined, alongside any initial financial considerations such as commission and expenses. Harrison (2021: 36) explains that trial periods are important because it takes time to build trust and to ensure that the partnership is functioning well. A manager would understandably want to confirm the working relationship before approaching others in the industries, so artists may be asked to sign a short agreement covering expenses and any deals achieved during the trial period.

Contractual relationships are a central driver of the music industries, and while there are no 'standard' management contracts as such, several clauses (as outlined below) are commonly seen (Anderton et al., 2013: 187). Independent legal advice from a specialist music lawyer is recommended to ensure that contractual terms and any conflicts of interest have been considered in advance by the artist, who can then decide the best course of action with confidence, based on a clear knowledge of the clauses. As noted above, artists should not be represented by the same lawyer (or law firm) as represents their manager, due to the conflict of interest that this creates. However, many labels, publishers and managers will provide an upfront payment for independent legal advice to ensure that the artist has been professionally advised and understands the contract (the cost of which will usually be recoupable from future earnings). Paying for an artist's initial legal advice provides protection to the company or manager where there are any future disputes, as it demonstrates that the artist was well-informed by a specialist legal expert in advance of signing a contract.

Some artist managers do not use contracts, demonstrating a high level of trust in their relationship with the artist. But standard industry practice is to have at least some written arrangement between the two parties, as is the case with publishing and recording companies seeking to protect their investments. Harrison (2021: 61–62) remarks that some artists refuse to commit to a contract. In such circumstances, the manager will need to proceed with cautious reluctance, since it will be difficult to prove the terms of a verbal contract or to claim recompense should a dispute later arise. The key elements and clauses found within management contracts are discussed below.

Implied obligations

An artist management contract is likely to include what lawyer Nick Kanaar (2007) refers to as 'implied obligations' on the part of the manager. These generally reflect that the manager will act in good faith on behalf of an artist, exercising 'due care and skill', such as the correct handling of confidential information and the maintenance of clear accounts. However, the artist must also play their part in committing effort, professionalism and reliability in building their career. This coordinated dual approach will ensure that the manager can also work to the best of their ability in supporting the artist.

Commission

Commission is a percentage of an artist's earnings, which is paid to the manager in return for their work. Commission rates usually fall between 15 percent and 25 percent, with the industry standard being 20 percent of gross income (prior to other costs being deducted). That percentage may be paid directly to the manager or to a management company that then pays the manager a regular salary (MMF, 2019b: 32). Touring and live shows are typically commissioned as net income (after other costs are considered), since the artist will encounter additional expenses during live work, such as agency fees, session musician payments and travel charges. More established artists will seek to negotiate lower rates (possibly as low as 10 percent) as they have a track record for generating higher and more consistent income. They may also be able to negotiate different percentages for different types of income (Thompson, 2012; Passman, 2019). In contrast, new and emerging artists may have to pay a higher amount (sometimes up to 25 percent) given the work involved in developing the artist at a time when revenues may be low (Baskerville and Baskerville, 2019). Morrow (2018b: 45) refers to this as 'the principle of deferred remuneration', which leads some managers to spread their financial risk by working with a small portfolio of artists at different levels of development (MMF, 2019b: 4). As a consequence, managers may pursue more than one job at a time, or seek involvement with other areas of the music business to build a sustainable career. The same is true of management companies (Thompson, 2012: 18), with diversification into recording and publishing companies, and the development of livestreaming companies and other opportunities.

The percentage commission model is beginning to be challenged, with artists and their managers occasionally agreeing a 'joint venture' or partnership arrangement (MMF, 2019b: 35). Furthermore, some well-known artists now choose to pay their manager a fixed salary rather than a profit share. For instance, artists such as Bruno Mars, Taylor Swift and Beyoncé have each adopted this approach at times, with superstar manager salaries ranging from $200,000 to $500,000 per year (Rys, 2016). Rys suggests that this strategy may only work for high-level artists, but cautions that it may not progress as planned: several high-profile artists, such as Prince and Queen, faced challenges with such an approach.

Accounting, auditing and expenses

Accounting clauses allow both artists and managers to keep track of finances; a significant challenge when there may be multiple sources of revenue, sometimes delivered informally in cash. For example, an artist may receive a payment directly from a concert promoter, which should then be declared to the manager. Vice versa, some payments may be made to the management team via digital means (such as royalty payments) and should then be declared to the artist. A bank account may be operated by the artist or manager, with other parties invoicing for their shares as appropriate. If either the artist or the manager is uncomfortable with controlling the central account, an accountant should be employed to manage it on their behalf (Harrison, 2021: 62–63). The management contract should state specific timeframes for issuing accounting information to the artist and/or manager, depending on who controls the central account. Artists are also entitled, as they are with a recording or publishing contract, to negotiate the right to audit a manager's accounts. Audits allow the artist to check that they have been receiving the correct level of income but, as they can be prohibitively expensive, this option should be considered carefully by the artist. Regarding the manager's expenses, Harrison (2021: 63) advises that these should not include the general costs of running a business, but that fees directly relating to the artist should be recoupable. It is therefore important for managers to retain receipts as proof of expenditure, which helps to support financial transparency and trust. Accounting and business structures are discussed further in Chapter 10.

Term

The standard duration of a management contract is typically a maximum of five years. The provision of a fixed term offers managers and artists certainty about the length of their working relationship, and the initial term may be followed by an annual 'rolling contract' that is automatically extended until one or other party decides against renewal. Term clauses may also include specific aspirations or benchmarks, sometimes known as 'hurdles', such as achieving a certain level of income (Harrison, 2021: 56–57). Artists can seek a break clause should these hurdles not be met, though Passman (2019: 39) notes that issues may be caused by the errors of others in the artist's team (hence beyond the remit of the manager), and that hurdles may be deliberately manipulated by an artist: for instance, by turning down work in order to avoid meeting the agreed target. Such issues may be considered by managers in advance of negotiating a contract, perhaps by requesting that artists take work opportunities similar to those that they have accepted in the past (Passman, 2019: 39).

Termination

A termination clause may be included, whereby the artist and manager may part company if certain conditions or expectations are not met, or where there has been unprofessional behaviour. Disputes leading to termination may include financial disagreements, poor communication, lack of prioritisation, insufficient effort, lack of trust or criminal activity. A manager may also negotiate post-contract commission (sometimes referred to as a 'sunset clause'), meaning that they are entitled to a percentage share of commissionable income even after their working relationship with an artist has come to an end. The length of such a period is negotiable in advance and can range from several years to decades. Thus, one consideration for artists is not to set too long a period for such post-term commission, as this may have the dual impact of deterring future managers and limiting income. An alternative is to introduce a declining scale, whereby the share taken by the manager is gradually reduced year on year for a set period. Harrison (2021: 60–61) notes that UK-based managers generally accept that such post-term commission should only be based on 'what was recorded or written during the management term'. However, there is currently much debate within the sector on the fairness and timescale of sunset clauses. Some argue that they are onerous to the artist, whereas others suggest that the manager should be fairly compensated in perpetuity for the work that they contributed (MMF, 2019b: 37–39). This debate is likely to continue in future, so both managers and artists should seek legal advice before agreeing to such clauses.

Exclusivity and key person clauses

Managers are likely to insist on exclusivity in their working relationship with the artist. This is standard practice, as working with multiple managers may result in confusion and a smaller percentage of earnings for all parties. One exception is where a co-management agreement has been negotiated across several territories (as noted later). The artist may request, vice versa, that the manager's work for other clients does not impede the artist's progress in any way. Furthermore, if an artist signs with a large company, they can request a 'key person' clause where they have the right to terminate the contract should that individual leave the organisation. However, companies are likely to push back against such a clause, given the power that it provides both to the artist and the key person involved (Harrison, 2021: 55–56).

Permissions

Contracts are likely to include a clause that allows the manager to give permission on behalf of an artist in relation to accepting performance opportunities and deciding on matters related to artistic direction and finance. Some artists may be happy to allow the manager to approve such key choices, but others will insist on limitations, such that significant decisions must be fully discussed and collaboratively approved by the artist and their team. Examples of such contractual limits may include a requirement to receive an artist's approval regarding financial payments, musical collaborations (such as remixes), media appearances, sponsorship opportunities and festival slots.

Territory and co-management

The territory clause refers to the geographical area covered by a management contract. Most managers will seek worldwide representation for an artist, resulting in greater royalty income and full control of the artist's career plan. The US market is, as Harrison suggests, 'very different' from the UK, so a specialist in that territory may help to improve an artist's overall prospects (2021: 52–53). However, the decision to co-manage an artist across territories brings both advantages and disadvantages. For instance, a key advantage of co-management is the pooling of resources and skill sets, allowing an artist to benefit from multiple personnel, each of whom has their own expertise and contacts (Morrow, 2018b: 45). A potential concern is that there may be communication challenges between the different managers and their teams, especially when operating across different time zones (2018b: 45), or where the strategies recommended for different territories may be contradictory.

Activities beyond music

It is increasingly common for managers to take commission from an artist's activities beyond their musical career. These may include related artistic activities, such as literature, presenting, acting, modelling, teaching, or product launches, such as for food or clothing items. Commission rates for such activities may differ from that of the core music income and can be negotiated when drafting the contract. Managers understandably argue that an artist's success in music (which they have helped to facilitate) justifies this additional commission. It also appears reasonable when considering the ongoing symbiosis of previously separate media forms within the music industries.

CONCLUSION

Numerous industry reports and books are available on the roles undertaken by artist managers, yet more academic research is required. Such research could help music fans and audiences better appreciate managers' significant contributions as cultural intermediaries by further explaining the vital roles they play in helping to develop the music that we enjoy. Contemporary music management encompasses an ever-growing list of skills and responsibilities, so it is important that managers are multi-skilled in the early stages of their careers. It is also crucial for them to assemble a professional, efficient and reliable team to work with them. To build such a team, aspiring managers should create connections by networking both online and at music industry events. Although this initial phase of profile building may be difficult, polite persistence and a professional attitude will help to shape a positive reputation. Contractual relations define the relationships between artists and managers, as well as with other members of the team, so these contracts need to be clearly written and mutually beneficial. Furthermore, specialist independent legal advice should be sought by both artist and manager to ensure that all terms have been understood and that the artist's career can develop successfully.

Key discussion points

- How could the music manager role change in the next decade?
- How can an artist best decide on the most appropriate management style and structure to develop their career?
- How can artists, managers and lawyers best negotiate conflicts of interest when they arise?
- Which elements of a management contract may be revised in the next decade?

FURTHER READING

To learn more about the current roles and responsibilities of a music manager, please see the MMF's *Managing Expectations* report (2019b). To discover more about management contracts, we recommend two books by music lawyers: Ann Harrison's *Music: The Business* (2021), and Donald Passman's *All You Need to Know about the Music Business* (2019).

3

ARTIST DEVELOPMENT STRATEGIES

SUMMARY

In this chapter we examine the process of artist development, considering the multiple strategies that may be employed for successful career progression within the music industries. In an era when labels are less likely to work with acts during the initial stages of their careers, we discuss the many other personnel who fulfil this early process of artist development. We also explore what artists themselves can do to develop their music, image and persona. Finally, we examine different routes for releasing music and the common terms found within recording and publishing contracts.

Chapter objectives

- To provide an overview of the artist development and A&R process and to consider the many individuals and organisations involved.
- To explore the various routes available for releasing music and to understand why artists may choose to release their music independently rather than seek traditional recording contracts.
- To consider how recording contracts may adapt to take account of this industry shift.
- To examine the key types of recording and publishing contracts.

Record companies and other music businesses face significant challenges in deciding on which artists to work with, because public tastes are ever-changing and difficult to predict (Negus, 1999: 31–32). In addition, launching a new artist is expensive due to the high fixed costs of recording, marketing and video production that need to be covered prior to revenue being generated. The music industries have typically dealt with this by focusing on star-making activities, whereby a small number of hit artists produces enough revenue to offset the losses produced by those who fail to recoup their initial expenses (Negus, 1999; Hesmondhalgh, 2019). In contrast, many small independent artists fund their activities from their day jobs, family loans or live performance income. They may augment this approach by calling in favours from their network of creative friends to help produce recordings and videos that can be posted online.

The system adopted by the larger record companies aims at achieving economies of scale: by focusing on a small number of high-profile artists, overall fixed costs are reduced but greater profits can be achieved due to the low marginal costs of distribution (Anderton et al., 2013: 6). In other words, it is better to sell a lot of one product than to sell smaller amounts of multiple products. It is in this sense that the economist Alan Krueger (2019: 78, 81) refers to the music business as 'a textbook example of a superstar market', where the 'ability to scale' allows superstar artists to reach larger audiences and generate larger profits for the company. The gap between superstar artists and other musicians is stark, with the top 0.1 percent of artists accounting for over 50 percent of album sales in 2017 (Krueger, 2019: 83). Likewise, in the live music sector, the top 1 percent of artists took 60 percent of total concert revenue in 2017 (2019: 84). Krueger suggests that such gaps in success are due to a 'band-wagon effect' (2019: 86), whereby audiences draw on recommendations from family and friends. By engaging in this process, audiences share common social experiences of engaging with the same music. Hit songs therefore build in popularity via such close networks, while also being strengthened through repetition in the media (2019: 86–87). Krueger argues that music consumption is likely to remain 'largely socially determined' (2019: 94), particularly in the mainstream pop music market, and so favourable to a relatively small number of highly successful artists. The increased use of algorithms, curated playlists and other data by streaming platforms will also contribute to maintaining the gap between superstars and other artists by enhancing these social effects, though they also allow for niche artists to find their audiences (2019: 94). See Chapter 7 for more on the role of digital platforms.

As noted above, artist development activities do not need to be highly capitalised in the initial stages of an artist's career. They may be undertaken in a relatively cost-effective manner in the short term (see Table 3.1). However, to achieve high-quality results on a consistent basis and to reach a wider potential market, artists and their teams will often require the additional funding and support available from a record company or external investors (as discussed below).

Table 3.1 Organisations and others involved in the initial stages of artist development

Organisation type	Role
PR companies, lawyers, pluggers	May work with an artist at an early stage, in anticipation of a long-term partnership. May also act as an initial manager.
Funders	May provide financial support in advance of the artist working with a manager or record company. Examples include Help Musicians UK, PRS Foundation (UK), Factor (Canada) and ASCAP Foundation (USA).
Specialist artist development agencies	Commercial companies that may provide a range of services aimed at aspiring artists, including vocal coaching, songwriting support, music production, image consultancy and advice on marketing, social media and interview techniques.

Charitable artist development agencies	Charitable organisations that provide artist development services for public benefit. Examples include Generator (UK) and MADE (Canada).
Trade bodies	The MMF's Accelerator programme (partnered with YouTube) provides funding and guidance to music managers in the UK. Other trade bodies providing education and networking events for artists include PRS for Music, the Music Publishers Association and UK Music.
Non-music companies	Many well-known brands play a role in developing artists. For example, Coca-Cola's 'Coke Studio' artist-based show in Pakistan. Red Bull ran a worldwide music academy for 20 years, providing educational content and development opportunities for artists.
Media companies	BBC Introducing allows artists to upload music for producers and presenters to hear. This may result in radio play, with some artists being elevated to a national playlist. But many other opportunities typically adopt a talent show format (including television competitions such as *The X Factor, America's Got Talent* and so on) that often result in short-term careers for the winning artists.
Recording studios	Studio personnel, such as owners or producers, may offer initial assistance and contacts, which sometimes progresses to a production deal (discussed later).
Live music promoters	Venue and festival promoters often help an artist develop by providing performance opportunities, advice and contacts. Backstage areas of festivals can be particularly useful for networking.

Artist development, particularly at the initial stages, is often a shared task. While some people or organisations may only be involved for a short time, they may nevertheless make a crucial contribution, such as a gig offer, initial radio play or providing introductions to other industry personnel. The African proverb that 'it takes a village to raise a child' can thus be applied to a music industry context, in acknowledging the importance of many individual influences on an artist's career development. Such contributors may not receive (or even desire) any credit or income further down the line – they offer support simply because they believe in the artist and their music. Aspiring artists should nevertheless take care to fully research the various people and organisations that may offer assistance. There are companies and individuals who seek to extract short-term profit from the excitement and naivety of singers and bands, while promising outcomes that they are ill-equipped to deliver (as discussed in Chapter 2). This situation again demonstrates the importance of making connections, networking with others, and becoming aware of who does (or does not) have a good reputation and track record.

ARTIST DEVELOPMENT PLANNING

In this section we focus on the role of the 'manager', by which we mean anyone who is engaged in supporting an artist in a managerial capacity (including the artist themselves). In the UK, research by the Music Managers Forum (MMF) – based on surveys and interviews with managers active in the country – notes that in today's digital-dominated culture, record companies anticipate that artists will already be 'developed', and expect that there will be 'genuine momentum behind them before a deal is offered' (MMF, 2019b: 8). As noted in Chapter 2, this means that the manager has a responsibility to develop (and perhaps invest in) their artist to the best of their ability from an early stage, possibly before any other team members are involved. Well-connected managers will understand the potential market position of their artists, both in terms of audience development and of the record companies and others who might be interested in working with, and investing in, them. The manager's role is, as noted by Tim Clark of ie:music, to 'sell' the artist's 'vision' to the audiences and industry personnel who they deem will be receptive to it (MMF, 2019b: 9). Paul Hitchman, President of the distribution and services company AWAL, agrees that 'managers are increasingly taking charge of the artist development process' (MMF, 2019b: 19). He also highlights their innovative use of social media, their key role in creative development, and the adaptations that have been made to the traditional artist–management business model (MMF, 2019b: 19). Moreover, artist manager and MMF board member Ellie Giles (interview with authors) refers to artist managers as 'dot-joiners' and 'business developers' who provide contacts, support and experience to guide the early stages of an artist's career, thus reinforcing the networking role discussed in Chapter 2.

Artist development activities are many and varied. The list of activities given in Table 3.2 is by no means exhaustive, but provides an overview of the multi-faceted and ongoing processes that may be seen throughout a musician's career.

Strategies for encouraging and managing artist creativity are also crucial to developing the artist brand and to achieving a sustainable career. Creative approaches can be utilised to identify new development opportunities, with Ellie Giles (interview with authors) warning against overtly 'risk-averse' strategies. Instead, artists should be encouraged to go beyond their comfort zones to make the most of new ideas, with the manager ensuring that the process is made as smooth as possible. The increasingly entrepreneurial role of managers (Hesmondhalgh, 2019) in developing their artists means that, as discussed in Chapter 2, many provide their own investment or seek sources of funding beyond the traditional record companies and publishers. Indeed, managers have become more adept at accessing such funds, or making partnerships with other companies to support an artist's development (MMF, 2019b: 9; PRS Foundation, n.d.). We will discuss funding opportunities and issues in further detail in Chapter 10.

Artist development can be tailored in a number of ways, taking account of genre, personality, available funds, and the team's level of ambition. Artists should consider their overall career aims at an early stage, whether self-managing or working alongside a manager. This process will ensure that their goals remain in focus when deciding strategies and forging relationships with other parts of the industry. Alongside this, artists are recommended to engage in self-appraisal activities, which involve an honest assessment of their status, fanbase, health, level of commitment, financial priorities, training needs, musical development and so on. Ellie Giles explains (interview with authors) that such a process can also be used by managers to develop their own skillsets. Such appraisals should not be a one-off exercise, but regularly updated as circumstances change and the artist (and manager) further develop their goals.

Table 3.2 Artist development activities and tasks

Activity	Examples of tasks
Live show development	Rehearsals, working with an agent, booking gigs at relevant venues with appropriate line-ups (perhaps also including house shows, showcase events and DJ sets), and working on stage design, choreography and so on.
Branding and image	Considering digital strategy, photography, artwork, music videos and brand partnerships in order to strengthen the artist's public image and brand.
Recording	Selecting studios, engineers and producers, preparing material in advance, ensuring high-quality recordings, and collaborating with remixers and other musicians as needed.
Marketing, press, and promotion	PR, plugging and advertising, including interviews and performances on radio, television and the internet as well as reviews and feature interviews in magazines and newspapers.
Songwriting	Collaborations, remixes and co-writing sessions, writing for others, and writing music specifically for use in video games, television shows, films and so on.
Financial development	Funding applications, crowdfunding, securing other investment, engagement with collection societies, protecting copyright, agreeing commission rates and fees, negotiating and signing contracts, and monitoring sales/data.
Maintaining connections	Ensuring good relations with the artist's team, in addition to other industry personnel and artists. Networking at gigs, industry events and award shows.
Maintaining a fanbase	Regular music releases, live performances, email lists and social media updates (text, image and video).
Data collection	Collecting and analysing data from social media, streaming platforms, ticket sales and mailing lists in line with consumer law.

Allen (2018: 188) also notes the importance of goal-setting, suggesting that specific aims should be attached to a variety of activities. He also recommends that artists create both a project budget and a personal budget at an early stage (2018: 92). Setting these budgets allows for more effective planning of periods when an artist may be 'out of cycle' (not releasing music or performing live). Artist manager Niko Michault (2019) acknowledges the importance of planning, advising that timelines as long as a decade will help an artist to develop a sustainable career. He also explains that building and maintaining a fanbase should be a particular priority. Similarly, manager Adam Tudhope notes the importance of focusing on 'audience retention and growth', both in terms of recorded output and live performances. He also highlights the importance of understanding the ticketing process, which can be a rich source of audience data (MMF, 2019b: 26). Ellie Giles is equally positive about the creative use of available data, suggesting that artists and managers should invest in data at an early stage in order to build audiences (MMF, 2019b: 30).

A&R manager Briony Turner suggests two main priorities for new artists: to be prolific in writing and recording songs, and to expand their creative networks (Music Business Worldwide, 2018). Being prolific gives greater choice both to the artist and those working with them, while also improving their song craft. This may help to avoid the 'difficult second album' syndrome that has affected so many artists in the past, whereby their best songs were included on their first album, leaving little time while on tour or promotional duties to write new ones of a similar quality. Artists can build their networks not only by approaching potential managers (as discussed in Chapter 2) but by approaching other musicians, producers and artists working in other artforms. This can lead to the development of new ideas and collaborations. In ideal circumstances, such collaborations would offer mutual benefit, with each artist or collaborator learning from the other. As an example, artist manager Matthew Thornhill describes the powerful role of group creativity when recounting the development of Mercury Prize winner Sampha. The artist and his team enhanced his profile via a series of well-selected collaborations, guest appearances and co-writes with high-profile artists, including Solange Knowles, Frank Ocean, Kanye West and Alicia Keys (MMF, 2019b: 12). Such an open-minded approach encourages greater experimentation and creativity, also building a larger audience for each collaborating artist. Indeed, *The Economist* (2018) notes that collaborations are popular for both artists and fans, citing data from the Billboard Hot 100, which shows that such musical partnerships accounted for over a third of US chart hits in 2017. Of course, this practice has long been utilised by jazz and hip-hop musicians, but it has become ever more important due to the dominance of streaming platforms and the algorithms that determine playlist placements and recommendations (as discussed further in Chapter 7).

Whether collaborating or not, an essential early step is to make high-quality recordings of the artist's songs, which can then be distributed online or pitched to record companies, publishers and others. Artists should ensure that any demos or potential releases are recorded, mixed and mastered to broadcast standard, as first impressions are important. However, if an artist later signs a recording or publishing contract, it is possible that A&R representatives will suggest remixing or re-recording earlier work. Such a process is undertaken partly for aesthetic reasons and partly to gain ownership or control of the master recordings. Initial distribution of the recordings can be achieved by uploading them to a Soundcloud, Instagram, YouTube, Bandcamp, or similar page owned by the artist, each of which has slightly different connotations in terms of musical genre and expected audience. For instance, Soundcloud is particularly important for rap music and a youth audience, while Bandcamp has become synonymous with artists and audiences who give preference and validation to the album format (Hesmondhalgh et al., 2019; see also Chapter 7). But to achieve distribution across high-profile streaming platforms and apps, and to help achieve inclusion on their most important playlists, a digital distribution deal with a specialist company is required. This is because direct uploads to Digital Service Providers (DSPs) such as Spotify, Apple Music, Deezer, Beatport and so on are not permitted. Digital distribution companies will place songs onto all of the major platforms around the world in exchange for either a flat fee or a commission percentage of the royalties earned (around 10–15 percent on average). Popular online distributors include AWAL, DistroKid, TuneCore and CD Baby. Major record labels are also active in digital distribution, with Universal's Spinnup and Warner's Level offering similar services. In 2019, Spotify experimented with offering independent artists the opportunity to upload their music directly to its catalogue, but it has since retracted the offer, preferring to work directly with distributors and to develop its data-centric Spotify for Artists and playlist pitching tools. A digital distributor remains, therefore, an essential partner for artists who want to release their music on the most popular streaming services.

Artist manager John Watson notes the difficulty that artists have in sustaining audience interest due to the voracious appetite of the public for new entertainment (Morrow, 2018b: 46). Similarly, Harrison (2021: 5) stresses the importance of 'discoverability' – the ability to rise 'above the noise'. Other contacts can of course help with this process, but an artist's own hard work is essential. Rising above such noise is challenging. We now live and work within an attention economy, with both individuals and companies vying for our eyes and ears. Academic Tim Wu (2017: 178) cites the warnings that television executive Fred Friendly gave as early as 1970 regarding the fragmentation of media audiences, and how competing companies formed 'a cacophonous attempt to attract the largest audience'. The splintering of the media landscape has given unparalleled choice for audiences and lower barriers to entry for artists. Yet, as Wu argues, the attention economy has since created a 'grand bargain that has transformed our lives', describing our collective attention as a commodity on a par with other consumer goods (Wu, 2017: 5–6). The need for artists and managers to compete in such conditions clearly creates pressure on both parties. The MMF (2019b: 27) states that many managers are 'pushing back against the "always-on" culture of social media and round-the-clock promotion' despite the high public demand for new content (see also Chapter 11). Managers must nevertheless strike a balance between the artist being 'available' to the public and ensuring that they are not over-exposed or posting consistently dramatic or over-the-top content. Such content may become 'a continual diet of the purely sensational', which may ultimately put off audiences (Wu, 2017: 100). Gauging the balance to achieve a sensibly managed public profile should be discussed at an early stage alongside other members of the team, such as record company and PR staff, ensuring that artists are not unduly pressured to create constant content.

As discussed in Chapter 2, managers may also take a commission of an artist's earnings in the wider entertainment industries, including income from acting, producing, podcasting, modelling, writing and presenting. Managers should therefore consider the potentially lucrative opportunities available to develop an artist's overall media profile in addition to their musical output. However, artists and managers should again ensure that such developments are appropriate and not counterproductive or potentially disruptive to the artist's musical career or fanbase. Examples of musicians who have succeeded in other artistic areas include Yoko Ono (visual art), Lady Gaga and Ice-T (acting), Jools Holland (presenting) and Patti Smith (writing). Many have also added radio DJ or podcaster to their resumé, including Jarvis Cocker, Amanda Palmer, George Ezra, Cerys Matthews, Iggy Pop and Alice Cooper, while others have featured in their own reality television programmes or documentaries, such as Ozzy Osbourne, Taylor Swift, Ted Nugent, Flavor Flav and Snoop Dogg.

Building a sustainable, long-term career is difficult, with very few artists remaining in the spotlight for decades. Even artists who enjoy a high level of success with their first few releases can rapidly fade from mainstream public interest, though some are able to leverage their fanbases and build significant niche audiences who continue to support them. Of course, notions of success and sustainability vary between artists. Some may seek a full-time career supported entirely by their musical work, while others adopt a portfolio approach, financially supporting their musical ambitions by maintaining a non-musical 'day job' or an allied career. For instance, record producers, music teachers, studio engineers and others often release music, as do workers in many other professions and roles, yet they are not dependent on their music-based income. Indeed, some choose to make their music available online for free or on a donation basis, with the personal satisfaction of making the music available being more important than generating profits (see Anderton, 2019c). To achieve a long-term career (whether full-time or part-time) usually involves careful planning of live performances, release schedules, media positioning, authentic fan interactions, and ongoing consideration of the artist's financial situation and well-being.

Harrison (2021: 45) references the short-term profile of television talent show participants, noting that most fail to build on the momentum generated during the weekly broadcasts. Indeed, some music industry personnel refer to such rapid, up-and-down experiences as 'firework careers', with many such artists subsequently dropped by their labels or seeking work in other areas of the entertainment sector. One issue that partly accounts for this lack of ongoing success is that contestants have not built a solid long-term fanbase beyond the talent show audience, resulting in limited interest and minimal loyalty from the public in subsequent years. Conversely, artists who have rehearsed, recorded, toured and built their profile more organically over a longer period will typically benefit because they have fostered a more engaged fanbase. Krueger (2019: 68) discusses the heavy metal band Metallica as an example of a group that has enjoyed significant longevity. The band's manager Cliff Burnstein suggests that this is due to a combination of artistic talent, outstanding organisation, a wide-ranging fan base, and a strong live act (2019: 68–69). Krueger also explores the concept of luck in relation to sustainable careers, arguing that a combination of musical subjectivity, chance incidents and other random factors often result in artists of equal talent being at different levels of success and income (2019: 81).

THE A&R PROCESS

A&R is an abbreviation of 'artists and repertoire', a term taken from the music industry of the early twentieth century. Songwriting and performing were usually separate activities at this time, hence A&R personnel acted as matchmakers finding songs for performers to record. The A&R role today is somewhat broader, involving the discovery of new talent, advising on song development, and making decisions about an artist's collaborators, producers and promotional strategies. The role is still typically associated with record companies, but A&R staff work at various other businesses, including music publishers. Managers also consider themselves to be a part of the process, with multiple MMF survey interviewees stating that A&R is now an essential part of the artist management process (MMF, 2019b). A&Rs often receive recommendations from other music industry contacts but will also attend shows and look for content and data via online platforms such as Shazam, Soundcloud, TikTok, YouTube and so on. In most cases, it is unlikely that unsolicited demos (unrequested material submitted directly to the company) will be acted upon by high-level industry professionals. Indeed, some labels even state on their websites that they will not listen to such submissions. Instead, A&R staff encourage artists to submit recordings only after hearing the music elsewhere (at a showcase or a concert) or following personal recommendations from trusted industry contacts. Such contacts may include promoters, venues, broadcasters and other artists, thus reinforcing the importance for artists and their managers of building a wide-ranging and supportive network. Larger companies may also make use of regional A&R scouts who give feedback based on the artists they work with or see in their local area. Many of these scouts are aspirant music industry workers, who are often not paid for their work. Instead, they use the role to build their contact base while seeking opportunities to move into a full-time position. Others are industry workers or musicians who have full- or part-time jobs, but like to operate as tastemakers within their local scenes. They may also help to promote artists who they think demonstrate potential.

A&R is a much desired and potentially rewarding career, with a high level of competition for roles. Academic (and former A&R) Ben Wardle (2016) notes that the role requires a varied skillset, including a wide musical knowledge, business acumen, negotiation skills and sales ability, in addition to the personal traits of grit and resilience. These personal traits are important because the role is often precarious, with A&Rs judged by the quality of their recent signings (Harrison, 2021: 7) and past successes soon fading. Wardle (2016) notes that A&Rs are often blamed if an act does not 'break'; however, this could be due to numerous reasons outside the A&R's control, including a lack of prioritisation by the record company, poor scheduling or a lack of commitment from the artist.

Factors likely to appeal to A&R teams will include great songs, a good live act, a strong visual identity, a distinctive sound, an interesting backstory, and the potential to build an artist and sell records. In addition, Capitol Records' UK President Nick Raphael lists his three essential artist qualities (in order of importance) as likeability, ambition and talent, noting that public appeal and hard work are arguably more important than musical ability (Rennie, 2015). These various factors are, of course, highly subjective: academic Keith Negus (1999: 34) refers to a 'mystical' attitude to A&R, in which 'great music will always find a home' and the A&R manager's gut instinct and personal judgement is highly valorised. In contrast, he says, record company executives and accountants seek a more predictable set of criteria. Hence, we see A&Rs consulting a wide range of industry data sources to help justify their decisions, including social media engagement, radio and streaming playlists, and data analytics from companies such as Soundcloud, Shazam, Spotify, YouTube, Live Nation, and so on. As record companies may be accessing similar data to each other, there is a potential for 'bidding wars' to occur where an artist and their manager achieve a significant level of hype. An alternative to seeking new artists through recommendations and scouts is to 'manufacture' groups through an audition process, with 'boy bands' and 'girl groups' being the most obvious examples of this. A highly developed version of the process can be seen in East Asia, where J-Pop, K-Pop and similar genres recruit and train their artists from a young age (see Box 3.1).

▬▬▬ BOX 3.1 ▬▬▬▬▬▬▬▬▬▬▬▬▬▬▬▬▬▬▬▬▬▬▬▬▬▬▬

A&R in K-Pop

A&R processes in the K-Pop genre have been explored by journalist John Seabrook. He describes how talent agencies recruit young people aged between 12 and 19, using both talent scouts and an audition proceess (Seabrook, 2015: 156). The companies exert more control over artists than is typical in Western markets (2015: 155), with performers undertaking several years of training before being assigned to a group (2015: 157). Concerns have been raised over working conditions, pressure to undergo plastic surgery and restrictive contracts (Lie, 2012; Seabrook, 2015).

(Continued)

Lee Soo-Man (the founder of leading K-Pop company SM Entertainment) seeks significant control over artists (Russell, cited in Seabrook, 2015: 151), which is partly achieved through a development process referred to as 'cultural technology' (Seabrook, 2015: 151). This process sets a goal of creating 'the biggest stars in the world' (Lee, cited in Seabrook, 2015: 154), with Lee providing SM employees with an accompanying 'manual' featuring guidance on selecting songwriters, production styles, chord progressions, dance moves, camera angles and make-up (Seabrook, 2015: 153). Seabrook describes Girls' Generation as 'the group that represented cultural technology in its highest form', succeeding both at home and internationally (2015: 151–153). Indeed, K-Pop is explicitly global in its outlook and 'business concerns consistently trump musical or artistic considerations' (Lie, 2012: 357). John Lie suggests that this accounts for the music being based on American-style chart pop and production techniques, and the use of simple English language phrases in the lyrics, which focus on the 'hegemonic pop-music theme of love' (2012: 356–358). He also notes that agencies focus on groups rather than solo artists, as groups act as their own backing dancers, and their members are easily interchangeable – for instance, when some are ill or busy on other projects such as acting, fan conventions and so on. Furthermore, Krueger (2019: 86) highlights the differences between artist agreements in South Korea as compared to the US. In the US system, artists and their teams are relatively independent, being able to plan their own touring schedules and fees. Conversely, K-Pop groups are more likely to sign lengthy and restrictive contracts. Krueger (2019: 86) also describes different systems in Japan (with musicians usually operating on a 'work-for-hire' basis) and China (where labels also commonly take a significant share of an act's live music income).

STRATEGIES AND ROUTES FOR RELEASING MUSIC

There are now multiple routes for releasing music, offering a range of options to artists of all genres and career stages. The do-it-yourself (DIY) approach, allied with direct-to-fan (D2F) distribution, has grown in recent years, with artists such as Skepta, Dolly Parton, Radiohead, Chance the Rapper and Frank Ocean achieving notable chart success outside a traditional record company structure at various stages of their careers. Such an approach can also be branded as 'artists direct', neatly summarising the process of artists selling directly to fans (Mulligan, 2021b). It should be noted, however, that many record companies are also enjoying a period of significant growth thanks to rising streaming revenues, with such businesses benefiting from high audience demand for both current and 'heritage' artists. They are also collaborating with DIY artists in 'label services' deals. In this section we consider the main options available to aspiring artists, as well as the potential advantages and disadvantages of each approach.

Do-it-yourself (DIY)

One effect of the digitisation of the music industries is that there is greater potential for democratisation, meaning that artists are increasingly able to reach their audiences without the mediation and support of a record company (Hesmondhalgh, 1998). Some DIY artists are entirely self-managed, while others are surrounded by professional teams including a manager, publisher, agent and lawyer. The benefits of a DIY approach include: retaining ownership of the music; earning a greater share of any revenues that are generated; and having direct access to data metrics about audiences. But it may be argued that artists are also turning to the DIY route due to the ease of digital distribution, the declining influence of radio promotion and the ability to build a fanbase online (Passman, 2019: 76). As such, niche artists are often better served outside the major label system, as they can target their fans in a much more direct and focused fashion (Passman, 2019: 76). However, while artists can now upload, promote and sell their own work entirely online, making a success of that process is somewhat harder (Haynes and Marshall, 2017). Stormzy's manager Tobe Onwuka explains that success via the DIY route understandably takes longer to achieve, also noting that it is a gruelling process. He nevertheless describes the notable benefits of such an approach, such as a lack of external interference and control of copyright (Jones, 2017). Furthermore, the MMF notes that the 'declining relevance of the "traditional" label system is especially true for acts who have already achieved a high level of commercial breakthrough and who may be out of contract' (MMF, 2019b: 16). Those who have adopted a DIY approach following a successful major label career include Dolly Parton, Radiohead and Frank Ocean, whereas those who have built 'from the ground up' include Chance the Rapper and Stormzy (although the latter signed a joint venture deal with Warner in 2018).

A DIY artist's activities may be separated into three broad areas (though there is considerable blurring between them): creative work, managerial processes and information systems (Oliver, 2010). Creative work includes songwriting, recording and live performance, though this may be extended to include other creative activities – for instance, aspects related to marketing and distribution (artwork, design work, promotional ideas and so on). There are clearly cross-overs here with both 'managerial processes' and 'information systems', as some aspects of music marketing and distribution require administrative skills, such as registration with royalty collection agencies, and dealing with digital distributors and the data they provide. For academic Paul Oliver (2010), such 'managerial processes' also refer to networking, collaboration and financial management. Financial management can incorporate the day-to-day business of managing a career, dealing with booking agents, journalists and so on. But it can also refer to the project management work required in setting release schedules, planning and running marketing and social media campaigns, and strategising tours. Once again, there are cross-overs here with 'information systems', as DIY artists need to deal with the technical aspects of websites, social media, collection societies, distributors, and a variety of data sources that may aid managerial processes. Such data can also feed into creative work, by helping artists to understand which songs gain the greatest traction and why. The data can also show which countries are engaging the most with their music, while playlist analysis may help to identify potential collaborators. Furthermore, digital consultant Jessie Scoullar (2015) notes that the administrative approaches mentioned by Oliver should include the prioritisation of mailing lists and the nurturing of fan relationships. In addition to promoting audio streams and downloads, these can also aid in driving merchandise sales and direct ticket sales, something which is becoming increasingly important as the livestreaming model is monetised (Anderton, 2022; see also Chapter 8). Furthermore, we should note that DIY artists often hold down day jobs to support their endeavours and may be involved in other money-making activities, such as instrumental tuition.

Label services

As noted earlier, DIY artists may not be as independent as they might at first seem, since they may choose to collaborate with record companies, distributors and others through a label services model. This approach helps artists to gain expertise and support in areas such as distribution, marketing, brand partnerships, playlist pitching and data management. Such deals may be offered by subsidiaries of the major record companies – such as The Orchard and AWAL (both owned by Sony Music Entertainment) and Virgin Music Label and Artist Services (owned by Universal Music Group). Alternatively, artists may work with independent companies such as Absolute, Believe, Horus Music and Integral. Artists must be of a high standard to be considered, yet the popularity of the model means that artists and managers are also 'increasingly demanding either outright control or reversion [of their copyrights] after a certain period' when negotiating record company deals (MMF, 2019b: 17). Manager Niamh Byrne notes, moreover, that managers may try to delay working with a record label, instead choosing to further develop an artist themselves in order to build momentum and create a stronger negotiating position (MMF, 2019b: 10). She also remarks that while a traditional label deal can provide the required funding for a campaign, it may be preferable to make use of alternative funding sources (if available) before seeking a label services deal (MMF, 2019b: 16). The popularity of the label services route is noted by the MMF, which argues that there are 'many instances of artists sustaining a career within the label services model' rather than a traditional recording contract (MMF, 2019b: 17). In some ways, such a service-based model may be viewed as an extension to the common practice of international licensing seen for both independent artists and independent record companies (discussed below).

However, one clear advantage of the DIY and label services systems is that artists retain both artistic and financial control of their careers, generating money from multiple income streams and retaining a higher share of royalties. Revenue splits for such deals may be in favour of the artist, but can be higher or lower depending on the quantity of services being supplied. A strong business knowledge is therefore required to ensure that the greater profit share achieved by being a DIY artist or signing a label services deal will be financially effective, especially as revenues for DIY artists will be smaller and more intermittent than receiving record company advances (see below).

Major record companies

Some artists may be offered a recording contract with a major record company (or 'major'), defined as a company which has more than 5 percent global market share in recorded music. However, recording contract offers are understandably rare. Millions of artists aspire to be signed to a major, yet only a few hundred are accepted by these companies (or their sublabels) each year. At the time of writing, the major record companies are Universal Music Group, Sony Music Entertainment and Warner Music Group. In terms of global market share, they represent more than two-thirds of the recorded music industry. This may be described as an oligopoly: where a small number of businesses dominate a market. Each major is *horizontally* integrated, meaning that it operates numerous subsidiary labels (also known as divisions or 'sub-labels') within a portfolio management strategy that allows labels to be bought, sold, merged or closed (Negus, 1999). Indeed, many of the subsidiary labels began as independent companies before being bought out by a major. Their original label names are often retained, since they have cultural resonance and brand recognition as, for instance, labels that supported well-known or highly respected artists in the past (The Beatles with Parlophone, Bob Dylan with Columbia, and so on). These subsidiary labels may experience tight financial control from the centre, but operate on a daily basis with loose creative control, hence each is likely to manage its own marketing and A&R functions, with the understanding that those working for them have a closer understanding of the markets they are operating within. Regular reports to the parent company will be expected, with sub-labels closed or merged with others in response to their commercial performance (Negus, 1999: 50). The majors (and their parent corporations) are also *vertically* integrated. This means that they own or control other companies within the music production chain, such as recording studios, distribution companies, music publishers, merchandisers, management companies and media businesses. This integrated structure allows them to benefit both financially and in terms of market share by minimising risks and reducing overall costs through rationalisation (Wall, 2013: 127). The majors are continuing to diversify their activities: for instance, WMG bought the youth culture website Uproxx and runs WMG Boost, which offers seed funding for music industry start-ups. The major record companies offer many potential career options for those seeking a music business career. These include, but are by no means limited to, the following areas:

- A&R/artist development.
- Brand partnership management.
- Promotion, marketing, social media and PR.
- Physical and digital distribution.
- Legal (copyrights, trademarks, contracts, etc).
- Arranging artwork and packaging.
- Audio-visual production (such as videos and social media content).
- Accounting and administration (including royalty management).
- International departments.
- Licensing and synchronisation (including music for film, TV and advertising).
- Artist management.

Independent record companies

Independent labels (or 'indies') are often considered as producing, manufacturing, distributing and selling records without the help of a major. But many indies rely on the majors either for funding (many are part-owned) or, acknowledging the global power of the major labels, for access to distribution networks and licensing deals in other territories. For instance, it is common for an independent label in one country to license its catalogue to a major label (or large independent) based in another. The licensee company then takes on responsibility for releasing and marketing the independent label's catalogue because they have specialist knowledge and contacts within their own territory, and can service that territory more effectively. Furthermore, independents may work with the majors on 'upstreaming' deals, where in-demand artists may be quickly transferred to the larger business. Such deals are usually agreed in advance of a release, thus relieving the need for lengthy licensing negotiations if the artist enjoys rapid success (Passman, 2019: 207). The interconnectedness of small and major companies leads the Association of Independent Music (AIM) to define an independent label as a record company that is less than 50 percent owned or financed by a major (AIM, n.d.). Artists signed to independent record companies meeting this definition may be included in the 'indie' record charts even though they may receive significant support from a major (Hesmondhalgh, 1998; Stanley, 2009).

Music industry executive Don Rose (2005) argues that independent labels have played an essential role in ensuring 'cultural diversity and innovation in music'. Numerous studies have made similar claims about record labels that have, for example, been pioneers in promoting rock and roll, British punk-rock and US indie-rock (Chapple and Garofalo, 1977; Hesmondhalgh, 1998; Azerrad, 2001). There are many stereotypes that surround independent labels, including assumptions that they have limited money, reject corporate approaches or are more 'authentic' in their operations and dealings with artists (Wall, 2013). Industry executive Darius van Arman (of US label Secretly Canadian) notes that indies are often categorised as more 'underground' or 'arty', while others assume that they are motivated less by achieving financial success than by supporting the music and artists that they believe in (PIAS, 2016). But van Arman argues that such stereotypes do not create an accurate picture of a wide-ranging sector. He points out that many independent companies are commercially ambitious, and that their significant sales revenue promotes wider competition in the music business (Ingham, 2016). Furthermore, there are many independent labels that have focused predominantly on chart pop: artists such as Kylie Minogue, Britney Spears, N-Sync and Taylor Swift were all initially signed to independent labels.

The independent sector is multi-faceted and highly diverse, ranging from small home-based labels with a limited number of signings (Strachan, 2007) through to multinational entities such as Beggars Group, Rough Trade and Domino. There are also numerous genre-focused labels that have provided a launchpad for successful careers, including London-based grime label Boy Better Know, created by brothers Jamie and Joseph Adenuga (better known by their stage names JME and Skepta). Jason Rackham, Managing Director of the large independent label PIAS, suggests that working with the independent sector can be beneficial for artists, arguing that there is lower staff turnover, hence a higher level of commitment to both artists and the label. Moreover, there is less pressure for an artist to achieve a quick success in comparison to a major. For Rackham, this means that the artist is more likely to build a sustainable, long-term career while working with 'like-minded' staff and fellow musicians (Rackham, 2016). van Arman concurs, suggesting further that independent labels have the ability both to scale up an artist's ambition and to reach a wider audience than might be achieved by taking a fully DIY approach (PIAS, 2016).

RECORD COMPANY CONTRACTS

If an artist signs a recording contract with a record company, the company typically agrees to pay the artist an advance: an upfront financial payment to support both living costs and creative activities. This advance must be paid back from the artist's future royalties under the contract, a process known as recoupment. Some services, such as recording, marketing, music video production and so on, may be paid for by the label but later recouped, so artists and their legal teams should check their contracts thoroughly to identify all recoupable costs. An artist's royalty percentage can vary considerably, so it is the artist manager's role to negotiate the best deal possible in relation to their artist's specific needs and their 'bargaining power' within the industry (Anderton et al., 2013: 194). More established artists, and those with an industry 'buzz' around them (as seen, for example, with the UK band Arctic Monkeys and the Norwegian artist Sigrid), will have greater bargaining power, hence may secure better terms. Once an artist has signed to a label, managers and artists must ensure that they become (and then remain) a priority for that label, to ensure that marketing budgets and time are assigned to them rather than to other acts. Prioritisation is based on the artist's public appeal, their potential for internationalisation and cross-over between genre markets, and their marketability across different media (Anderton et al., 2013: 40). To ensure continued prioritisation, artist managers need 'buy-in' from the various teams that work within a label, so must use their negotiation and social skills carefully. In some cases, a key figure within a company may provide this 'buy-in'. But as staff regularly move job roles and companies, it is important for the manager to build wider support to protect their artist's interests. Failure to do so may lead to de-prioritisation should that key figure leave the label.

Royalty rates vary considerably, depending on the type of label, artist career stage and the type of release (digital or physical). Royalty payments are only paid to the artist once the advances paid out under a contract have been fully recouped (i.e. repaid) from the artist's royalty share. Hence, if a recording sells poorly, it will likely be the case that the artist receives no income under the contract, even though the record label itself may have recovered its costs from its (much larger) share of the revenues generated. Even where a record does sell well, income from that recording may also be offset (cross-collateralised) against advances related to other elements of the contract. Artists may therefore be in debt to a record company for a very long time, though it should be noted that advances are not typically repayable in the manner of a personal loan, only from royalty income. Single-song deals are also possible, with the artist assigning rights to a company for just one track, leaving them free to sign other deals elsewhere for the remainder of their catalogue. Such deals may relate to novelty songs, summer holiday successes, social media trends or club hits promoted by DJs.

Recording contracts in the independent sector often work in a different way: a 50/50 split of revenues between label and artist once the initial costs related to the project are recouped. Multiple rights (or '360') deals have also been commonplace over the past decade (in both the major and the independent sectors). In such a deal, the label may take a percentage of live ticket sales, merchandise income, sponsorship income, work in other creative areas (such as acting or presenting) and publishing income. Harrison (2021: 93–94) notes that such revenue-sharing deals are still commonly offered to new artists looking to sign an exclusive deal, although there are tentative signs of a decline. Indeed, Harrison (2021: 95) suggests that the labels' previous justification for such deals has been weakened by the significant income now generated for them through streaming platforms. Yet despite such successes for labels, the majority of record company signings do not recoup their advance payments (Krueger, 2019; Osborne, 2021), hence highly successful artists effectively subsidise other signings and label activities. This is a potentially dangerous position for an independent label, should those high-profile artists leave the company or release commercially unsuccessful music.

There are some signs that the traditional recording contract may be changing. Artist manager Ellie Giles suggests that some labels' historic request for rights over the 'life of copyright' (70 years) should no longer apply in the streaming age, where albums never go out of print (MMF, 2019b: 17). However, the record company would understandably argue that the risks of investing in artists means that they have a right to long-term royalties in order to recoup their financial outlay (MMF, 2019b: 17). Nevertheless, artist managers contend that the traditional terms of recording contracts are no longer fit for purpose, and they are increasingly seeking more 'equitable contract terms' from record labels, including a shift away from the system of an advance being exchanged for 'lifetime ownership of their client recordings' (MMF, 2019b: 14–15). Artist manager Kilo Jalloh explains that artists now expect an indie-style deal offering a 50/50 profit-share and are less willing to sign away their live income (MMF 2019b: 18). As an example, Taylor Swift's current deal with Universal Music Group (UMG) appears to allow retention of the 'master' rights while licensing them to UMG on 'a relatively short-term basis' (Ingham, 2019). Artist manager Pat Corcoran signed a seemingly similar deal with Warner for two of his artists, whereby the artists retain their master rights and engage in profit sharing as opposed to royalty payments (Ingham, 2019). As a result, such deals are akin to the label services and independent sector deals noted earlier, and perhaps reflect the growing bargaining power of the artists involved.

Despite these improvements in flexibility, artists and their teams should still be aware of potential 'options' clauses in recording contracts. Such clauses give the record company the option to extend contractual terms by a set number of albums or other releases, as agreed in the contract. For example, a company may guarantee to release one album, but retain the 'option' to release another two (or more) based on the first album's success. Passman (2019: 108) explains that such clauses provide a record company with the smallest obligation possible if the artist's music fails to sell well, while keeping the option to benefit from the artist's potential long-term success.

PUBLISHING COMPANIES AND CONTRACTS

As discussed in the introduction, publishing companies play a key role in the music industries. Whereas a record deal focuses on the *sound recording* of a song, a publishing deal focuses on *the song itself*. Thus, publishers sign songwriters, who may or may not be performing artists as well. Publishing income includes performance royalties, mechanical royalties and synchronisation, all of which are considered in more detail in Chapter 10. A publisher's role is multi-faceted, involving duties such as: printing sheet music, administering copyrights, organising writing sessions, pursuing legal cases related to plagiarism and piracy, and working with collection societies to ensure that royalties for both artists and the company are maximised. In addition, they promote songs to record labels and performers who may be interested in recording their songwriters' music, and seek synchronisation (also known as 'sync') licences. Publishing income, including performance royalties, mechanical royalties and sync licensing, is discussed in more detail in Chapter 10.

In a typical exclusive publishing contract (sometimes known as a 'co-pub' deal), songs are assigned to a publisher for a set amount of time, known as the 'rights period'. Once signed, an artist can expect a publishing company to actively promote their music through the variety of approaches outlined above. An exclusive contract is similar to a recording deal in several aspects, with the artist receiving an advance which must be recouped before royalties can be paid. However, publishing contracts usually allocate a far higher royalty percentage to the artist, who may take as much as a 75–80 percent share (Harrison, 2021: 152). Some publishers may request an additional 5–10 percent for royalties earned from sync licences negotiated by the publisher (Harrison, 2021: 153).

The rights to an artist's catalogue can be assigned either for the life of copyright (typically 70 years after the last surviving writer's death), or for shorter periods, varying widely from 2–20 years. Rights periods of 12–15 years are likely to be offered for exclusive publishing deals (Harrison, 2021: 147–148). Although rights periods can be lengthy, terms (in which the publisher actively promotes the artist's songs) can be shorter, sometimes covering an initial period of one year, with several option periods potentially added (Harrison, 2021: 148). Related to this, Passman (2019: 293–294) recommends that artists should negotiate levels of creative control, considering issues such as changes to the music or lyrics, translations, sync licence permissions and the use of lyrics in advertising. Such considerations also align with the concept of moral rights, an area which is discussed in Chapter 10. Passman (2019: 291) notes further that some recording companies may request that an artist signs with their aligned publishing company as well. He recommends that artists should strongly resist this (thus remaining free to sign other potentially better deals), though it may be the only option available for a new artist.

Rather than assigning an artist's songs to the publisher, an alternative is to opt for an administration (licensing) deal. In this form of agreement, the publisher will collect royalties and carry out general administrative duties, but will not actively promote the songwriter's music. The artist is likely to retain around 85 percent of the royalties, due to the publisher's lower workload. An advantage of this agreement is that copyrights tend to be licensed for only a few years, rather than being assigned for a longer period of time. A downside is that the artist will need to promote their own song catalogues. A further option is self-administration, yet this DIY approach is arguably more difficult to achieve than its recording equivalent (i.e. releasing music through a distributor). This is due not only to the sheer complexity of the publishing and copyright sectors, but also to the additional work required in administering copyrights, chasing international royalty payments, and pitching music to other artists and companies. As a result, many artists who undertake the DIY recording route still sign with a publishing company to help maximise their songwriting income. As is the case with recordings, single-song agreements are also possible. The songwriter will likely have less control over the use of the song than in the other deals, but is free to sign with other publishers for other songs (Harrison, 2021: 143).

CONCLUSION

This chapter has considered the broad area of artist development, from creating an initial plan to building a sustainable, long-term career. We have considered A&R processes at recording companies, and the increasingly similar activities undertaken by managers, publishers and others. More research is required into A&R and artist development, particularly regarding how these processes operate in different cultures and territories. More analysis of how online communication and promotion is changing artists' routes to market would also be welcome. Artists and their managers need to carefully consider the potential advantages and disadvantages of seeking a recording contract with either a major or independent company. They should also weigh up the options for a label services deal or selling directly to their audiences (also considering how best to manage their publishing). These choices are not simple ones, but relate strongly to the career goals and aspirations of the artist. Whichever routes are chosen, it pays for the artist to understand the implications of their choices. If signing contracts with record companies and publishers, independent legal advice should be sought to protect artists' interests.

Key discussion points

- How can record companies continue to amend their contracts to make them more appealing to artists?
- What are the key benefits and challenges of artists adopting a DIY approach to releasing music?
- How can managers effectively balance an artist's personality, level of ambition, business acumen and genre when creating a development plan?

FURTHER READING

To discover more about practical elements of the artist development process, we recommend Paul Allen's *Artist Management for the Music Business* (2018), alongside *Understanding the Music Industries* by Chris Anderton, Andrew Dubber and Martin James (2013). To learn more about the changing aspects of recording contracts and the many options available to artists and their teams, we suggest reading MMF's *Managing Expectations* report (2019b).

4

CREATING A BUZZ

SUMMARY

In this chapter we explain the process of building a 'buzz' around an artist, an important area that has received relatively little academic attention. Buzz feeds (and is fed by) coverage across a range of platforms, including social media, magazines, websites, blogs, TV, radio and video games. It can be found particularly in the passionate discussions of friends and fans, both online and in person, about songs, videos, photographs, live performances and interviews. Buzz creates a compelling narrative and a strong sense of anticipation aimed at driving conversation about an artist, event or release. Here, we discuss it in relation to visual and verbal identity, and the important roles played by both audiences and data analytics.

Chapter objectives

- To examine the various ways of creating buzz, along with the preparatory work and tools required.
- To gain an in-depth understanding of artists and to show how this understanding feeds into the creation of campaign strategies.
- To explore the visual and verbal identity of artists, and the importance of photography, logos and names.
- To consider the important role of audiences in creating buzz.

Buzz is the momentum that drives an artist to 'the tipping point' (Gladwell, 2000) of success, though it may not take them over it. For the music consumer, it is a feeling that one must find out more and not miss out (see Bauman, 2005). Buzz is viral. It is 'contagious talk' (Carl, 2006: 602): the noise, chatter and palpable excitement that vibrates through relational networks like electricity through circuits. It cannot be ignored. Buzz is created to raise awareness and interest among the public, thus helping to build new audiences, drive sales and to develop a fan base. However, it is also used to secure the support of personnel in all strands of the music industry ecology, such as media, managers, record companies, live promoters, booking agents, journalists, games developers, music supervisors and brand sponsors. Buzz typically results from 3–12 months of thorough research and strategic planning by an artist's team in discussion with the artist. The key messages and objectives of the campaign are agreed, and the target audience is identified. The messages must be consistent across all promotional routes, and clearly define and reinforce the artist's brand in order to achieve the objectives set. Key objectives include awareness and music discovery among fans, and to pique the interest of record companies and media.

Artists and fans have an important role to play. As Nancy Baym (2018: 19) notes, artists are now engaged in 'relational labo[u]r': 'the ongoing, interactive, affective, material and cognitive work of communicating with people over time to create structures that can support continued work'. This revolves around the creation and maintenance of social connections with fans, media and industry figures. Additional time commitment is needed from artists, as is the development of 'communicative, self-presentational, entrepreneurial, and technological skills' (Baym, 2018: 6). For instance, Lil Nas X applied his experience as a meme creator to become a chart star (Rambarran, 2021: 153–154). Fans' roles have changed too since the 'internet made fan activity more public and put the distribution of media content into the hands of ordinary computer users' (Duffett, 2013: 382). Such an environment produces 'artists as entrepreneurs, [and] fans as workers' or 'co-creators', thus 'changing occupational and creative roles for artists and fans' (Morris, 2014: 273).

This chapter explores the discussions which take place between artists and their teams regarding the promotional options available to them. It also considers the processes that need to be developed, in addition to the assets that are required to achieve success. These form the building blocks that will, if used correctly, set solid foundations not only for specific campaigns but also for the ongoing careers of both artists and their teams. Much of this work revolves around the artist's visual and verbal identity, which is cultivated through the various strands of the media. This is where the conversation begins and where connections start to be made (see also Chapters 5 and 6). For this to be effective, detailed research and knowledge in a number of areas is required, beginning with an in-depth understanding of the artist being promoted.

UNDERSTANDING THE ARTIST

Following the relationship model outlined in Chapter 1, an artist's team must develop a nuanced understanding of the artist, and build a supportive and productive working relationship on a social and professional level. A rigorous analytical assessment of the artist from business, creative and psychological perspectives should also be undertaken. This will help an artist manager and their team to decide whether they wish to work with the artist, and to understand how they might proceed if they do. Songs are clearly central to this in terms of music, lyrics, instrumentation, arrangement, sound and production. What audience will they appeal to? Could they be played on the radio or go viral on social media? What do they say about the artist? Do they provide angles for media stories? Live performance also needs to be considered, with attention given not only to ticket sales but to an artist's stagecraft and visual presence (audience engagement and reactions will also provide useful feedback). In our visually-oriented culture, it is vital to consider how an artist's image (clothing, hair-styles, attitude) will work in relevant media and connect with audiences. Linked to this are their personal interests (politics, film, literature, sport, art and so on), and the media that they regularly consume, which provide a rounded picture of the artist and suggest promo-tional opportunities. Similarly, does the artist have other talents (acting, painting, blogging, podcasting and so on) that could be drawn upon in media coverage and social media posts? For example, Chloe Walsh of Grandstand Media (interview with authors) notes that, when taking on new clients:

> I ask them who they think their musician peers are, what outlets they read and what kinds of interests they have outside of music. The more I know about them the better I can represent them to the media. And whether they have a passion for muscle cars, soccer, poetry or sustainable fashion, I can pitch profiles tailored to their interests and provide them with the kinds of profile-raising press that will help lead people to their music.

Furthermore, the team should ask the artist how they see themselves as being positioned within the broader music market, though research should also be undertaken to establish an impartial view on this. Finally, an artist's current media and social media presence should be analysed in relation to the number of followers, types of stories, nature of fan responses, and fan engagement.

Understanding artists' personalities and the relational nature of group dynamics first helps to determine their marketing/promotion. For instance, analysis of any teen-pop band from Spice Girls and One Direction to the various East Asian idol groups shows that band members are presented as clearly characterised personalities. This allows audience identification with individual performers as well as with the group. Second, it determines how best to deal with and pre-empt future problems. An understanding of psychology is useful here. How does the artist operate? If the artist is a group, how stable are the interpersonal dynamics? Are the group members compatible, or are there rivalries, ego battles and potential causes for resentment? Is there a leader, and who is the principal songwriter? Does the songwriter share the publishing money with the rest of the band? Even groups of friends with shared experiences and interests can fall out with each other over business matters such as these. It is therefore important, whether the artist is a solo performer or a group, to establish the following:

- What are their ambitions, inspirations and motivations (AIM)? (Hopkins, 2016).
- Do they have the work ethic and commitment to match their ambitions?
- Do they have the self-confidence and self-belief to push themselves forward?
- How will they handle media interviews and will they need media training?
- How would they deal with success or failure?
- What are their limitations?
- How is their mental and physical health? How will they handle the workload, the touring, the reviews and social media comments (both positive and negative) and being in the public eye? (see also Chapter 11)
- Are there any stories that might appear in the press when they become successful that might under-mine their image?

If the answers to these various questions are established early in the process, those building the artist's campaign are in a position of strength and can plan accordingly. Similarly, if the artist is self-managing, then it would be worthwhile for them to carry out an honest and reflective self-analysis. It is important for the artist to find their focus, voice, presence, identity and confidence – in themselves, on stage, in their songs and on social media – before stepping things up. To move an artist from writing and demoing songs in their bedroom or rehearsal space into the public and media spheres is a delicate process, and many need the guidance of industry professionals and others to help them do so successfully. Indeed, in some respects, an artist does not fully 'exist' until they have come into contact with an audience and the press – until they have defined themselves through photographs, live performances and online content, as well as through their interactions with fans and critics. It is here that a crucial stage in meaning-making and star-making happens: when the artist becomes 'real' and develops confidence in their presentation.

Preparing the artists thoroughly is a key stage of any campaign. Team members often perform an educative, mentoring role for their clients, expanding their knowledge (of music, film, literature, politics and so on), inculcating new ideas, and encouraging them to challenge their own assumptions and those of others (Hopkins, 2016). This is aimed at developing them as stars: to give them confidence and something to talk about in interviews and social media posts, enabling them to make connections and contextualise themselves. Music journalist Lois Wilson was the first manager of psychedelic band Temples, who reached number 7 in the official UK charts in 2014 with their debut album *Sun Structures*. She states, in Hopkins (2016):

> The role of a band manager for me is to facilitate and enable the band's potential, to help their musical ideas grow. You use the music industry … drawing on all resources available to reach that potential. It's a guiding, mentoring role. … As a manager I gave knowledge and guidance, I even gave homework – go see this band and see how they use their guitar as a weapon not just to make music. We would watch YouTube videos – see what the lead singer says in between songs to engage the audience – how will you do that? We planned everything, from image, to what venue and why, support bands, DJs, researching what had gone before us and what we wanted to take from that and build on.

VISUAL AND VERBAL IDENTITY

Popular music is understandably viewed, primarily, as an aural experience. Yet songs are consumed, to varying degrees, with visuals – publicity photos and posters, magazine covers and website banners, album artwork, social media posts and teasers, and promotional films and videos. For Keith Negus (1992: 72), such 'visual marketing involves an attempt to articulate the authenticity and uniqueness of an artist … [one that] operates as a metonym for an act's entire identity and music'. Indeed, Australian academic Guy Morrow (2020) suggests that we adopt the term 'design culture' – drawn from the work of Guy Julier (2006) – as a way to think about an artist's identity. For Morrow (2020: 2):

> [D]esign culture offers a way to understand music product milieus and the visual and multisensory storytelling practices that stem from these. … [T]he visual and multisensory artefacts featured are a part of popular music as an artform – they are not just tacked onto music to market it.

These visual elements are part of a package, integrated, to varying degrees, with the music. Thus, they are a key part of an artist's overall image and the subsequent experience of their fans. It is therefore crucial that photographs, videos and artwork should match and enhance the music, to reinforce it with a consistent message that works in tandem with verbal elements such as PR stories (discussed in Chapter 6).

With an ever-increasing number of media platforms and cheaper, more advanced hardware and wi-fi access, we are increasingly consuming music with a range of visuals. Some of the more sophisticated examples are: Beyoncé's visual albums *Beyoncé* (2013), *Lemonade* (2016) and *Black is King* (2020); and Björk's *Biophilia* (2011) and *Vulnicura* (2015). Beyoncé's albums feature extended videos for every song, helping to reconceptualise their meanings and connect further with social and political issues. Björk's *Biophilia* was released as a smartphone app where tracks were accompanied by animations, gameplay and additional information for fans to engage with while listening. Of course, these were expensive productions by established stars, yet the accessibility of cheap, advanced technology, such as smartphones and GoPro cameras, has created new opportunities. In 2009, the grime star Giggs established an audience via YouTube with the video for 'Talkin' Da Hardest', which was filmed on a third-generation mobile phone – a practice that quickly became standard in the genre (James, 2021: 84). The DIY nature of early grime videos matches what Monique Charles identifies as grime's 'lo-fi sound' (cited in James, 2021: 97). Alternatively, emerging stars might connect to audiences through livestreamed performances or by posting cover versions on YouTube. Through the latter approach, R&B sisters Chloe X Halle earned a recording contract with Beyoncé's Parkwood Entertainment in 2013. Such activities may secure fan, industry and media interest, thus becoming a key part of an act's origin story – part of their 'buzz'.

In the music industries, close attention should be paid to the visual, verbal and musical identity of an artist. Chloe Walsh (interview with authors) states that:

> The media are inundated with pitches, [so] knowing what specific editors, critics or producers respond to will make your pitches more successful. Wast[ing] their time having them listen to things that don't make sense for their outlet or TV show will just make it harder for you next time you have something you'd like them to listen to.

In the following sections we examine the visual identity of artists as developed through photography, and through the careful design and choice of artist logo and name. We then focus on broader aspects related to verbal identity. We will return to visual identity again in Chapter 5 (with a focus on single and album artwork) and in Chapter 6 (the production of video content and its integration with social media platforms).

Photography

Music publicity photos are a mix of communication, seduction, and sometimes provocation. They carry a message, tell a story, start a conversation, and make a connection with the viewer. The guiding principles of a good publicity photograph are:

- Is it newsworthy?
- Does it tell a story? And does that story align well with the artist's image and music?
- Will it stand out and catch the attention of the media and public?
- Will it be shared on social media, and secure major space on websites and print media?

Photography is part of the star-making process and, according to Marco Livingstone, shapes 'our perceptions not only of [the artist's] appearance at the peak of their inventiveness but of the particular qualities of their own creativity' (cited in Rock, 1995: 8). It is crucial in establishing the iconography of popular music, with the best images evoking emotions and igniting engagement and connection. Photography is a 'central part in the culture of celebrity' (Bull, 2010: 167), being used to document the activities and lives of artists in live performance, studio reportage, backstage footage and so on. Depending on the needs and image of an artist, it can be used to increase their relatability to an audience (Adele, Ed Sheeran) or to create a larger-than-life fantasy persona (David Bowie, Lady Gaga).

Photography is readily understandable to modern audiences in our visually-oriented culture, though cultural theorist Stuart Hall (1999: 309) notes that 'all images are multi-vocal and are always capable of bearing more than one interpretation'. Moreover, as the art critic John Berger (1972: 8) states, '[t]he way we see things is affected by what we know or what we believe' : in other words, by our cultural conditioning and experiences. With this in mind it is important to consider the context in which a photograph may be seen and how the audience might interpret it. Given the globalised nature of the modern music industries, and the circulation of images through social media platforms, it is therefore crucial to be fully aware of cultural differences between different territories. Will the references and meanings embedded in the photo be understood as intended? Might they cause offence?

If a photograph is to act as a 'metonym for an act's entire identity and music' (Negus, 1992: 72), it is crucial to establish what needs to be communicated, how this can best be achieved, and which media outlets will be most suitable for reaching the desired target audience. Without this knowledge it will be difficult to create the elusive buzz that artists and their teams seek. Photographs should show 'what the band are all about ... to make it look to the viewer [that] they know what's going on in the mind of the artist ... some sort of contact ... a kind of magic' (Tom Sheehan, interview with authors). This is one of many reasons why it is vital for the team to analyse and understand the artist first. It also points to the importance of location in framing the artist and giving them context. As Negus (1992: 67) states, the 'background provides a series of connotations which reinforce the artist's musical identity'. Hip-hop and punk-rock artists might use locations featuring city streets and graffiti, while folk and country music artists might choose bucolic countryside locales. Yet such approaches conform somewhat simplistically to the genre rules, conventions and expectations (Fabbri, 1981; Frith, 1996) associated with these genres. Instead, it may be more interesting to act counterintuitively to create a sense of disjuncture that makes the media and public pay attention. This is by no means always easy to achieve. One occasion where counterintuition proved successful was with Billy Childish. In 2002, when most acts were making use of photographers with new digital cameras, he produced a photo of himself on a pinhole camera he made from cardboard. As the photo was grainy black and white, the media were not initially keen on using it. However, when it was explained that the photo was consistent with Childish's creative practice (using vintage Vox amps rather than PA systems) and image (Victorian and Edwardian military/workwear), they agreed. Indeed, the photo was used extensively and contrasted sharply with the usual high-resolution, glossy and full-colour photographs found in print and online media.

Other important choices include the following, each of which will result in different connotations or meanings being ascribed to an artist:

- Should the images be in colour or black and white?
- Should they be oriented as portrait or landscape?
- Will the artist be carefully posed? Or presented in an informal way?
- Will it be a full body shot or head and shoulders?
- Should the artist be static or photographed in motion?
- Are props required to make a point?
- When photographing a band, where should each member stand in relation to the others?

Photographer Tom Sheehan (interview with authors) notes that: 'Record companies want all bases covered … images for all sorts of uses. Mags want a more direct, specific image … normally one that is close to the edge/doing something that the artist wouldn't normally do.' A creative brief may be provided to the photographer, outlining factors such as location, mood and message, as well detailing the fee, deadline, format and intended uses of the photos (for example, print press only, social media only, or all uses including album artwork).

Logos and names

If we see artists as brands (see Chapter 9), we should carefully consider the component parts. Mollerup (1997: 56) states that a 'brand is a product … including its trademark, its brand name, its reputation. … When we talk about a brand we talk about verbal, visual and conceptual aspects of product identity.' These three strands usually come together in an artist's logo, which needs to be both instantly recognisable and communicate the cultural positioning and meanings to be ascribed to an artist. The logo may be the artist's name presented in a font that reflects the artist and their music. For instance, Taylor Swift's handwritten logo connotes elegance and accessibility, qualities that are key to her appeal. The logo may also be presented as a graphic. Examples include Prince's gender-fluid symbol and the Rolling Stones' lascivious lips and tongue – based on singer Mick Jagger. Public Enemy's logo features a silhouetted figure adopting a B-boy stance in the crosshairs of a gun, symbolising, for lead rapper Chuck D, 'the black man in America' (Grow, 2014), thus mirroring their name. An effective logo should work successfully in various settings: as a social media icon, poster, artwork, t-shirt and across other, more creative, contexts. For instance, Radiohead achieved much media coverage and social media traction when their bear logo appeared as a crop circle, teasing their announcement as headliners for Glastonbury 2017.

Sometimes artists adapt letters in their logo to create visual interest and to communicate something about them: for instance, the dollar signs that replace the letter 'S' in the names of rappers Joey Bada$$ and A$ap Rocky indicate their entrepreneurialism. Artists may also avoid using letters altogether to create instant graphic logos. An example is ††† (Crosses – a band led by Chino Moreno from Deftones).

Artists and managers should take care to avoid using names that have already been used, or any that are the same as an existing corporate business, as any subsequent lawsuit may prove costly and time-consuming and put the artist's career on hold. An artist's name plays a crucial role in conveying meaning. As Dave Laing (2015: 55) states: 'Whether a name is familiar or new, it can set up expectations of the music which is to come, through what the name positively connotes but also through what it appears to exclude.' Names are at the frontline of publicity, and a well-chosen name can make an instant connection with, and pique the interest of, potential fans and the media. Conversely, a badly chosen name can put off a potential fan entirely, depending on the associations it might trigger. Hence, names are important for indicating what an artist might sound like, what they might be like as people, and how they might fit into a fan's social world and personal identity (i.e. what does it say about them as fans?).

Taking a stage name gives an artist space in which to create a new persona and step out of their everyday lives and into other characters, enabling them to push themselves on stage and to perform in ways that perhaps they could not have done otherwise. For instance, Faruk Bulsara (lead singer of Queen) became Freddie Mercury, a name well-suited to the fantasy world of the glam rock era. In contrast, artists such as Sam Smith, Ed Sheeran and Dave play on the ordinariness of their given names and image. Changes of name need to be managed carefully as they can sometimes backfire. A good example is Lana Del Rey. When it was revealed before the release of her debut album that she had previously released material as Lizzy Grant, some fans and media felt deceived and there was significant backlash in print and online (Harris, 2012). Nevertheless, the name Lana Del Rey was very well constructed, with layers of meaning that matched her American 'retro' look at the time of launch. The key reference points are: Lana Turner (a glamorous Hollywood actress from the 1940s–1960s), Marina Del Rey (a glamorous seaside resort on the outskirts of Los Angeles), the Chevrolet Delray (a classic curvy space-age 1950s American car complete with tail-fins and shiny chrome), the Brazilian Ford Del Rey car (whose logo features in her debut video), and the El Rey theatre, an influential Art Deco music venue in LA.

Bands also draw on pop culture references that have strong associations and resonances, thus seeking to make meaningful connections with their intended audiences. Films, books and comics have been a rich source for this. Examples include: Bring Me The Horizon (taken from a line in the film *Pirates of the Caribbean: Curse of the Black Pearl*), Black Sabbath (taken from an obscure Italian horror film of the same name), and Duran Duran (adapted from a character name in the cult sci-fi film *Barbarella*). Some names are deliberately designed to be offensive and court controversy, such as the Sex Pistols, Jesus & Mary Chain, Dead Kennedys, Butthole Surfers and Deicide. More recently, several artists have chosen to draw on the influence of text messaging and social media conventions by removing the vowels from their names or re-spelling their names in eye-catching ways (something which also helps with search engine optimisation). Examples include the Canadian R&B artist The Weeknd, the Hull dream pop band bdrmm (pronounced 'bedroom') and the Scottish electronic pop group Chvrches.

Verbal identity

Verbal identity extends beyond an artist's name to describe all the language-based activity associated with an artist – activity that helps to build an artist's story and image while explaining who they are. Indeed, as Laing (2006: 333) notes: 'Popular music is never entirely "itself". Almost every context of performance or listening is framed by language. This language may prepare an audience for the musical experience, provide background information or seek to persuade listeners to become consumers ...' An artist's verbal identity is constructed through social media posts, press releases, media stories, advertising copy, sleeve notes, reviews and interviews, and many people contribute to this dialogue: PRs, marketers, journalists, bloggers, fans and the artists themselves. Their contributions form a 'metatext' around the artist and their music, affecting how we listen to and understand them (Taylor, 1995: 510). They also help 'to structure that listening, taking it from the "natural" physicality of sound to the "cultural" state of sounds endowed with human meaning' (Blake, 1997: 7). This is why PRs and marketers are so important in establishing the artist's verbal identity through the astute and appropriate choice of words, tone of voice and storytelling. Identifying the artist's genre(s), making comparisons with other artists positively or negatively, and including 'for fans of' indicators help to situate an artist within the broader music market.

Descriptions need to be informative, create excitement and curiosity, and deliver agenda-setting messages that address the question of what the music sounds like, how it makes the listener feel, and what imagery it evokes. Furthermore, it may detail the experience of seeing an artist live or offer insights into what the musicians are like as people. Points of connection and intrigue may be provided. For instance, mentions of cult musicians, films, authors or photographers can be relatable for some fans, or encourage others to find out more: a form of initiation as the fan travels from outsider to insider. Praising or criticising other musicians can also position the artist within the market and connect with fans and media. These references, phrases and opinions can then be drawn upon to inform the content of social media posts, press releases and artist biographies. Brainstorming keywords during the campaign planning phase can also influence visual elements such as the look and mood of album or poster artwork, or of videos and photos.

When Bon Iver's debut album *For Emma, Forever Ago* (2007) was released, a compelling (true) origin story was circulated about how it was recorded by Justin Vernon in a Wisconsin log cabin after a relationship break up and bouts of depression and illness. The location spoke to romanticised views of rural America. The overall story pointed to a record that would offer an intimate and lo-fi musical experience. However, care needs to be taken here as artists such as the rappers Akon, Rick Ross and the 'hobo' blues artist Seasick Steve have been exposed for over-exaggerating their back stories, thus harming their credibility. Other artists have succeeded through fiction and gamification. The rock band Creeper have proved themselves repeatedly in this approach, using clues, teasers and mysteries in their stories of the missing James Scythe (2015). A further example is Nine Inch Nails' campaign for *Year Zero* (2007), which made use of coded messages on t-shirts and on USB sticks left at gigs. These led fans to telephone numbers and websites that drove online conversations as fans tried to decode their meanings (Montgomery, 2007; Deacon, 2018). As Ann Powers (2007) notes, the campaign was 'a total marriage of the pop and gamer aesthetics that unlocks the rusty cages of the music industry and solves some key problems facing rock music as its cultural dominance dissolves into dust'. Increasingly the stories, narratives and games created by such campaigns are disseminated through social media as well as through press releases and press stories, with cross-referencing of elements across the different platforms. Creating engaging and appropriate content to support these narratives is a primary skill for music PRs to acquire, and we will discuss this further in Chapter 6.

UNDERSTANDING AUDIENCES

Understanding fandom, the levels of commitment involved, and the nuanced differences that may be identified between and within genres, are crucial concerns for both musicians and their teams. Such considerations will help them to determine the activities that fans will respond to and how best to communicate with them on both a day-to-day level through social media, and in broader marketing and promotional campaigns. Furthermore, it is important to be fully conversant with the rapid 'shifts in the media' and how these may reshape fandom (Duffett 2013: 28).

Fans buy artists' music, concert tickets, meet-and-greet access and merchandise, or support them in their recording and touring activities through crowdfunding. Yet, being a fan is rarely as simple as this. Indeed, while such financial investments are important to the ongoing sustainability of an artist's career, there are emotional and (sub) cultural investments that must also be considered. Emotional investment relates to how the music makes us feel as individuals, as well as how we feel about the artist. Here, it is worth borrowing the phrase 'felt relationships' from John Fiske's (2016: 87) study of sports fans, and applying it to the dynamic between music fans and their favourite artists. The cultural investment of being a fan says something about us – our identity, lifestyle and fashion – as well as our broader interests and belief systems. Ultimately, our emotional and cultural investments in artists and genres may shape the things we talk about in person or on social media, the friendships and communities that we build, and where we connect with others, such as gigs, clubs, skateparks, record shops, social media and gaming platforms.

Allied to this are the many emotional, cultural and practical roles that music plays in our lives (Sacks, 2008; Hesmondhalgh, 2013). Knowledge of all these elements is vital for the artist and their team when trying to develop marketing and PR campaigns to create a buzz. For instance, if they know where the target audience tends to gather (both online and in the real world), they can make informed decisions on the best locations to place advertisements. They will also gain important knowledge about fans and their consumer habits and behaviours that can be used to understand them in greater detail. *Dazed Media's* 2020 report 'The Future of Youth Culture' shows that Instagram, Sina Weibo and TikTok are the most influential social platforms globally for Generation Z and Millennials (Farmiloe and Cohen, 2020: 93). Fifty-six percent of global respondents stated that Instagram had the most influence, while 58 percent of Chinese respondents selected Sina Weibo (2020: 91). However, the mediascape is constantly changing, so an artist's team must monitor new platforms and trends, as well as their artists' audiences and their evolving use of social media.

A community of fans, such as Lady Gaga's Little Monsters or Yungblud's Black Hearts Club, represents an active community of consumers who can be drawn into an artist's marketing campaigns. They are, potentially, listeners, readers and followers/subscribers for radio stations, podcasts, magazines, newspapers and websites, and for YouTube channels, influencers, blogs and other 'publications' in the social media sphere (e.g. *GRM Daily*, *The Needle Drop*, *LADbible* or *Popjustice*). Hence, once identified, these communities become target markets for advertisers, which drives sponsorship endorsements and deals that may be beneficial to an artist's marketing and financial goals. Thorne and Bruner (2006: 53–55) note that fans have a 'desire for external involvement': to display their fandom through clothing, hairstyles, tattoos and wearing/using merchandise. There is a 'wish to acquire' which can be seen in the ownership of records and limited-edition products, as well as memorabilia such as tickets, wristbands and autographs. Likewise, there is a 'desire for social interaction' – the need for connection and conversation with other like-minded fans – thus building a self-supporting community of fans at gigs, club nights, fan club meetings, meet and greets and online. Thorne and Bruner (2006: 68) suggest that marketers should incorporate these factors into their thinking and plans, and we argue that this should happen early in the process in order to drive grassroots promotion and the fan-led buzz that may develop from it.

The grassroots activity noted above can be regarded as a form of 'fan labour', in which fans work to promote an artist but receive no direct financial benefits from doing so. Tiziana Terranova (2000: 37) refers to this as 'the moment where this knowledgeable consumption of culture is translated into productive activities that are pleasurably embraced and at the same time often shamelessly exploited'. While a fan might wear an artist's t-shirt (thus acting as a visible advertisement), others may operate at a higher level of commitment serving as vocal evangelists for the artist, particularly online. They are knowledgeable about their favourite artists and skilled in the use of social media, and combine these in promoting the artists, thus publicly displaying their fan credentials, and creating or enhancing grassroots buzz about an artist. Baym and Burnett (2009) call these fans 'amateur experts', while the term 'data fandom' is used in reference to East Asian fan communities (see Chapter 5). These fans are engaged in 'hidden' and unpaid work, yet that work carries the kudos of subcultural capital and personal validation. The 'symbolic creativity' (Willis, 1990) of this work includes, for example, fan art and fan fiction shared through social media, artist- and genre-centric websites, blogs and discussion lists. These are rich areas of fan activity that have blossomed in the digital age. For instance, fan-created work features in Daisy Asquith's insightful film about fandom *Crazy About One Direction* (2013). Other examples of 'symbolic creativity' include Snapchat images, TikTok videos, memes, tattoos, and the bricolage inherent in the clothing subversions and adaptions (Hebdige, 1979: 104) seen in genres such as mod, punk, goth and emo.

A key area of amateur productivity, or 'vernacular creativity' (Burgess, 2006), is to return to an earlier theme, fan photography. Martin Hand (2012: 3) notes that we live in a time of 'unprecedented levels of visual mediation' facilitated by 'a vast proliferation in the numbers of visual technologies and images circulating within advanced capitalist economies' (2012: 11). Thus, with the prevalence of smartphones and wireless technology, fans are able to instantly post a photograph of an artist (perhaps spotted in a supermarket or airport), a selfie taken at a meet and greet, or an image or video taken at a gig, to the platform of their choice. This practice displays their physical proximity or access to an artist, or shows their attendance at a particular event. While this may be regarded as jostling for position in a fan community, it is also a way of demonstrating that fandom, connecting with others and starting a conversation.

Data analytics

Before social media, labels and managers could discover where an artist was popular (or not) by analysing ticket, vinyl and CD sales (du Gay and Negus, 1994: 396). They could find out the specific record shops where an artist's music was bought and in what quantities. They might compile fan addresses from fan club mailing lists or competitions, but there was little other information available. Now, however, we are at what Lev Manovich (2018: 473) calls the 'media analytics' stage of media development. Here, the data available from digital platforms and social media sites goes far beyond plain figures to provide rich detail that helps to build a clear profile of an artist's audience and their activity. Social media data is no longer just about the numbers of followers and likes that are accrued on artists' pages. It is more about the quality of engagement and interaction, about sharing, commenting, creating content and making a commitment.

Data analytics has become an essential tool across the music industries, generating information that is invaluable for understanding fans, their music consumption habits and their levels of engagement. Data can be gleaned from a variety of sources, including (though not limited to) an artist's social media and website (and those of their record label and management company), YouTube (via YouTube Studio), Spotify (via Spotify for Artists) and other audio streaming sites, rights management companies (such as Kobalt), and live promoters and ticketing companies. There has also been a proliferation in specialist analytics companies, such as Next Big Sound (in conjunction with Pandora), Chartmetric, and Soundcharts, which provide data analysis to labels, artists and managers for a fee. Spotify, Live Nation, Shazam and other companies identify and publish details of trends based on the artists and genres their customers listen to or engage with, giving artists, managers and labels a clearer understanding of audiences and markets that can be used to inform their plans. Data is not only available to the major companies, since the 'increased popularity of direct-to-fan platforms and self-release tools [have] put more data into the hands of more artists' (Mulligan, 2018: 153). An example of this is Bandcamp for Artists and Labels (see also Chapter 7).

Negus (2019: 378) notes that the data analytics available from streaming services can give an artist and their team knowledge of:

> ... location, time of accessing music, repeated listens to the same track or artist, adjustment of volume, range of musical preference ... hardware and software use, and Internet activity. Listener engagement with specific genres, artists or songs can be cross-correlated with significant events (military conflict, royal wedding), controversial news stories, marketing campaigns or a performer's touring and promotional activities.

Companies like Awario offer social media monitoring and social listening, tracking mentions of artists both online and in the media. This important area of data collection facilitates 'semantic analysis' of internet conversations: analysing 'the words used and descriptions about musicians and bands in articles, reviews, blogs, forums and across social media platforms' (Negus, 2019: 378). Data can then be 'reduced to recurring keywords, and dissected to construct networks or webs of connections between artists, between songs and between listeners in different places' (2019: 378). Artists and their teams may carry out a social media audit themselves or engage an external company or consultant to do so. The results of such an analysis can then feed into the planning of marketing campaigns, the timing of release dates and the routing of concert tours, as well as to A&R, production and remix choices, and retail targets. It will also guide the team regarding platforms to be used, where to advertise, and how to communicate effectively with their fans.

Data analytics is also crucial in building business-to-business (B2B) 'buzz' – i.e. between businesses within the various sectors of the music and media industries. Emerging artists not only need to secure media support but also, as discussed in earlier chapters, the support of managers, record companies, booking agents and so on. FOMO (fear of missing out) characterises fan behaviour, yet it is also felt by industry personnel: the more that the industry is brought onside, the further the momentum builds, thus making it easier to persuade others to get involved. This is achieved by presenting a convincing argument about the viability of an artist, by building a buzz through conversations at music industry conferences and events, and by working with the tastemaker sections of music industry publications and blogs. Industry personnel are likely to ask questions such as: What's the level of fan engagement? Who are their fans in demographic and psychographic terms? What are their fans' social media and music consumption habits and broader consumer behaviour? The answers to such data-led questions can have a significant impact on decision-making, since labels, managers and other professionals are less likely to take a risk on a new signing without a positive data narrative being presented. When it is, a buzz about the artist can build and result in a bidding war between record labels, thus putting the artist in a stronger negotiating position and allowing them to request more funding, more creative control and so on. See Chapter 7 for further discussion of the role of data in the music industries.

CAMPAIGN STRATEGIES

In the early stages of an artist's career the campaign strategy may revolve around a carefully timed and integrated process. This is driven by research-informed decision-making. Behind-the-scenes preparation includes assembling the right selection of songs for performance and recording, learning stagecraft through open mic nights, rap 'battles', busking, local support shows and livestreamed performances, and developing visual and verbal identity. Taking the initial steps revolves around positioning the artist within the market by building a story and an engaging presence on social media platforms that the target audience uses, driving traffic between platforms, and placing representative tracks on SoundCloud and videos on YouTube. Allies must be cultivated in the traditional media and music industries, including managers, booking agents and record labels. To build the PR strategy, suitable media outlets must be chosen, including local and student press and radio, blogs and streaming playlists. Jamie Woolgar (Head of Press at Rough Trade) favours grassroots media like student press, and early tastemakers such as *So Young, Clash, The Quietus, Loud and Quiet, Line of Best Fit, The Guardian, iD, Dazed*, and 'new band of the week' introductory features (interview with authors). These work well together with airplay on local radio stations and international internet radio stations, as well as with support, in the UK, from BBC Introducing. These activities should build buzz and help to secure slots at industry conferences/events such as The Great Escape (UK) and South by Southwest (SXSW) (USA).

Catherine Fitterman-Radbill (2017: 323) defines music industry entrepreneurship as 'opportunity, creativity, innovation, and a "what if?" attitude'. This approach should also drive artists' buzz-focused campaigns. In Box 4.1 and Box 4.2, we discuss two examples, relating to the South London dubstep producer Burial and the indie rock band Black Midi, each of which has developed their career by staying true to themselves and marking out their difference. We then explore two innovative approaches to staging live performances that have proven successful in creating buzz.

■■■■■■ **BOX 4.1** ■■■■■■

'I want to be unknown': Burial and anonymity as strategy?

Genres such as pop, rock and hip-hop tend to revolve around personalities or personas (Kanye, Lady Gaga): 'the star'. In dance music, the superstar DJ and producer may also take on this role (David Guetta, for example), but it is perhaps more common to take a more anonymous approach, like Daft Punk and Deadmau5. Burial went further, maintaining total anonymity through the release of his first two albums, thus refusing to follow the 'star' model of promotion and marketing. There were no gigs, no DJ sets, no radio shows, and hardly any photographs. The few images available were taken by Georgina Cook, a dubstep insider (Hancox, 2007). None revealed his face, yet they successfully created an atmosphere that matched his music: he is shown only in silhouette or as an obscured reflection in a rain-soaked pavement. Nevertheless, word began to spread due to the quality of his music and a small but influential network of tastemakers and their niche blogs: Hyperdub label boss and producer Steve Goodman's *kode9*, Martin Clark's *blackdownsoundboy* and Mark Fisher's *k-punk*. Interviews with Burial were exceedingly rare and when they appeared, they focused only on the music, not the life of the artist, such that rumours about his identity abounded: was he, perhaps, Thom Yorke, Damon Albarn, Kode9, Aphex Twin or Kieran Hebden? (Marino, 2017: 177–178). In an interview for *The Wire*, he states: 'Most of the tunes I like, I never knew what the people who made them looked like, anyway. It draws you in. You could believe in it more ...' (Fisher, 2007: 28). The music critic, Simon Reynolds (2017) argues that:

> Burial's initial intent was always to stay true to the radical anonymity and facelessness of rave culture and underground techno ... he grew up fascinated by the enigmatic and outlandish artist names—LTJ Bukem, Rufige Kru, Foul Play, 2 Bad Mice, Dr S Gachet—that offered no clues to the color or class of these shadowy operators, no hint of where they came from, or even how many people were involved.

(Continued)

However, when Burial's second album, *Untrue*, secured a Mercury Prize nomination, the race was on to unmask the producer, with *The Sun* newspaper even offering a reward to anyone who could reveal Burial's true identity (Marino, 2017: 177). He finally revealed (via his Myspace page) his real name of Will Bevan, yet he still gave little away about himself as a person, the focus remaining firmly on his music. For Mark Fisher (2007: 28), Burial's refusal to be 'a subject of the media's promotional machine is in part a temperamental preference, and in part a resistance to the conditions of ubiquitous visibility and hyperclarity imposed by digital culture'.

▬▬▬▬ BOX 4.2 ▬▬▬▬

Black Midi and 'anti'-social media

Black Midi were one of the most successful British buzz bands of the late 2010s, securing magazine covers and a Mercury Prize nomination for their debut album *Schlagenheim* (2019). Their profile was initially fan-driven, built through comments boards, live performance (playing over 200 concerts) and the approval of another band, Shame. Black Midi had more or less no official social media presence (despite being on Facebook since 2016) and no music online when the buzz started building. They did not join Instagram until the week of the Mercury Prize (September 2019) and still post only rarely. They were, as Jamie Woolgar notes 'very reluctant to use social media' (interview with authors). The lack of information, music and accessibility worked in their favour to build mystique. The band also 'turned down quite a lot press', so Woolgar made strategic choices to secure press coverage in specific publications: *Mojo* ('for the older market – the record heads'), *The Crack* and *Loud and Quiet* (for the younger early adopters), the online style magazine *The Face* (for the tastemakers) and *The Times T2* magazine. The fact that the band members had attended the BRIT School could have been problematic given their 'cool' image and their experimental indie sound, but as Woolgar (interview with authors) says:

> we had to be up front about it and it was a positive for the mainstream media which led to them securing [The] *Times T2* magazine cover – unheard of for a new band. But the BRIT School link worked because of Adele and Amy Winehouse. The editor had heard of the BRIT School.

The band also had creative ideas beyond the music. Woolgar explains that they 'had strong feelings of how they wanted to be perceived. ... They're from the computer game generation, so they wanted to be animated in the style of *Grand Theft Auto* [GTA]'. The photos and video for 'Ducter' (2019) were produced by Anthrox Studio, known for their work on GTA and Red Dead Redemption. These visuals created a distinctive image for the band that linked to their (and their fans') interest in gaming.

Guerrilla gigging and gigjacking

Giacomo Bottà (2018: 4) defines guerrilla gigging as 'impromptu events in public spaces, often with marketing purposes'. While guerrilla gigs are not always impromptu, they are certainly designed to achieve the maximum buzz, while also building a community of fans through shared experience. This was demonstrated by the relationship built between bands such as The Libertines and The Others and their fans in the early-mid 2000s. The Libertines would regularly hold guerrilla gigs in their flats or those of friends or fans, even when they were selling out large London venues. This was, in part, about breaking down the metaphorical barrier between stars and their fans, while delivering a memorable and intimate experience. They also achieved considerable media coverage and genuine excitement around the band. Developing the idea further, The Others staged a series of guerrilla gigs in unusual locations, strategically chosen to gain attention. These included gigs held on a London Underground carriage, on the Abbey Road zebra crossing made famous by The Beatles, in the foyer of the Radio 1 building in London, and on the dodgems ride at the Leeds Festival (Barton, 2004). Central to their success was the active role of text messaging, fan forums and websites – an early use of networked connectivity in the music industries context. These guerrilla gigs turned functional everyday spaces into the chaos and anarchy of Hakim Bey's (1991) 'temporary autonomous zone': a short-lived space of heightened awareness and peak experience that mocks traditional authorities and hierarchies. The excitement and potential of guerrilla gigging can also be seen in the 'secret' or 'surprise' gig format, where established artists stage under-the-radar gigs or festival appearances to promote album releases or cater to fans. Examples include the Foo Fighters, Prince, Radiohead, Kanye West and Skepta.

Gigjacking, like guerrilla gigging, can be regarded as a form of 'street spectacle' (Serazio, 2013: 60) – the 'hijacking' of a conventional concert performance organised by a successful or compatible artist by staging an unofficial live performance outside the venue. Gigjacking developed into a scene in mainland Europe, taking particular root in Germany. Sophie Labrey regularly gigjacked across Europe with her band Shoshin between 2011 and 2018, and the band was able 'to fund, promote and rehearse our album through gigjacking, before we went into the studio to record it' (interview with authors). Shoshin did not directly pre-promote the details of their street shows for fear of alerting the authorities. However, 'it was a sort of game for our more "hardcore" followers, as they'd notice via Instagram that we were in a certain city, and would ... try and guess what concert we would be jacking. ... [A] big part of the success is down to the element of surprise...' (interview with authors). Moreover, once the band had safely moved on to the next town, they would use social media to 'post videos of crazy street shows, or tour diaries, which would entertain a lot of people' (interview with authors). This helped to extend the memory of the event and build a feeling of community. As a result of their activities and the 'buzz' it generated, the band was able to secure a booking agent and a record deal in the US. While artists and their teams can draw inspiration from these examples, they must bear in mind that while guerrilla gigging and gigjacking may be relatively easy and cheap to organise, they must comply with local and national laws and health and safety regulations.

CONCLUSION

This chapter has shown how the creation of buzz requires methodical research and planning, the identification and generation of opportunities, and a detailed understanding of the artist, the market and the competition. It also requires skills in networking and creative ideas, the development of a visual and verbal identity, and management skills in bringing all of the assets together. Activities need to be scheduled in an integrated and holistic way, using social media and other promotional routes. Schuyler Brown (2006: 223) argues that 'No brand can maintain buzz indefinitely' and it would be wrong to try to do so. Besides, '[w]e live in a neophiliac culture' where everyone is searching for the next new buzz artist (2006: 223). Creating buzz and reaching the tipping point is an important achievement, but as noted at the start of this chapter, it does not necessarily secure success. Chapters 5 and 6 show how artists' careers can pivot beyond that point, and be further developed and maintained through strategic marketing, PR and promotion.

Key discussion points

- How can the visual and verbal identity of artists be explored and developed using emergent technologies and platforms?
- What new ways might fans use to express their fandom?
- How might the energy and connections of fans be harnessed to work for the mutual benefit of artists and fans?

FURTHER READING

To understand the power of music and the impact it has on fans' intimate and collective emotions, we recommend David Hesmondhalgh's *Why Music Matters* (2013). On fandom specifically, the work of Mark Duffett is essential, including *Understanding Fandom: An Introduction to the Study of Media Fan Culture* (2013).

5

MUSIC MARKETING

SUMMARY

In this chapter we define marketing and promotion in the context of the modern music industries. We propose the *5Cs of music marketing* and the *9Cs of music marketing communication* as aids for strategic planning, and underline the importance of market research, planning, strategy and consistency in key aims and messages. We also discuss the roles and responsibilities of music marketers and important aspects of content creation. We conclude with a discussion of emergent practices of 'data fandom', as pioneered in the East Asian music industries, and consider their implications for music marketing in the Western music industries.

Chapter Objectives

- To explore the broader context of marketing and to define the operations of music marketing within it.
- To introduce and update marketing models and theories as relevant to the music industries.
- To explore the roles and responsibilities of music marketers.
- To acknowledge the associative, affective qualities of recorded music products, and their emotional and cultural significance.
- To investigate Chinese 'data fandom' and its implications.

The marketing of music operates within the wider contexts of what Zygmunt Bauman (2005: 2) characterises as the 'liquid life' that we lead, defined as:

> ... a precarious life, lived under conditions of constant uncertainty. The most acute and stubborn worries that haunt such a life are the fears of being caught napping, of failing to catch up with fast-moving events, of being left behind, of over-looking 'use by' dates, of being saddled with possessions that are no longer desirable ...

This resonates with the concept of FOMO (Fear of Missing Out) and the popular music fan's 'wish to acquire' (Thorne and Bruner, 2006) the latest record release or piece of merchandise, to experience the latest gig, to discover the next 'buzz' artist, or to become accepted as a member of a fan community. Music marketing is driven by the need to engender these desires and wishes. It walks the line between detailed planning, organisation, analytics and structure on the one hand, and instinct and creativity on the other. The best marketing involves all of these elements.

The Chartered Institute of Marketing (CIM) – the trade body for the marketing industry – defines marketing as 'the management process responsible for identifying, anticipating and satisfying customer requirements profitably ... the customer is at the heart of marketing, and businesses ignore this at their peril' (CIM, 2009: 2). To anticipate and satisfy audience needs successfully, music marketers must identify, analyse and understand what those needs are, and shape and deliver the artist and their music in a way that meets those needs while remaining true to the artist. This requires rigorous research into the artist, their vision, their competition, their target audience and wider market trends. Clearly, for artists, managers and labels to survive and thrive, they need successful and well-planned marketing campaigns.

Marketing is an ongoing and evolving journey. The emotional and associative qualities of music, and the marketing built around it, 'allow the musician and consumer to connect at the interpersonal level' (Ogden et al., 2011: 120). Indeed, unlike most other commodities, 'recorded music is characterised by emotional and experiential responses/needs rather than strictly utilitarian ones' (Anderton et al., 2013: 104). Clearly, fans make cultural and emotional investments in their favourite acts that extend well beyond the financial.

This chapter begins by introducing and updating the theoretical models which underpin music marketing and assist in strategic campaign planning. We then explore the roles and responsibilities of music marketing personnel, before looking more closely at content creation. We argue that one of the central aims of music marketing is to create a compelling and immersive environment, a 'discrete world' around an artist and their music. This is achieved through visual and experiential elements such as artwork, guerrilla and viral marketing, advertising and publicity, online gaming, geo-location technology and record stores. The final section looks at the rise of 'data fandom', particularly in China, and its implications for Western marketing practices.

THEORETICAL APPROACHES: MARKETING MODELS

The marketing mix: from the 4Ps to the 5Cs of music marketing

The marketing mix was originally devised by Jerome McCarthy (1960/1975) and consisted of four elements (the 4Ps): product, price, place and promotion. It was not designed specifically for the music industries, but can be easily applied to them. The *product* must have the right sound and look, and it must entertain its target audience, affect their mood, and meet their interests and expectations; hence it is important to get the music, the packaging and the overall design right. The *price* must be right for both the consumer and the artist, whether this is free, at a standard price point or at a premium price point (see Box 5.1). *Place* refers to how consumers will access the product, and marketers must ensure that music, merchandise and tickets are all available through the most appropriate channels for their target market to access them (and in a timely fashion to allow maximum impact related to marketing, PR and live activity). *Promotion* through the most relevant media channels (online, radio, television, press) is required to tell the target audience that the product is available.

━━━━ **BOX 5.1** ━━━━━━━━━━━━━━━━━━━━━━━━━━━━━

Alternative pricing strategies

In 2008, Nine Inch Nails and Radiohead released albums with notable but very different approaches to pricing. For *In Rainbows*, Radiohead took a donation approach, allowing fans to pay what they liked to download the record, or even to pay nothing. In contrast, Nine Inch Nails' *Ghosts I–IV* was made available in a number of formats, including a free download of *Ghosts I*, a high-quality audio download of the full album priced at $5, and 2,500 copies of a deluxe set priced at $300 (which included a hardcover book, two limited edition art prints, and the full album on CD, DVD, Blu-Ray and vinyl). Following the success of the campaign, the band later released another album for free, *The Slip*, as well as high-definition live footage, as a thank you to the fans (Ogden et al., 2011).

In 2017, the Australian psychedelic rock band King Gizzard and the Lizard Wizard announced their new album *Polygondwanaland* on their Facebook page. Here they encouraged people to not only download the high-quality audio files and digital artwork for free, but to make copies and sell them if they wished to. The band proclaimed: 'Make tapes, make CD's [sic], make records. Ever wanted to start your own record label? Go for it! Employ your mates, press wax, pack boxes. We do not own this record. You do. Go forth, share, enjoy' (King Gizzard and the Lizard Wizard, 2017). The post generated an impressive level of engagement and interaction for a band their size, and garnered significant media coverage. Effective marketing often goes unnoticed, but sometimes, as here, it is specifically designed to be a story in itself.

The strategies pursued by Radiohead and King Gizzard acknowledge that it may be productive to give music away for free, as it helps in marketing the artist and drives other strands of their creative and business activities (see also Anderson, 2009). In contrast, Nine Inch Nails' approach can be viewed as an attempt to re-establish monetary value for recorded music products by introducing different packages at a range of price points. This strategy has also been used by Eminem, who released a range of bundles in 2013 for *The Marshall Mathers LP 2*, including a $300 limited edition. Rapper Nipsey Hussle built his career on this approach, winning plaudits from *Forbes* magazine (Robehmed, 2013). Inspired by Jonah Berger's (2013) business book *Contagious*, he decided to manufacture a limited edition of his 2013 mixtape *Crenshaw*, which he retailed at $100 each. All 1,000 copies sold within 24 hours. This funded further creative activity. He went on to launch his Proud2Pay campaign, which incentivised hardcore fans 'with concerts, priority access to new material, and one-of-a-kind gifts, like an old rap notebook or signed photo' (Robehmed, 2013). A similar logic is seen in the crowdfunding and fan-centric platforms discussed in Chapter 7.

McCarthy's marketing mix has been extended by various authors (such as Nickels and Jolson, 1976; Booms and Bitner, 1981) to include further considerations related to the provision of services: people, physical evidence, process, packaging and payment. However, these extensions, and the original model, remain producer-focused. An alternative, proposed by Bob Lauterborn (1990), is the 4Cs model, which inverts the 4Ps to place the customer at the centre of marketing activities. Product becomes 'consumer wants and needs'; price becomes 'cost to satisfy'; place becomes 'convenience to buy';

and promotion becomes 'communication'. In so doing, the 4Cs model pushes market-ers to think more closely about how consumers engage with products and services – to see the whole process from their point of view. Lauterborn's model offers a useful approach for the marketing of music, but we argue that a fifth element needs to be added: community.

Community is central to the experience of music fandom and is often a key driver of it, largely due to the emotional nature of music as well as the social and cultural relationships that fans have with it. Social media also revolves around notions of community and the circulation of information, opinion and conversation through dedicated fan groups and accounts focused on specific artists or genres. When creating campaigns, marketers should be sensitive and responsive to the community that they are targeting – to understand their needs and to mobilise that community through appropriate channels of communication. With the addition of 'community', we have the *5Cs of music marketing*, as shown in Table 5.1. We argue that the community element is a crucial addition, as it acknowledges fans' need for social interaction. Music marketing should therefore nurture fan communities and involve fans in an artist's ever-developing story.

The 9Cs of music marketing communication

Lauterborn's (1990) model, like the traditional marketing mix, considers the broad market-ing picture, while Jobber and Fahy (2009) focus specifically on marketing communication, stressing the importance of 'clarity', 'credibility', 'consistency' and 'competitiveness'. To make their approach more relevant to music, we suggest five significant additions to their model: content, channels, conversation, connection and commitment. These additions help to fine-tune the messaging to engender conversation, connection and commitment, and to reach (potential) music fans most effectively. Together, they form the *9Cs of music marketing communication* (see Table 5.2).

Taken together, the *5Cs of music marketing* and the *9Cs of music marketing communication* allow artists and their teams to analyse their music, marketing strategies, messages and audi-ences – as well as those of their competitors. This enables them to learn from and develop their future strategic plans and to build strong fan engagement and commitment.

Table 5.1 The 5Cs of music marketing (adapted and extended from Lauterborn, 1990)

Element	Description
Consumer wants and needs	Highlights the fan-focused approach and makes a clear distinction between their wants and needs.
Cost to satisfy	Pricing based on necessity (free/cheap) or status (expensive/exclusive).
Convenience to buy	Is the song/album or merchandise easy to buy online or in a shop? Yet some music fans like a challenge to secure rare items – e.g. on Record Store Day.
Communication	This emphasises the channels that fans prefer to use, rather than simply the marketing content being created.
Community	This reflects the communal nature of music fandom and social media.

Table 5.2 The 9Cs of music marketing communication (adapted and extended from Jobber and Fahy, 2009)

Element	Description
Clarity	Clear and simple messaging.
Credibility	The message must resonate with the intended audience and 'fit' with their understanding of the artist and genre, and enhance the artist's standing.
Consistency	Across all relevant media channels.
Competitiveness	An innovative idea or angle that helps the message to stand out.
Content	The way that verbal and visual content is created, chosen and delivered is vital to its success in reaching audiences.
Channels	The channels chosen to disseminate the content – for instance, advertising, as well as viral and guerrilla marketing.
Conversation	The content of any communication should instigate a conversation between the artist and their fans, and also among fans.
Connection	This conversation should create a stronger connection between the artist and their fans, and also within their fan community.
Commitment	The development of connection should instil a greater sense of commitment between the artist and their fans, and also within the fan community.

MUSIC MARKETING: ROLES AND RESPONSIBILITIES

Major record labels, larger independent labels, artist management companies and the larger live promoters all have marketing departments with teams of managers and assistants, often led by a director. Each marketing manager will be responsible for their own roster of artists, with the assistants supporting their work. Sometimes the assistants, once they have proven themselves capable, will be given responsibility for a new act. Music marketing personnel are responsible for a range of activities, as shown in Table 5.3. Those working in marketing often bring experts together from the various fields they work with to build (with artists and their managers) overarching and synchronised marketing campaigns. The marketing manager will coordinate regular meetings with the wider team to develop creative and practical ideas, as well as to agree consistent objectives and messages.

At some companies, marketing managers are called *product* managers. Allied to this is the industries' perception of music as 'product'. We suggest that this is an area that needs attention, and a change of language, mind-set and approach. Music plays multiple roles in our lives (Sacks, 2008; Hesmondhalgh, 2013). 'Product' undervalues this as well as the affective and associative qualities of music, the emotional and cultural investments fans make in artists and their music, and the often-intense connections that fans feel with artists and other fans in their communities. In the more competitive, fan-focused market of the twenty-first-century music industries, it is crucial to think about how to tell a story and how to deliver an engaging, immersive experience rather than to simply sell a 'product'. This reflects the needs of the 'experience economy' (Pine and Gilmore, 2011; see also Krueger, 2019), in which consumers seek entertaining and absorbing activities

Table 5.3 Music marketing activities

Music marketing activities
Market research.
Campaign planning, coordination and strategy.
Generating creative ideas.
Product positioning and packaging, including limited editions and the bundling of products.
Pricing policy.
Overseeing sales and distribution of music products to both physical and digital retail and/or streaming sites.
Taking responsibility for advertising campaigns, writing advertising copy and working with advertising agencies.
Working with brand sponsors on co-branded campaigns.
Commissioning key campaign assets, such as artwork, videos and photography.

that may engage them creatively and emotionally. Of course, music recordings, and the musicians who make them, are, in some ways, commodities, but to focus on them as products is to ignore the crucial fact that they represent a web of songs, stories and experiences loaded with personal, cultural and emotional significance both for the artist and their audience. These are significant assets within marketing due to their ability to connect artists with audiences, and audiences with each other. Thus, there is a need to develop more nuanced understandings of specific audiences, artists, songs and albums. Furthermore, music marketers should aim 'to understand the emotional underpinnings of consumer decision-making' (Jenkins, 2006: 61–62), and use that understanding to be creative in how they approach their campaigns. We suggest that the use of the 5Cs and the 9Cs can help in this form of 'affective economics' (Jenkins, 2006).

Market segmentation describes how the potential audience for an artist and their music may be defined, described and accessed. As Keith Negus (1999: 32) states: 'markets have to be carefully constructed and maintained; a process requiring investment in staff and systems for monitoring and researching the purchase and use of recordings'. Examples of such monitoring include the work of Nielsen Soundscan in the US and the Official Charts Company in the UK, each of which tracks sales and streams. Segmentation involves analysis and understanding of the market and is a way of refining and streamlining campaigns, saving human and financial resources, and making marketing more effective. It involves both demographic data, which describes age, gender, occupation, education, marital status, income, location and class, and psychographic profiling, which is focused on 'lifestyle, personality, opinions, motives, or interests' (Hutchison et al., 2010: 39). Here, as elsewhere, the benefits of social media, digital ticketing and other online analytics are clear, since an increasing range of data about consumer demographics, behaviour, activities and preferences is more readily available than ever before. Clearly there are privacy concerns related to data collection, so companies' actions must be transparent and comply with the current regulations. Hutchison et al. (2010: 21) suggest three broad categories of people: fans, potential fans and non-fans (the first two being the target market for campaigns). To this, we should add 'superfans': those who engage most avidly with the career of an artist and who actively share their engagement and fandom with others. Further segmentation is conducted within these broad categories using different sets of criteria. Such segmentation aims at constructing identifiable markets that can be targeted through marketing campaigns. Artificial intelligence (AI) technology is creating more personalised content and valuable insights, such as identifying 'audiences who have a high likelihood of deepening their engagement and becoming long-term fans of individual artists' (Stassen, 2020a). It is also enabling labels to 'make much better decisions, spend your money more wisely, and respond to marketing opportunities more quickly' (Roback, cited in Stassen, 2020a).

As with literature and film, music is divided into genres and subgenres: 'a series of apparently intuitive, obvious and common-sense categories which do not so much involve an understanding of "reality" as a construction and intervention into reality' (Negus, 1999: 19). Music industry personnel use the concept of genre to help them contextualise the music that they are working with, and to make it easier to align it with a potential market. It also helps them to market the artists to other areas of the music industries, as well as to the media, advertisers, syncing companies and the public: to construct connections between particular artists, genres and their audiences. Marketing staff differentiate between similar artists within a genre by emphasising the nuances and unique characteristics in their sound, look, image, personality or beliefs. Thus they help to continually construct, reconstruct and develop genre definitions that change over time. To follow a genre too closely might seem to lack inspiration, while a creative twist on a familiar formula may work well to connect with an audience, appearing as fresh and new.

The media are also often organised around genres, as they need to link artists, audiences and stakeholders (such as commercial advertisers). For instance, the magazine *Kerrang!* essentially writes about rock/metal, while *XXL* focuses on hip hop. Each has a specific target audience, and the advertisers that make these publications commercially viable are attracted on the basis that their marketing messages will be seen by a receptive and relevant audience. Similarly, radio stations and the schedules of specific shows are also differentiated, with the US market in particular focused very narrowly around 'formats' (such as country, classic rock, urban adult contemporary) (Shuker, 2016: 140–141; Anderton et al., 2013). This can also be seen in Digital Audio Broadcasting (for instance, Classic FM, Absolute 80s and Planet Rock) and on streaming platforms, where playlists can be organised not only around genres, but on lifestyle factors (revising, exercise, cleaning and so on) (see also Chapter 7). Music marketers must therefore ensure that they focus their research and planning on the most appropriate media channels and mood and activity-based streaming playlists to maximise their potential audience reach.

MUSIC MARKETING AS A 'DISCRETE WORLD'

In Chapter 4 we introduced Guy Morrow's (2020) discussion of 'design culture' in relation to music. Here, we bring it into dialogue with an insightful observation from the cultural commentator, Jon Savage, who in a piece for *The Face* in 1983 noted a turning point: 'These days, it is not enough to sling out a record; it has to be part of a discrete world, the noise backed up by an infrastructure of promotion, videos and record sleeves that has become all-important ...' (reprinted in Savage, 1989: 171). Visualising these creative outputs as forming a 'discrete world' is instructive in recognising how they create an environment which frames the meanings associated with an artist and their music. It is important to understand how the 'infrastructure' is built through the coherent, credible and immersive content commissioned by marketing professionals. In this section we discuss album artwork, guerrilla and viral marketing, advertising and publicity, online gaming, geo-location technology and record stores. Video production, playlisting, promotional activities and the role of the public relations (PR) professional are considered in Chapter 6.

Album artwork

David Machin (2010: 32) states that artists are able to communicate meaning about who they are as an artist 'not just through the kinds of sounds they make, but also through the way they look and move, through the photographs in which we see them and the artwork they use on record sleeves'. The vinyl record, in particular, has become a 'cultural icon' that retains 'totemic power in music communities' (Bartmanski and Woodward, 2018: 171), despite the peak sales of the format being in the 1980s. The more recent vinyl revival seen since the 2010s was not dependent solely on the nostalgia and purchasing power of fans aged 40 plus, but also on 'teenagers and students' (Tomkins, cited in Osborne, 2012: 1). Sales of record players have also grown, in part due to the efforts of companies such as Crosley, which have placed their turntables in a range of retail outlets, including the influential fashion and lifestyle one-stop shop Urban Outfitters. Crosley's retro aesthetic draws on the portable record players of the 1960s, appealing to both younger and older music fans.

A recording's artwork is an important way to establish a meaningful connection with an audience, and of communicating key ideas about an artist and their music. In Mike Alleyne's study of the design agency Hipgnosis, which produced iconic record covers for Biffy Clyro, Black Sabbath, Foo Fighters and Pink Floyd (among many others), he states that the agency was responsible for making 'the album cover more integral to a record's artistic totality, effectively translating sonic experiences into still images' (Alleyne, 2014: 251). This comment could also be applied to the work of other major album designers, such as Peter Saville (Joy Division, New Order) or Neil Krug (Tame Impala). Richard Osborne (2012: 176) notes how the record sleeve 'became an essential and entwined part of the listening experience', with fans often exploring the visuals, reading the liner notes and analysing the lyric sheets as they listened. The sleeve has multiple roles: as advertising enticement, as decoration, as information and as protection for the record inside. For many years, albums and their sleeves 'have been considered indivisible' and it has been claimed that they 'share an intimacy beyond that of other formats' (Osborne, 2012: 177, 178). In the twenty-first century, sleeve artwork must work across all possible formats from CDs and vinyl LPs through to their reproduction on the small screens of mobile phones. The artwork may also have a myriad of other uses on posters, t-shirts, merchandise and concert backdrops.

Physical records also provide a sensory experience absent from digital streaming (Morrow, 2020): some use smooth cardboard, others rough, and some are textured (e.g. embossed), or feature cut-outs and other features. The Durutti Column's debut album *The Return of Durutti Column* (1979) was housed in a sandpaper sleeve so that it damaged the records it was filed next to – an idea borrowed from a Situationist book by Guy Debord and Asger Jörn. Pop-up sleeves have also been popular, such as Hawkwind's *Warrior on the Edge of Time* (1975), and the cassette version of the Oasis single 'Cigarettes and Alcohol' (1994), which came in a cardboard flip-top box simulating a cigarette packet. The Pop Art legend Andy Warhol, who began his career providing illustrations and lettering for jazz albums in the 1950s, later made several landmark record sleeves. Johannes Voelz (2017) states that:

> Warhol turned the record cover into a pop art version of Marcel Duchamp's urinal. While Duchamp had used a signature to claim art status for an industrial ready-made, Warhol repeated the gesture for an image that undeniably served illustrative (i.e., non-autonomous) purposes.

For instance, he used tactile devices such as a peelable banana sticker for the cover of *Velvet Underground and Nico*, while for the Rolling Stones' *Sticky Fingers* sleeve he incorporated a real zip into a close-up picture of a pair of jeans (when unzipped the model's underwear was revealed). More recently, Stormzy's *Heavy is the Head* (2019) features, in part, the Banksy-designed stab vest (featuring the Union Jack flag) that he famously wore at the Glastonbury Festival. This links well with his political activism, relates strongly to moral panics in the media about race and knife crime in London, and, through the use of the flag, highlights institutional racism and the rise of nationalism. As Osborne (2012: 184) notes, such design elements help 'to make sound visible'. Other leading visual artists who have designed album covers include Takashi Murakami (Kanye West, J Balvin), Peter Blake (The Beatles, Paul Weller), Richard Hamilton (The Beatles) and Jeff Koons (Lady Gaga). Conversely, some musicians are skilled visual artists and have designed their own sleeves (e.g. Laurie Anderson, Daniel Johnston and Billy Childish).

Guerrilla marketing and viral marketing

Guerrilla marketing can be defined as 'advertising through unexpected, often online, interpersonal, and outdoor' routes (Serazio, 2013: 3). Viral marketing is essentially word-of-mouth re-tooled by digital technology: where traditional word-of-mouth communication is linear and one-to-one (or, at best, one-to-several), viral marketing is many-to-many in the form of likes, shares, memes and so on. Viral and guerrilla marketing are clearly interconnected, but the line between them has become increasingly blurred. Indeed, more or less any marketing, promotion, PR, video or press article has the potential to become viral.

The artwork and packaging of an album or single release can also become a prompt for fan-driven guerrilla marketing, with stickers a common example of this; for instance, fans can display these stickers on their computers, books and bags. A more unusual example was the packaging created for two of Kasabian's early singles; the vinyl versions (available only on a 10-inch format) came with different giveaways that encouraged fan labour on the group's behalf. First, 'Club Foot' (2004) came with a stencil attached to the front. This led to Kasabian's logo being stencilled in the streets, raising an awareness of the band, creating a sense of subversion around them, and making the participating fans feel more involved and invested in their success. Second, 'Processed Beats' (2004) came wrapped in a flag featuring the band's logo. These flags recalled those of Italian football fans, thus linking to one of the band's main interests (football) and the Italian heritage of one of their guitarists. Inevitably, fans displayed and waved their flags at gigs, clubs, festivals and in the streets, creating a sense of identity and community. The repetition of the logo through the stencils and the flags at this early stage of their career acted as effective promotion and ensured brand recognition.

The cover of Travis Scott's 2018 *Astroworld* album, created by photographer David La Chapelle, features a golden reproduction of Scott's head. For the marketing campaign, replicas of the head were produced and placed in strategic locations, including a Los Angeles branch of Tower Records. In the UK, a larger version was made by Diabolical and, on the day of the album's release, taken on a boat trip down the River Thames. Fans were encouraged via social media to join the ride and to post about it online (Diabolical, 2018). This was, perhaps, a deliberate echo of a similar publicity campaign for Michael Jackson's *HIStory* album in 1995, but on a humbler scale and benefiting from the connectivity of social media. The following week the head was installed at Shoreditch Boxpark, East London, located on a busy commuter route in an area populated by many companies, tastemakers and influencers in the creative industries. Here, people could interact with Scott's model head, go inside it, and pose for sharable photographs that added further to the conversation and excitement around the release of the album.

Much cheaper, and arguably just as effective, was the Stone Roses lo-fi poster campaign that appeared in several bars and shops across the hip Northern Quarter of Manchester city centre on the morning of 2 November 2015. While the posters did not feature the band's name, nor indeed any words, the large slice of lemon that dominated them was a recognisable reference to previous Roses artwork, including their debut album. The posters were simple two-colour items, typically arranged into blocks of 16 to create a strong visual impact. Social media images of the posters led to free online word-of-mouth promotion alongside speculation about whether there was an imminent new album or gigs. This was then picked up by traditional news platforms such as *NME* and the *Daily Mirror*. At 7pm on the same day, a radio news story announced that the band would be playing reunion gigs in 2016, making sense of the choice of 16 posters.

These interventions can be viewed as examples of 'street spectacle' (Serazio, 2013: 60), and are forms of both viral and guerrilla marketing. Inevitably, such campaigns are particularly successful when targeting youth markets, which is one of the reasons this approach is so effective in a music context. This is advertising as entertainment through disjuncture, surprise and clever content. It is aimed at engaging those who have become sceptical or immune to traditional marketing approaches. Such guerrilla tactics not only raise awareness and engagement, but can also, as Serazio (2013: 19) notes, confer valuable 'subcultural capital' (see also Thornton, 1995). These intriguing visual interventions in public spaces are necessary in our advertising-saturated environments, within which we become immune to traditional marketing approaches, often walking past billboards without looking, as they are part of the clutter of everyday life. Thus, when someone tries a new approach, it can draw in fans, potential fans and non-fans who will then share stories and images on social media. Each of these interventions guide the viewer through the key stages of the AIDAR marketing model: awareness (seeing), interest (experiencing), desire (interacting), action and advocacy (taking and sharing photographs), and retention (extending the story, reinforcing the loyalty) (Fortenberry and McGoldrick, 2020).

Advertising and publicity

Advertising takes many forms in the modern music industries. Usually, this amounts to the strategic booking of adverts on social media at times when most of the artist's audience will be online. Alternatively, marketers may target advertising at relevant magazines, newspapers, radio shows, podcasts and websites. The adverts will usually feature the relevant single or album artwork alongside key information, such as release date and format, perhaps accompanied by media quotes and additional text aimed at raising interest. Labels will sometimes collaborate with a retailer, whether a major chain or a local independent, to produce co-op advertising (Hull et al., 2011: 183). Such partnerships promote particular price deals or exclusive editions, and draw fans to shop at the store. Fans are thus incentivised to visit particular shops at particular times, which can increase first week sales and a release's subsequent chart position. Artists and labels with major budgets may also book advertising slots on strategically chosen television programmes and commercial radio shows. However, advertising through social media is much more cost-effective and is generally more successful in reaching suitable music audiences. This media planning process is carefully devised by a record company's marketing department or is contracted out to an advertising agency.

Al and Laura Ries (2004: xx) state that: 'Advertising doesn't build brands, publicity does. Advertising can only maintain brands that have been created by publicity. The truth is, advertising cannot start a fire. It can only fan a fire after it has been started'. However, as discussed above, a well-thought-out advertising campaign can generate its own publicity and lead to social media sharing across multiple platforms in tandem with press coverage. The campaign for Chvrches' 2015 album *Every Open Eye* involved a billboard based on the album sleeve, but with fresh flowers embedded into it, making it a three-dimensional advert (Diabolical, 2015). It was situated by a busy road in London's Hammersmith and quickly became an Instagrammable site of pilgrimage for fans who would visit, take photos and post on social media. This led to subsequent news stories in the traditional press. The billboard resonated with contemporary green-thinking about establishing living walls of plants to improve air quality in cities – which was appropriate given the huge carbon footprint from the volume of traffic on that particular road. This shows the value of look-ing at wider societal trends, not just in music, when marketing and positioning artists and creating campaigns.

The benefit of a campaign such as that for Chvrches (and for those of Travis Scott and Stone Roses discussed above) is that it has the potential to engage 'non-fans' (Hutchison et al., 2010: 21). Such a grouping includes the curious public (often not even music fans), who feel com-pelled to post photos to their social media whether or not they are invested in the artist. This is valuable but free promotional labour that drives viral marketing and increases the reach of a campaign, such that more fans and potential fans may become aware of it.

Online gaming

The links between music and online gaming have been growing for many years. Where once music acted purely as a background soundtrack to the action, musicians are now centre stage. In 2019, 100 Gecs staged a concert in Minecraft, and returned with a festival in 2020, while Roblox has staged virtual performances from Ava Max, Lil Nas X and Royal Blood. Marshmello's 2019 concert in Fortnite was, at the time, the largest in-game event with 10.7 million concurrent players during its 10-minute duration – a level of engagement that far exceeds most other platforms for music, with only mega-events such as the US Super Bowl offering greater exposure. It was also widely reported that the performance led to a 20,000 percent rise of Marshmello's audio streaming figures. Statt (2019) called it 'a glimpse into the future of interactive entertainment, where the worlds of gaming, music and celebrity combined to create a virtual experience we've never quite seen before'. Fortnite's developers followed this with the launch of Travis Scott's 'Astronomical' single (2020), which set a new record of 12.3 million concurrent participants (Shanley, 2020). Fortnite's team has also ven-tured into K-pop, making an exclusive skin of Jung Chan-woo from boy band iKon available to buyers of the Samsung S10 mobile phone (Liao, 2019). iKon also played launches for the Samsung S10. Fortnite plans to provide opportunities for less established acts in order to help widen its audience and services, and to reposition itself as a social entertainment platform (Shanley, 2019): an immersive one-stop metaverse of gaming, music and social interaction rather than simply a game.

There is also huge potential for in-game monetisation, such as virtual merchandise and collectibles, with 68 percent of the sector's £138 billion value coming from in-game pur-chases (Mulligan et al., 2021). The customisation available in online games far exceeds any-thing that is currently possible through audio streaming sites, hence marketing campaigns can be extended into this virtual space in more diverse and innovative ways that will more strongly engage fans and potential fans.

Geo-location technology

Geo-location is another technology that is gaining more traction in the music industries as it is interactive and focused on engagement. In 2010, Arcade Fire debuted an interactive video for 'We Used To Wait' on a dedicated website called *The Wilderness Downtown* – a phrase taken from the song. The video was designed in conjunction with Google Creative Lab/Google Chrome, which was then fairly new. It made use of HTML5, Google Maps and Google Street View, also fairly new, to match the suburban/downtown theme of the song and album. Fans were encouraged to enter the postcode of the place where they grew up, with the video then taking them on a semi-animated journey from their current location to their childhood home. At the end of the video fans were asked to complete a virtual postcard that might later be used in a backdrop montage for the song during the band's tour. In 2018, Bury Tomorrow won Music Ally's Best Use of Geo-Location award for their 'Black Flame' campaign. The campaign team used Google Maps and location tracking technology to create a band-branded map, hosted on the band's official website. They encouraged fans to '*Claim Their Flame*', in which they pre-saved the album playlist on streaming services and put the *Black Flame* logo on their location. This created dialogue between fans on social media, as they took screenshots of their own flame and shared them on the map, enabling them to connect with others nearby. Initiatives were created to find fans in more remote locations and to reward them for being fans of the band. Streaming figures quadrupled due to tweets sharing the streaming link and the band's subsequent tour sold out quickly. Following this campaign the band achieved its highest album chart position in the UK, while the band's management team increased fan engagement and gained a clear visual representation of the distribution of Bury Tomorrow fans globally, which aided future planning.

Record stores

While some people like the convenience of buying from Amazon, Bandcamp, or an artist's own website, others trust large music/entertainment stores, such as Best Buy (USA) or HMV (UK), or specialist independent record stores, such as Rough Trade (London, Bristol, Nottingham, New York) and Piccadilly (Manchester, UK). Independent record stores are, in particular, a space for knowledge exchange and recommendation, and many provide a social experience in a (sub)cultural community space (Jones, 2010; Hracs and Jansson, 2017). Customers are encouraged not just to listen to and buy music, but to browse through the racks and explore magazines, fanzines and books, with some offering café services. Because of the unique position held by these stores in many music consumers' lives, they are an important consideration within marketing campaigns. They may not sell large numbers of records, but they sell to the tastemakers and committed fans on which the music industries rely.

Record stores are factored into the planning of marketing campaigns, as the release dates of singles and albums provide a fixed focus for promotional activities. For fans, these release dates become important events in their schedules, around which their lives may be (re) structured. Buying the new album by a favourite artist is still a thrill for many fans young and old, providing the opportunity to meet up and talk with like-minded music obsessives. During the week of release there may be in-store performances and signings, with some shops specifically designed to include a performance space. These intimate and exclusive shows will attract fans and the media to the shops to buy and promote the record at a strategic time and create a sense of excitement. In planning these promotional events, marketers and distributors have a hit list of key record shops, such as Beggars (London, UK), Resident (Brighton, UK), Third Man (Detroit and Nashville, US; London, UK) and Drift (Totnes, UK), and even during the Covid-19 lockdowns many staged virtual in-store performances. Moreover, despite the dominance of audio streaming over physical formats, there has been a rebirth in the sector (Jones, 2010). Indeed, in 2015, Resident more than doubled its physical retail space (DJ Mag, 2015) and new independents such as Vinilo (Southampton, UK) and Pie & Vinyl (Southsea, UK) launched in the 2010s. Record shops are further embedded in the wider music industries through the promotion or co-promotion of live events, aimed at publicising the shops as well as the artists. For instance, Resident has collaborated with promoters One Inch Badge to produce 'outstores' at local venues featuring Idles, Yungblud, Melanie C, Celeste and Fontaines DC.

Record Store Day (RSD), founded in 2007, has been key to the sector's revival and provides a specific focus for fans and marketing teams alike. In relation to RSD, Eliot Bates (2020: 690, emphasis in original) notes that 'the vinyl record gains value when the *lived experience of materiality* becomes an *event* and enables the *performance of self* in social contexts'. Such is the excitement surrounding RSD, and the 'wish to acquire' (Thorne and Bruner, 2006) limited edition releases, that fans often queue outside stores for a day or two before. The queue becomes a newsworthy event in the media, with local cafés supplying coffee to fans in the queues and to any buskers entertaining them. Social media also comes into play, with fans posting photos of the queues and uploading unboxing videos of their purchases to YouTube (Bates, 2020: 690).

Through delivering the visual items, tactile pleasures and immersive experiences discussed above, marketers build the infrastructure and 'discrete world' around the artist and their music.

DATA FANDOM

In Chapter 4 we considered the importance of data analytics in informing the decisions and actions of artists and their teams. Here, we explore how fans use data to contribute to an artist's success and achieve connection with them. The global growth and success of East Asian pop music (including K-Pop, J-Pop and C-Pop) beyond their traditional bases of South Korea, Japan and China have brought new knowledge, understanding and approaches to music marketing. The Chinese development of 'data fandom', in particular, gives valuable insights into the contemporary use of data by the music industries and fans, as well as into emerging trends of cultural production and consumption. Data fandom reflects the 'datafication of listening' (Prey, 2016) through streaming services, as well as the 'algorithmic culture' (Yin, 2020) of social media platforms like Sina Weibo (similar to Twitter) and the impact of social media in facilitating a range of new fan activities. Data fandom illustrates most clearly how the music industries have been 'reconfigured by digital social media platforms' (Zhang and Negus, 2020: 493). Similarly, the lives and activities of fans have been reconfigured, creating a more integrated and committed fandom.

In data fandom, '[d]ata fans understand how their online activities are tracked, and adopt individual and collective strategies to influence metric and semantic information reported on digital platforms and social media' (Zhang and Negus, 2020: 493). Thus, rather than passively accepting being turned into data, fans are actively and creatively involved in developing tactics that manipulate the use of data (van der Nagel, cited in Zhang and Negus, 2020: 494). As such, data fans are modern-day 'prosumers' (Toffler, 1980): consumers who also produce value. They are engaged in 'fan labour', yet while it is tempting to view fan labour as exploitative (Terranova, 2000; see also Chapter 4), the fan–artist relationship may also be seen in a more positive light. For instance, Patryk Galuszka (2015: 26) regards fans as 'sponsors, co-creators of value, stakeholders, investors, and filters'. This parallels the alliances constructed between artists, fans and music companies (management, record labels, streaming services) in East Asia – alliances that suggest a collaborative enterprise with an active, integrated, focused, organised and professionalised fandom at its centre. This sense of collaborative enterprise has produced data fan groups, some of which have evolved organically, while others have been instigated by music entertainment companies. Either way, data fan groups are keen to be involved in their favourite artists' success, and have been harnessed by these companies, integrated into the artists' marketing campaigns and incentivised with rewards.

Baym (2018) discusses how social media has made the connection between musicians and fans closer and stronger, creating a sense of obligation between the two parties. Data fandom extends on this, as their activities aim to affect artists' chart positions and the content and quantity of traffic on social media platforms. In doing so, they offer benefits to the idols they follow, while also enhancing their own agency and 'sense of achievement' (Zhang and Negus, 2020: 493). Data fans, like digital prosumers generally, produce economic value (James, 2021: 90) the constant circulation of data hypes traffic and statistics by affecting the algorithms used by social media sites. This has helped to create 'data traffic stars' such as Lu Han, Kris Wu, Yang Yang and Li Yifeng (Zhang and Negus, 2020: 501). Three key areas of data fan activity may be identified: 'chart beating', 'fan clubs' and 'data teams' (2020: 501). The outputs of these factors are 'data contributions' (Yin, 2020: 481), and we will examine them in turn here.

'Chart beating'

Chart positions and their related sales figures have always been markers for commercial success in the music industries across the globe, but in data fandom charts take on greater significance for the fans with 'an expanded idea of "charts" as a visualisation of an idol's success' (Zhang and Negus, 2020: 501). 'Chart beating' enables fans to play an active role in the artist's success, buying more than one copy of a release, perhaps from more than one retail outlet, or through downloads and streams, to help build up sales figures. While the practice is not new, it never really had a name, nor has it operated on such an organised, extensive and industrialised scale. Data fans further engage in chart beating through the various 'types of voting, comment and feedback' (2020: 502) afforded by social media and streaming. They actively try to influence the charts in key territories such as Korea (MelOn, Hanteo and Gaon), Japan (Oricon), China (Fresh Asia Music Chart) and the US (Billboard, Spotify, Apple Music). The 2018 number 1 iTunes chart success of Kris Wu's *Antares* album has been credited to such chart beating activities (2020: 502). Ultimately, chart beating requires 'strategic planning, coordinated cooperation, and investment in time and resources through which fans act collectively and individually' (2020: 504). It relies on the commitment and motivation of data fans as well as the organised structure of data fan clubs.

Data fan clubs

Chart beating and other such fan activities are organised through fan clubs, and each idol may have many clubs. These fan clubs adhere to 'an ethics of responsibility, approaching idols with a sense of duty or moral obligation; values that informed their commitment to rewarding and supporting an artist' (Zhang and Negus, 2020: 504). This often involves organising grand gestures such as light shows, flying banners across a city, or, more simply, greeting stars at airports or hotels *en masse*. Clearly, this often requires a large financial investment by fans, who often use platforms like GoFundMe to raise the money and mobilise other fans. The fan clubs 'operate less as conventional membership clubs and more as data information hubs and focal points for action, within and across social media platforms such as Sina Weibo, WeChat, QQ and Douyin' (2020: 505). Fan clubs are highly organised and incorporate 'formal departments such as Core Management, Art Design, Copywriting, Data, Comment Control, Public Relations, Finance and Frontline – the last of which deals with direct, offline engagement' (Shuhong, 2019). Money is raised for their activities through membership schemes and calls for donations, with active fans able to receive early access to tickets and other benefits. As noted above, these fan clubs operate on trust and passion, which may leave fans in a rather vulnerable position. Indeed, there have been accusations of 'fraudulent accounting and overpriced products' against some clubs, including claims that fan club leaders have used the money raised to buy themselves new cars or houses (Shuhong, 2019).

The data team

As noted above, one of the key departments of each fan club is its 'data team', which is 'a group of dedicated, skilled fans with extensive knowledge of digital platforms, and who understand the technical processes driving algorithms' (Zhang and Negus, 2020: 505). The data team also understands the principles of connectivity, and draws on the available data both to create strategies and to guide those fan club members without in-depth technical understanding to implement them. For instance, they help to coordinate fans in order to boost the numbers of re-posts and related content on social media, to manipulate search trends on popular internet search engines and social media platforms, to counter any criticism made about idols, and to organise 'voting blocs' in online competitions (Shuhong, 2019). Such activity is important to the success of the idol. For instance, popular artists may have over 20 million followers, and they can receive more than 1 million reactions to their social media posts (Yin, 2020: 479). In return for rewards from an idol's management or record company, the data team gives instructions to fan club members on:

...how to play or stream tracks repeatedly; how to use more than one account; how to use overseas proxies to bypass [China's] great firewall; how to use systems of online voting to influence ratings on various platforms and social media. The data team may also suggest the wording of statements that should be posted against 'enemy fans' and give advice on how to remove online negative remarks about idols. (Zhang and Negus, 2020: 505)

The data team is also involved in creating memes and videos, writing and managing fan blogs, posting social media gossip, and creating fan art and photography (Zhang and Negus, 2020: 505–506). All these activities require significant investments of time and, thus, they align with Thorne and Bruner's (2006) point about how committing to be a fan requires a restructuring of one's life and the creation of a schedule to accommodate the range of fan activities that one wishes to become involved with. Indeed, such activities and schedules become part of a fan's 'daily routines' (Yin, 2020: 488). Due to the roles that they play in fostering their chosen idol's success, data team members have reported feelings of personal and collective achievement, similar to those seen in activities such as sport (Zhang and Negus, 2020: 506). Indeed, the sport analogy is appropriate, considering the strongly competitive focus of chart beating that represents the gamification of fandom. These various fan activities may sound like a regimented and industrialised form of fandom, yet fans 'also continue to participate in the fun and frustrations of being a pop fan' (2020: 508).

These East Asian developments offer potential lessons for the future marketing of other music genres in territories across the world. In some ways the foundations have always been there. For instance, active fan clubs were a key part of the successes of Lonnie Donegan in the 1950s and The Beatles in the 1960s. Further, Western music companies have become increasingly data-driven and the promotional and financial value of data fan labour is clear to see. Some Western fans of East Asian idols are already members of data fan clubs. Would more Western fans feel comfortable taking part in these fan activities? Would these activities comply with the chart rules in Western countries?

CONCLUSION

Music is never consumed on its own. It relies on the 'discrete world' of visual elements built around it. These help record labels and management companies to market their artists and products to audiences, and help fans understand and fully experience the music, to become immersed in its world. In recent years, music marketing has become more inventive, as illustrated by the examples of 'street spectacle' (Serazio, 2013: 60) discussed above. Advertising has been reinvigorated to meet the challenges. Gaming, geo-location and other digital features, all aided by cutting-edge technology, are creating new ways of building these 'discrete worlds' and engaging fans. Chinese data fandom points to a potential future for the artist–fan relationships and for fan labour, with potentially significant benefits for artists, music companies. and the fans themselves.

Key discussion points

- How can music marketing make the best use of emergent technologies and platforms to evolve and keep audiences engaged?
- How might marketing roles develop in the ever-changing music industries?
- How could AI be further employed to enhance music marketing?
- In what ways could geo-location technology be further applied in music marketing?
- What could be the benefits of data fandom for Western artists, music companies and fans? What are the social and cultural constraints that might need to be overcome?
- How can the 'worlds of gaming, music and celebrity' (Statt, 2019) be further integrated to benefit artists and fans?

FURTHER READING

We recommend Pine and Gilmore's *The Experience Economy* (2011) and Alan Krueger's *Rockonomics* (2019), as well as Henry Jenkins' prescient *Convergence Culture* (2006) and Jonah Berger's *Contagious* (2013), which introduce many instructive ideas. To stay up to date with technology developments relating to the music industries, we suggest reading *MIDiA Research* articles and reports, *Music Business Worldwide* and *The Verge*.

6

PUBLIC RELATIONS AND PROMOTION

SUMMARY

In this chapter, we examine and demystify the roles, responsibilities, practices and strategies of the industry professionals whose work falls within the broad field of Public Relations (PR) and promotion. These professionals operate as 'cultural intermediaries' (Bourdieu, 1984; Edwards, 2012), who negotiate with the gatekeepers of media organisations to secure strategic exposure for artists and their music. The chapter also considers how key audio, visual and verbal assets can be circulated productively by PRs and pluggers through both social and traditional media, and addresses the important role of crisis management.

Chapter objectives

- To explore how PR and promotion intersect with traditional media (newspapers, magazines, websites, blogs, radio and TV), social media and streaming playlists.
- To discuss the concepts of 'connectivity' and 'transmedia storytelling'.
- To show best practice in devising and executing campaigns and strategies.
- To demonstrate the importance of music video and other assets.
- To explore how to manage a PR crisis effectively.

Digital technology blurs the distinctions between press, radio, TV and social media. The connectivity between the different forms of media means that information and content may be teased across a selection of platforms like a puzzle that fans feel compelled to solve. Such 'transmedia storytelling' creates (fictional) worlds where 'consumers must assume the role of hunters and gatherers, chasing down bits of the story across media channels, comparing notes … and collaborating with each other to ensure that everyone who invests time and effort will come away with a richer entertainment experience' (Jenkins, 2006: 21). Ultimately, the aim of most campaigns is to translate the momentum created through press and social media coverage into radio and TV exposure that may generate further social media conversation and garner a larger audience.

The mediascape continues to evolve rapidly and is increasingly both global and integrated. For instance, in the US, NPR (National Public Radio) has developed podcasts and the acclaimed *Tiny Desk Concert* video series, while in the UK, the BBC makes radio and TV shows, podcasts and other content available through its BBC Sounds app. Streaming service Apple Music has broadened its remit to include three radio stations, and YouTube works with artists to create short films for their Artist Spotlight Stories. Furthermore, the traditional 'production-to-consumption' model of the media has been restructured by Web 2.0 social media to become 'circuits of content that integrate industries and audiences' (Zhang and Negus, 2020: 493). As Shara Rambarran (2021: 10) notes, 'the digital virtual era erases the barrier between the artist, industry and fan or consumer' such that fans are 'virtually part of "the music industry"' and 'are now "the media"'. This represents a significant shift in the power relations of content creation and distribution, with fans regarded as prosumers or 'producers of promotion' (Edwards, 2018: 24). Hence, the networks created by and between fans and the industry allow content to flow in a circular rather than a linear manner.

Public Relations (PR) forms both the underpinning structure and the overarching message of the activities and campaigns that connect artists to audiences/fans, whatever media channel is used. While it could be seen as simply securing artists space in the media, this cannot be done without strategy. Effective PR requires attention to both narratives (stories) and tone of voice, and must be directed to relevant media outlets. It should also operate to a schedule that supports the development of an ongoing campaign. The PR strategy should therefore align closely with marketing and plugging activities and be appropriate to the artist's image, ambitions, strengths and weaknesses (as discussed in Chapter 4). Furthermore, music PR may also be about keeping artists *out* of the media, in order to avoid over-exposure or to protect the artist's reputation and well-being at times of crisis.

PUBLIC RELATIONS

According to the Chartered Institute of Public Relations (CIPR), PR 'is about reputation – the result of what you do, what you say and what others say about you' (CIPR, n.d.). It relates to the actions, opinions and impressions delivered about artists and their music, as well as the dialogue and reputation that circulates around them. Moreover, PR is a 'planned and sustained effort to establish and maintain goodwill and mutual understanding between an organisation and its publics' (CIPR, n.d). It is therefore an ongoing process that requires planning and negotiation to embed trust and to produce meaning. Drawing on Manuel Castells' theory of networks (2013), Lee Edwards (2018: 18) states: 'Public relations may be understood as an attempt to program networks by framing communication in particular ways, but practitioners may also be switchers, creating connections between networks as they communicate with different audiences'.

Roles and Responsibilities

PR professionals act as 'cultural intermediaries' (Bourdieu, 1984; Edwards, 2012) who seek to shape media and public opinion. They are communicators, storytellers and creators of conversations, as well as curators, gatekeepers and salespeople who need skills in negotiation, strategic planning and crisis management. They define key messages, write press releases, artist biographies and PR plans, and devise campaigns which should 'engage us in 'conversations' [and] promote "relationships"' (Edwards, 2018: 1). Five broad audiences are addressed: media, industry, fans, potential fans and the curious public. Their main outlets are newspapers, magazines, fanzines, websites and social media. PR has always been about setting the news or conversation agenda, but it now has more control than ever before due to the direct-to-fan nature of social media. In addition, both social and traditional media outlets are often busy and understaffed, so may publish a pre-packaged story created by a PR if it includes relevant information, news angle, headline and photo, and meets the needs of the publication/site. In Box 6.1, Chloe Walsh (interview with authors) describes her everyday PR work.

BOX 6.1

Interview with Chloe Walsh, Independent PR

Chloe Walsh is a publicist at Grandstand Media. Of her role, she says:

> ... since the music realm works in album and touring cycles, the vast majority of my work is project specific, but my responsibility overall is to the client's public image in general. ... [I]t's my job to make sure that each project of my clients gets widespread attention, but also that the messaging is consistent for every aspect of their work. Everything from writing the clients' Playbill blurb for fundraising events to tweaking the press releases from Apple or Spotify promoting their content. ... I frequently advise on how they use [their social media] and help craft any direct-to-fan messaging.

As an independent PR rather than a record company PR, Walsh has other responsibilities:

> Many of my clients also have non-music related projects – be it acting, fashion/brand partnerships, books, visual art or other endeavours like podcasting or philanthropy. I help them navigate the media to best help them achieve their goals, whatever they may be.

This is important, as artists are increasingly involved in a broad range of creative and entrepreneurial activity. Farmiloe and Cohen (2020: 56–57) call these artists 'the modern polymaths', listing Kanye West and FKA Twigs as examples. Among many others, we could add the increasing number of artists who are now producing their own podcasts, such as Jessie Ware, Questlove and Yungblud. Walsh notes that it's 'a full-time job keeping up with the chaos that is the modern media', with rapidly changing publications, platforms and contacts. She continues:

> Staff writers and editors are frequently doing the jobs of what would have been two or three people a few years ago. They don't have time to listen to everything they're sent. ... They certainly don't have time to look for things to cover that aren't presented to them by a known source.

Walsh also underlines the continued importance of PRs and their expertise:

> Who will make sure they've negotiated the best amount of space, the best writer for the piece, a photographer and make-up artist who fits with their aesthetic? Who will come up with angles for the writer to focus on that are engaging to readers and show the artist in the best light possible? Who will be there to make sure the writer isn't taking advantage of the access or the time given to them? Who's to make sure they don't go round to their house, stay too long, and root around in their bathroom cabinet when they go to the loo? Or stop them when they try to track down their deadbeat dad for a response to a song lyric? (True story!) It's the publicist's [PR] job to carefully manage every aspect of media coverage. Without someone shepherding the artists through all of it things can go very badly wrong.

Lee Edwards (2018) argues that the PR role is not simply commercial work. Instead, she stresses its cultural impact, which works through framing, contextualisation and persuasion, and serves to build an artist's image and the story around them. This 'symbolic work' (2018: 441) of connecting specific meanings and artistic/cultural value to particular artists and songs/albums is illustrative of the PR's role as a tastemaker and opinion shaper (see also Edwards and Hodges, 2011: 4). While PR is usually outward-facing, PRs may have to advocate for the artist within the record/management company or related businesses to persuade doubters. This may lead to increased budgets, or potentially save an artist from being 'dropped' from their contract.

The 3 'I's of music PR

PR campaigns should 'inform, inspire and incite' the media and public through communication and storytelling (Hopkins, 2016). PRs must inform media and fans of key details, including song titles, release dates and tour dates. They must inspire the reader to listen and to believe in the artist and their music, and through the framing and meaning-making activities they adopt, they should incite strong feelings leading to action. PRs know that if an artist and/or their music provokes passionate opinions, positive and negative, this polarisation of opinion is a valuable indicator of potential success. For many years, these have been called 'Marmite artists', about whom strong opinions will always be voiced, and especially so through social media. Polarisation creates a dialogue between the two sides, creates excitement and generates questions that rattle around playgrounds, pubs, clubs and online.

We can see this when an artist changes their sound or image, as exemplified by the development of bands such as Bring Me The Horizon, Paramore, and Fall Out Boy. Such changes may create cognitive dissonance for both fans and media as the new look or sound no longer matches the expectations that were previously built. As a result, fans may reject the new version of the artist, so PRs must minimise this cognitive dissonance by presenting a viable case for the change. As Chloe Walsh suggests: 'It's fine for them to come back with a new album with an entirely different personality. It's our job to parlay that to the media. ... We just work to find a new story for them' (interview with authors). For example, Rapper Lil Nas X successfully presented his country-trap song 'Old Town Road' within the context of the country music genre on SoundCloud and iTunes, leading to a US Billboard Hot Number 1 and a deal with Columbia/RCA (Rambarran, 2021: 154).

Social relationships and 'music worlds'

The PR role is based on strong collaborative professional relationships which exist within what might be termed 'music worlds' (Finnegan, 1989: 31–32). Like Howard S. Becker's 'art worlds', music worlds rely on the 'collective action' of various 'support personnel' (Becker, 1974, 1976) who form 'networks of working relationships' (Peterson and Anand, 2004: 317) and conducive environments for cultural production. Nick Crossley develops the 'music worlds' idea further, drawing on Durkheim's concept of 'collective effervescence', to explore the 'web of interaction whose participants encourage, stimulate and provoke one another' (Crossley, 2015: 87–88), creating opportunities for synergy. Trust and transparent intra-team communication are key, with PRs, pluggers and marketers who represent the same clients sharing news of their progress as soon as they become aware of it. This may be the support of a key journalist, an article, a positive review, airplay, radio playlisting, TV performance or streaming playlists and statistics. These achievements show that there is demand for an artist or song, thus providing vital evidence when negotiating with media contacts.

Progress is also communicated through weekly reports that are circulated within the team. Music professionals earn (sub)cultural and social capital through the success of their work (Barna, 2018: 255), building their professional brand and gaining trusted connections that help them to secure media coverage and playlists. It is important that the personalities, motivations, musical tastes and other interests of these connections – such as films, books, sport, politics, food – are understood. This enables them to successfully match artists to their media contacts in a constructive manner. Media and PR personnel may bond over current buzz acts, tips for the future, and obscure or canonical music of the past. This confers (sub)cultural capital, helping to build trust and to validate a PR's opinions. If the media trust a PR's taste in music, they will pay more attention to that PR's clients.

Balancing the competing needs of media contacts, artists, managers and labels is a skill that must be acquired and developed over time. Likewise, understanding the changing power dynamics between media and music industries is important. For instance, when a new artist is trying to break through, the media hold the power, but when that artist becomes successful, the scales tip in favour of them and their team. Music PRs must also follow new trends in music, media, technology, fashion, film, popular culture and the wider world of, say, politics and sport, in order to remain relevant and to inform their campaigns.

PR CAMPAIGNS

Research and preparation are key to creating PR campaigns. The PR must analyse the needs of the artist, client, media and fans, as well as the project to be promoted, current and future trends, and any competition in the marketplace. Potential issues must be identified and dealt with ahead of launch, with clear short-term and long-term objectives set. These objectives will give the campaign focus, direction and purpose, and allow the PR to evaluate its effectiveness.

Objectives may be informational (raising awareness) and/or motivational (invoking action and commitment). Media targets must then be targeted and negotiated with, and a time-based plan created for the release of creative content and media activities. A good example of this is provided by Stormzy's campaign for the 2019 album *Heavy Is The Head* (see Box 6.2). Jamie Woolgar (Head of Press, Rough Trade Records) notes that there has been a shift to 'rolling campaigns' that produce 'a continuous story, rolling every day' through the drip-feeding of press stories, videos on YouTube and social media teasers. The upshot of this is that campaigns may be 'less structured around releases' with minimal front-loading of media coverage and sometimes more singles (interview with authors).

▬▬▬ BOX 6.2 ▬▬▬

Campaign case study: Stormzy – *Heavy Is The Head*

On 7 November 2019 at his Stormzy x Relentless takeover at Thorpe Park theme park, Stormzy announced onstage that he had just finished the vocals for his new album. On the night of 18 November, the initials 'h.i.t.h.' in a gothic font were projected onto prominent London locations (a long-standing promotional tactic), such as St Paul's Cathedral. These initials had also been trailed in the video for Stormzy's previous single 'Wiley Flow'. Inevitably there was much rumour and speculation online as to what the initials stood for. Following various news stories about the projections, which linked them to Stormzy, on the morning of 19 November he confirmed the story through his social media account. In so doing, he revealed the track listing, album art and title (*Heavy Is The Head*), making sense of the previously trailed initials, which inevitably featured on the album cover. That the story was not confirmed straight away served to hype rumours in the media and online, with photographs of the projections widely posted by the public, fans and media. Soon after, on 22 November, 'Own It', a single featuring Ed Sheeran and Burna Boy dropped, going to number 1 on the UK charts, with the album following on 13 December, also securing the number 1 spot. This coordinated campaign was successful due to the way that information was intriguingly drip-fed across various channels, and because it utilised both traditional promotional activities and the connectivity of online platforms to embed consistent visual and verbal messages.

Campaign assets

In music, photos and videos are a powerful persuader and have become increasingly important PR/marketing assets. Yet, as Edwards (2012: 441) notes, language is the 'raw material' of PR, with written and spoken communication central to assets such as press releases and artist biographies. Care is needed with both the choice of language and the tone of voice, as these elements affect how messages are understood, believed and connected with. One of the most effective ways of engaging an audience is by asking questions in press releases and social media posts. Questions help to set campaign and media agendas by lodging the idea/artist/music in readers' minds and encouraging the audience to think about the subject and perhaps respond. Press releases should also answer the 5Ws: Who, What, When, Where and Why. As with artist biographies, press releases should provide an engaging headline, and key phrases and points that can inform, inspire and incite journalists to take action. Campaign assets – including music samples, visuals, press cuttings, quote sheets and so on – are typically provided to journalists as electronic press kits (EPKs): a downloadable or emailed zip file, a press release with embedded links, or a short documentary that uses video clips and interviews to create a narrative and understanding of the artist. Print journalism has contracted as a sector, yet online publications are flourishing. Indeed, incisive reviews and quality long-form features remain via publications/sites such as *Pitchfork*, *Mojo*, *The Guardian*, the *New York Times*, *The Quietus* and *Louder Than War*. Social media may now be central to processes of music discovery and the circulation of information and opinion about music, yet music journalism still exerts an 'ideological influence'. This influence extends to the music industries. As Simon Frith (2001: 40) has noted: 'the way in which music writers respond to a new act or sound feeds back into the way in which the record company markets them [and] informs the coverage of non-specialist press, radio and television, [and] influences retail campaigns, stage performances' and, thus, broader society. Effective PR campaigns will make use of both the press and social media, with these sectors working in tandem. As Chloe Walsh (interview with authors) explains:

> Since most entertainment media is now digested via social media ... we work closely with media outlets to make sure that whatever content we're arranging with them ... will also be shared on their social platforms. For artists, the value is to be appearing in people's feeds as they scroll in the queue at Starbucks. Being written about on a website without additional social media promotion is often a complete waste of time. ... It's lovely to get a lengthy feature in the *New Yorker* but that's going to reach a very specific demographic of people. The real worth of the piece in the *New Yorker* is the amount of times they tweet it. The real worth of the *Rolling Stone* coverage is getting onto their socials. It's FAR more significant to be on *Vogue*'s Instagram than it is to be in *Vogue*. ... When I negotiate a piece in a magazine, I try to negotiate what it means for socials at the same time. ... [I]t's as important ... as the size of the piece they're offering, or the calibre of the photographer they're hiring.

The value, then, is in combining a print/web publication's brand reputation, writers and content with the audience reach of their social platforms, which is then magnified by readers who recirculate it through their accounts.

Connectivity, stickiness and spreadable media

When crafting content for social media, it should be both compelling and memorable. Six principles have been suggested for why some messages 'stick': simplicity, unexpectedness, concreteness, credibility, emotion, stories (SUCCESs) (Heath and Heath, 2008: 16–18; see also Gladwell, 2000). Moreover, Jenkins et al. (2013) argue that these messages should also be 'spreadable': telling a story or forming part of an ongoing narrative. Social media posts are often written or vetted by a PR before being posted, as managers and record companies want to ensure that their artists do not go 'off message'. Yet, some artists are adamant that they retain control of their preferred platforms in order to connect more directly with their fans.

Compared to verbal content, visual material is more likely to create 'affective resonance with an audience, and is therefore more likely to be engaged with, circulated and shared' (Carah and Louw, 2015: 158). In addition to his musical output, DJ Khaled also built his success through regular informal, visual posts on Snapchat, in which he came across as both funny and approachable. Music-related memes also make engaging content; for instance, the use of Kendrick Lamar's *Damn* album artwork, or Lil Nas X's meme videos for 'Old Town Road' (Rambarran, 2021: 151–154). Of course, a combination of verbal and visual elements usually has the most impact in drawing viewers' attention and communicating information and stories, as does a well strategised campaign (see Box 6.3).

BOX 6.3

Social media campaign for Ed Sheeran's *Divide* album

Sheeran's campaign made creative use of transmedia storytelling and the connectivity between platforms to present a puzzle to solve, driving fan traffic and media across platforms to find out more. This created eager questions and chatter online, while encouraging fans to fill in the gaps, create their own versions of the songs and share. This engaging campaign primed fans and media for the imminent release of the album and became a media story in its own right. The timeline was as follows:

- 13 December 2015 – Sheeran announces a break from social media so he can take time out from music to go travelling.
- 13 December 2016 – Sheeran enigmatically posts a light blue square with no words or message on his Twitter account.
- 1 January 2017 – Sheeran posts a short video announcing new music for the following Friday.
- 4 January 2017 – a six-second teaser of the blue square plus the lyric 'the club isn't the best place to find a lover' (the opening line of new single 'Shape Of You') is followed by a short snippet of the beat with some lyrics on Instagram and a Snapchat filter with 30 seconds of a finished song.
- 6 January 2017 – two singles are released: 'Shape Of You' and 'Castle On The Hill'. These rise to number 1 and number 2 on the UK charts. The artwork for both singles features a light blue background, as did the album.

However, not all artists make use of social media. For instance, Woolgar (interview with authors) notes that the acclaimed New York group Parquet Courts:

> ... still have no social media, fans just listen ... or see them live. Fans have to make an effort to find the music and experience it. It feels special. There's no day-to-day coverage or insights and it's not hindered them. ... [However] a lot of fans talk about them on Reddit. So they did a Reddit Q&A.

Music video

In the 2000s, music video became ubiquitous online, thanks to the accessibility of cheaper and more advanced technology (such as smartphones, GoPro action cameras, etc.) and the spread of social media platforms like YouTube, TikTok and Triller. Artists now talk about releasing a video rather than a single; likewise, websites and social media provide links where viewers can 'see' or 'watch', rather than 'hear'. From a PR perspective, social media has enhanced the virality of music video and drawn fans into extended roles as both sharers and prosumers (via user-generated lip-sync videos and so on). From the platforms' perspective, video content is valuable for keeping viewers engaged with the site for longer, making the platform more attractive to advertisers. Thus, Instagram, Facebook, Twitter and so on have created features that encourage the creation and sharing of video content.

Music videos help to build, maintain and enhance an artist's visual identity (Negus, 1992: 96) or even to reinvent it. For instance, Joseph Kahn's 2017 video for Taylor Swift's 'Look What You Made Me Do' transitioned her from the long-established apple-pie/cookie-cutter image of 'the good girl' in Kristin Lieb's (2018) lifecycle model of female popular music stars, to a forthright individual who answers all the accusations levelled at her by the media and her peers. The strategy behind the release of the video achieved maximum impact through a teaser released on the *Good Morning America* television show, with a full première at the 2017 MTV Awards. The power and reach of music video and social media in the contemporary mediascape are such that the video secured more than 40 million YouTube views in its first 24 hours of availability.

Music videos must operate effectively on televisions, computers and smartphones, and compete with the busy contexts in which they are seen (Vernallis, 2013: 24), hence they should engage the viewer's attention immediately, and maintain it throughout the song. Many feature intertextual cultural references, themes and pastiches (drawn, for example, from film, television, art or other artists' videos) that help to deepen meanings and connect further with the audience. For instance, David Meyers's 2017 video for Kendrick Lamar's 'Humble' references Leonardo Da Vinci's painting 'The Last Supper'. Artists or their team will approach video directors with a budget and a brief from which the director will design 'images with the song as a guide' (Vernallis, 2007: 112). In the age of social media, the brief is now likely to stipulate that the video includes scenes that are suitable for use as sharable teasers or clips. Kim Gehrig's infectious and dynamic dance video for Chaka Khan's 'Like Sugar' (2018) appears tailored specifically for this.

New technologies are facilitating innovative video work. For example, Pussy Riot's 'Panic Attack' was created using augmented reality (AR) technology and 'rendered through a video game engine' for an immersive viewer experience (Minsker, 2021). The 1975's 'The Birthday Party' used computer-generated imagery (CGI) and animatronic memes, while Aphex Twin's 'T69 Collapse' was inspired by artificial intelligence (AI) and also created using CGI. Björk, often at the forefront of new sound and presentation possibilities, released her *Vulnicura* as a virtual reality (VR) album in 2019, in which the viewer 'drives the narrative, through their own spatial movement' (Morrow, 2020: 180). Not only are these videos technically advanced (which made them media stories in themselves), but they are also conversation starters that play out in music fans' discussions and on social media: 'Did you see that video?'; 'What did it mean?'; 'How did they make it?'. They are also irresistibly shareable and ripe for exploiting the connectivity of social media.

Social video and TikToxicity

YouTube (among other platforms) has been central to the spread of music video (Morrow, 2020): for the 16–24 age group in the UK, it is the most-watched platform, more so than television (Ofcom, 2019). For grime, a genre initially marginalised and ignored by much of the mainstream media and recording industries, the expansion of YouTube, after its acquisition by Google, enabled a range of channels like GRM Daily, LinkUp TV and Jamal Edwards' SBTV to emerge (James, 2021: 81). This instantly provided artists with a global audience, while the integration of digital hardware and social platform meant that videos could be created and uploaded cost-effectively, then consumed and prosumed through the use of smartphones.

Social entertainment platforms such as TikTok and Triller have also risen in importance, with short-form user-generated videos and memes helping to promote songs. Indeed, many artists actively encourage users through hashtag challenges to create their own dance videos to audio clips. For example, Doja Cat's song 'Say So', prompted by a teenage fan posting a 15-second clip dancing to the chorus, now has over 20 million user-generated videos of the chorus and several million for other sections of the song (Zhang, 2020). The success of the viral videos meant that Doja Cat was able to extend the lifespan of her *Hot Pink* album, and enabled the release of seven singles from it (Torres, 2021). Heritage acts such as Abba, Dolly Parton and Fleetwood Mac have also successfully made use of TikTok, with record companies now strongly promoting back catalogue songs through the platform to support both sales and tours. TikTok's power and reach can be illustrated by the fact that by October 2020 there were 732 million monthly active users, who watched on average of 89 minutes of video content per day (Ingham, 2021a).

Drawing on Malcolm Gladwell's (2000) theory that ideas and products can spread like a virus, we can talk about the virality of music videos and TikTok. To extend Gladwell's concept to music videos, we can argue that 'Say So' succeeded because of what might be termed its 'TikToxicity': its contagiousness and suitability for the format of TikTok and the audiences that gather there. Key to Doja Cat's success was the way that fan-created videos – examples of user-generated content (UGC) and prosumption – operate alongside official videos in the promotion of artists when shared on YouTube, TikTok and Triller. For this reason, we have seen the rise of video-making competitions and challenges that incentivise fans to take part. This strengthening of artist–fan bonds builds ongoing engagement and keeps the music on playlists for longer than might otherwise have been the case.

Music documentaries

Music documentaries are an extension of the star-making and storytelling processes of PR. Frith (2001: 42) notes that 'the cinema has probably had more effect on the sales of specific records than television', partly because they are 'star vehicles which can be kept under greater promotional control and which have a greater global reach'. In the twentieth century, this usually benefited established stars such as Elvis and The Beatles, yet this expanded considerably in the 2010s (White, 2020). The daily work of artists at all career stages is constantly being recorded by themselves and their teams. This enables them to create documentary videos in a variety of formats: short-form or long-form, a tour diary, a studio diary or something more elaborate. These can then be disseminated through a variety of channels: their socials, website, YouTube channel or the cinema. Documentaries reinforce an artist's image, narrativise their life and career, and position them as stars worthy of public attention. According to Edgar et al. (2013: xi), music documentaries have 'risen in prominence ... to [become] a component fundamental to contemporary popular music'. Prominent examples include *Oasis: Supersonic* (2016) and *Billie Eilish: The World's A Little Blurry* (2021). Historic, niche or less well-known artists can also be showcased through documentary formats, bringing their music to new and broader audiences. Examples include *MC5: A True Testimonial* (2002), *Anvil* (2008) and *Lawrence of Belgravia* (2011). Music documentaries are not just promotional storytelling opportunities, they can also be big business. For instance, Apple TV+ paid $26 million for Eilish's film (White, 2020).

RADIO, TV AND ONLINE: PLUGGING AND PLAYLISTS

If PR is about the artist's story and image as well as the music, plugging is almost entirely focused on the suitability of the songs, whether on radio, on television or online. While radio and TV programmers pay attention to stories that create buzz, they are unlikely to play an artist's record (or schedule a studio performance) unless the track sounds right for their show. This is particularly true of radio as it is fundamentally an audio medium so, as Marc Brown notes, 'the sound of the record needs to sell itself' (interview with authors).

Radio

The demise of radio has been predicted regularly since its arrival in the 1920s (Percival, 2011), yet the move to online broadcasting has helped to reposition and globalise radio as a format (Wall, 2016: 260). The coronavirus pandemic of 2020–21 had the perhaps surprising effect of increasing the popularity of radio (as well as TV streaming) 'at the expense of music streaming' (Jopling, 2020). This was due partly to radio's traditional strengths: 'the sense of a live listening experience, localized content and strong presenter personalities' (Wall, 2016: 263) – qualities that services like Spotify and Last.FM cannot deliver. Apple and TikTok's diversification into radio backs this up and bodes well for the future.

Even though listening habits have changed and radio may often just be background sound while we engage in other activities, it still has a subliminal or direct influence on our lives and tastes. As Marc Brown suggests: 'even though people [now] discover music in different ways the radio is where records [can] become really popular', because, like television, it can access older or more mainstream audiences and promote cross-platform success (interview with authors). Thus, the music industries continue to value the format, while musicians themselves also like to hear themselves on the radio – as demonstrated in the UK by the popularity of BBC Introducing, where up-and-coming bands can upload their songs with the intention of gaining radio play.

Commercial radio stations (such as Capital, Heart and Kiss in the UK) are funded partly through advertising. Thus, they are focused on matching advertisers to audiences and 'tend towards a coherent musical sound' (Frith, 2001: 41). In contrast, public service stations (such as those of BBC Radio 1, 1Xtra and Asian Network in the UK, NPR in the US or Triple J in Australia) are state-supported and tend to offer far more variety, 'with specialist programmes defined by reference to musical rather than demographic differences' (2001: 41). Indeed, the BBC uses its specialist music shows to justify its public service status (Wall and Dubber, 2009). Marc Brown notes that both types are dominated by playlists: 'As a general rule most of what you hear during the day is part of a playlist with DJs having very few choices. ... In the evening things get more relaxed so ... it is the best chance you have of getting new music on the shows' (interview with authors).

Television

Television continues to have a significant role in music promotion, albeit undermined by the shift to online viewing, social media and on-demand services. More than radio, television 'offers audiences events, the sense of being there while the music happens, partly because star-building needs people to see performers as well as hear them' (Frith, 2001: 41–42). Indeed, TV provides memorable, much-discussed moments. Examples include Beyoncé's half-time show at the Super Bowl in 2016 (which featured references to the Black Panthers and the Black Lives Matter protests in the US) and Future Islands' 2014 performance on *The Late Show with David Letterman* (which became a viral hit and the show's most viewed clip on its YouTube channel). However, the evolving mediascape has created challenges, given that YouTube, TikTok and vodcasts all give fans instant access to visual musical content. The long-running weekly show *Top of the Pops* was cancelled in the UK in 2006, and there are now relatively few opportunities for music performance outside shows such as *Later... with Jools Holland* and *Gary Barlow: I'm with the Band*. Artists may be booked for chat shows, including *The Graham Norton Show*, or may make guest appearances on reality TV competitions such as *The X Factor*, but such opportunities are very limited – in both number and the variety of music that is showcased. There are more options available in the US, where performances and interviews are included on *Jimmy Kimmel Live*, *The Tonight Show Starring Jimmy Fallon* and *The Late Late Show with James Corden*. Corden's regular 'Carpool Karaoke' slot is an inventive idea, taking stars like Adele, Kanye West and Sia away from conventional performance spaces, presentation and structure into a more informal and intimate environment, singing karaoke-style in a car. These short slots are tailor-made for online consumption and are disseminated through the show's own YouTube channel, often achieving over 100 million views, and being widely shared by fans.

Radio and television plugging

Pluggers are primarily responsible for nurturing relationships with radio and television producers, playlisters, programme researchers and DJs, in order to secure their artists radio airplay and playlisting, or television performances, interviews and video broadcasts. These activities are crucial for campaigns that require an artist and their music to reach broader and more mainstream audiences, and are supported by PR-generated stories alongside social media and streaming data. Campaign strategies are planned both nationally and regionally (Percival, 2011), and may target broad-based media outlets. Some strategies, however, may focus more closely on specific channels or shows that appeal to particular demographics or musical tastes. Successful radio pluggers will often have considerable say over what songs are chosen as singles due to both their contacts and understanding of radio. They know what could be played (or not) by particular DJs at any given time, bearing in mind current tastes and trends.

Playlist plugging involves both formal and informal routes, including attendance at radio playlist meetings. It may also involve conversations with radio personnel while socialising in venues, pubs and restaurants, or via phone calls, emails and social media. As with PR, it is important for pluggers to carry out thorough research into the musical tastes and opinions of key decision-makers. As Marc Brown (interview with authors) notes, this helps to:

...[u]nderstand the records and the bands that you are working with. Everyone discovers music through different sources, friends, etc. It's the same with the media, the shows you listen to for enjoyment are most likely the ones that would play a new band you like too.

The plugger will build an artist's radio presence through airplay on suitable shows and stations, with the aim of being playlisted – which guarantees a certain number of plays per week on a particular station (Anderton et al., 2013: 117–118). Airplay and playlists primarily drive album sales and streams, but may also have an impact on ticket sales for tours and festivals. Other strategic objectives include interviews, news stories and live sessions. Interviews and sessions 'build a sense of the artist as a "real" person or band with whom the DJ-presenter (and thus, by proxy, the audience) may interact' (Percival, 2011: 459). If the plugger represents an established star, being able to offer these opportunities gives them leverage in their negotiations about that star or, indeed less-established artists. When asked about targets, Marc Brown (interview with authors) states:

With pop music the target is generally to get it played as much and as quickly as possible as that genre really isn't built by gaining legitimacy with specialist DJs or shows. With other music like guitar or dance one starts by encouraging those specialist areas (shows in the evening or overnight) who are ... 'specialists' in their respective genres and who, through word of mouth, encourage fans and other media to take an interest in the new things they play. So early on it isn't about volume of play but the right plays.

Each week, radio station staff are sent more music than they can realistically process. So, to encourage them to prioritise an artist's release, it is useful to discuss media coverage and buzz, as well as social media data and sales figures (live and recorded), as the artist's online traction may help the radio station to maintain and grow their own audience. A plugger might also offer access to the artists or free gig tickets and merchandise.

Playlisting on streaming sites

There is an assumption among some musicians that if they put their songs on Spotify (or another streaming platform) people will flock to listen in their droves. Yet streaming does not, in itself, guarantee awareness and interest, let alone success. Indeed, data from Forgotify demonstrates that around 20 percent of tracks loaded to Spotify receive no plays at all (Eriksson et al., 2019: 98). Playlist pluggers (also referred to as streaming marketers) must devise creative ways to increase streams on online platforms and, as with radio and television, build relationships with playlist curators. As we discuss in Chapter 7, playlists are created by a mix of data algorithms and human curators (artists, media organisations, members of the public or staff employed by the service). Playlists primarily offer publicity, in the sense of raising awareness of particular songs. Hence, they fit into the overarching narrative of PR, but provide little context about a musician's life, personality or story. Indeed, an individual song may gain millions of streams via playlists, but may fail to build a loyal connection between listeners and the artist. Such a situation may negatively impact both the artist's overall revenue streams (low ticket sales) and the sense of community that underpins the development of fandom.

Nevertheless, playlist curators hold increasing power. They have become 'taste entrepreneurs' who earn financial and 'symbolic power' through their activities (Barna, 2018: 255, 266). As playlist curators act as tastemakers, pluggers must carefully choose the playlists they target to ensure that the song may be heard by its intended audience. However, targeting a particular playlist is no guarantee of securing it. Pitching and negotiation are both required, so this process will be aided by the story being built more broadly by the PR, while also considering data and the success of other promotional activities on a range of platforms. These activities will also help to drive traffic to the playlist and promote streaming activity for the song. Streaming services mark 'the shift from commodity ownership to commodified experience' (Eriksson et al., 2019: 1). Some users want the discovery work to be done for them: they pay their monthly subscription and listen to the playlists often with minimal commitment and involvement (see also Chapter 7). Thus, the playlists, whether organised around genres, activities, moods and so on, frequently act like daytime BBC Radio 1 in the UK or Top 40 radio in the US, albeit without the interjections of DJs, news and other elements commonly found on radio. In this way, they almost remove choice, creating convenience consumption – something which is also seen in the integration of music streaming into online exercise applications and internet-enabled equipment such as Peloton. The lack of a playlist presenter may also be driving growth in podcasting where, as in traditional radio, the connection made by the DJ's voice is powerful, giving the impression that they are addressing the listener as an individual – 'synthetic personalisation' (Fairclough, 2015) – or as a member of an 'imagined community' (Anderson, 2006) of listeners.

CRISIS MANAGEMENT

As musicians exist in the media spotlight and often live fast lifestyles, a crisis is never far away. These may be of different levels of severity, including accusations, bar room brawls, Twitter feuds, infidelities, divorce, intra-band fights, altercations with paparazzi, drug busts, sex tapes (fake or real) and even death. In the digital age, leaks have become more likely, and sensitive information is more readily accessible and shareable, clearly presenting challenges (Edwards, 2018: 14–15). For instance, smartphones enable the instant dissemination of photographs or films of an incident via social media, potentially turning it into a full-blown crisis. An artist's 'accumulated reputational capital' (Cornelissen, 2017: 215) is often carefully constructed and hard-won. It is a major asset for them, so crises can significantly threaten their public image and the goodwill felt towards them by fans. However, for some artists there may be advantages in the negative stories that are told about them, so long as they can be constructively used to enhance their bad boy/girl image or to mark a new phase in their career, thus turning a negative into a positive. However, the artist and their team must be prepared to take instant and decisive action (Cornelissen, 2017: 212). If left, a crisis will create further damage; hence, crisis management is essentially about both damage prevention and damage limitation. It is also fundamentally about 'planning, managing and responding' (Coombs, 2012). It is therefore important to know everything about an artist upfront in order to pre-empt potential issues (as discussed in Chapter 4). Contingency plans should also be developed (Cornelissen, 2017: 211, 219) with communication strategies for probable and possible situations. This includes decisions about who would be responsible for updates and what communication channels should be used. Some crises cannot be prevented, but if the PR has pre-planned strategies and responses ready, they can seek to manage it. This is essential given the volatile nature of some artists, the pressures of stardom and the intrusive tendencies of some media companies. It is worth carrying out a risk assessment in advance: What could happen? How likely is it? What/who could it involve? What would be the impact on the artist and other interested parties (label, management, fans)? What would be the best way to manage the situation? And who will manage it?

Urgent research is also necessary to inform the response. The PR must quickly establish what actually happened by speaking directly to those involved to gather as much information as possible in order to build a clear picture of events and identify whether there were any witnesses and what evidence is out there. In some cases, the person who witnessed, experienced or recorded the incident seeks money and publicity, so may have approached a tabloid newspaper or a scandal website. These publications will often contact the artist's PR for an official comment, which enables the PR to attempt damage limitation by negotiating and scaling down the story or attempting to stop it entirely. One way the PR may achieve such objectives is to offer the publication an exclusive story that is more positive or more fitting to the artist's image: to control the media narrative.

When it comes to crisis communication, diligence, clarity and honesty are vital, as is following the 9Cs of music marketing communication (see Chapter 5). Cornelissen (2017: 219) identifies six strategies that may be used as relevant:

- 'Non-existence strategies' – in effect, denial, clarification and attack.
- 'Distance strategies' – excuse and downplay.
- 'Association strategies' – reminding media and public about the positives of the organisation or person.
- 'Suffering strategy' – showing how the organisation/person is suffering from the situation.
- 'Acceptance strategy' – full apology, compensation, 'asking for forgiveness'.
- 'Accommodative strategy' – taking appropriate steps to resolve the situation and prevent it happening again.

Whichever strategy is chosen, it will be disseminated via a statement within a press release (often with quotes from the artist) circulated to the media, as well as through the artist's website and socials. In writing the press release, the PR should use appropriate language and tone of voice for the circumstances, and ensure that all of those impacted by the crisis are addressed – whether fans, public, media or other stakeholders. On some occasions it may be necessary to hold a press conference to address the concerns. Chloe Walsh (interview with authors) discusses her approach to crisis management:

> My philosophy is to watch it closely and always tell the truth. Tracking whether a story is growing or shrinking is instrumental in knowing what to do. I have always handled coverage of a tricky situation directly with the outlet covering it. I don't believe in blowing a story even wider by making public announcements or declarations. If a writer is writing something inaccurate based on false or muddy information, get them on the phone and let them know the facts, ask them if you can provide them something on the record and talk to them about it. You can never break your clients' trust, but you will better navigate the media for them if you're able to have a dialogue with the people covering the story. ... Talk to them and work with them to get a clearer picture of the situation. It may mean putting your client on record in response, but you could go on record on their behalf and clear it up without making it into a bigger story.

CONCLUSION

This chapter has shown how PR is the underpinning structure and the overarching message of the promotional activities and campaigns discussed above. It has evolved and expanded by finding more routes through which to control the narrative, particularly via social media (with the virality of music video being central to this development). Music radio has shown resilience, while music TV and journalism both face challenges. What is clear is that both media coverage and media-based content have their power magnified when spread via social media. Within our participatory culture, fans play an increasing role in PR campaigns by creating and sharing content (effectively operating as unpaid prosumers). Indeed, underlining the importance of fan-made YouTube videos, the company's Global Head of Music, Lyor Cohen, states that of 'the $4 billion plus generated for artists and songwriters and rights holders in the last 12 months ... 30% of it has come from UGC [user-generated content]' (cited in Stassen, 2021a). PR campaigns should be coordinated and consistent, entertaining and engaging, as well as firmly grounded in research and appropriately strategised. They should inform, inspire and incite the media, the industry and the public. Clearly, there can be crises, but these must be pre-empted, planned for and managed in order to protect the artist's reputation.

Key discussion points

- What new tactics could PRs devise to make the most of the changing communication channels?
- What might the next stage of social media innovation offer musicians and their teams?
- What are the implications of the shift away from performer identity to streaming playlists?
- How will the popularity of playlists impact fan loyalty and the album format?
- How might music journalism, radio and television evolve?

FURTHER READING

We recommend Manuel Castells' *The Rise of the Network Society* (2010), Henry Jenkins et al.'s *Spreadable Media: Creating Value and Meaning in a Networked Culture* (2013), and Shara Rambarran's *Virtual Music* (2021) for broader theoretical insights and examples related to social media. For further detail on crisis management, it is worth consulting Timothy Coombs' *Ongoing Crisis Communication: Planning, Managing and Responding* (2012). Trade publications such as *Billboard* and *Music Week* often discuss PR campaigns.

7

ONLINE MUSIC: MEDIA PLATFORMS, MUSIC STREAMING AND MUSIC RECOMMENDATION

SUMMARY

The music and media economies are increasingly platform-based and platform-reliant in terms of distributing content, accessing audiences and earning revenues. Digital platforms have not only changed how music and media reach audiences, but are continuing to influence the working practices of musicians and music companies who must alter what they do in order to benefit from their potential (Nieborg and Poell, 2018). In this chapter we discuss the contemporary platform economy, the remuneration models employed by music streaming platforms such as Spotify, and the problems raised by YouTube in terms of music piracy and the 'value gap'. We also examine how media gatekeeping has changed and how both curated and automated music recommendation systems operate.

Chapter objectives

- To explore how the platform economy of crowdsourcing, crowdfunding, and music streaming operate within the music industries.
- To understand how revenues are typically generated and distributed through on-demand streaming, and to consider some of the alternatives to current systems.
- To question the 'value gap' as it arises in relation to YouTube's user-generated model of music streaming.
- To consider the changing nature of media gatekeepers and the growing importance of music recommendation systems.

Online platforms and affordable digital technologies are transforming how musicians and music businesses can create, distribute and earn revenue from music. It may be argued that these changes have eroded 'the power of the major labels' (Hracs, 2012: 442; see also Wikström, 2019). For example, musicians can record music using increasingly sophisticated software tools, and can mix and master their recordings in home studios using relatively inexpensive Digital Audio Workstations such as Apple Logic Pro, Ableton Live and so on. They can upload their music for distribution, sale and streaming through online platforms, and can promote it through social networks and dedicated music portals (as discussed below). They can also independently produce video recordings, create livestreamed concerts and manage their own ticket sales and online presence through a variety of online platforms and apps. This can be regarded as the democratisation of music industry production and promotion. Alongside this, we have seen growth in disintermediation, where the gatekeeping models associated with journalists, radio and television are increasingly challenged by social media platforms, music distribution websites, blogs, online fanzines, e-commerce stores and 'citizen critics' (listeners and fans), whose user-generated reviews and ratings may have as much impact as the those of traditional media sources.

However, research suggests that independent musicians continue to find it difficult to translate their online engagement and attention into financial income, and to develop new fans, rather than simply catering to their existing ones (Haynes and Marshall, 2017: 11–12). For instance, there is an over-saturation of music online (2017: 12), with data from Spotify suggesting that more than 60,000 new tracks were being added to the platform each day in early 2021 (Ingham, 2021b).

We begin this chapter with a discussion of the platform economy through which the music industry increasingly operates, before focusing on the major streaming platforms and their revenue models. We then examine the transformation of the gatekeeping function through playlisting, platform architecture and algorithmic recommendation.

THE PLATFORM ECONOMY

We define digital platforms as online websites or apps that facilitate interaction between consumers, advertisers and cultural producers (such as the music industries), and encourage users (such as musicians, record labels and listeners) to engage creatively with them. The latter is particularly important, since platforms differ from older e-commerce retail sites in that they typically give access (at varying levels) to Software Development Kits (SDKs) and Application Programming Interfaces (APIs) (Nieborg and Poell, 2018: 4287). These allow for customisation of the platform, the development of new features by external software developers, and the opportunity for music fans and music companies to communicate, trade and earn revenue directly through them (Langley and Leyshon, 2017: 17). For instance, Chinese sites such as Tencent Music allow users to donate directly to the artist (a virtual tipping jar) – an innovation that Spotify adopted and adapted in its Artist Fundraising Pick feature launched during the coronavirus pandemic of 2020–21.

Platforms are an extension of the read-write logic of Web 2.0, where users become producers and can directly amend the platform (in contrast to Web 1.0 where users could only read what a webmaster made available). Social media applications that rely on user-generated content (UGC) are the most commonly understood aspect of Web 2.0 (e.g. Facebook, Insta-gram, YouTube and TikTok), as are early music-based platforms such as mp3.com, Napster, Myspace and SoundCloud. However, the platformisation of the online sphere leads to many more opportunities, such as crowdsourcing, crowdfunding and integration with online and console-based gaming platforms such as Xbox and PlayStation. Furthermore, there is increasing integration with video on demand (VOD) subscription television platforms such as Amazon TV, Apple TV+, Netflix and Roku, as well as smart speakers such as Amazon Echo and Apple HomePod. Another emergent trend is for non-fungible tokens (NFTs) – see Box 7.1. The following section discusses crowdsourcing and crowdfunding, while later sections focus on music-centred platforms and their issues.

BOX 7.1

Non-fungible tokens (NFTs)

Non-fungible tokens (NFTs) are a form of virtual merchandise which comes with a guaranteed proof of ownership, as their unique data cannot be duplicated and is verifiable via Blockchain technology (see Chapter 10). NFTs therefore reinstate a form of scarcity and value that had previously been una-vailable for digital products. In 2021, many artists launched NFT offers. For instance, Kings of Leon released the album *When You See Yourself* as an NFT in March 2021, with additional NFT auctions of special artwork and 'golden tickets' that guarantee front-row tickets for their future live concerts. The Weeknd released new music and limited-edition digital artworks (the 'Acephalous' series, created with Strangeloop Studios), while digital artworks, tracks and/or tickets to special live gigs have been offered by Steve Aoki, Gorillaz, Grimes, Deadmau5, Lewis Capaldi and many others. The potential financial benefits for the artists are considerable, with NFT sales raising millions of dollars in some cases. However, there are questions to be asked. Will these NFTs retain value in the long term? Are the high prices for NFTs exploiting an artist's superfans, or are they being bought by rich internet speculators who have no real interest in the artist, only the potential profit they might make in the future? For NFTs to filter down into the mainstream market, prices need to be lower and the com-plexity involved in purchasing them needs to be simplified. In terms of virtual merchandise, we are also likely to see developments beyond NFTs, such as making artist-branded avatars, skins and other accessories available for fans to purchase in virtual reality applications/events and in online gaming.

Crowdsourcing and crowdfunding

Crowdsourcing platforms bring people and/or businesses together in order to exchange goods and services or to provide introductions between people who may want to work together. For example, musicians can collaborate on music projects online through sites such as Kompoz and Splice, while audiences can club together to request artists to perform in specific venues using platforms such as WeDemand, youbloomConnect and MyMusicTaste. There are also sites connecting musicians with producers, festival promoters with equipment suppliers, and concert organisers with promotional street teams. Such sites promote a Do-It-Together approach of match-making that is potentially democratising and inclusive, and could lead to network effects if reproduced at scale; in other words, accumulating significant economic value as more and more people engage with it.

Crowdfunding is focused on the collective financing of music projects (recording, promoting, touring and so on) in the form of fan-led patronage; an alternative to the traditional self-funding or record company contract models that have long been the bedrock of the recording industry. In the crowdfunding model, individual donors (patrons) pledge a sum towards the overall project total. If enough money is pledged, the artist will be able to undertake the project. Patrons are offered a range of incentives depending on the amount they pledge, ranging from signed CDs and memorabilia to bespoke house concerts, 'meet and greets' and the opportunity to perform on an artist's recordings. The crowdfunding platforms (such as ArtistShare, Indiegogo and Kickstarter) do not take ownership of the copyrights or products created or offered through their platforms, but do charge a percentage fee (between 5 and 15 percent) on the money raised. Many artists have made use of crowdfunding services. The most famous example is Amanda Palmer, who was the first musician to raise over $1 million to support the recording and release of her 2012 album *Theatre is Evil*. Her success was no doubt assisted by her pre-existing music profile (she had previously been signed to Roadrunner Records) and her work on marketing her campaign. The same is true for the many other artists who have successfully adopted the crowdfunding path since the early 2000s (whether through direct leveraging of their fans or through crowdfunding platforms). Examples include the rock bands Marillion, Protest the Hero, and Dream Theater, singer-songwriter Julianna Hatfield, and jazz composer Maria Schneider.

Crowdfunding is, however, not without its difficulties. Previously unknown artists may find it difficult to raise interest in their campaigns, especially as there is relatively little marketing support from the platforms themselves. In addition, there is always the potential for a platform to fail. Pledge Music is a prominent example: it went into administration in 2019 owing an estimated $9.5 million, leaving both artists and fans out of pocket. One response to this has been the growth in fan-engagement platforms such as Patreon, FanCircles and Ampled: sites that focus on smaller and more regular rewards and payments (micro-patronage) that offer artists a more consistent income. Unlike the producer-oriented platforms discussed below, these patron-led sites are always behind paywalls, with minimum subscription tiers. The aim is to establish ongoing and interactive fan communities rather than to fund specific projects.

Producer-oriented music platforms

A distinction may be made between those music platforms which are 'producer-oriented', such as Bandcamp and SoundCloud, and those which are 'consumer-oriented', such as Apple Music and Spotify (Hesmondhalgh et al., 2019: 2). The producer-oriented model encourages music creators to upload content that can later be streamed, commented upon or downloaded by users who they hope will be converted into fans. Downloads may be locked behind paywalls, but most artists will make their streams freely available in order to maximise their promotional potential. For some artists, a platform's pages will become their primary 'shop window', providing information, storage, distribution and retail opportunities in a one-stop location, complete with external links to an artist's social media presence. This relatively static model differs from the consumer-oriented model outlined later, where the emphasis is on circulation – on guiding users to listen to more and more artists and music: to act as consumers rather than fans.

Bandcamp and SoundCloud make an interesting contrast. Hesmondhalgh et al. (2019) argue that Bandcamp is modelled on an indie rock aesthetic which gives preference to the album as an artistic concept and positions ownership (through downloading) as an important mode of consumption. This maintains the emphasis on music as art rather than as product, which is reinforced by the lack of advertising banners and the relative lack of customisation tools or social media integration (Hesmondhalgh et al., 2019: 7). Early criticism of the site for its lack of artist marketing has been addressed through artist-curated 'recommendations' – a search engine based on genre – and links to Bandcamp Daily: long-form editorial articles that focus on particular music genres and offer numerous links to artists on the platform. In contrast, SoundCloud places greater emphasis on social and interactive tools, including the ability to follow other users' profiles, to leave/send messages between users, and to post comments at specific moments on a visualised waveform of a song. Tracks may be downloadable, but are more often streamed, with a website widget available so that tracks can easily be shared and embedded in blogs, social media posts and websites. Whole albums may be uploaded, but it is more usual to find single tracks loaded sequentially, with the most recent at the top of the page. The simple design of the platform downplays the artist's image, making it particularly suitable for electronic dance music (EDM) and hip hop, where multiple aliases and a dynamic, ephemeral aesthetic are more highly revered than indie rock's emphasis on the album (2019: 3).

Consumer-oriented music platforms

Consumer-oriented music platforms are also referred to as Digital Service Providers (DSPs). They focus on single tracks and playlists, rather than artists and albums, which makes them attractive as 'shop windows' and for music discovery, but makes it harder for artists to build sustainable careers through the cultivation of fans. The unlimited inventories of the DSPs (such as Spotify, Apple Music and Deezer) are made possible by the 'near-zero marginal costs' (Waldfogel, 2017: 195) of online distribution. Music is no longer regarded as a 'product' that is 'manufactured, packaged, promoted and purchased', but as 'content' that is 'uploaded and circulated in the hope that it will be "used" in a manner that allows it to be "monetised"' (Negus, 2019: 371). Redefined as 'content', it becomes clear that music is valued less for its artistic merits than for its ability (taking the inventory as a whole) to attract people to the DSP, where their personal details and usage data can be analysed, packaged and sold to record labels, music publishers and advertisers (2019: 378). Seen in this light, the music industry is no longer simply a copyright industry (Wikström, 2019) but part of a growing data analytics industry.

Following on from this, we can see an emphasis on 'discoverability' (McKelvey and Hunt, 2019) and the growing significance of online curators over music creators (Negus, 2019: 371). In other words, the playlist takes the place of the album as a cultural artefact, and the playlist editor supplants the radio producer (and journalists) as a media gatekeeper (2019: 372). We will explore such issues later in the chapter. A further consequence of shifting attention to playlists (rather than artists and albums) is that it disrupts the music industries' attempts to build sustainable careers for artists – something which has long been central to their star-making business model (see Chapter 3). This is exacerbated by the licensing of music to social media platforms and video sharing apps (social entertainment platforms) such as Facebook, Snap, Tencent, TikTok and Triller, which again shifts attention away from the artist. Instead, music becomes a soundtrack to a user-generated video or photo slideshow, rather than something to be enjoyed on its own terms. There may be single-track breakthroughs from such an approach, but it is unlikely that artists will gain significant long-term traction.

STREAMING MUSIC: REVENUE MODELS

Search online and you will find numerous articles providing estimated data regarding the per stream income available from different streaming platforms and online debates using the hashtags #brokenrecord and #fixstreaming to question the amount of money coming to performers and songwriters from their audio streams. For instance, it is often claimed that music-specific DSPs such as Spotify, Apple Music, Deezer and TIDAL will pay in the region of $0.004 to $0.013 per stream. Such figures are useful in that they demonstrate that economies of scale are of vital importance: if a track at the lower end of those figures receives a million listens it will generate $4,000, whereas a track with 250 streams will only generate $1.00. However, such statistics fail to account for the rich complexity of the mechanisms and calculations through which revenues are generated and paid, and the methodologies underlying the statistics are typically glossed over by media reports that are more interested in clickbait headlines, ranking the different platforms and providing royalty calculators that are often inaccurate. In this section, we explore the difference between the commonly used pro-rata revenue share model and the user-centric per-subscriber model. We also demystify some of the complications inherent to the streaming model, and will discuss how the major labels in particular have asserted their dominance within streaming distribution such that the playing field between major labels, independent labels and independent musicians is anything but fair.

Pro-rata model

The pro-rata revenue share model is currently employed across the majority of music streaming services (such as Spotify and Apple Music). Each month, royalties are calculated on the number of streams that a track receives as a percentage of the total number of streams achieved on the platform. It is a system that benefits those songs and artists that are streamed the most, with the British Phonographic Industry (BPI) suggesting that around 1,800 artists achieved over 10 million streams each in the UK in 2020, of which 400 achieved in excess of 50 million (BPI, 2021). In the same year, Spotify reported that 90 percent of all streams were shared by just 43,000 artists, yet there are millions of artists on the platform (Ingham, 2020a). Further details about the pro-rata model are given in Box 7.2, but it is worth noting here that while short-form video apps such as TikTok also use the pro-rata model, royalty payments are based on the number of times a song clip is used to soundtrack videos posted to the app, rather than on the number of times those videos are viewed.

━━━ **BOX 7.2** ━━━

Explaining the pro-rata model of streaming

Under the pro-rata model, calculations are typically made each month. In a simplified version of the calculation, we can understand the process as follows. Each month the total number of streams that a track receives is divided by the total number of streams made on the DSP as a whole, then multiplied by the total monthly revenue (subscriptions and advertising) of the DSP. For instance, if a track receives 1,000 streams in a month that saw total streams on the platform of 5,000,000, then that single track could earn 0.0002 (1,000 divided by 5,000,000) multiplied by the platform's revenue. This pro-rata revenue share is then typically split as follows: 30–35 percent to the platform (to cover its running costs), 55–60 percent to the recorded music licence holder (typically a record company), and 10–15 percent to the songwriting licence holder (usually a publisher) (Muikku, 2017: 4).

In reality, however, the calculations are much more complicated (Songtrust, 2019; Cooke, 2020). For instance, it is usual for record companies to license entire catalogues of music to a DSP, hence a bulk payment is made each month in relation to their catalogue as a whole. This is typically managed by a Collective Management Organisation (CMO), such as MCPS in the UK or Harry Fox Agency in the US. The label then splits the revenue it receives according to listener share and the terms of an artist's contract. Publishers also license entire catalogues to the DSPs, but they collect revenue in a different way. This is because each song may have multiple authors who own different percentage shares and who may be represented by different publishing companies (Cooke, 2020: 16–17). As a global database for songwriting and publishing information does not yet exist, revenues must be claimed in an alternative manner. The solution is to send the streaming data to a Performing Rights Organisation (PRO) that represents the publishers, such as PRS for Music in the UK, SECAM in France or ASCAP, BMI, SESAC, and others in the US. This monthly data is then matched against the information held by each publisher. Each publisher then returns an invoice to the DSP requesting payment. Needless to say, this can slow the entire process down considerably, especially if there are mismatches between the records that are held by different PROs or where there is legal action in relation to ownership disputes, such as the unlicensed use of music samples or where there are claims of plagiarism in relation to a song (MMF, 2019c: 15–16).

In addition to the complexities discussed in Box 7.2, there are a number of broader issues related not only to the pro-rata system, but to how the streaming market currently operates, including questions about whether online streaming should be treated as a form of public performance. If it were, performers in the UK, for example, could also gain revenue from what are known as 'equitable remuneration' rights. This issue is discussed further in Chapter 10. Four other issues are worthy of consideration here. First, while the DSP may operate as a global business, revenue collection is typically carried out on a country-by-country (or territory-by-territory) basis, with a spider's web of PROs and CMOs in place to collect and administer the income. A related point is that revenues collected in different territories will be in different currencies (leading to exchange rate issues), and there are large variations in the amount charged per subscription. For instance, in 2021 a Spotify Premium subscriber paid $9.99 per month in the US, but an equivalent of less than $2.00 per month in India. Spotify and other DSPs are aggressively targeting countries around the world to achieve maximum market share, but the lower subscription rates agreed in these countries serve to reduce the Average Revenue Per User (ARPU) for each service. There are also variations in the statutory licensing rates and calculations used by different countries since each country sets its own rules.

Second, DSPs account for their revenues on the basis of different subscriber types, from free (advertising-supported) plans, to individual, family and student subscriptions (and so on). Artist revenue is therefore calculated on the relative pro-rata share of streams and income per customer plan. This means that an artist whose streams mainly come from users on the ad-supported plan will likely receive very little income, since the advertising income to which it is connected is only a small fraction of a DSP's overall revenue. Third, DSPs are experimenting with new promotional services, such as Spotify's Marquee (which creates pop-up ads) and Discovery Mode (which boosts tracks in auto play recommendation algorithms). These are provided to artists and their labels either at a cost-per-click or in return for a lower royalty. For artists and their teams, there will be a trade-off between the cost implications of these services and the potential boost in streaming numbers that may be achieved through their use. Will their return-on-investment be worth it? Or is it, perhaps, uncomfortably close to a pay-to-play arrangement?

A final issue is that the major recording companies and publishers (and some larger independent labels) have brokered special deals with the DSPs when licensing their catalogues. These deals are hidden behind non-disclosure agreements (NDAs), so the details are unknown to the artists and their managers – a lack of transparency that makes it hard for them to know whether or not they are receiving the correct revenue. This was brought sharply into focus in 2015 when a licensing contract made between Spotify and Sony Music in 2011 was leaked to the online magazine *The Verge*. The contract contained a number of clauses that increased the amount of money Spotify had to pay. For instance, upfront payments were to be made irrespective of the number of tracks actually streamed, and a per-stream minimum payment was demanded that could exceed the label's actual revenue share (Singleton, 2015). If, as suggested by the article, such terms are replicated across the other major record companies, this would give them considerable power over the means of online distribution. It is also unclear, due to NDAs, whether any additional (unallocated) revenue generated through such deals is distributed to artists signed to the label and, if so, on what terms. Is it retained by the label? Or applied pro-rata to artists on the same basis as that month's user data? An important outcome of the terms negotiated by the major record labels is that the pool of revenue available for other copyright holders (independent artists, labels and publishers) is reduced, hence driving their revenue per stream downwards.

User-centric model

An alternative to the pro-rata model is the user-centric (or per-subscriber) model, whereby a user's individual subscription revenue is distributed only to those artists they actually listened to. If the user only listened to tracks by one artist during a month, then that artist would receive the entire subscription fee of the user less DSP costs (Maasø, 2014; Dimont, 2018). This would seem to offer a fairer payment distribution as it is based on the listening preferences of users, and could feasibly assist independent record labels and artists in earning more money from streaming. Research has, however, suggested that the outcome of this model may not be so clear-cut, since it relies on the independent artist or label driving significant traffic to their streams. For example, if a user listened obsessively to three artists, their subscription would be split three ways. Yet, if a user listened to many different artists, or predominantly listened to compilation playlists, there would be relatively little benefit to the individual artists streamed (Muikku, 2017: 10). Furthermore, if the model was introduced across all streaming platforms, it is likely that the revenues currently earned by the major record labels would reduce. This is not a situation that those labels would welcome. Nevertheless, in 2019 Deezer announced its #MakeStreamingFair initiative, which includes a pilot user-centric scheme in its home country of France (Deezer, 2019). At the time of writing, the scheme has yet to launch, as it has proved difficult to get the record companies (both indie and major) to agree to it (Cooke, 2020: 69).

An alternative system was launched by SoundCloud in April 2021. Its 'fan-powered' user-centric system includes around 100,000 artists who monetise directly with the platform (i.e. independent artists who are not tied into record company contracts). According to SoundCloud's website, royalties will be paid from a pool of paid subscriptions and advertising income. Each artist will gain a percentage royalty from the pool based on their share of overall listening time each month. Such a system would seem fairer, yet it should be remembered that the royalty pool available via SoundCloud is a lot smaller than that for the major streaming sites, so the potential benefits for participating artists are yet to be seen. What these developments do show, however, is that alternative ways of accounting for royalties are possible, and that we are likely to see new, and possibly more ethical, systems introduced to the streaming music sector in the future (see Box 7.3). Nevertheless, a key issue remains for both artists and labels when distributing through streaming platforms: how to attract listeners to their streams in a sustainable manner in order to produce a regular monthly income. This places particular attention on the role of marketing and promotion, as discussed in previous chapters.

BOX 7.3

Alternative streaming models

A number of alternative streaming models have been introduced that aim to pay artist royalties in a fairer manner. We look at two here: Primephonic and Resonate.

Initially launched in 2017, the subscription-based Primephonic.com (acquired by Apple Music in 2021) catered to the classical music market. The problem that the platform addressed is that classical music pieces tend to be lengthy in nature, yet the pro-rata system of the market-leading DSPs means that one play of a three-minute pop song earns the same as one play of an hour-long symphony. Primephonic addressed this through a pay-per-second system (its Fair Payout Model): the longer a track was streamed, the more money it would earn, thus offering a potentially more equitable payment structure.

Resonate.is describes itself as a 'community-owned music network' and operates a pay-as-you-play model with no regular subscription fees: instead, users purchase credits as and when they wish. First established in 2015, it was relaunched in 2019 with a stream-to-own model that sees the cost of a download split into nine micro-payments. Each time a track is played by a user the cost of the micro-payment increases. Once it has been played nine times, the user will own the track and can play it thereafter at no additional cost. By splitting the per-track costs in this way, users are encouraged to sample more tracks on the site in the knowledge that the micro-payments will directly benefit the artists. The site argues that even a few listens to a track will generate revenue in excess of that available from a comparable pro-rata streaming service. Resonate runs as a cooperative, meaning that artists and users can choose to become official members for a small annual subscription, and will then receive a share in any profits that the company makes.

YOUTUBE, SAFE HARBOUR AND THE 'VALUE GAP'

YouTube has been subject to criticism by musicians, record labels and publishers for many years, since its average revenue per stream (even considering the difficulties in determining such figures) is markedly lower than that received from music-centric streaming services. This disparity is known as the 'value gap', and results from 'safe harbour' provisions introduced in the 1990s. At that time, Internet Service Providers (ISPs) and website hosts were concerned that they could be made liable for copyright infringement if and when their users distributed copyrighted material through their platforms without permission or licences from copyright owners. Political lobbying led to global treaties that gave the technology companies immunity from liability ('safe harbour') so long as they created 'takedown' systems through which copyright owners could request removal of unlicensed content. It was also agreed that rights holders would be allowed to sue uploaders directly for damages. These terms (and others) were subsequently passed into national laws through the implementation of regional treaties, such as the US Digital Millennium Copyright Act of 1998 and the EU Electronic Commerce Directive of 2000. Following further pressure from the music industries, YouTube created Content ID in 2007, a system for detecting user-generated videos that incorporate copyrighted material. Content ID offers rights holders the opportunity to request the removal of unlicensed videos, to monetise them by adding advertisements or to access viewer statistics. This has produced a new revenue stream for the music industries, but the system has been criticised for its failure to identify all instances of unlicensed use, for errors in content recognition and for its inability to account for fair use (where, under certain exceptions to national copyright law, the use of music tracks may be allowed without permission or licence).

A US study using 2015 data estimated that the value gap in the US alone (i.e. between YouTube and other music-based subscription services) was in excess of $650 million per year (Beard et al., 2017). Furthermore, YouTube was an important contributor to online music piracy, as copyrighted tracks and albums that had been uploaded to the platform could be downloaded using 'stream ripping' software. For the music industry, Content ID was no longer enough, so further action was needed to address the problem. One solution was the creation of music-matching companies such as Pex and Breathe, which offer a similar service to Content ID but operate across all user-generated content platforms and are able to identify musical content with much greater accuracy. Such services will be increasingly important in the future, as rights holders seek to track every possible use of their content across streaming services, podcasts, livestreams, video apps and so on. However, this does not address the underlying issues created by safe harbour laws, so music industry organisations have continued to lobby for legislative action aimed at eroding the protections that benefit YouTube and other UGC platforms.

The counter-lobbying efforts of Google and other technology companies in the US mean that discussion and amendment of the Digital Millennium Copyright Act 1998 is in its infancy. Nevertheless, there have been some important developments. The Protect Lawful Streaming Act 2020 increases the criminal penalties for operators of unlicensed streaming services, while the proposed Digital Copyright Act (DCA) seeks to replace the current 'notice and takedown' system (where rights holders have to monitor internet traffic and issue takedown requests for each infringement) with a 'notice and staydown' system that puts the onus on the streaming provider to monitor and remove infringing content once it has been identified. Some legislative success has also been seen in Europe, where the European Union's 2019 Directive on Copyright in the Digital Single Market now states that sites such as YouTube will no longer receive complete protection from liability. Instead, they will have a conditional exemption from liability that requires them to take further action (beyond, for example, the existing Content ID system). The lobbying power of the major technology companies meant that the original terms of the Directive were watered down, and media reports that YouTube would need to implement draconian upload filters can no longer be supported. EU member states will design their own national laws and regulations based on the Directive, following which negotiations will need to take place between those governments and YouTube to determine how best to implement the new rules.

During the course of the EU negotiations, YouTube launched a music subscription service (YouTube Music) which has licensing deals similar to those of the major DSPs. Indeed, testimony from YouTube at a UK government enquiry in 2021 claimed that YouTube had paid out $3 billion to the music industry in 2019 and that this figure was rising year on year (Paine, 2021a). However, revenue from its advertising-supported tier remains low, and after over 15 years of offering its content for free, it remains to be seen whether YouTube's user base as a whole will be willing to pay for a subscription. Yet, there are signs that YouTube has turned a corner in terms of revenue generation for the music industries, with reports that premium channel subscriptions and the monetisation of user-generated content are rapidly increasing (Stassen, 2021a). The shift to online streaming and entertainment (with associated growth in advertising revenue) during the coronavirus lockdown may be one driver for this change in fortunes, as well as pressure from potential legislation.

GATEKEEPING ONLINE

The concept of gatekeeping has long been used to discuss the music industries (for example, see Hirsch, 1990). Gatekeepers are theorised as cultural intermediaries who make decisions that have profound consequences for the relationship between artists and audiences. For example, A&R directors choose who will or will not be signed and marketing managers prioritise funding and support for some promotional campaigns but not others. Similarly, radio producers decide which songs will or will not be played, and music supervisors guide programme makers in the choice of music to appear in films, video games and television shows. All of these decisions limit the music that will be made available to the public, while further gatekeepers, such as journalists, act as tastemakers whose praise or criticism can potentially affect consumers' listening and purchasing decisions.

Digitalisation has transformed this model. Artists can record, release, promote and sell their music directly to the public, and the public can comment on the music directly through personal blogs, message boards, rating sites and retail sites (by leaving feedback and writing reviews). In this respect, they extend into the digital sphere the pre-existing independent and alternative media of paper-based fanzines and amateur journalists that co-existed alongside the old model. This online alternative media of crowd sourced opinion is a form of 'citizen journalism' (Atton, 2009) that would seem to reduce the power of the music industries by bypassing the traditional industry gatekeepers. Yet, despite this disintermediation, it is still relatively difficult for independent artists to get their music played on a national radio station, to be interviewed or perform on television, or to gain coveted home page promotional slots on the major music streaming services. In other words, access to the means of production, distribution and promotion does not necessarily mean that a broad audience will come to hear the music that is made (Haynes and Marshall, 2017: 11). Instead, the financial, marketing and networking power of the major labels still has an important role to play, and traditional media outlets such as radio and television are adapting to the online environment by integrating their services across the new platforms. For instance, the radio sector has expanded to incorporate live streaming, podcasts, video content, music recommendation and integration with internet TV, as well as bespoke apps such as BBC Sounds.

Artists continue to value radio airplay, not only as a source of income and promotion, but as a validation of their work (perhaps because there is a gatekeeper involved). Radio producers and music industry pluggers embody a symbiotic relationship in which radio airplay may be guided by spikes in listening statistics seen on music streaming platforms, video sharing apps or music recognition apps (particularly Shazam). Similarly, a song that is promoted strongly through radio may subsequently be shared across social media and through DSP playlists. Where traditional and online exposure aligns, there is potential for creating a significant global hit, so record companies and artists focused on mainstream success in the singles charts work hard to manage their campaigns across multiple media platforms.

Gatekeepers continue to exist across the music and media industries, but the gatekeeping function has changed, particularly with respect to how DSPs use music recommendation software. For some commentators, this makes the major DSPs the pre-eminent form of gatekeeper, since they can 'set the "listening agendas" of global music consumers' (Bonini and Gandini, 2019: 2). The major DSPs have both human gatekeepers (curators) and automated systems based on algorithms (discussed below), though human curators have only been added to the mix since 2014. There are now hundreds of curators working across the DSPs, with some responsible for a platform's overall playlist strategy for specific genres, and others for creating and updating the playlists themselves (2019: 3–4). As a result, a 'cottage industry' of playlist pitching companies has emerged which claim to have contacts with key DSP playlisters in much the same way as the traditional model of radio and television plugging (2019: 4). It is also possible for artists to pitch their tracks directly to playlisters through, for example, Spotify For Artists. Here, an artist can upload a track for consideration in a playlist, so long as that track has not previously been released. It is therefore important to ensure that there is sufficient lead-in time with the distribution company so that the track can be pitched prior to it going live on Spotify or other DSPs. This is beneficial for Spotify in that it gains first choice for playlisting a track ahead of other DSPs. It is also beneficial for artists in that they may gain significant exposure if chosen. An unintended consequence may be that artists write songs with the intention of fitting in with specific playlist formats and expectations, or that artists who are not easily categorised may find it difficult to gain playlist inclusion at all.

It may be argued that the addition of human curators in the mid-2010s was a response to increased competition for customers and a burgeoning growth in the quantity of music available via each DSP. Increased competition, allied with an offering that is almost otherwise identical across the main DSPs (they all offer access to more or less the same catalogues of music and charge much the same price), meant that new ways were needed to enhance usability and create a differentiated product experience. The creation of bespoke playlists is one way to do this, and it has the advantage of perhaps counteracting what Eli Pariser (2011) has termed the 'filter bubble' effect: where automated systems continue to recommend music that users have already heard or are aware of, rather than introducing them to new music. Some playlists, such as Spotify's Rap Caviar, are entirely curator-driven, while others, such as Apple Music's For You are entirely algorithmic. More typical, perhaps, are those playlists which make use of both data analysis and editorial taste making, which are described as 'algo-torial' by Spotify (Bonini and Gandini, 2019: 6). It is also possible for popular playlists to expand into brands that cross over into other opportunities. A good example is Spotify's Who We Be, a specialist urban music playlist that has grown into a podcast (WWB Talks) and an annual live event (WWB Live).

Playlists are increasingly organised on the basis of moods and activities rather than genre, which reflects the different ways that consumers use music in their everyday lives. Music can be listened to at almost any time and in almost any situation, making music listening practices dependent on both the physical context of listening and the emotional state of the listener (Andjelkovic et al., 2019; see also DeNora, 2000; Bull, 2007). Recommender systems may therefore be characterised as both a technology of control (guiding the preferences of users) and as a technology of the self, where recommendations can help users transform and manage their everyday lives and emotions (Karakayali et al., 2018). The latter is enhanced by the ability of users to create their own playlists – playlists which become a further data element to be used by DSPs in their algorithmic systems. For instance, tracks that are saved to personal playlists from DSP-generated playlists are more likely to be retained in that DSP playlist or to be added to other ones, since personal playlist creation is regarded as a marker of popularity.

The ultimate goal of a DSP is to promote continued use of its platform by its users, with McKelvey and Hunt (2019: 5–6) defining three principal forms of experience: 'rabbit holes', 'carousels' and 'gorking out'. Users disappear down 'rabbit holes' when their curiosity leads them to follow the various links that the recommendation system is supplying – a fairly active form of listening that is nevertheless directed by the algorithmic recommendations presented. At the opposite end of the scale is 'gorking out', which involves passively accepting the choices that the recommender makes, such as the 'playing next' function on YouTube. Finally, there are 'carousels', in which users continually return to familiar content and recommendations, and are seemingly held in a room of mirrors equivalent to Pariser's (2011) 'filter bubble'. One of the challenges for the DSPs is to enhance the 'rabbit holes' in order to improve the discoverability of music on their platforms, whether of newly released music or back catalogue. Such discoverability is valued by record companies, publishers and artists, as it has the potential to increase their market share and revenues, and by the DSPs that seek to retain users by providing an ever-changing product offering that remains interesting and engaging.

PLATFORM ARCHITECTURE AND ALGORITHMIC RECOMMENDATION

The aim of any music recommendation system is to help users to navigate the huge and ever-growing catalogue of music that is available through a DSP, and to identify tracks that are likely to match users' personal preferences. This is carried out through the generation of algorithms that draw on the wide range of data available from users' interactions with the DSP and from contextual data that can be 'mined' from the internet. Three broad approaches can be delineated, though these are often combined in practice: content-based, collaborative-based and context-based. In content-based approaches, a database is created using descriptive data about the music itself. Two contrasting strategies illustrate this. In the first, typified by Pandora Internet Radio's Music Genome Project, human employees listen to and categorise music tracks using a wide range of musical attributes, referred to as 'genes' by Pandora (Prey, 2018: 1089). Pandora uses over 450 different attributes, ranging from the basics of musical key, tempo, rhythm, harmony and so on, through to aspects of instrumentation (types, registers, use of effects), the sound of a voice, the rhyme scheme of the lyrics and so on. Pandora's music recommendation system uses the genome data by comparing the attributes of a listener's current song to its database in order to choose the next track to be played. An alternative way to achieve content-based filtering is to employ acoustic analysis software that analyses the waveform or spectrogram of a track to categorise a variety of elements that can then be compared to a database of previously examined tracks. This system is used, in part, by The Echo Nest, which was bought by Spotify in 2014.

Collaborative-based filtering, such as the Matrix Factorization models used by Netflix, Amazon and Yahoo! Music draw on user and usage data rather than descriptions of the music itself. Recommendations are made on the basis of similarities between user profiles, hence on the basis of the listening profiles and activities of users, their personal demographic data and any user-generated content that a DSP allows, such as ratings, comments or saving to personal playlists (Cheng et al., 2017: 3654). The DSPs operate their own proprietary systems to support this. For instance, Spotify's PUMA (Playlist Usage Monitoring and Analysis) records the number of plays, skips and saves alongside data about age range, gender, geographical location, time of day, subscription tier, and so on (Bonini and Gandini, 2019: 6). Recommendation will improve with continued use, since data accumulates and builds a stronger picture of a user's individual tastes and preferences: a 'data shadow' (Andrejevic, 2014) of each individual user which represents them on the platform. Drawbacks of the collaborative-based method are that there is clearly a potential for the 'filter bubble' effect (due to reliance on historical usage data). Other risks are that new or occasional users gain poor-quality recommendations (due to the lack of data available), or user profiles become muddled if an account is shared with others.

Social-based recommendation uses data-mining techniques to enhance the contextual information available about individual tracks – to reach beyond musical attributes and usage data. The Echo Nest offers a good example of such an approach as it scours millions of internet reviews, blogs, social media posts, and ratings sites to learn about the cultural positioning and descriptions of tracks through semantic analysis. In other words, online conversation is converted into 'quantifiable data' (Prey, 2018: 1091) that can enhance that collected through content-based and collaboratively-based methods. At Spotify, this hybrid information is used to create a visualisation and taste preference tool called the 'Taste Profile'. This creates detailed 'data shadows' of individual users that are constantly updated, helping to drive personalised recommendations on the Spotify home screen. Further developments in recommendation software will extend the socially-based contextualisation of the music to the specific social and contextual uses of the users, with smartphones and wearable 'smart' devices offering new opportunities to learn more about when, where and how users listen to music (Prey, 2018). For instance, data about traffic conditions, the weather, a user's mood, and activities such as jogging or revising, and so on may be collected or implied through context-aware devices that can map how people use music throughout a day. This may then allow the DSPs to amend and improve the quality and timeliness of their recommendations (Cheng and Shen, 2016).

Automated and algo-torial recommendation systems place constraints on what users might hear, so that a manageable selection is promoted and the user does not become overwhelmed by choice. Another form of constraint is provided by the design of the user interface, which we regard as a form of platform architecture (a new form of gatekeeping). McKelvey and Hunt (2019) provide a useful way to consider this architecture by referring to 'surrounds' and 'vectors', though we prefer to use the terms 'content framing' and 'content networking'.

Content framing refers to how the pages of the platform are structured to guide listeners towards some tracks rather than others, and to provide a curated and directed selection of music. For instance, the home page will invariably contain a banner for a new release that has likely resulted from the digital plugging of a major record label, together with popular playlists. These drive listeners to hear new music, while the playlists themselves embody a cultural hierarchy of taste and quality: tracks placed near the top will be deemed more important than those placed lower down (Bonini and Gandini, 2019: 7). Content networking (or 'vectors') refers to 'the interactive pathways we take through data, guided by software' (McKelvey and Hunt, 2019: 2). This may be seen through the provision of personalised automated playlists created on the basis of the user's own listening habits. These give the appearance of the platform knowing and understanding the individual user's own music taste, which can in turn foster a sense of loyalty to the platform. However, they also constrain the user by pushing them towards music that the platform has recommended, with the user largely unaware of how the music has been chosen for them.

A final aspect of platform architecture is that the major DSPs all offer gigantic catalogues of music, the majority of which their users will never hear. In this sense, they are what we would call 'horizontally oriented' DSPs – offering a broad base of music in order to attract a broad base of users. In contrast, there are indications that 'vertically oriented' DSPs are beginning to expand within the music streaming sector. Here, the catalogues available are more closely curated towards niche music markets, such as jazz or classical music, rather than the one-size-fits-all aesthetic of the major streaming sites. These newer DSPs may be able to offer better targeted music recommendations, as well as additional curated content, such as written features, interviews, podcasts, exclusives and so on that are directly relevant to the (narrower) user base. Examples include Primephonic (discussed earlier) and the jazz music specialist Jazzed, which launched in 2020. Both also offer high-resolution subscription tiers to cater to the audiophile tendency found within these markets.

CONCLUSION

In the twenty-first century, the platformisation of the music industries has led to significant changes in how artists make, distribute, market and sell their music online. These changes drive processes of democratisation and disintermediation, affording greater control to artists and a more direct relationship between them and their audiences. However, it is often difficult for up-and-coming artists to take advantage of these changes to create a sustainable living. The existing copyright system, together with the market dominance of both the major record labels and the major DSPs, means that the playing field remains unequal, while accounting practices and contractual terms serve to benefit record companies more than artists. The widespread use of non-disclosure agreements means that artists and their managers are unable to properly understand how revenue is generated and distributed, and how their music is being used. There may be considerable benefits for audiences, including access to huge catalogues of music for a relatively low cost, the convenience of a digital archive available through cloud services and increasingly personalised systems of recommendation. Yet such benefits do little for the artists unless those artists are being streamed many millions of times, or have been able to cultivate a fanbase that can be leveraged beyond the streaming services themselves. Nevertheless, the success of producer-oriented platforms such as Bandcamp, fan-centric sites such as Patreon and FanCircles, the emergence of vertically-oriented genre-centric platforms such as Primephonic and Jazzed, and the push for alternative revenue models to be adopted by DSPs suggest that there are more developments to come in this sector. It is also possible that new, more equitable models will be developed alongside the well-known mass market DSPs and social media platforms. The challenge, as ever, will be in convincing audiences to engage with these platforms, and in finding revenue models that can work at a scale substantial enough to be sustainably profitable for all parties concerned.

Key discussion points

- How can fan engagement be promoted through digital platforms for both established and up-and-coming artists?
- What opportunities and challenges are opened up by user-centric models of revenue generation and distribution?
- How can music recommendation systems be improved?

FURTHER READING

To learn more about the platform economy as it relates to music, gatekeeping and recommendation, we recommend the October–December 2019 edition of the journal *Social Media + Society*. For more detail about music streaming revenues, collection and contractual terms, please see the Music Managers Forum's *The Song Royalties Guide* (MMF, 2019c) and Chris Cooke's *Dissecting the Digital Dollar* (2020).

8

CONCERTS AND FESTIVALS

SUMMARY

In this chapter we examine the concert and festival industries in three main sections and acknowledge the changes brought about by the coronavirus pandemic of 2020–21. In the first section, we look at the value of live music from the point of view of artists, host locations and audiences: all important elements of a broader live music ecology. The second section extends on the metaphor of a live music ecology to show how key aspects of that ecology (venues, promoters, booking agents, tour managers and media companies) operate and interact with others. The final section explores a range of issues and campaigns found within the live music and festival sectors.

Chapter objectives

- To explore the value of live music for artists, hosts and audiences.
- To expand the metaphor of a live music ecology, explore the different aspects of that ecology, and to consider some of the changes that have occurred due to the coronavirus pandemic that emerged in 2020.
- To show how the live music and festival sectors can be used as campaigning platforms for a range of issues.

THE VALUE OF LIVE MUSIC

This section focuses on three broad approaches to valuing live music – the economic, the instrumental and the social – and applies these to artists, event locations and audiences. The economic approach looks at revenue generation for artists, the spill-over effects for locations playing host to festivals and venues, and the financial costs of audiences attending events.

The instrumental approach focuses primarily on specific localities and the way that local, regional and national music policies affect the health of the live music sector. Finally, the social approach looks at the impacts on local, regional and national communities, and the cultural benefits of live performance for both artists and audiences.

Artists

For many artists (though by no means all), live performance is the lifeblood of their craft, with life 'on the road' offering not only income, but the excitements of travel, meeting new people and seeing new places. Simon Frith (2015: 272) notes that 'the live show is the truest form of musical expression, the setting in which musicians and their listeners alike can judge whether what they do is "real"'. The ability to play songs and to play them well is an important part of live performance for genres such as rock and jazz, though the increasing use of electronic instruments and pre-programmed musical elements would seem to negatively affect notions of an authentic live performance (a point we will return to later). Nevertheless, live performances act as research and development engines for artists, helping them to develop both their music and their on-stage presence. This is particularly useful for artists who are starting out, since there is considerable competition in the market: if others are also trying to get noticed, how can an artist ensure that they stand out from the crowd? In addition, in some genres there remains a strong emphasis on artists 'paying their dues' on the concert circuit – particularly at the start of their careers.

The myth of a band gigging hard and inevitably being picked up by a record company may have always been just that – a myth – yet it is an enduring one that is also mobilised when discussing the importance of grassroots music venues to the live music sector (Hesmondhalgh, 1999; Cluley, 2009a). Furthermore, gatekeepers such as radio DJs, critics and bloggers like to say that they 'discovered' an artist through live performance (even if they were already aware of them through industry contacts), and this can be useful for promoting the artist in the future. Regular gigging can, if handled well, lead to growth in an artist's fan base and social media statistics, and consequently to increased status among venue owners, promoters and other music professionals, such as booking agents. This is particularly the case where they are able to extend their reach into regional and national touring, as they can draw on the contacts they develop to establish long-lasting and mutually beneficial business relationships. For instance, a band that plays a support slot for an established group might be picked up by that band's manager or be recommended by them to another, thus leading to enhanced opportunities in the future. Furthermore, where artists are predominantly performing their own music, they should check the requirements of their national copyright collection agency (such as PRS for Music in the UK, or BMI, ASCAP or SESAC in the US) in order to claim live performance royalties for their songs. These can be quite lucrative for larger festival appearances, since royalties are typically based on a percentage of the event's overall ticket income.

An artist may draw on their concert and other revenues to create merchandise that can be sold on tour or online, including recordings, clothing, badges and other memorabilia, thus developing an additional income stream. Artists might also consider 'bundling' their tickets with other products (such as digital downloads or CDs/vinyl records) or offering VIP benefits, meet and greets, and other added-value activities to the ticket price. Further opportunities to extend the potential marketing reach and impact of live performance include regular social media updates before and after concerts, the use of endorsement deals and sponsorships (see Chapter 9) and pay-per-view (PPV) livestreaming. The latter sector grew significantly in 2020–21 as the lockdowns and social distancing measures introduced by governments to control the coronavirus pandemic made bricks-and-mortar performances untenable. Livestreaming has advantages in terms of reducing costs (as touring is an expensive activity) and for reaching a more geographically diverse audience than is possible in traditional concert tours. However, as artist manager Murray Curnow (interview with authors) notes, the livestreaming market is most likely to benefit larger-scale artists:

> Personally, I have reservations that these events work so well for emerging/mid-range bands – whereas your Harry Styles, Niall Horan, Dua Lipas can do so at great financial gain and success. I think there is some virtue in preserving your live fanbase, yet still releasing content. For example, a ticketed livestream event – versus releasing a great live vid on YouTube – I don't think financially you see an upside unless you're expecting 10–20k ticket purchasers – and the live vid on YouTube can effectively do the same job.

The PPV livestream market generated $0.6 billion in 2020 and is set to grow as the market matures from the early adopter phase into a wider audience (Mulligan, 2021c). The industry has recognised its potential, with numerous livestreaming companies launched by a range of management companies, record companies, PR companies and concert promoters. No single company or platform has yet achieved market dominance, though VenewLive, Mandolin and eMusicLive have all developed one-stop platforms for production and distribution. Livestreams are also available across multiple social media platforms (including YouTube, Twitch, Instagram and Facebook), meaning that the market is, for the moment, open to new entrants and innovative ideas (Anderton, 2022).

Event locations

In the UK, local governments have long used cultural events to promote both civic pride and economic growth (Frith et al., 2013: 40–41). Since the 1980s (and earlier in the US and Europe), urban cultural strategies have proliferated: the creation of cultural districts or clusters within cities; support for high-profile 'flagship' arts events to encourage urban regeneration and cultural tourism; and the establishment of 'music cities' (see Smith, 2012; Ballico and Watson, 2020). However, different forms of event have attracted varying responses from those in charge of public funding. For instance, in the UK, national and provincial orchestras, opera companies and ballet companies (as well as the venues and organisations that support them) have been typically regarded as 'good for consumers but could not survive the market' (Behr et al., 2016: 17). In other words, to survive commercially they need support from state subsidies, and such support is given validation by stressing the intrinsic cultural value of the art itself (Behr et al., 2014: 406; see also Levine (1988) on the emergence of the highbrow/lowbrow divide in the US). Owen McNeir (2016) suggests that ticket sales for arts festivals rarely cover more than 40 percent of their running costs, with the result that such organisations have become experts at fundraising. He argues that such events no longer rely solely on state support and ticket income, but also seek funding from private trusts and foundations, membership schemes, media partnerships and bequests.

In contrast, popular music performance and the venues it takes place in have historically been viewed by many arts funding organisations, especially in the UK, as commercially led, and thus not suitable for support on intrinsic grounds. Instead, the venues succeed or fail on their ability to make profits from their businesses and tend to rely on 'personal capital and retained profits' (Cluley, 2009a: 214). Robert Cluley (2009a) argues that small and medium-sized venues often lack the skills and knowledge to apply for the funding that may be available to them, though there are examples of those that have been successful. For instance, both In the Woods and the Green Man Festival received funds from the PRS for Music Foundation, Arts Council England, and the National Lottery (Anderton, 2019a: 82). The coronavirus pandemic saw a much broader range of British music businesses applying and receiving state support from the UK Cultural Recovery Fund, so it may be that commercially run popular music venues will be more proactive and more successful in seeking funding support in the future.

Festivals and venues seeking funding need to show how they might benefit the locality in which they are based. For this reason, we have seen numerous economic impact surveys focusing on data related to the numbers of jobs an event has created or supported, the added-value economic benefits for local businesses, and the tourist numbers attracted (Behr et al., 2014). Similarly, UK Music's *Wish You Were Here* reports (from 2013 to 2017), documented the economic benefits of music tourism to the UK. In contrast, the Music Venue Trust and Independent Venue Week (both based in the UK) consistently refer to the value of grassroots venues in both economic terms and the less easily quantifiable cultural well-being of audiences and musicians, and the development of future stars. In so doing, they help to reinforce the notion that small venues are the lifeblood of the industry and for developing talent.

Audiences

Live music is an intangible, experiential activity, produced and consumed simultaneously in a specific time and place, and presented to the public as unique – even though the same set list of songs might be played by an artist on every night of a tour (Holt, 2010; Cloonan, 2012). While the performance may be livestreamed or recorded for later consumption, the social atmosphere and lived experience of the event can never truly be replicated. Fabian Holt draws on the work of Walter Benjamin to describe this as an event's 'aura', noting that 'even the most perfect reproduction is always lacking presence in the here and now' (Holt, 2010: 256). Survey research of both venues and festivals has suggested a wide variety of motivations for attendance, yet it is clear that live events are valued for much more than the performances themselves (Webster and McKay, 2016; AIF, 2018; Webster et al., 2018). For instance, as Jim Mawdsley of the Association of Independent Festivals (AIF) noted with regard to festivals: there are people at one extreme who want to 'turn up and buy a beer and watch a few bands', while at the other there are those who seek a 'truly immersive' experience, to 'experience new things, [and] almost to step out of reality' (AIF, 2018: 11). Any attempt to generalise the motivational factors and experience of live events is therefore fraught with difficulty, yet it is useful to delineate some broad parameters, as we shall do below. It is also useful for concert and festival promoters to do their utmost to understand the needs and desires of their particular audiences in order to tailor their offerings and promote repeat attendance.

Socialisation and belonging

In 2018, the AIF published a *Ten Year Report* that showed the increasing importance of 'camping with friends' and of 'people attending the festival' as primary motivations for attendance across the audience surveys carried out over the previous decade (AIF, 2018: 18). In the same year, Webster et al. published the results of the 2017 UK Live Music Census. This report also showed how spending time with friends, making new acquaintances and sharing an experience with others were key motivations for British concertgoers (Webster et al., 2018: 28). Furthermore, respondents felt that concerts were 'energising, exciting and uplifting', with health and well-being benefits that were enhanced by the emotional connections felt between artists, audiences and music. Socialising in groups is particularly important at camping-based music festivals, where emotional attachments and a sense of belonging can develop between festivalgoers and the events that they attend (Wilks, 2011; Tjora, 2016) – especially where there is repeat attendance on an annual basis, and where groups of friends and generations of families attend together (Anderton, 2019a: 144). A sense of belonging may also develop for some venues, particularly where they become the centre of a subculture or scene (Bennett and Peterson, 2004; Bennett and Guerra, 2019). This can lead to enhanced loyalty and may be fostered by the booking habits of the promoter, who acts as a trusted tastemaker within the scene. This typically happens with independent rather than corporate promoters, since they are recognised as being a part of the communities in which they work, and they develop strong social relationships with the audiences who attend their shows.

Authenticity

The music itself is also, of course, a primary motivation for attendance, and feeds strongly into the second main theme: the search for authentic experience. This is fostered by the intangible, one-off nature of live events, of sharing physical space with musicians as they create music. This is stronger in concerts than in festivals, for as Dave Laing (2004: 7) has noted, at festivals 'the key thing is to be present at the event [for the social atmosphere and so on discussed above] ... not necessarily to see or experience a particular act. The latter is the motivation to attend a concert'. The festival experience (particularly for those events held outdoors and over a weekend) is far broader than the concert experience, while notions of authenticity at concert events differ in line with the 'genre worlds' within which those events are positioned. Simon Frith (1996: 207) argues that all performances are 'framed' by genre rules 'which determine how both performer and audience should behave' (see also

Auslander, 2008). These rules, or conventions, also help audiences to evaluate whether performances are good or bad (Frith, 1996: 208) and, we might argue, how authentic they may feel a performance to be. Authenticity is also connected to the sensory experience of live music, and there has long been a split between 'music for dancing' and 'music for listening' (Anderton and Atton, 2020). For some events, a sense of authenticity is connected to how a performance moves people to engage in their own physical movement and expression, from singing and clapping along with the music, to dancing, head banging or moshing. For others, quiet appreciation and attentive listening is the expectation, with applause restricted to the completion of featured solos or to the ends of songs.

One commonly discussed aspect of authenticity is its 'liveness' (Auslander, 2008; Holt, 2010; Danielsen and Helseth, 2016): the quality of 'seeing and hearing a performance with other fans at the time of its occurrence' (Westgate, 2019: 3), and the feelings of intimacy, immediacy and uniqueness that come with it. In live performance, the audience can see the work that has gone into the creation of the music – connecting the movements and actions on stage with the sounds that they hear, and witnessing both the emotion of the singer and the technical proficiency and stage presence of the musicians (Frith, 1996: 207; Auslander, 2008: 90–91). Philip Auslander (2008) has suggested that the authenticity of live performance is undermined by technologies that allow artists to use pre-programmed musical elements, sequencers, samplers and backing tapes. Yet, this is now a commonplace practice for many artists. Danielsen and Helseth's (2016: 36–37) research found that the use of pre-recorded elements was generally accepted so long as there were some musicians on stage who were visually representing aspects of what was being heard. Those musicians and their performances have a symbolic role to play in representing the liveness of the event, to evoke 'the overall soundscape of the music rather than to actually create it [all] in the moment' (2016: 37). What counts, then, is who is seen to be making the performance, and how this communicates a sense of authenticity. One fairly constant element is that the lead singers of both rock and pop groups are typically expected to perform live: to prove that they can perform and communicate the emotional content of the music. Where the singers do not perform live, they are likely to be criticised.

Freedom from everyday life

The third theme – of experiencing a sense of freedom from everyday life's routines and expectations – is most strongly associated with music festivals (Falassi, 1987; Ehrenreich, 2006; Anderton, 2019a), though it may also be connected to concerts (Webster et al., 2018). Camping festivals in particular are occasions where, for a few days, an individual's usual behaviours, social norms and identity may be safely and playfully changed or overturned, without adversely affecting their wider social lives (Ravenscroft and Gilchrist, 2009: 36; see also Robinson, 2015a; Anderton, 2019a). For many, this break from everyday social routines offers a period of personal renewal spent among family and friends, the opportunity to meet new people and try new things, and to socialise with others who share a similar set of interests and attitudes. Yet, there is also a hedonistic or carnivalesque aspect to outdoor festivals, where behaviours that might usually be frowned upon within everyday life are given temporary licence (Anderton, 2008, 2019a). We will discuss some of these behaviours later in the chapter.

THE LIVE MUSIC ECOLOGY

The use of ecological metaphors has become commonplace within both academic studies and music policy documents (Behr et al., 2016: 5), and may be regarded as extending Howard Becker's description of 'art worlds' as 'a large network of cooperating people, all of whose work is essential to the final outcome' (Becker, 1974: 769). This is clearly the case for the provision of live music performance, where concerts and festivals involve a wide range of roles, responsibilities, people and places. These are shown in Figure 8.1 where there is an inner core responsible for the show itself and a range of external organisations and factors within the broader business environment.

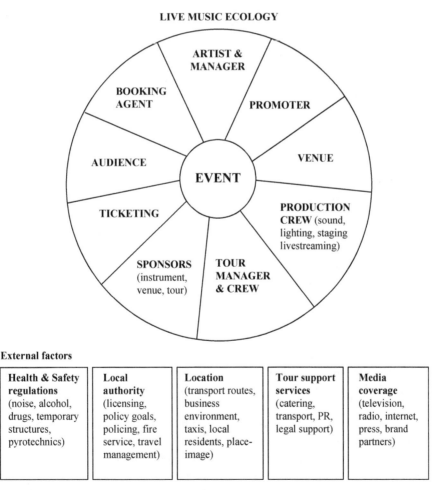

Figure 8.1 The live music ecology framework

We have adopted the metaphor of a live music ecology for two main reasons. First, it helps us to visualise the interactions and interconnections found within the live music industries, which helps us to understand the varying ways that they impact each other. Second, the approach implies other environmental metaphors, such as evolution: the recognition that the roles, responsibilities and interrelationships are not fixed, but will change over time. In the previous section we discussed artists, locations and audiences, while the role of the media was covered in earlier chapters, and sponsorship will be examined in Chapter 9. For this section, we will focus primarily on four other aspects of the live music ecology: venues, promoters, booking agents and tour managers.

Venues

Live music venues vary enormously in style and size – from the smallest-scale pubs, clubs and house concerts to 'grassroots' and 'platform' venues, mid-range national touring venues and large-scale stadia and festivals. 'Platform' venues are described as ones that provide 'a step up for bands at the start of their careers … the first place a touring band will play in [a] city' (Behr et al., 2016: 9). There may be some cross-over with 'grassroots' venues, which are local venues that focus predominantly on the provision of live music, rather than venues that offer music as an additional attraction (such as pubs, clubs, restaurants and hotels). Platform and grassroots venues are seen as crucial to the musical health of a city, providing opportunities for local musicians to learn their craft and play alongside touring bands. At the mid-range level, we find a variety of local and regional venue operators, including, in the UK, the Academy Group, which now manages nearly 20 venues across the country. The Academy Group is majority-owned by Live Nation Entertainment, which, through financial relationships with SJM Concerts, Metropolis Music, DF Concerts and Ireland's Gaiety Investments (among many others), is the single largest corporate organisation within the UK live music industry. In the US, Live Nation owns both the House of Blues and The Fillmore venue chains, and also owns, operates or controls a large number of other venues and music festivals worldwide. As we will see later, Live Nation also owns ticketing agencies, tour management companies and many other companies involved in the live music ecology, making it difficult for smaller and independent venues and festivals to book artists that have been locked into financial arrangements by the corporation.

Venues, depending on their size, typically earn their revenues from the concert promoter: through hire fees, a percentage of ticket sales or a combination of the two. Many venues also book and promote their own shows (known as 'in-house' booking), which increases their share of the ticket income, but also increases their exposure to risk should the event fail to make a profit. Venues add to their revenues through a variety of ancillary income routes, including, perhaps, a percentage of any on-site merchandise sales, charging for parking and for cloakrooms, selling food and drink (often vital to a venue's profitability), and securing sponsorship deals. According to the UK Live Music Census report, over 85 percent of small venues also hire out their space for activities beyond the provision of live music concerts, such as educational programmes, band practice, film viewings, art exhibitions, and theatre and dance shows (Webster et al., 2018: 32) – a mixed income approach that reflects the difficulties that small venues have in meeting their financial commitments through music alone. Venues work to foster and maintain relationships with artists, bookers, promoters, tour managers and audiences in order to provide a good experience that can help to build a solid reputation and foster future repeat business. Whether they book in-house or accept/rely on outside promoters, small venues undertake valuable 'curatorial work on the music side', as they work with a larger number of booking agents and artists than the larger-scale venues that mostly cater to established pop and rock stars (Holt, 2012). However, as we shall discuss later, the economic challenges of this sector are significant, even before the disruption caused by the 2020–21 coronavirus pandemic.

Promoters

Promoters operate at a variety of levels. Three broad types may be distinguished – enthusiast, state-funded and professional (Cloonan, 2012) – though the boundaries are blurry. Enthusiasts are less concerned with making profits from their events. They want to bring like-minded people together to provide 'great moments for their audiences' (Cluley, 2009b: 377) and support their passion through income from other jobs. Enthusiast promoters typically operate in local venues, but may also be found in the music festival sector and in the house concert circuit. House concerts initially developed in the hardcore punk scenes of the US (Makagon, 2015) but can now be found across a range of genres (see houseconcerts.com or concertsinyourhome.com). These small-scale concerts (typically 15–50 people in attendance) are usually held in the host promoter's own home and are, effectively, a kind of private party. As a result, the host cannot charge for tickets, but will suggest a minimum donation that can be given to the performer.

State-funded promoters are often associated with genres such as jazz, folk and classical music. Such genres may find it difficult to be staged commercially (Behr et al., 2014: 404), yet their work is justified as 'underpinned by a sense of the public good' (Cloonan, 2012: 154). Success is not necessarily judged through profits, but through the provision of positive benefits to local, regional or national culture, or to the host community, such as social inclusion and local economic development. In addition to financial support from governments, such promoters may also seek additional income from private funders, philanthropists and corporate sponsors. In contrast, professional promoters (in other words, those who are commercially motivated and seek to make a living from their work) are strongly associated with commercial genres such as rock, pop and dance music. Those who are active at the platform venue level are described by Adam Behr et al. (2016: 8) as 'invest[ing] in emerging artists who have been endorsed by agents at the start of their careers'. As we will see in the next section, booking agents do not work with all artists – only those where there is a likelihood of regular touring work that can provide an income to the agent. Promoters therefore work closely with agents to book these acts as headliners, as they will reduce the risk (uncertain ticket sales) inherent in putting on a live show. They will typically insist on exclusivity clauses for a similar reason, as these prevent artists from playing other, potentially competing shows within a specified time frame and geographical range.

Another common tactic for reducing the risk of a show is to book local artists as support acts at a lower cost. However, booking agents and managers may insist on tour packages that include a specified support act to help an up-and-coming artist gain exposure. In some cases, these acts have to 'buy on' to the tour (paying for the privilege) in order to gain the promotional reach and kudos of supporting a particular headliner. This may increase the risk profile of the event for the promoter, but they must, like venues, keep the artists and their intermediaries (manager, booking agent, PR) happy in order to build social capital and to enhance 'loyalty, reputation, and favors' (Behr et al., 2016: 8) in the future.

Promoters work closely with booking agents and artist managers to determine the ticket prices that will be charged for a concert, and to agree the contractual terms under which the artist will play. For larger shows, these terms will be formalised through a written and signed contract, while smaller shows may operate more informally – for instance, through an agreement via email. The latter is reliant on a trust relationship between the promoter and the booking agent, with unreliable promoters being barred by agents, and new promoters finding it difficult to gain a response. Promoters liaise closely with tour managers to ensure that the arrangements are in place to bring the artist to the venue/accommodation and to meet both the technical specifications of the show and the band's hospitality requirements (the contract's 'rider') (discussed later; see also Kielich, 2022). They also advertise and sell tickets to the public (typically through online ticket agencies or through their own website), and will be present before, during and after the event to look after their financial and business interests. If the show sells out and the ticket price and costs have been calculated well, the promoter stands to make a healthy profit. If not, the venue and band will typically be the first to be paid, which may leave the promoter making a loss. The promoter will aim to reduce their risk profile through the methods discussed earlier, and by promoting multiple shows, whereby profitable shows will hopefully cover any shortfalls on those which are not.

Further methods for reducing risk, though frowned upon by many artists, include the 'free gig' model operated by in-house promoters and the 'pay-to-play' model. In the free gig model (such as 'open mic' nights), live music is used as a promotional tool to attract people to a venue that primarily makes its profits from food and drinks sales. Musicians may or may not be paid for their time under this model, though the venues will sell the opportunity as a chance for artists to gain experience and start building a fanbase. The pay-to-play model is often justified in the same way (or with promises that record company scouts will be in the audience), and involves artists and DJs purchasing discounted tickets from the promoter and then selling them themselves at full price. The onus is therefore on the artists, rather than the promoter, to bring the audience to the gig, while the promoter is guaranteed upfront revenue. It is a practice that the Musicians' Union, among others, has fought hard against in the UK (through its #worknotplayMU naming and shaming campaign).

Festival promotion differs from concert promotion both in terms of scale and responsibility. The venue for an outdoor festival needs to be created from scratch, so festival promoters are not only responsible for booking, ticketing and marketing. For instance, they must hire stages, technical equipment (sound, lighting and so on), security staff, portable toilets and arena fencing, as well as securing/managing food, drink and retail outlets. They also need to liaise with local governments and emergency services and meet stringent health and safety regulations. The risks are significant, since a considerable financial and insurance burden is payable prior to revenue being available from ticket sales. For example, artists and suppliers will typically request 50 percent of their fee upfront.

The 2020–21 coronavirus pandemic led to lockdowns and restrictions that effectively closed concert venues and festivals for many months. Socially distanced events could not be managed in a financially sustainable way, yet livestreaming emerged as a viable alternative for musicians seeking to replace lost revenue, and as a source of funding for venues that could host them. Livestreaming is not a new phenomenon, but the pandemic accelerated a trend that, in contrast with the gaming and eSports industries, was underdeveloped within music (Thomas, 2020: 83). Many companies have adapted their business models to accommodate livestreaming, including ticketing companies such as Ticketmaster, Songkick, Bandsintown and Dice, management companies such as Driift, and entertainment companies such as Big Hit Entertainment. The latter, famous for the South Korean group BTS, joined forces with YG Entertainment, Universal Music Group and video technology company Kiswe to launch VenewLive in 2021 – a global livestreaming platform that presages a wave of such developments as companies seek to gain dominance within the emerging marketplace. At a smaller level, the British company Scruff of the Neck (which encompasses concert promotion, publishing and a record label) has partnered with the gaming platform Twitch. Chris Brierley (Head of Live at Scruff of the Neck told *Music Week* that:

> We hope that we can develop a space for new music discovery, while at the same time building an online community for those looking to immerse themselves in a gig experience and become part of the conversation around some of the most exciting talent on offer. (Paine, 2021b).

Virtual reality (VR) is also beginning to enter the mainstream of live music. For instance, in 2019, MelodyVR partnered with Academy Group sponsor O2 to provide O2 customers with access to VR experiences of concerts held at Academy Group venues. The sector expanded markedly during the global pandemic, with the electronic music festival Tomorrowland launching *Tomorrowland Around the World* – an online festival that recreated many of the stages found in the real-world event as well as interactive participatory activities, virtual fireworks and laser shows. Virtual recreations of real-world concert and club venues have also been developed. For instance, Sony's Immersive Studios has recreated the Sony Concert Hall in New York, with artists appearing as 3D virtual avatars in concerts livestreamed through PlayStationVR and OculusVR.

Booking agents

New and emerging artists typically book their own shows, directly contacting venues to gain bookings or to organise small tours. However, as artists become more established and seek to perform at larger venues, they will need to work with a manager and seek representation from a booking agent (sometimes referred to as a 'talent agent'). This is made easier where there is a pre-existing relationship of trust between the manager and a booking agent, and where there is a 'buzz' about the artist (see Chapter 4). Perhaps most important of all, the agent should believe in the potential of the artist and their music; after all, it is part of their role to convince promoters that they should book the artist. Booking agents earn their revenues from the performance guarantee (discussed later) – typically around 10 percent – so it is not in their interest to work with artists who are unlikely to command good fees. There are, however, many booking agencies and booking agents, who may specialise in specific genres and/or geographic regions, so artist managers must carefully research the options. Booking agents can help to secure support slots with higher-profile artists, and use their knowledge of venues and promoters to successfully route tours and maximise performance guarantees. As artists gain further fame and begin to play larger venues, so managers will look to create new relationships with booking agents that are at an appropriate level; hence, while artists may typically sign with only one agency, they will move from agency to agency as their fortunes rise or fall. At an international level, key agencies include the US-based Creative Artists Agency, William Morris Endeavor Entertainment and Live Nation Entertainment.

Booking agents work with artist managers to set the basic terms of a show or tour and to determine a minimum ticket price. They then negotiate with promoters on behalf of the manager to secure dates and to agree the contractual terms under which the artist will perform. Contracts are generally in two parts. The first details the overall parameters of the agreement, including the date, time, location and length of the performance, the artist's position on the bill (should there be more than one act performing), and financial details regarding the calculation of the artist's fee. Fixed-fee deals are often found for festival events that involve tens to hundreds of performers, and for events offered free to the public. Under such deals, a guaranteed payment is received by the artist irrespective of how many people actually attend, with up to 50 percent of the guarantee paid upfront. On tours and one-off ticketed events, it is more common to find variations of the 'guarantee plus percentage gate' deal. Here, there is a minimum guarantee (again, partly paid upfront), plus an agreement to pay a percentage of any profits received from ticket sales after the promoter's costs have been accounted for. The percentage can vary enormously, with superstar performers demanding the highest rates (sometimes 90 percent or more). A number of other variations exist, including the 'versus' deal, where the artist receives either the fixed guarantee or the percentage gate (whichever is greater), and the 'percentage net' deal (common in smaller venues) where the artist receives a cut of ticket receipts after event expenses have been paid.

The second part of the contract is the 'rider', which gives detailed information about technical specifications (including amplification and lighting, special effects, power supplies and staging) and an artist's hospitality requirements. The latter typically relates to overnight accommodation, dressing rooms, catering, security arrangements, and extras such as free access to the internet, clean towels, flowers in the dressing room and a whole range of requests which can, in some cases, seem rather bizarre (Croft, 2007). Promoters will do their best to either meet the demands made of them or to negotiate them out of the contract. In some cases, clauses such as the famous request on a Van Halen tour for a bowl of M&Ms with the brown ones removed, are there to see whether the promoter has read all the terms correctly. If the requirement hasn't been met, it may mean that other, more important, requirements have been missed (The Smoking Gun, 2008).

Tour managers

Tour managers are required for artists undertaking national and international tours and are responsible for a wide range of activities – financial, logistic and interpersonal. Prior to commencing the tour, they work with the artist's management to create a tour budget and to hire the crew who will undertake the various technical aspects of the tour: sound engineers, lighting technicians, instrument technicians, transportation, catering and so on. They then take responsibility for the day-to-day running of the tour, ensuring that artists, equipment and crew make it to each venue in good time to set up the stage and equipment, complete a sound check and manage a smooth performance. Organisation, communication and adaptability are key attributes for a tour manager, as they need to liaise not only with their own crew, but with transportation and accommodation companies, the venues and promoters where the artist is performing, and with any merchandising company or brand sponsors involved in the tour. They will also have to deal with potentially difficult artists, promoters, venue owners and others, mediate between band members, and look after the emotional well-being of the artists and crew with whom they work.

The terms of the performance contract need to be checked at each venue to ensure that the technical requirements for the show are met and that the personal riders for the artists are properly supplied. Tour managers will negotiate and pay crew wages and may also work with the artist's manager and the promoter to arrange for payment of artist performance fees, including checking ticket receipts with regard to 'percentage gate' deals. A considerable amount of paperwork is involved in the role, which includes 'advancing' the show: clear communication about travel times, routes and parking arrangements, the load-in/load-out times for equipment and arrangements for sound checks. They will also be responsible for submitting set lists to the promoter to ensure that the relevant performance royalty collection society is informed. Additionally, they must ensure that all artists and crew have relevant backstage passes for the shows, as well as identity papers and work visas for international travel.

The international transport of equipment typically involves the use of carnets – a temporary customs document that details all the equipment and merchandise that is crossing the border and ensures that import duties and taxes are not charged. These tour carnets can cost anything from a few hundred to a few thousand pounds and help to avoid delays at border crossings (UK Music, 2018b). At the time of writing there are significant concerns for British bands intent on touring Europe. The freedom of movement previously granted the UK via membership of the European Union (EU) was lost following Brexit, adding restrictions, delays and expenses related to carnets, work visas, customs checks and cabotage (how many times a UK haulier can make stops in the EU). British concert promoters are also concerned by this, as European artists will find that their paperwork and expenses have increased when seeking to perform in Britain. The industry will adapt to the new arrangements, as it currently does when touring countries outside the European Union, but there are campaigns to streamline the post-Brexit process via a relaxation of EU cabotage rules and the introduction of pan-European work visas and carnets that avoid border checks, paperwork and payments being required for UK tours at each European border (ISM, 2018; UK Music, 2018b).

ISSUES AND CAMPAIGNS

Grassroots venues

As discussed above, the grassroots sector (typically venues with attendance capacities of fewer than 500 people) is regularly lauded by musicians, industry organisations and governments as being vital to the health of the music industry as a whole. Despite this, the first two decades of the twenty-first century have seen increased divergence in the fortunes of locally-based, independent grassroots venues in comparison to corporately-owned venues and promoters. The latter are increasingly oligopolistic in nature, as a small number of interdependent national and international companies now dominate 'high-level gig promotion' (mid-range venues, arenas, stadium gigs and festivals) (Behr et al., 2016: 10). For instance, in the UK market, there are complex ownership deals between Live Nation, Gaiety Investments, Academy Music Group, SJM Concerts, DF Concerts and Metropolis Music (which between them operate the vast majority of medium and large-scale venues and festivals), while in the US, Ticketmaster (owned by Live Nation) has around 80 percent of the ticketing market for the nation's Top 100 tours. Furthermore, companies such as Live Nation are vertically integrated, with different parts of the same company looking after booking, promoting, ticketing, venue ownership, artist management, tour management, merchandising and sponsorship. This gives the company a tremendous advantage, as it offers a one-stop range of services, while also managing entire national and international tours. The bargaining power this offers makes it harder for independent venues, promoters and festivals to compete, with top-selling performers consistently unavailable due to contractual relationships and exclusivity clauses.

The market for live music at a grassroots level suffers from a lack of investment due to shifts seen in music consumption since the 1990s. Fans are now more likely to save up for large-scale arena shows than to attend their local venue on a regular basis, and are more likely to discover new bands through a streaming site than a live performance. Hence, while ticket prices are rising for large-scale shows, they are stagnating at the grassroots level, making it harder for these venues to make a profit or to invest in better-quality facilities or bookings. In addition, there have been further pressures, particularly in the UK, caused by rising rents and rates (DCMS, 2019a), especially for venues located in inner-city locations that are the target of gentrification. New property developments, such as the conversion of old office blocks into residential flats, raise local land prices, while noise complaints from new residents have, in the past, been the cause of venues closing down. Such pressures have also been seen in other countries, with the Australian state of Victoria being the first to successfully act on the issue by adopting the Agent of Change principle into law. Under this system, property developers take on the financial responsibility for meeting the costs of noise management rather than the nearby venue and should, if correctly applied, prevent noise complaints from being used to close venues in the future. In the UK, the Music Venue Trust worked with other stakeholders, such as UK Music, to lobby the government to introduce the Agent of Change principle into British planning law. It has since been adopted, though it remains to be seen how effective the new rules will be.

In parts of Europe, the intrinsic importance of music venues and live performance for local and national culture and tourism has long been recognised. A 2018 report suggests that over 35 percent of the European venues surveyed received a state subsidy, rising to over 50 percent for venues in France (Dee, 2018: 11). However, in the UK, the grassroots commercial sector rarely qualifies for state support, leading the Music Venue Trust (MVT) to lobby both the major live music promoters/venue owners and Arts Council England (ACE) for action. In 2018, MVT launched the Pipeline Investment Fund with a Statement of Intent which sought funding from music industry organisations to support grassroots venues. In so doing they mobilised the mythology of small venues as the creative powerhouse and future of new music. Over a dozen organisations signed the Statement of Intent, while further lobbying led ACE to launch a 'Supporting Grassroots Live Music' fund worth £1.5 million. These developments aim to make tangible improvements to small venues, from investment in modern sound and lighting systems and facilities to repairing crumbling infrastructure and developing apprenticeship and training programmes. This marks a considerable change in state funding policy in the UK, which is now more open to supporting commercially-run venues and a wider range of genre interests.

Primary and secondary ticketing

Digital technologies are transforming the live music ecology – with developments in gig discovery and interactivity, and in the growth of both augmented reality (AR) and virtual reality (VR) applications. One area that has already transformed markedly, and which affects both concerts and festivals, is the digitisation of the ticketing industry and the dominance of a small number of major ticketing companies. Primary ticket sellers (who sell face-value tickets directly to the public), such as Ticketmaster, have been criticised for their high processing fees and for a range of 'predatory practices' that disadvantage ticket buyers (Z. Klein, 2010: 187). One of these is the 'bait and switch' tactic of diverting potential purchasers away from the primary ticketing website to a secondary ticketing website owned by the same company (where prices are much higher) – even though face-value tickets are still available on the primary ticket seller's own website. Unsuspecting purchasers may therefore pay prices considerably higher than face-value on the mistaken assumption that this is the only way to get a ticket to a show. This tactic came to light through court cases in the US and Canada, with Ticketmaster agreeing to change its business practices and compensate purchasers who had overpaid for their tickets (Z. Klein, 2010: 185–186, 195–196).

Another issue is a lack of transparency about the availability of tickets. For instance, potential customers will not know whether a venue/promoter has retained a tranche of tickets to be released at a later time; hence, there is artificial scarcity until that tranche is released. Furthermore, large concerts typically have a ticket allocation ('holds') set aside for sponsors, artists/managers, media outlets and high-profile guests. The size of these allocations is not known, although the US Government Accountability Office suggests an average figure of 16 percent for stadium concerts (GAO, 2018: 7). It may be that unused tickets find their way back to the primary market at a later stage or are instead pushed onto the secondary market, with the intended recipients of the 'holds' profiting significantly from this practice (Z. Klein, 2010: 197). Even more worryingly, a 2012 British television documentary exposed how secondary ticket sellers Viagogo and Seatwave were 'actually engaged in industrial scale ticket purchases specifically for the purpose of reselling at large mark-ups' (Behr and Cloonan, 2018: 4). It showed that these companies (and others) were not only purchasing directly from primary ticket sellers, but that primary ticket sellers were allocating tranches of tickets directly to the secondary site in order to reap higher profits.

When secondary ticketing sites first entered the market in the early 2000s, Ticketmaster was highly critical of what is essentially an online form of ticket touting (known in the US as ticket scalping). Yet, as legislation to control the sector was not forthcoming, the company bought into the secondary ticketing market instead, beginning with the purchase of GetMeIn! in 2008 (Behr and Cloonan, 2018: 3). Both primary and secondary ticket sellers have fought to prevent legislation being enacted, while organisations representing consumers, such as the FanFair Alliance, the Ticket Trust and FEAT (Face-value European Alliance for Ticketing) have lobbied for change. Some success has been seen. For instance, Ticketmaster closed its subsidiaries GetMeIn! and Seatwave, and both the UK and the US have enacted legislation to ban the use of 'bots' (automated computer programs that purchase tickets as they come on sale and make it harder for legitimate buyers to access primary tickets) (Behr and Cloonan, 2018; GAO, 2018). In 2020 the European Commission announced proposals for the Digital Services Act, aimed at regulating the secondary ticketing marketplace in the European Union. FEAT continue to lobby for ticket personalisation (which requires attendees to display matching identification) and for legal, face-value resale (and re-personalisation) methods to allow ticket owners to transfer ownership of their tickets should they be unable to attend a concert or event (FEAT, 2021). Moreover, it is likely that smartphone-based digital and contactless ticketing will be adopted across the sector, partly to make secondary ticketing a more difficult proposition but also to streamline food and drink orders through venue-specific apps.

Festival-led campaigns: Sex, drugs and environmental sustainability

In the past, outdoor music festivals were 'frequently at the centre of the generational anxieties that gripped those in authority' (Nita and Gemie, 2019: 5; see also Clarke, 1982; Worthington, 2005). This was, in large part, because of issues related to illicit drug use, unsafe sex, the acceptance of squalid conditions and the potential for disorder (Clarke, 1982; Anderton, 2019a). However, as the sector has commercialised and professionalised since the mid-1990s, so the perception of music festivals as radical spaces has diminished. Festivals are a key part of the summer leisure-time experience for people of all ages and is an increasingly mainstream activity. Nevertheless, issues regarding sexual behaviour and drug use continue to be raised. Festival promoters and organisations are, of course, keen to present their events as safe, welcoming places in order to increase attendance figures, stage trouble-free events and secure continued support from licence-granting authorities. They have, therefore, taken concerted action on these issues with high-profile campaigns and 'digital blackouts' – where festival websites are replaced for a day by links to relevant information and resources – in order to raise awareness and promote potential solutions.

The 'anything-goes', 'free love' stereotypes of the countercultural festivals of the 1960s continue to have resonance in the contemporary music festival sector, yet attitudes have changed. Events now commonly include welfare tents where sexual health advice may be sought, and there is an increased focus on challenging the use of sexualised language, flashing, sexual assault and sexualised photography. This has been driven by high-profile cases of sexual assault at events, the use of social media in the wake of the #MeToo movement and by the campaigning of organisations such as Girls Against, Safe Gigs for Women and The White Ribbon Campaign. In the UK, the Association of Independent Festivals (AIF) launched the Safer Spaces campaign in 2017. Signatory events agree to enforce a victim-led, zero tolerance policy towards reports of sexual assault (defined as 'any unwanted sexual act or activity') and to promote the key messages of 'hands off unless consent' and 'don't be a bystander' (AIF, 2018: 33).

In the late 1960s and 1970s, festivals became synonymous with the open use of illicit drugs (Clarke, 1982: 27–28), with ecstasy use at illegal raves in the 1980s and 1990s extending the connection. Contemporary festivals often warn festivalgoers about the dangers of drugs in their terms and conditions, and actively dissuade drug use by working with the police. Nevertheless, for many festivalgoers, the perceived freedom of outdoor festivals includes the ability to take drugs, and it is both impractical and costly for organisers to attempt to find and arrest all drug users. Indeed, such a strict approach might adversely affect the overall atmosphere and experience for festivalgoers in general, hence affecting the overall viability of an event (Robinson, 2015a: 81).

While this may be the case, it is also important for promoters to be seen to be taking action, particularly as highly visible drug use and cases of overdose and death are damaging not only for those involved, but for the event in terms of its public image and its ability to secure an event licence in the future. In the UK, the AIF successfully campaigned to make the sale of so-called 'legal highs' (chemical compounds with a psychoactive effect) illegal. Moreover, several festivals now work with a charity called The Loop to implement Multi Agency Safety Testing (MAST) on site, which tests drugs brought in by festivalgoers (without fear of being arrested). The service helps to educate users, issue warnings about potentially dangerous substances, and to offer useful information to the emergency services dealing with drug-related cases (Measham, 2016).

The presence of thousands, or tens of thousands, of festivalgoers in one place over one weekend inevitably places significant pressure upon the environment; for instance, in terms of the carbon footprint of festival travel and onsite energy use, and the creation of huge quantities of waste, including tents that are left behind when festivalgoers leave. Environmental sustainability has increasingly come to dominate the mainstream political agenda, with music festivals seen as good places to campaign for action. Indeed, some festivals, such as Shambala in the UK and Bonnaroo in the US, have made the 'green' agenda a key part of their overall ethos and marketing. A number of initiatives have been adopted in the UK, including the Love Your Tent campaign (aimed at reducing landfill waste), Drastic on Plastic (aimed at ending the use of single-use plastics on festival sites) and Powerful Thinking (offering advice on sustainable energy solutions for outdoor events). In addition, organisations such as Julie's Bicycle and A Greener Festival publish reports and guidance for festival organisers and suppliers, and run accreditation schemes such as Industry Green Certification.

The actions available for festivals include educational activities for festivalgoers, such as the use of 'green ambassadors' who patrol the arenas and give advice, and 'green' clauses added to suppliers' contracts. They may also introduce enhanced recycling schemes, the use of compostable materials, and the monitoring and reduction of energy and water usage. Many have adopted renewable energy sources to varying extents or offer car share/public transport initiatives aimed at reducing carbon emissions from festival travel. Research at Bonnaroo festival in the US suggests that festivalgoers understand and engage in 'waste diversion' practices, such as recycling, but are less knowledgeable about other environmental strategies (Kennell and Sitz, 2010). A disconnect has also been seen in UK festivals, with the AIF reporting that while festivalgoers increasingly say they support sustainable transport, average car use actually increased across the same survey period of 2008–17 (AIF, 2018: 15). One of the main issues for festival organisers who are not ethically or ideologically driven is that environmental policies may well increase costs. As a result, we see festivals choosing to adopt practices that meet the 'triple bottom line' of planet (environment), people (society) and profit (economy) (Elkington, 1997; Gration et al., 2011), with profit perhaps being the key motivation. For instance, an increase in recycling means a decrease in landfill costs and potentially an income from the recycling of waste collected. Similarly, allowing companies onsite that promote 'green' toilets will provide a concession rental for the promoter and reduce the number and cost of urinals and portaloos that it needs to hire.

CONCLUSION

This chapter has demonstrated the importance of live music to the music industry ecology in social, cultural, political and economic terms. Further work is needed on the various elements of the production chain (bookers, promoters, agents, tour crew, sound and lighting technicians and so on), as well as on the marketing and experience of live concerts and festivals. New technologies, such as augmented reality and virtual reality, are continuing to develop, and there is still a lot of potential for integrating social media and smartphone apps into the overall event experience. There will be resistance from some concert and festival attendees because the use of such technologies may be viewed as disrupting the intimacy and authenticity of the live music experience. Yet, others are likely to embrace the potential offered, thus creating a different kind of live music event; something foreshadowed by the shift to livestreaming models during the coronavirus pandemic. Whether this will aid the sustainability and success of grassroots venues, or whether further state action is required to support this part of the sector, is yet to be seen. However, what we learn from histories of the sector (see Frith et al., 2013, 2019, 2021; Anderton, 2019a), is that, like the recorded music industry, there are times of growth and times of stagnation. However, the sector remains a vitally important part of the music industry as a whole, and of the social and cultural life of both musicians and audiences. The coronavirus pandemic may have been debilitating for the live music sector, but a latent demand for live music performance will see a newly configured version of the industry emerge in the future, one in which livestreaming and physical venues operate alongside each other.

Key discussion points

- How have the different sectors of the live music ecology developed as a result of the disruption caused by the coronavirus pandemic?
- Are technologies such as livestreaming and VR disruptive to the existing live music ecology, and will they become mainstream?
- What is the fairest way for the secondary ticketing market to operate?
- Can the gap between the grassroots live music sector and the top-earning live music artists be reduced? Should international corporations or national governments take more action?

FURTHER READING

For further discussion of the outdoor music festival sector, see Roxy Robinson's *Music Festivals and the Politics of Participation* (2015a), Gina Arnold's *Half a Million Strong: Crowds and Power from Woodstock to Coachella* (2018) and Chris Anderton's *Music Festivals in the UK: Beyond the Carnivalesque* (2019a). These books examine a range of historical and contemporary perspectives related to the social, cultural, business and media value of outdoor events. The following books examine concerts as well as festivals, and delve deeper into the various job roles and technologies found with the sector: Ewa Mazierska et al.'s *The Future of Live Music* (2020), and Chris Anderton and Sergio Pisfil's *Researching Live Music: Gigs, Tours, Concerts and Festivals* (2022).

9

BRANDING AND SPONSORSHIP

SUMMARY

Branding and sponsorship have become increasingly important to the modern music industries. This chapter examines two main areas of impact. The first is artist-centred brand activity, typically carried out by music professionals in collaboration with artists and external partners, such as corporate brands, other musicians, media, fans and so on. Such partnerships help to position the artist within the broader music marketplace, and to provide funding, marketing and other mutually beneficial outcomes. The second is the role of branding within the live music sector, with a particular focus on music festivals, where sponsorship deals have been an important driver in the commercialisation and professionalisation of the sector. We highlight potential issues with regard to ownership, control and 'brand fit': the degree to which the values espoused by an artist or event match those of a sponsor, and those of their fans and audiences.

Chapter objectives

- To explore definitions and meanings of branding and sponsorship, ranging from endorsement deals through to brand ambassadorships and immersive brand experiences.
- To analyse notions of 'brand fit' and return on investment.
- To apply a cultural economy approach to the notions of 'artist-as-brand' and 'festival-as-brand'.
- To examine critiques of sponsorship and branding.

Branding and sponsorship have been present in the broader music and media industries for well over a hundred years (Meier, 2017: 5), with record labels, artists and managers increasingly viewing them in positive terms (MMF, 2019b). Indeed, UK Music (2020a: 8) regards the revenue derived from an 'artist brand' as one of the four most significant assets to be held by an artist, alongside songwriting, master recording and live performance. However, some musicians raise objections about the 'selling out' of artistic integrity when music becomes aligned with a commercial or corporate brand (Harrison, 2021: 238), especially when it affects artists considered to have been 'authentic' in their early careers (Bridson et al., 2017). Naomi Klein (2010: 3) describes the 1980s as a watershed moment for the relationship between artists and multinational corporations, when management theory of the time re-situated the principal work of corporate businesses as marketing rather than manufacturing, as a process of building 'brands, as opposed to products'. At the heart of this was brand differentiation based around lifestyle marketing and image, since traditional marketing tactics – such as price differentiation and product promotions – could easily be imitated by rivals (2001: 14). To gain competitive advantage they increasingly sought sponsorship deals with the cultural industries: adding value to their products by associating them with specific cultural icons, musicians, sporting events and so on. As Klein notes, this made the 1980s 'music's decade of the straight-up shill', in which artists such as Eric Clapton and Genesis sang in beer adverts and pop stars appeared in Coca-Cola or Pepsi adverts (N. Klein, 2010: 46; see also Meier, 2017: 38–39). It also led Neil Young to respond with the song and video 'This Note's for You' (1988, directed by Julien Temple), which lampooned a then-contemporary Budweiser advert and featured looka-likes of Michael Jackson, Whitney Houston and others. In the video, the hair of the Michael Jackson lookalike catches fire, as it famously had for the real star during the filming of a Pepsi advert in 1984. This sort of response, and the countercultural attitudes underpinning it has, as Bethany Klein (2020) notes, largely waned since the late 1990s, though there are still some artists who retain a strong antipathy to corporate branding, such as Trent Reznor (of Nine Inch Nails) and the singer-songwriter Tom Waits.

In the live music sector, brand sponsorship has been present at least since the emergence of commercially-run music festivals in the 1960s and 1970s, when promoters made use of sponsorship tie-ins to help fund their events (Anderton, 2019a: 83–85). Event-based sponsorship has since become not only a conventional practice, but one which is often necessary to the financial success and sustainability of what is a highly risky business (Anderton, 2019a, 2019b). In North America alone, live music sponsorship was valued at $1.61 billion in 2018, which represents a 48 percent increase on 2010 (IEG, 2019). Sponsorship spend will no doubt be re-evaluated following the coronavirus pandemic of 2020–21, but events will remain an important sponsor category. Valuations about artist-based sponsorships are more difficult to ascertain, yet high-profile endorsement deals such as Beyoncé's 2012 deal with Pepsi can run into millions of dollars, while smaller endorsement deals of $50,000 to $300,000 are perhaps more typical (Lieb, 2018: 87). The level of funding achieved depends on the bargaining power of the artist involved. Lesser known, up-and-coming or independent artists are likely to receive considerably less than this, or nothing more than the perceived kudos and marketing benefits of the association (Meier, 2017: 114).

BRANDING, SPONSORSHIP AND ENDORSEMENT DEALS

A distinction may be made between branding activities that relate directly to an artist and/or event brand (the core brand) and those which relate to deals made between the core brand

and external partners (co-branding). It is important to those managing the core brand that any campaigns and partnerships made with others will reinforce the core meanings of the brand rather than conflict with them. The same is true for the partner brands, which also need the branding relationship to be perceived as credible by their own target market of consumers (Meier, 2017: 103). This issue of 'brand fit' will be considered later in the chapter, though it is worth noting here that brand partnerships and sponsorships should provide mutual benefits for both parties to the deal (ICC, 2003: 2): they are not philanthropic gestures made by the sponsor brand, but business transactions that are expected to provide a return on investment (ROI). ROI objectives range from enhancing awareness, sales and loyalty (including digital media content and data capture), to repositioning the brand with respect to its intended target market and demonstrating corporate social responsibility or community integration.

The underlying meanings associated with specific brands (whether artists, events or business partners) are typically intangible in nature, but are represented symbolically through a variety of markers, such as names, logos and images, as well as interviews, social media interactions, product packaging and so on. These provide shorthand ways to communicate brand identity, and help both consumers and industry representatives (including record labels, managers and journalists) develop a brand image around the artist or event (O'Reilly et al., 2013: 16). Some of these branding elements, such as names, logos and images, may be considered as forms of intellectual property and gain protection through copyright or trademark legislation (Harrison, 2021: 237). Indeed, it is not unusual for record companies to request ownership and control of artist websites and domain names (Harrison, 2021: 237). More broadly, it is important for live music venues and festivals to do the same, as websites and apps are the primary methods for fans to learn about and interact with them, and ticket sales are now commonly driven by social media activity.

Branding encompasses a range of deals through which the brand of the artist or event is linked to a commercial (or charitable) brand via such things as endorsements, product placements, advertising campaigns, merchandising, sponsorships and brand ambassadorships. These deals are contractual relationships with terms which must be negotiated and met by both sides. The sponsor brand will provide cash or in-kind support of varying kinds to the artist or event promoter 'in return for access to the exploitable commercial potential associated' with them (IEG, 2000: 1). At the most basic level, this might refer to product endorsement or product placement, where an artist agrees that their image, name and/or logo will be used for on-product, print and digital advertisements, or a product will be visible in a video, social media post or other public forum such as an awards ceremony. With regard to the latter, it is common for artists to be loaned clothes for live shows or photo shoots, in return for a name check for the manufacturer (Harrison, 2021: 261). If the artist is also a social influencer on an online platform, they will need to be wary of the product placement rules that govern sponsor endorsements. For instance, guidance from the US Federal Trade Commission suggests that artists should declare whether they have been paid to post messages. This may be achieved through the use of hashtags, such as #ad or #sponsored (Harrison, 2021: 262). Brand endorsements and sponsorships may be extended in a variety of ways, with artists giving special performances for clients of a brand, attending product launches, participating in instrumental clinics to demonstrate musical equipment or starring in video advertisements. In some cases, there is a cross-over between an advert and the official music video of a track. For instance, Paloma Faith's brand partnership with the car manufacturer Škoda led to an advertising video that featured her cover of the song 'Make Your Own Kind of Music'. The video was first aired in March 2018 during an advertising break in the show *The Voice* on the British television channel ITV. The song was a hit on Shazam and on streaming platforms, leading Faith's record company to add it to her album *The Architect* and to officially class it as a single.

The line between endorsement and sponsorship can be rather fluid, but sponsorship deals typically require the artist to engage more directly in marketing campaigns, while endorsements may be relatively passive in nature. Some artists and event organisers operate with multiple sponsorship deals, with exclusivity granted to particular product segments. Artists will typically have fewer deals due to the difficulty of meeting the expectations of each brand sponsor, though it is not uncommon for individual band members to have endorsement deals relevant to their particular instruments. The benefits to the band of such deals are likely be 'in-kind' rather than in cash, with equipment (and perhaps servicing) provided free of charge or at a discounted price in return for a mention on the band's website or tour programme, or the right to use the image and name of the musician in advertising campaigns for the brand's products. This can be especially useful for emerging artists who may not be on the radar of the larger brands or may not write and perform music that is suitable for those brands.

Small-scale endorsement and sponsorship deals may be brokered directly with a sponsor brand by an artist or their manager, or by an event or festival promoter, though the likelihood of success by taking such a direct approach will reduce as the size of the sponsor brand increases. When approaching a potential sponsor, it is important that the artist or promoter focuses not simply on what they might gain from the relationship, but on what benefits they might offer the sponsor. Such an approach is commonplace in crowdfunding campaigns, but can also be adopted with respect to corporate sponsors who need to be convinced that the deal is a good one for their business. On other occasions, the roles might be reversed with the sponsor brand seeking out the artist, event or festival for a deal, as they regard them as relevant to their target market and a good 'fit' with the needs of their marketing campaigns. For instrumental equipment manufacturers, this may lead to 'signature' products named after the musician concerned. For larger-scale deals, it is more common for artist managers, record companies, event promoters and sponsor brands to deal with each other through sponsor brokers who specialise in matching clients' needs for specific campaigns, tours, venues and festivals. Such agents typically charge between 5 and 15 percent of gross sponsorship income, which is calculated not only on the amount of cash received (if any), but on the value of any in-kind support supplied (Harrison, 2021: 263). This is an important consideration, as the agent may request 50 percent or more of the fee to be paid upfront. The growing importance of sponsorship as an income route has led some record companies, artist management companies and live music promoters to form in-house brand departments that deal directly with brand partnerships. Examples include Universal Music Group & Brands, ATC Management and Live Nation Entertainment. However, specialist branding consultants are also hired for specific projects, with smaller and medium-sized companies drawing on their expertise.

As noted earlier, sponsorship deals need to be managed carefully to ensure that the right products and services are linked with the right artists. These deals are typically exclusive (within particular categories) and will specify an artist's policy on prior approval – to ensure that marketing materials are not released without the artist's management agreeing to it. The deals may also dictate that certain photographers, videographers or designers are hired for the production of the marketing campaign. Furthermore, and to ensure that artists are not over-exposed within any particular country, sponsorship deals will specify the timeframe of the campaign and the geographic territories or platforms which will be targeted. Brand partnerships that work in one territory may not work in another (due to the social, political or cultural attitudes of audiences and/or regulators within that territory), so artist managers need to bear this in mind when negotiating deals. Alternatively, some deals remain strictly digital and global, targeted at particular audience segments that will respond best to them, but largely unseen by others. The enhanced data made available through social media makes sponsorship deals less risky than in the past – or, at least, gives the appearance of being supported with better information about an artist's fanbase or an event's audience. This includes not only data about age, gender and geographical reach (demographics), but about consumption patterns, behavioural expectations, and social and cultural values (psycho-graphics). This data is readily available to in-house brand departments, which can also work with sponsor brands and other parts of a record company or event promotions company to develop achievable campaigns: from creating viral content of various kinds, through to bespoke recordings and immersive, interactive events. Large-scale event promoters are better placed to work with such data, though smaller-scale festival organisers will also have data from ticketing sites. If seeking sponsorship support, they should survey their audiences to provide insights that will not only help to secure sponsorship deals, but can also be used to enhance the overall event experience.

ARTIST AS BRAND

This section focuses on the idea of the artist as a brand, both in terms of how that brand is initially constructed, and how brand partnerships may enhance the audience reach and meaning of the brand. As noted earlier, this is fraught with potential issues since the brand of an artist is intrinsically linked to their personal and professional reputation. An ill-chosen partnership can harm the perception of an artist both with the consuming public and within the industry, though well-managed ones can yield significant benefits for both artist and sponsor. In seeking to understand how the brand of an artist is created, communicated and negotiated, we have adopted a cultural economy approach. This approach recognises that the image and meaning of a brand lies at the intersection of a range of music and media businesses, personnel and fans, and is co-created through them (see Figure 9.1). Further to this, the image and meaning of the artist brand should be regarded as an ongoing process. As O'Reilly et al. (2013: 99) suggest, these 'meanings are continually produced, negotiated and consumed through social and economic interaction'. This is even the case where the meanings have become almost stereotypical or self-parodic, as we might regard such heritage artists as The Rolling Stones or Dolly Parton. Their image may now be relatively static, but it needs to be consistently reinforced and renewed in order to maintain relevance to their audiences and to attract new fans.

Cultural economy approach to artist branding

A broad-based cultural economy approach is one that recognises how music businesses and professionals are not only involved in creating culture but are themselves influenced by the culture(s) within which they live. Our approach is inspired by Jason Toynbee's (2000) work on musical creativity, which adapts the concepts of 'field' and 'habitus' that were first introduced by the sociologist Pierre Bourdieu (1984). Where Toynbee's discussion principally relates to the field and habitus of musicians' lives and work as it relates to their musical output (Toynbee, 2000: 36–42), our analysis will extend to include music and media business personnel and music fans. This is because we contend that there is an ongoing negotiation between artists, industry and audience which drives the creation, reception, meanings and development of an artist's brand.

In Figure 9.1 we present the 'artist–brand matrix', a visual representation of our approach which places the artist as our central focus. The artist is surrounded by a space we have termed as 'cultural positioning and influences', which is analogous to Bourdieu's notions of field and habitus (as discussed below). Surrounding this space of cultural positioning and influences we have placed a non-exhaustive selection of music business and consumer roles that may contribute to how an artist's brand is perceived. The cultural workers and audiences involved in this outer ring will each have their own cultural positioning and influences. Therefore, the middle space is not simply shared between them, but should be conceived as a space of intersection – where different understandings of an artist's brand may be constructed.

For Bourdieu (1984: 170), an individual's habitus is a set of dispositions, ways of thinking and ways of approaching social life that are acquired 'without any conscious concentration' during that individual's early years. As Toynbee (2000: 36) suggests, the habitus acts as 'a mediator between social relations – class, race, gender, education and so on – and what people think and do'. These dispositions (to which we might add language, geography, religion, politics, and other factors) may change over time, but they provide a primary foundation that underpins how we think about, and behave in, the world. Toynbee (2000: 36) suggests that artists are therefore more likely to 'play, write, record or perform in a particular way', to which we might extend that they are also likely to be drawn towards particular ways of expressing and branding themselves. Furthermore, the habitus associated with individual music business personnel, as well as with individual audience members, will also underpin how they conceive the cultural and business world around them, hence affecting their working relationships and understandings of an artist's brand. Some people will be drawn to work with, or to consume, the music of an artist, while others will not, and, as noted earlier, changes to an established artist's brand and music may appear to lack authenticity or credibility if it comes into conflict with the underlying dispositions held by audiences. This will be exacerbated by the relationships that exist between each individual's habitus and the 'fields' of cultural production within which music is made and heard: the space of 'cultural positioning and influences' shown in Figure 9.1.

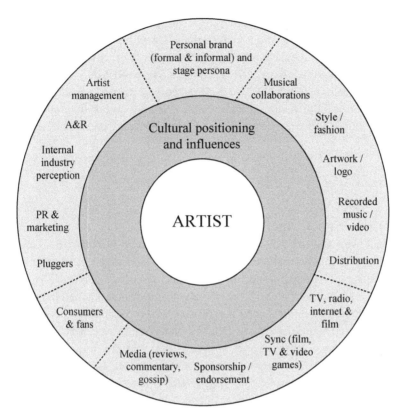

Figure 9.1 The artist–brand matrix

Bourdieu's (1984) concept of 'field' refers to the broader social, cultural, political and economic contexts within which, in our case, music-based activities take place. Within these fields, artists and their representatives must negotiate varying power positions and structures in order to find success. For artists, and for music or media industry personnel, that success may be theorised in terms of financial rewards and economic sustainability, of star power and influence (which Bourdieu refers to as cultural capital) or as 'a utopian drive to make the world better through music' (Toynbee, 2000: 37). In the music and media industries there is a wide range of fields in play, each with their own rules and expectations – including recording, publishing, distribution, sponsorship, traditional media and social media (and many more). Within these varying fields there will be guidelines, norms and assumptions related to such things as musical genre, corporate culture, fandom, language, image, geography, demography and censorship, that act to define what has previously been done within a field, and place commonly held limitations on what might be achieved or expected within that field in the future. As Toynbee notes of musical creativity, it is often the mismatch between habitus and field that sparks new musical variants; variants that are regarded as innovative because they play with and extend the previously accumulated norms found within a field, while retaining enough similarities to them to be accepted as belonging to that field. We argue that the same is true of the broader cultural production of an artist's brand. For instance, Keith Negus (1992: 67) discusses how an artist's marketing may initially copy 'existing styles' and 'visual clichés' in order to place that artist within genre expectations related to clothing, hairstyles, poses, make-up and environment. He warns that artists must 'feel comfortable with and committed to their image in some way' so that they appear authentic and the audience will believe in it (1992: 70–71). More recently, Kristin Lieb (2018: 18) has argued that there are 'music industry norms, societal norms and fan norms' that restrict how female pop artists are promoted, with a 'heavy emphasis on their clothes, bodies and representations'.

The 'artist–brand matrix'

O'Reilly et al. (2013: 100) argue that an artist's personal brand is comprised of a stage 'persona' and a 'private personality', yet the use of social media blurs the distinctions between them. Instead, we argue that the personal brand is produced in both formal and informal ways, and that our understanding of an artist is always mediated – whether through music industry campaigns, media appearances, journalistic exposés or social media posts. There will always be a core individual (an artist or individual members of a band), but choices are made regarding the level of access that is provided to their (ostensibly) 'private' lives. Some artists are highly active on social media, posting what seem to be personal stories that offer insight into their personalities beyond the formal mediation of music videos, live performances and photoshoots. This 'public' version of their 'private' brand can be instrumental in constructing 'audience identification' (Lieb, 2018: 14) and in promoting the appearance of credibility and authenticity. Their personal lives, humour, opinions and issues make them seem more 'real', and provide narratives that connect with the daily experience of listeners in much the same way that we see in television soap operas.

The outer circle of Figure 9.1 includes numerous other routes through which the brand of an artist can be developed and communicated, with dotted lines showing where these may be loosely grouped together. Brand development is typically driven by artist managers or as a collaboration between managers, artists and other music professionals. However, it is increasingly common for artists themselves to undertake this work in the initial stages of their careers, as they have become increasingly 'savvy about the business. From the moment an artist starts posting music to, say Soundcloud or Facebook, they are in effect developing their own "brand"' (MMF, 2019b: 12). To an extent, this has always been the case, since artists have performed live, constructed stage shows, sold merchandise and made demo tapes in the offline environment for many years. Yet, the increased significance of digital platforms, social media and image to the music industries means that artist managers, record companies and publishers are increasingly looking to work with acts who have already built a profile and fanbase online. Artist managers then work with artists and others to further develop the brand to draw the attention and interest of other industry sectors, such as recording, publishing, sponsorships and media. Indeed, one of the strategic aims of a manager may be to build a sense of 'buzz' around an artist that can spark bidding wars between potential recording companies and publishers in order to secure the best deal for an artist they work with. It is within this brand development work that we can identify the intersection of both habitus and field, with the artist, the manager and others all viewing the development of the artist–brand through their own particular lenses. It is also where negative narratives of manipulative managers and of artists 'selling out' in pursuit of commercial gain may come from; particularly if the existing audience of an artist detects changes in that artist's work and brand. Yet, the creative negotiations that occur between the different fields and dispositions of an individual's habitus may also work to create unique music and brands that resonate with a wider audience and help an artist to achieve success.

The artist–brand is an ongoing process rather than a fixed outcome, with other parts of the music industries having an impact on its development over time. A range of collaborators will be employed to bring the brand image to life, including stylists, art designers, record producers and musical collaborations with other artists. The latter are important in bringing an artist to the attention of new audiences, especially where those new audiences lie beyond the usual habitus and field associated with the artist. The same may be true of sponsorship, synchronisation and media coverage, so managers and artists should not only target a core audience, but understand potential cross-overs into new audiences. They should also keep track of newly launched social media platforms that act like new 'fields'. Successful early adoption of a new platform can prove useful for the marketing of an artist, as has been seen in the past with sites such as Myspace, YouTube, Snapchat and TikTok. Put simply, there is less competition during the early adoption phase of a new platform, so a breakout artist can make a bigger impact. One concern that managers will have is the potential for monetisation rather than simply promotional reach, with more recent entrants such as Byte (a micro-video sharing site launched in 2020) offering direct revenues through partner programmes whereas others, such as TikTok, do not. Another is that platforms regularly go in and out of fashion, so artists should avoid becoming overly reliant on any one of them.

The final part of the artist–brand matrix shown in Figure 9.1 relates to the consumers and fans of an artist, including both an artist's own core products (recordings, concerts, merchandise and so on) and the many other products and services that may have been connected to them through sponsorship and endorsement deals, film and television synchronisation, and the wider media. The importance of synchronisation and sponsorship has led Meier (2017: 86) to refer to brands and the music supervisors that work with them as the 'new gatekeepers' within the music industries. Furthermore, the rise of interactive social media as an important grassroots marketing tool also means that there are 'citizen gatekeepers' acting within the field of music consumption. Their influence can also be very important in communicating ideas about an artist, whether through blogging sites, fan-managed websites, personal playlists, online reviews or collaborative genre-based special interest sites and discussion boards. On a wider level, artists can leverage fandom through the provision of meet-and-greet events, competitions and direct engagement with fans through social media, though not all artists will be comfortable with this level of contact. As noted in Chapters 3 and 11, the pressures of being 'always on' can be very draining.

Forms of sponsorship and issues of 'brand fit'

Sponsorship activities may be categorised as passive or active, though there are cross-overs between them, and campaigns may include elements of both. Passive sponsorship refers to the use of an artist's name, logo and/or image on static advertisements for products or services. The term might also be used to refer to how an artist's music is used on a television, film, video game or advertising soundtrack, or to product placement in an artist's photoshoot or music video. Active sponsorship is more involved, with the artist engaging in new activities specifically designed to benefit the sponsor brand. Examples include instrumental music clinics, product launches and competitions, newly recorded songs, jingles and cover songs used in advertisements, and the use of radio, video or social media interviews, posts and advertisements that specifically endorse a product. Artists may also be engaged as brand ambassadors and curators that have creative control with regard to a sponsor company's product development – in effect, a co-branding exercise that fully integrates the brand of the sponsor with that of the artist.

When sponsorship deals are managed well, they can extend the narrative and image of the branded artist, reinforce preferred meanings and expand the reach of an artist's marketing. However, the merits and potential problems of a deal should be examined in detail, with consideration of what similar artists are or have been doing, and how successful they have been. As sponsorships and endorsements are essentially testimonials that promote the benefits of a sponsor's product or service, it is important that the product or service is of good quality, as a poor product will reflect badly on the artist. Furthermore, it is imperative that there are no conflicts between the personal values of the artist and the values or actions of the sponsor (part of their 'brand fit'). For instance, for an artist with a strong and public anti-war stance to accept a sponsorship deal from a company that is later shown to be involved in the supply chain of an arms manufacturer could be very damaging to the artist's reputation. The reverse is also true, with brand sponsors having expectations regarding the conduct and opinions of the artists they work with. A poorly thought-out interview response or a hastily made social media post could lead to negative consequences not only for the artist but for the brand. Such considerations are increasingly important in the online environment as fans, activists and trolls have much greater access to information than ever before, and the means to communicate their views to a much broader audience through social media. The team may be able to request creative control or prior approval related to branding activities in order to protect the brand of the artist, though their ability to obtain this will depend on the bargaining power of the artist relative to the sponsor. Furthermore, as Harrison (2021: 267–268) notes, management teams should take care to ensure that their artists are not over-committed to multiple brands or to activities that may be onerous or overly time-consuming.

The power relationship between artist and sponsor lies at the heart of Meier's argument that sponsor brands are the 'new gatekeepers' (2017: 86). For Meier (2017: 87), music is used to 'deepen the cultural relevance of and build emotional bonds with the consumer or … brand promoted', hence will be subordinate to the needs and objectives of the advertising and branding campaign. There is less mutual benefit or reciprocity than might be imagined in this relationship, with the marketing objectives of the artist subsumed within those of the commercial brand being advertised, and perhaps reduced to a riff, hook, chorus or specific lyric (2017: 88). These may be enough to spike a viewer's interest or to prompt them to use Shazam or a similar app to track down the original song. But Meier argues that the idea of a sync 'breaking' an artist or song to a wider audience is actually rather rare, despite a few high-profile examples, such as Moby licensing all 18 tracks of his 1999 album *Play*. She also extends the argument to television and film placements, suggesting that only a minority have led to commercial success for an artist (Meier, 2017: 98). Nevertheless, syncs may be a useful source of revenue and validation for an artist. Furthermore, music supervisors are increasingly looking to unsigned or newly signed artists for their advertising placements in order to differentiate their brand (2017: 89), so this offers a good promotional opportunity to help create 'buzz'.

The mechanisms associated with artist branding are laid bare in somewhat dramatised and stereotypical ways by reality television contests such as *The X Factor*, *America's Got Talent* and *The Voice*, where the image of the contestants is manufactured and developed on screen, and the audience is encouraged to identify with and support particular singers or bands. The artist–brands created through these shows remain subservient to the brands of the shows themselves, with the artists having little bargaining power at the beginning of the process when they are asked to sign recording, sponsorship and merchandising contracts as a pre-condition of participation (Harrison, 2021: 234–235). They are also, like the manufactured boy bands and girl bands of the pop music sphere, likely to have relatively short shelf-lives. Thus, sponsorship, endorsement and advertising deals are a common way for revenue to be generated quickly (2017: 215). Kristin Lieb (2018: 18) has argued that female pop stars in particular have short careers and must 'achieve cultural resonance quickly and deeply or risk fading into oblivion'. For Lieb, this is a structural problem within society, with both music industry personnel and audiences choosing to focus primarily on female artists' bodies, their ability to cross-market other products, such as fashion and cosmetics, and then (and perhaps only then) their music. She defines a range of female-centred artist–brand types, from the talented 'insignificant seller' (unlikely to gain the interest of a major record label) to the 'indie star' (loved by critics and fans, but having an influence which is greater than their sales), and through to the 'flash in the pan' (briefly successful before disappearing) and the 'career artist' (multiplatinum-level artists who have gained much greater control over their careers). She argues that such artist–brand types serve to reduce the potential narratives available for female pop stars in comparison to male stars (Lieb, 2018: 16), which then restricts how music industry personnel work with them. However, we could argue that such a logic exists more generally, as implied by the artist–brand matrix introduced earlier in this chapter, where the cultural codes and norms of artists, managers and others (their 'fields') serve to guide expectations about their narratives, images and activities.

BRANDING AND SPONSORSHIP IN THE LIVE SECTOR

Brands have been involved in the live music sector for a long time, though the 1980s again serves as an important marker for developments, as it did for the artist-centred sponsorship activities discussed earlier. Naomi Klein (2010: 47) identifies the Rolling Stones' 1981 tour as one of the first tour sponsorships (with Jovan perfume) to be arranged without record company support, while Anderton (2019a: 84–85) notes how brewers such as Theakston, Newcastle Breweries and Guinness all brokered 'title' sponsorships for outdoor music festivals in the UK during the 1980s: deals in which the name of the sponsor brand was incorporated into the name of the festival itself. An early example of festival sponsorship in the US is the Bumbershoot Festival, a non-profit event which adopted corporate sponsors in the mid-1980s in order to keep ticket prices low (Fitterman-Radbill, 2017: 186). Key drivers for festival sponsorship include escalating production costs, rising audience expectations and significant growth in artist fees, with corporate sponsorship becoming common throughout the 1990s despite opposition, especially in the UK, from festivalgoers who felt that corporate involvement was contrary to the true meaning and ethos of festival culture (Anderton, 2019a: 98–99). By the 2000s it was uncommon to find a festival that was not supported by sponsorship in some form, since sponsorship funding provides a degree of financial security in what is a highly volatile and risky market (Anderton, 2011, 2015, 2019b; Arnold, 2018). Title sponsorships are also a common sight within live music venues, with both venue chains and arenas typically being named after sponsor brands, while mid-scale and large-scale touring artists often broker sponsorship deals to reduce financial risk and extend their marketing reach. In the following sections, we will discuss the brand matrix of music festivals, how branding campaigns have developed over time, and what issues have been raised by them.

The brand matrix of music festivals

Rock and pop music festivals first gained broad popularity in the mid- to late-1960s, where they helped to popularise countercultural ideals of peace, love and communal living alongside a broadly pro-environmental, anti-establishment and anti-corporate stance. In the UK, stereotypes associated with hippie culture became more strongly attached to the 'free festivals' scene of the 1970s and early 1980s, and later to the free party raves of the 1990s (Clarke, 1982; McKay, 2000; Partridge, 2006). A narrative of corporate co-optation is often allied to such histories, which tend to downplay the co-existence of commercially motivated and commercially run festivals throughout the same time period. As a result, there has been relatively little discussion of music festivals as brands, and it may even seem antithetical to the countercultural ethos associated with them (Anderton, 2019a). However, we feel that it is useful to think of music festivals as brands, not only for newly launched events seeking to find space within the market, but for longer-lived events whose brands have developed organically. Anderton (2019a) regards such events as situated within a 'brand matrix' (see Figure 9.2), where the meanings associated with a festival brand are produced through the interaction of a festival organiser's own personal beliefs and interests (as shown through site design, booking policies and event marketing), the pre-existing meanings of the host location, and the activities of commercial and media sponsors and artists. To this we may also add the influence of audiences and local authorities (whose interpretation of licensing law will have a significant impact on what a festival organiser can achieve with their event). Audiences are especially important because festivals tend to rely on word-of-mouth marketing, and because the unofficial social media activities of festivalgoers help to develop and define public perceptions of an event just as much as an event's official media presence.

Festivals which develop a strong brand are able to foster ongoing repeat attendance and to offer 'early bird' tickets that help to give financial stability to their organisers. These advance tickets, typically available for sale for a limited period soon after an event has

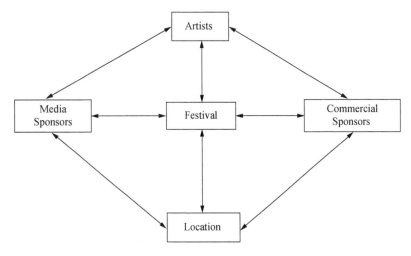

Figure 9.2 The 'brand matrix' of music festivals (based on Anderton, 2019a: 75)

finished for the year, are bought without any knowledge of the following year's line-up of artists. This signifies considerable trust in the festival organiser, but also indicates that it is not necessarily the line-up of the festival that is driving attendance. This is especially relevant for smaller events which may struggle to book popular headline artists (due to the exclusivity deals brokered by major concert promoters); hence, we have seen growth in the smaller-scale 'boutique' festival market where music is only one of many other activities and attractions available (Robinson, 2015a; Anderton, 2019a). Festivals may also be focused around specific music genres, though larger events tend to be multi-genre and headliner-focused in order to drive ticket sales. In some cases, the prior history of a festival may cause conflicts for booking policies. A good example is the reaction that Glastonbury Festival saw when it began to book hip-hop acts such as Jay-Z and Kanye West to headline the Pyramid Stage. For some commentators, including Noel Gallagher of Oasis in 2008, the festival was regarded as principally a rock music event, with hip-hop artists such as Jay-Z deemed to be out of place. A similar reaction greeted the announcement of Kanye West in 2015, when an online petition called the booking a 'musical injustice' and garnered over 130,000 signatures (Anderton, 2019a: 78).

Festival brands are attractive to potential sponsors because they represent strong and consistent markets that are readily delineated in terms of both demographics and psychographics. Potential sponsors are therefore able to evaluate whether a particular event is a good 'fit' for their marketing campaigns, while event organisers can pitch for sponsorship support with a ready-made market in mind. At the present time, the key business sectors involved in large-scale event sponsorship are telecommunications, financial services and drinks companies (alcoholic, soft or energy). There are many opportunities for brand sponsors to engage in branding activities at or with festival partners, as discussed shortly, while the media coverage which festivals attract can allow the brand a potentially larger promotional reach than a brand's own marketing budget can manage. The final say on brand fit will, however, lie with festivalgoers themselves who will evaluate the presence of a brand with reference to their own subjective understandings of the event (Drengner et al., 2011: 27–28). Such understandings will be 'influenced by marketing, mediation and word-of-mouth', as well as by their prior experiences of an event and their beliefs about the more general cultural positioning of music festivals (Anderton, 2019a: 76). In Bourdieu's terms, this is the intersection of their particular habitus with their understanding of the field.

It is not only large-scale events that attract sponsorship deals. Events of all sizes often require sponsorship support, with smaller events courting local companies and councils for their sponsorship rather than multinational corporations. A direct approach outlining the potential benefits to the sponsor is important at this level of the market, so event organisers should be encouraged to collect data on their attendees to help support their case. Larger events will be targeted by national and international brands, either directly or via sponsor brokers. In all cases, the event organiser must not only provide the sponsor with demographic details and potential benefits, but also be clear about what it is they are seeking (either monetary or non-monetary support) and the level of involvement or control that will be granted to the sponsor. For instance, will the sponsor have a say in artist booking or in the staging of the event? Will they require a particular part of the site to be branded exclusively to them, and how will this be managed if there are multiple sponsors at an event? Will the sponsor have an exclusive deal for their particular product/service category? These questions are important, as festivals may have deals with many sponsors, and there are many opportunities for branding (known as touch points). These include the ticket-selling website, the official festival website, the official programme, the festival wristband, festival stage designs, video loops on festival screens, and space in the backstage and VIP areas. The deal will also specify how the sponsor logo is to be used (size, positioning, prominence) and whether the sponsor will have other benefits, such as designated artist signing areas, an allocation of free tickets to give to employees or suppliers, or tickets to be used in competitions. The potential for audiences to be distracted by multiple sponsorship deals on site has led some companies to create their own events in order to control all aspects of branding to their own benefit. Past examples of companies that have organised their own festivals include Ben & Jerry's, Innocent Drinks, Vans and Corona.

Festival and event sponsorship: from badging to immersive experience

Festival and event sponsorships might also be classified on a continuum between passive and active, with badging activities being the most passive form. At its most basic, badging refers to the placement of a brand's logo on festival marketing and on-site advertising, but may extend through to stage naming, title sponsorship or media sponsorship (such as sponsoring television coverage). This straightforward badging activity is often 'leveraged' to make the sponsorship more active in nature. For instance, the brand might offer on-site product sampling or run co-branded competitions on its products. The brand may also create social media sites where festivalgoers can upload images of themselves or tag themselves in crowd photos. Social media integration is increasingly important, as access to social media involves the provision of personal data. Data mining techniques can then be used to further understand the audience of the event and brand, and to target that audience for future campaigns. Title rights might also be allied with 'pouring rights', in which exclusivity is given to provide on-site bars and drinks. A long-running example in the UK was the title sponsorship (1998–2007) of the Reading Festival (and later the Leeds Festival), which saw the event renamed *The Carling Weekend* after the Canadian brewery.

Badging and leveraging activities are regarded as a relatively ineffectual form of sponsorship, since there is often a lack of direct engagement with festivalgoers (Wakefield, 2012: 146). Where a title sponsorship is allied with pouring rights there are clear financial benefits in terms of product sales, but it is much more difficult to determine the value of a sponsorship when it is based purely on placing logos on marketing and merchandise or by naming stages. The festival environment is one in which there are often multiple and competing sponsors plus competition for attention from numerous other activities, so a cost–benefit analysis is difficult to assess. To tackle this, the terms 'sponsor activation', 'added value' and 'experiential marketing' began to appear in the marketing literature during the 2000s (Anderton, 2019a: 87). Early examples of 'added value' were relatively basic, including free on-site mobile phone charging and social media integration campaigns, such as Virgin Mobile's *Text the Fest* and *Foto the Fest* campaigns. These allowed festivalgoers to post messages and pictures to the stage-side screens of the Virgin branded main stage at the V Festival in the UK. Over time, such 'added value' tactics have become more sophisticated, with sponsors creating their own branded spaces within festival arenas. This offers them greater control, allowing them to provide more brand-centric activities, to engage audiences for longer and to promote further opportunities for the audience to share their experiences through social media. Where early versions of such activity were focused on drinks brands such as Strongbow and Bacardi, which provided exclusive DJ sets within their own branded tents, it is now common to find such branded spaces (Carù and Cova, 2007: 41) being created by other sponsor categories, such as catering and fashion. The activities are aimed not simply at raising awareness, but at immersing festivalgoers within an experiential environment that fosters positive feelings towards the brand and allows for promotion and sales of that brand's core products. For some sponsors, there is also an opportunity to enhance their corporate social responsibility (CSR) agenda by designing activities that link to environmental or social benefits. For instance, the New Zealand-based drinks brand Old Mout Cider set up the Kiwi Camp at British festivals in 2019 – a brand-centric area featuring interactive entertainments such as Disco Yoga and Rockaoke alongside 'do good' challenges, the opportunity to 'upcycle' unloved items and requests to donate to the World Wildlife Fund.

Issues raised by festival and event sponsorship

The vast majority of festivals and events make use of sponsorship deals in order to be commercially viable and to maintain ticket prices at a level acceptable to their intended audiences. For these events, the sponsorship activities and brands involved should offer 'added value' that will enhance the overall festival experience. Such ventures should also match both the demographic and psychographic interests of festivalgoers, and align with the beliefs of festival organisers. The latter is of particular interest to events with an environmental sustainability or social justice agenda, as certain categories of sponsor, such as car manufacturers, will be deemed inappropriate. Some event organisers will have local sourcing policies as part of their sustainability agenda, or will avoid using corporate brands because they feel that they detract from the 'real' experience of a music festival. In the UK, this includes festivals such as Beat Herder, which has roots in the free party rave scene of the 1990s, and Shambala, whose guiding principles demonstrate their commitment to developing community, creativity and environmental solutions while remaining free from all external 'advertising and branding and mindless consumerism' (Shambala, n.d.).

Critiques of branding and sponsorship by audiences and media commentators were relatively common in the UK in the early 2000s, when corporate promoters were beginning to dominate the festival market and the countercultural free party raves of the 1990s were still fresh in people's memories. For some, festivals had become giant marketing experiments which represented the exploitative reproduction of capital and the loss of the countercultural freedoms of the past (Carah, 2010: 19). As Naomi Klein (2010: 51) has argued, 'when any space is bought, even if only temporarily, it changes to fit its sponsors'. However, we can also recognise a shift in festival audiences since this time, with a broadening of demographics and psychographics as the music festival sector has become more mainstream and increasingly professional in its organisation (Anderton, 2019a). Criticism of brand involvement has lessened, and audience surveys suggest that contemporary festivalgoers either accept sponsorship as necessary to help fund the events they attend, or believe that they actively enhance the event experience. Anderton (2019a: 97) argues that the mainstreaming of the music festival sector means that events are increasingly regarded as 'leisure spectacles' akin to the commodified environments of theme parks, shopping malls and casinos. They are part of festivalgoers' postmodern consumerist identities (Anderton, 2011: 154) in which the simulated and hyperreal environments of a festival and its branded spaces and attractions are treated as 'real' and enjoyed as such (Anderton, 2019a: 98).

CONCLUSION

Branding and sponsorship have become essential components for both the recorded and the live music industries. This is likely to continue in the future, even though confidence in the live music market will have been shaken by the disruptions of the coronavirus pandemic of 2020–21. Marketing spend in general will be reduced as brand sponsors seek to make savings as a result of the financial pressures imposed upon them by global lockdowns and social distancing. Moreover, uncertainty about when live music events would be allowed to return made sponsor brands nervous: they did not wish to commit support to an event that might be cancelled. However, the brand fit between music and a range of lifestyle commodities and experiences will ensure that these deals will return in the future and develop in new ways, especially in relation to the livestreaming of concerts and the creation of virtual reality applications and opportunities.

Key discussion points

- To what extent do you agree with Meier's (2017) suggestion that brand sponsors and music supervisors are the 'new gatekeepers' of the music industries?
- What are your views on brand sponsorship in relation to artists, venues and festivals? What do you think underpins your views?
- Think about your personal social and cultural background in order to describe – as per Bourdieu (1984) – your own habitus and field. How do you think these affect your music tastes and the kinds of music industry genres and work that you want to be involved in?
- How might music-related brand sponsorships develop in the future?

FURTHER READING

The increased significance of branding and sponsorship to music business activities has been acknowledged in a number of academic publications that examine music industry branding in detail, though it remains a growing rather than an established field of study. Important book-length contributions include Nicholas Carah's *Pop Brands: Branding, Popular Music, and Young People* (2010), Leslie Meier's *Popular Music as Promotion: Music and Branding in the Digital Age* (2017) and Kristin Lieb's *Gender, Branding and the Modern Music Industry* (2018). The latter is especially useful in demonstrating the gendered stereotypes that underpin so many music industry strategies. In live music, Anderton's work on music festivals (2008, 2011, 2015, 2019a) explores a range of examples in a British context, while Gina Arnold's *Half a Million Strong: Crowds and Power from Woodstock to Coachella* (2018) discusses the situation in the US.

10

COPYRIGHT, FUNDING AND REVENUE STREAMS

SUMMARY

An essential aspect of building a music career or company is to identify, sustain and manage multiple income streams. In this chapter we discuss practical matters such as budgeting and financial planning within a music industries context. We provide an overview of the current copyright and royalty collection system, analysing its many issues and inequities. In the process we discuss revenue streams such as record sales, streaming revenue and performance royalties, alongside other sources of income, such as synchronisation. We also consider the many options available for accessing music funding.

Chapter objectives

- To emphasise the importance of financial planning and budgeting for achieving success.
- To understand the role and impact of budgeting decisions made within music businesses.
- To explore the music industry as a copyright industry, critically analysing how copyrights generate revenues and how those revenues are then distributed between artists, record labels and publishing companies.
- To examine other forms of revenue, including music funding opportunities that exist beyond record labels and publishers.
- To explore how artists develop portfolio careers and multiple income streams.

FINANCIAL CHALLENGES FOR ARTISTS AND MANAGERS

Visual artist and writer Rod Judkins (2015) argues that creative practitioners should embrace monetary discussions rather than avoid them, commenting that creativity flourishes when it receives financial support. He explains further that many notable artistic movements have benefited from the support of philanthropic or state subsidies, suggesting that 'the history of art is inseparable from the history of money' (2015: 180–182). Singer-songwriter Paul Simon goes further, arguing that the music industry is 'completely tied up with capitalism' (cited in Krueger, 2019: 27). Indeed, even highly regarded composers of the Western classical tradition, such as Mozart and Tchaikovsky, often wrote letters to friends or patrons requesting funds with which to pursue their musical endeavours. But despite such clear historical links between art and commerce, many musicians and managers remain nervous about discussing financial issues, particularly in the early stages of their careers. Yet it is vital to create robust financial plans if an artist is to ultimately enjoy a sustainable career which allows them to work on music full-time. In addition, financial and budgeting skills are essential for acquiring early-stage career funding, whether via a charitable grant or a record company advance. Paul Allen (2018: 38–39) argues that music managers must develop a detailed understanding of both income streams and outgoings. Their financial overview and diligence relieves pressure on the artist, thereby allowing them to focus on creating music. However, he also recommends, as do we, that artists should develop their own financial skills and regularly discuss money issues with their managers; failure to do so may lead to financial disagreements that can end the managerial relationship.

Common financial pitfalls for artists, managers and companies include overspending, overconfidence in potential sales figures, amassing debts and falling victim to scams (as discussed in Chapter 2). Many famous musicians have entered bankruptcy proceedings despite their considerable success, including Toni Braxton, Willie Nelson, Marvin Gaye, Meat Loaf, Dionne Warwick, Mick Fleetwood and 50 Cent. The causes of an artist's bankruptcy may be many and varied, but common reasons include alcohol or drug addiction, legal disputes, restrictive contracts, a lack of songwriting credits and poor tax planning (Mokoena, 2015). The economist Alan Krueger (2019: 174–175) warns that musical earnings may be short-term, given the fickle nature of the industry, adding that many musicians fail to save when their incomes are relatively high, or assume that their income will continue at present levels or increase in the future. To exacerbate the situation, there is rarely a level playing field in terms of power dynamics, particularly at the start of an artist's career. Krueger (2019: 160) notes that this is partly due to the nature of music industry negotiations, where artists have relatively low bargaining power due to the sheer number who desire to succeed. In the following sections, we discuss issues related to budgeting, revenue streams, copyright, royalty collection, music funding and the many other income sources that artists may seek.

BUDGETING AND BUSINESS STRATEGY

For artists and their teams, both in their personal and professional lives, there are many benefits to creating, working with and tracking financial budgets. Budgeting can lower the likelihood of encountering unexpected costs and help to identify opportunities to make savings. This is particularly important for artists who may otherwise unknowingly amass significant debts under their recording contracts; for example, by ordering taxis, requesting travel upgrades, making full use of the minibar in hotels or requesting additional musicians to play on recordings (and so on). It is common for these expenses to be paid by the record company rather than directly by the artist, but they will often be recoupable expenses that will need to be paid from the artist's royalty share. As most artists have relatively short careers in the spotlight (Krueger, 2019; Passman, 2019), musicians and their teams should take care to stay within agreed budgets and to plan carefully for the future. Sensible budgeting can ensure an income during periods when the artist may be unable to release music or perform live, or when a release or tour fails to sell as well as expected. This was brought into sharp focus by the coronavirus pandemic of 2020–21, when touring musicians and tour support crews suddenly found their principal income stream denied them by lockdowns and travel restrictions (Anderton, 2022). This was exacerbated by the freelance nature of work within the music industries, making it harder for musicians and technical crews to claim government support in many countries.

An initial budget for a music project should prioritise essential spending and determine monthly operating costs, personal living expenses, and the likely costs relating to travel and entertainment (Allen, 2018: 39). If it is a recording project, the artist should also consider costs relating to producers (who may be due to receive a royalty – known as 'points' – for their work). Further costs relate to recording and mastering engineers, studio hire, rehearsal time, artwork and manufacturing. For a concert tour, costs might include equipment and musician hire, transportation, catering, road crew, pyrotechnics and so on, with the tour budget typically arranged by the artist manager and the tour manager (as discussed in Chapter 8).

Large music businesses tend to budget on both a quarterly and an annual basis in order to demonstrate the health of their underlying accounts, and they may assign entire teams to financial functions and royalty-tracking. The accounting process allows a company to identify which of their activities are exceeding expectations, which are on target and which are underperforming. Resources (both staff and funds) can then be allocated appropriately; for instance, record company divisions and labels may be merged or new ones created to cater for genres that have seen rapid growth. There are many stakeholders who make use of a music business's financial information, including investment analysts, competitors and government departments (McLaney and Atrill, 2020: 2–4), as well as journalists, artists and managers. However, detailed financial information at the artist level may be difficult to access, even for artists and their managers. This is because access is dependent on the terms of any recording, publishing, ticketing or other contracts that have been negotiated. Most contracts will include a right to audit the accounts, detailing both how often this may be requested and what rights of redress the artist may have should discrepancies be identified. It should be noted, however, that such audits are often expensive to undertake.

When allocating financial resources, companies will also create internal project budgets (such as those related to an individual artist's release). To be effective, they should be viable and realistic, covering all resources and staff required within a clear and achievable timeframe (Callahan et al., 2011: 141–169). They should also correlate with a company's broader outlook and market strategy, demonstrating a potential to increase revenues. However, as noted in Chapter 1 (and despite high investment in A&R), only a few artists manage to recoup their record company advances. Fewer still achieve a level of sustainable success that can subsidise the other artists signed to the label, while also providing funds to cover the label's running costs and investments in new signings. Record companies therefore engage in differential promotion of the artists on their rosters, with the focus typically on established acts who have a proven track record, or on other 'priority' acts that have a strong likelihood of success. As a result, smaller budgets are assigned to the remaining artists (Hirsch, cited in Anderton et al., 2013: 40). Priority artists, including superstars, face additional pressures to succeed. For example, Capitol Records boss Steve Barnett admitted to 'tough conversations' with Katy Perry after the relatively poor commercial performance of her fourth album *Witness* (Savage, 2018). The issue of focusing on a small number of priority artists or genres is called into question by Krueger (2019: 124), who argues that many music companies do not adequately diversify their portfolio of artists, genres or services. This lack of diversification may lead to financial difficulties if the priority artists do not achieve the success anticipated.

As discussed in Chapter 2, regular communication between team members is paramount when discussing financial information, allowing budgets to be reviewed and, where appropriate, amended. An important consideration, and one which many artists in the past have neglected to their cost, is to set aside monies to pay for their tax liabilities. In the UK, this can include income tax, corporation tax (based on a company's annual profit and investments) and business rates (payable to local councils where the company's premises are situated). A further challenge is to consider foreign exchange rates, particularly in relation to international royalties and touring, as changes in these rates can have both positive and negative impacts depending on how the currency markets move. An accountant can help with these key budgeting considerations, which is why we consider accountants to be part of an artist's support team (as discussed in Chapter 2). Budgeting also helps companies to borrow money, with even the most successful companies requiring occasional loans in order to launch new products, purchase property or grow the business in line with company ambitions. Common borrowing options include bank loans and credit facilities, in addition to loans from other companies. The latter, known as business-to-business lending, can include major record companies, publishers and live promoters making investments in independent companies, which may lead to successful artists or companies eventually becoming part of the larger business.

Other income-generating options for businesses include direct funding, whereby start-up companies pitch for investment in 'funding rounds' with larger corporations, venture capitalists (VC) and occasionally governments. For instance, in the early years of Spotify, all three major record companies and Merlin (which represents a consortium of independent record companies) bought a stake in the business (ranging from 1 to 6 percent). When Spotify launched on the New York Stock Exchange in 2018, Warner Music Group and Merlin sold their entire stakes, while Sony Music Entertainment sold 50 percent and Universal Music Group retained its full share. These sales created significant 'windfall' revenue for these companies, and we will return to these in a later section. Larger companies may also buy smaller businesses outright, as has been the case with Spotify's purchase of multiple podcast and podcast-related businesses since 2019, including Parcast, Gimlet Media, Anchor, The Ringer and Megaphone: such buy-outs are part of Spotify's strategy to diversify its content beyond its core music streaming service. Additional funds may also be raised by selling shares to the public via a stock market launch, with the shares of Spotify, Warner Music Group, Tencent, Yamaha, Universal Music Group and Avid all publicly traded. In some cases, such as the 2017 share-swap arrangement between Spotify and Tencent, and Tencent's purchase of 20 percent of Universal Music Group (completed in 2021), these deals are made to extend market reach. For instance, they may be used to introduce Chinese artists into Western markets or to help Western artists and companies benefit further from the expansion of the Chinese marketplace.

COPYRIGHT

Copyright and intellectual property (IP) are often discussed together, but they are in fact separate concepts. The World Intellectual Property Organization (WIPO) explains that IP 'refers to creations of the mind', whereas copyright is a *type* of IP that 'protects the creative or artistic expression of an idea' (WIPO, 2017: 4). Other forms of protected IP include trademarks, patents and design rights. IP in the music industries is typically owned in two main forms: (1) by creating and recording a piece of music, or (2) by assigning the songwriting or recording rights of that music to another person or organisation (who then becomes the *de facto* owner, rather than the songwriter or artist). We can see this in exclusive recording and publishing deals, and also when entire catalogues of music are bought and sold by different music companies. However, IP may also be licensed for a limited term of years, in which case the licensee company effectively acts as the owner. The licensee can then make decisions about how the IP should be used for that specific time period, but with ownership eventually reverting to the original copyright holder.

There are two primary forms of copyright within every recorded piece of music: (1) the copyright in the sound recording (typically owned by record companies), and (2) the copyright in the underlying music and lyrics (typically owned by publishing companies). If an artist's song is performed by another musician, the *performer* will earn royalties for their new sound recording, while the *writer or composer* of the original song will be entitled to royalties for having written or composed it. It is important to remember that, as discussed in Chapter 7, revenues are generated and collected from these two forms of copyright in different ways, leading to inequalities that are increasingly challenged by music industry organisations such as the Musicians' Union (MU), the Featured Artists Coalition (FAC) and the Music Managers Forum (MMF). We will discuss these challenges in the section on collection societies below, where we will also discuss 'performance royalties' and 'neighbouring rights'. Such rights relate to the public performance of songs and recordings, whether in bars, restaurants, sports grounds, shops and so on, or through radio and television.

Academic Patrik Wikström (2019: 21) describes the music business as a 'copyright industry', explaining that the copyright process commodifies musical works, which can then be transferred between artists and companies (2019: 27). Furthermore, the majority of the revenue earned by record labels, publishers and artists from recorded music results from the 'exploitation' of copyrights. Here, the term 'exploitation' refers to any commercial use:

from physical products and digital download sales, to digital streaming, radio and television broadcast, and the use of music in advertising campaigns, television shows, films and computer games (to list the primary sources of revenue). Copyright law therefore offers protection to rights owners (to stop other people making money from their copyrighted work without permission) and acts as an incentive to authors to create new copyrighted works from which they may benefit (WIPO, 2017). Copyright is, however, limited in term: in many countries it is 50 or 70 years after death because copyright legislation suggests that music is a public good (i.e. part of our shared culture). Hence, once the copyright term has elapsed, the music should become part of the 'public domain' where it can be used to enrich culture and society without requiring either permission or payment. Needless to say, the enduring popularity of past artists means that gatekeepers such as record companies, publishers and collection societies have secured extensions to the minimum copyright terms outlined in international treaties in order to protect their interests and earn revenues for longer (Carlisle, 2014). For instance, recordings released in the late 1960s in the US will not enter the public domain until 2067 (Jenkins, 2019).

There is an ongoing debate about the ideal length of copyright terms, which must balance artistic efforts, commercial considerations, legal impacts and the public interest. Many critics argue that the current level of protection is both overly long and too restrictive, and that copyright laws serve the interests of music industry gatekeepers rather than artists (Krueger, 2019: 230; see also Macmillan, 2015). However, copyright expert Stephen Carlisle (2014) notes that lengthy copyright terms provide a level of inheritance, as is found in other business sectors, that can benefit family members after an artist's death. National cultures also inform the global copyright debate, with many countries assigning artistic protection in theory while essentially following an approach based on collectivism and sharing (in line with their respective religious or moral viewpoints). As a result, some countries may simply not participate in the process for cultural, bureaucratic or financial reasons, hence copyright protection and royalty collection vary considerably throughout the world. In particular, Sami Valkonen of PRS for Music criticises governments in the Middle East Gulf region for not aligning with international standards on royalty collections (Nichols, 2019). As a result, PRS successfully brought a copyright claim in 2020 against Qatar Airways regarding their use of copyright-protected music for in-flight entertainment (Steyn, 2020).

The successful exploitation of copyright is reliant on detailed accounting practices and accurate data – something which is especially important with regard to digital distribution, where errors in the metadata attached to a track can mean that rights owners may not receive the payments they are due. This metadata includes, but is by no means limited to, information about ownership of the master recording rights and details about all songwriters and publishers (including percentage ownership where more than one songwriter/publisher is involved). Some songs (especially in chart-focused pop music) may be owned by many co-writers and, by extension, multiple publishing companies which represent each co-writer. This creates a potentially complex web of ownership that may slow down royalty payments related to songwriting copyrights, especially as there is no single authoritative database of this information, despite efforts to create one. For example, the proposed Global Repertoire Database project collapsed in 2014 after five years of development and investment of over

$13.7 million (Resnikoff, 2014a). On a smaller scale, the Mechanical Licensing Collective has been building a database in the US to deal with digital royalties from streaming services. Similarly, in Europe, ICE Services provides a copyright administration hub that integrates the databases of several national copyright collection agencies in order to identify and rectify any inconsistencies between them, and to speed up royalty payments. Two further complexities are that publishing catalogues are often bought and sold, so ownership information needs to be kept up to date, and if there are any copyright claims related to plagiarism, payments will be frozen pending the outcome of legal proceedings. A number of international standards have been adopted in an effort to simplify the data management process, and these are used by copyright collection societies to uniquely identify master recordings (International Standard Recording Code), compositions (International Standard Work Code) and artist names (International Standard Name Identifier), with the latter especially important for musicians who release music under a variety of different names.

As noted above, copyright laws are enacted by each individual country, and while many have signed international treaties aimed at 'harmonising' the rules between them, there are still variations in how these laws are written and enacted, since these treaties have to be translated into national law to take effect. Nevertheless, the treatment of some common terms remains relatively consistent across different territories. For instance, for a musical work to gain copyright protection it must be 'original', i.e. not a straightforward copy of something that already exists. Indeed, the UK Copyright, Designs and Patents Act 1988 (CDPA) includes 'no requirement for the work to be novel or inventive' in and of itself – a definition that is replicated across most territories. This leaves considerable scope for legal interpretation: to what extent is a song a 'copy'? This has increasingly been tested and exploited by artists, publishers and their legal teams in the twenty-first century, with lawsuits and threats of litigation made against musicians on the basis that they may have copied (plagiarised) elements of songs in their own releases. For instance, actions have been taken against Ed Sheeran, Justin Bieber, Taylor Swift and Kendrick Lamar. Some cases have been settled out of court, with additional songwriters being added to the writing credits of songs in acknowledgment that there was potentially a case to be made, while others have gone to court. A prominent example of the latter is the 'Blurred Lines' case involving songwriters Robin Thicke and Pharrell Williams. The case resulted from the perceived similarity of 'Blurred Lines' and Marvin Gaye's 1977 hit 'Got to Give it Up'. A federal jury in the US listened to both songs in court, then decided in favour of the estate of Marvin Gaye. In a later case, the Christian rapper Flame claimed that Katy Perry had appropriated the underlying beat of his song 'Joyful Noise' in her global hit 'Dark Horse' and, after listening to the two songs, a jury agreed with him and he was awarded $2.2 million. However, Katy Perry successfully appealed the judgement in 2020, and it is likely that US juries will no longer be allowed to compare recordings of songs and make a determination on the basis of how similar they sound. Instead, we are likely to see a return to paper-based analysis and evidence from musicologists. Nevertheless, the growth in such plagiarism cases has prompted concern among both artists and music business personnel, with Chic guitarist Nile Rodgers commenting that 'there is no such thing as a completely original composition' (Izundu, 2017) and producer Quincy Jones arguing that 'some overlap is inevitable' (Krueger, 2019: 207).

Copyright protection is both free and automatically assigned in the 177 countries, including the UK and the US, that are signatories to the Berne Convention of 1886. But such protection only applies when the music is 'fixed' in a tangible form (i.e. in a written form or as a recording that has been made either by the author or with their permission). Digital recordings may carry a time stamp, demonstrating the date of 'fixation', should any future legal dispute arise. Artists planning to release music in the US can also register their songs with the US Copyright Office, as this gives additional legal support should a plagiarism case be filed. In many ways, copyright is a negative right, in which legislation permits rights owners to prevent copying, distributing, renting or adapting a piece of music without permission and/or payment, together with the right to sue for damages where those rights have been infringed. Music copyrights may be licensed (time-limited, and with limitations on the uses to which the copyright may be used) or assigned (in effect, sold or transferred outright) to music publishers and record companies (among others). In addition to these economic rights, the Berne Convention also acknowledges what are known as moral rights, including the right of paternity (the right to be identified as the author when published to the public) and the right of integrity (providing songwriters the right to object to derogatory treatment of their work). These rights cannot be licensed or assigned, though it is common for record companies and publishers in some territories (such as the US), to request in their contracts that artists waive their moral rights. When artists waive these rights, companies are given greater control to exploit the copyrights without first seeking agreement from the artist. In other territories, such as Europe, moral rights are given far greater importance. For example, in the early 2000s, the US singer Tom Waits took legal action against production companies in both Spain and Germany because they used vocal imitators in adverts for Audi and Opel cars, giving the impression that he endorsed those brands. He won damages in one case and settled out of court in the other. A further example demonstrates some of the issues related to national laws: the US did not ratify the moral rights provisions of the Berne Convention, so it is not possible to pursue a moral rights case in the US because artists do not have this protection. This also applies to non-US-based artists, even if those artists would have enjoyed moral rights protections in their own countries. This was highlighted in a legal case brought against Jay-Z by the estate of Baligh Hamdi – a well-known Egyptian composer whose work Jay-Z had sampled in the song 'Big Pimpin'' released in 1999. Hamdi's family argued that the sample represented derogatory use, but the courts found against them, arguing that even though moral rights are present in Egyptian law, they cannot apply in the US because US law does not recognise them.

The copyright system discussed above can be described as an 'all rights reserved' model, which is a term often included when artists, publishers and record labels assert their ownership by using the copyright symbol © (for compositions) or ℗ (for recordings). An alternative to this is the 'some rights reserved' model proposed by Creative Commons, whereby rights ownership is maintained, but licences are available to allow other people to make use of those rights. This may include the use of music for non-commercial purposes, free sharing and the granting of permission to other musicians to remix tracks. Most of these licences specify that 'attribution' must be given when a track or remix is used, ensuring that the original creator is given credit. More detail on the licences can be found at creativecommons.org.

ROYALTY INCOME AND COLLECTION SOCIETIES

As noted previously, every recorded song comprises two principal forms of copyright: one related to the underlying composition, and one to the recording itself. We focus first on the recording, where revenue is payable whenever the track is streamed or sold. If the recording artist is signed to a record label, these payments will be made directly to the label, which will apply that revenue in accordance with the performer's recording contract. Artists without a label contract will be paid via their distribution company, which will usually deduct around 15 percent of the revenue to cover their operating costs. If a signed artist has yet to recoup their recording advance, the revenue will be applied to their balance and they will receive no payment; once the advance has been recouped, a share of the revenue (the artist royalty) will be payable. As an aside, Sony Music Entertainment launched its Artists Forward initiative in 2021, which tackles some of the issues raised by this. Legacy artists who signed with the company prior to 2000, and who have not received any further advances since that time, will no longer have their streaming revenues applied to their outstanding balances (Dredge, 2021).

It is vital that artists and managers fully understand how the contractual terms of a recording contract operate, as the headline royalty rate negotiated will often be reduced by them. For example, royalties are typically based on net sales, yet a range of deductions may be applied, including breakage clauses, packaging deductions and free goods clauses that were originally introduced in relation to physical products but may also be applied to revenue derived from digital sales and streaming. Such clauses are clearly anachronistic, and while common in older recording contracts, they are less likely (though this is by no means always the case) to be seen in contemporary contracts. For instance, the major record companies all confirmed to the UK government that breakage clauses were no longer included in their contracts (Paine, 2021c). Nevertheless, it reinforces the need for artists, managers and their lawyers to check the contractual terms carefully at the negotiation stage.

Artists should also check to see whether revenues received from digital streaming and downloads are to be accounted for as licences or as sales. The distinction is important, because if they are characterised as licences, the performing artist will be due a higher royalty rate than the standard one received for physical sales. For example, Tommy Boy Records offered the hip-hop group De La Soul a 10 percent digital royalty on their back-catalogue albums, but the group refused to accept the deal. This is why classic albums such as *3 Feet High and Rising* were for many years unavailable on streaming platforms. However, a deal was made in 2021 following Reservoir Media's purchase of Tommy Boy Records and renewed negotiations with band. Furthermore, as demonstrated by a leaked recording contract between Lady Gaga and Interscope (part of Universal Music Group), it may be that artists are not being paid because the licensing deal has been negotiated for a label's entire catalogue, rather than for each individual artist (Resnikoff, 2014b). However, some record companies have adopted a more ethical approach to how they manage royalty payments. For instance, Rupert Skellett (General Counsel to the Beggars Group label) says that Beggars Group has amended its deals so that artists can earn higher percentages for digital royalties, a decision that has also been reflected in their legacy contracts, which have been revised upwards. Furthermore, he argues that the major record labels should follow suit, stating that a 25 percent share to the artist would be fairer (Paine, 2021d), but they have yet to do so.

Royalty payments related to a song's *underlying music and/or lyrics* are payable to a music publisher (where the songwriter has licensed or assigned the rights to the song) or to the songwriter via a collection society – also referred to as Performing Rights Organisations (PRO) or Collective Management Organisations (CMO), depending on the particular rights they are involved in collecting. Collection societies distribute payments from two main sources: mechanical rights and performance rights. Mechanical royalties are payable when a song is copied in some way, whether as a physical product, a download or a stream. They are payable to songwriters and their publishers by record companies and streaming platforms, who essentially pay for the right to duplicate the artist's music. In most countries, mechanical rights are governed by statutory licences (set in copyright law or by a copyright tribunal), which determine a set payment rate, though rates and rules vary across different territories. Mechanical royalties are collected by societies such as MCPS (now aligned with PRS for Music) in the UK, Harry Fox Agency in the US, and AMCOS in Australia.

Performance royalties are payable when songs are performed at live shows or, as noted earlier, when recordings of those songs are 'performed' in public (i.e. when those recordings are played on radio and television or in settings such as restaurants, bars and shops). In the UK, businesses pay a licence fee to PRS for Music in order to play music on their premises, and there are numerous tariffs based on the size and type of business involved. There are also multiple reporting procedures aimed at identifying a representative sample of the songs played. Similar arrangements can be found in other countries; for instance, in France, such licences are issued by SACEM, while in the US, they may be issued by a range of societies, including ASCAP, BMI and SESAC. It should be noted that a licence fee is also payable in relation to the public performance of a recording of the song (not just the underlying song itself), with this revenue payable to performers and their record labels rather than songwriters. In the UK, this revenue is collected and distributed by PPL (Phonographic Performance Limited), which, since 2018, has issued joint licences with PRS for Music to prevent business owners from having to pay two separate fees.

In the US, as discussed in Chapter 1, performance fees are payable to songwriters when their music is played by terrestrial radio broadcasters, but not to the musicians who play on the recordings. In contrast, in the UK (and many other European countries), musicians are able to earn from the public performance of their recordings on radio, but not from on-demand streams. This is because UK copyright law does not regard online streaming as utilising the performance right, but what is sometimes referred to as the 'making available' right: the right of communication to the public 'by electronic transmission in such a way that members of the public may access it from a place and at a time individually chosen by them' (CDPA, 1988: S. 20/2/b (amended)). The aim of the 'making available' right was to allow uploaders of pirated music to be made liable for infringement – because they infringe the 'making available' right of the rights owner, who has not given permission for them to do so. However, as the making available right is assigned to a record company, the musicians who perform on the record will not receive a royalty as they would when their recordings are played on the radio or in shops. The growth in online streaming in the 2010s, aligned with the shuttering of the live music market in 2020–21, has brought this issue into high relief for performers, leading to calls from trade bodies and artists for 'equitable remuneration' (ER) – to create a royalty that is payable directly to performers whose work is represented in audio recordings (rather than to their record companies).

There are two main issues to be considered here. First, if such a right were to be introduced, it would need to be paid from the same revenue pot that is currently split between record companies and publishers, hence requiring an increase in subscription fees to fill the gap or a voluntary reduction in revenue share. This is made more difficult because songwriters feel that the publishing share of streaming revenue is already too small in comparison to that of the record companies (see Chapter 7) and needs to be re-balanced. However, this seems unlikely to happen, given that the three largest music publishers are aligned with the three largest record companies. Second, the current system of streaming royalties is based on market share – those artists who receive the most streams earn the highest rewards. This would likely be replicated in a system of equitable remuneration, with the most popular performers reaping the greatest benefits, so while all performers could potentially see a rise in their incomes, the system may retain an in-built bias towards major labels and their artists.

We discussed earlier how the creation of the US Mechanical Licensing Collective and Europe's ICE Services came about due to the prevalence of inconsistent and inaccurate data within music rights. Each country has its own national collection agencies that operate their own accounting procedures and databases of information, so the potential for conflicts is significant. Furthermore, they typically only license music within their own countries, so reciprocal agreements are in place between a worldwide network of societies in order that revenue can be allocated to the correct rights holder. For instance, when songs are played or sold in one country, it may be that the rights holders of those songs are based in another country, hence the local collection agency must work with the rights holders' agency to match data and make payments. This may be complicated further where songs are managed by multiple publishers and sub-publishers, creating what Chris Cooke (2019) has characterised as 'royalty chains'. The lengthier the chain, the longer it takes for revenue to flow through it, the greater the chance that there will be errors requiring resolution, and the greater the number of deductions for commission taken by each organisation involved. Cumulative errors and gaps in data mean that there are royalty payments that have been collected, but which cannot effectively be matched to their rightful owners. This undistributed revenue is then placed in what is colloquially termed a 'black box', awaiting resolution of queries or new data to be uncovered. These unclaimed royalties are eventually distributed by the collection agency to their rights holder members on the basis of their current market share (Cooke, 2019: 6). This is, of course, an area of contention for managers and artists, as it benefits major record companies even though the unclaimed royalties are unlikely to be related to their catalogues. Anabella Coldrick of the Music Managers Forum (MMF) suggests that black box revenues should be used more productively to fund data, education and grassroots initiatives instead (cited in Paine, 2021e).

Collection societies typically pay rights holders (record companies, publishers, performers and/or songwriters) around two to four times per year. In many countries, these societies operate as a near-monopoly, with few (if any) large-scale competitors. There is greater competition among collection societies in the US, with SESAC, AMRA, Sound Exchange, PRO, BMI and ASCAP all offering similar services and therefore providing a wider choice to rights holders. However, there are signs of change in Europe. For instance, while PRS for Music remains the predominant collection society in the UK, Eos was established in 2012 to support writers in the Welsh music industry. It was formed following a royalty collection disagreement, with around 300 Welsh rights holders moving to the breakaway society. A further example is the situation in Spain, where hundreds of rights holders departed the long-standing SGAE society in 2019, following several accounting scandals and the organisation's temporary expulsion from the international trade body CISAC. A competitor society, Unison, was formed shortly afterwards to offer an alternative.

The current royalty payment system has been criticised by Horace Trubridge (General Secretary of the MU), who argues that 'the artists and performers who write and deliver the music that the whole ecosystem depends on are, at best, the poor relations' (Musicians' Union, 2021). As we have demonstrated above, this is partly due to the way that recording contracts and licensing deals have been written in favour of record companies, and partly due to how the royalty collection system operates. Annabella Coldrick of the MMF has suggested that multiple areas in the streaming economy are ripe for change, including a need for greater transparency, for increased global cooperation, for faster payments and for fairer distribution of 'black box' royalties (Coldrick, 2019). As noted earlier in the chapter, the collection agencies tried to address these issues through the ill-fated Global Repertoire Database, but a more recent development has been the establishment of TOWGE (Technical Online Working Group Europe), which sets common standards for Europe's collection agencies, plus commitments from them to enhance their working practices (ICE Services, 2019). The potential of Blockchain technology is also being pursued, as the distributed ledger model that underpins Blockchain solutions would help to minimise discrepancies in data, prevent potential fraud or deletion and avoid issues with respect to currency fluctuations. For instance, ASCAP, SACEM and PRS for Music announced in 2017 that they were jointly investigating a new system that would better connect the data related to audio recordings and song publishing, while Spotify and Warner have also purchased, or invested in, a number of blockchain companies.

MUSIC FUNDING

Funding for artists is available from a variety of sources. Many musicians seek to secure advances from recording and publishing companies, but there are many other forms of direct investment available from streaming companies, consumer brands, individual philanthropists and music funders (both state-supported and private). In this section, we focus specifically on how musicians and their managers may apply for financial grants from specialist music funders. Such grants are aimed at supporting the creation, performance and promotion of music. They appeal to musicians because they are both non-repayable and non-recoupable, unlike a bank loan or a standard record company advance. Grants typically range from a few hundred pounds to five-figure sums for larger artist-led music projects, while world-famous music organisations, such as London's Royal Opera House, receive millions of pounds each year. Researcher Olivia Gable (2020) notes the importance of such funding, explaining that it has helped emerging artists to build full-time careers as musicians. The various funding organisations operate with significantly different criteria depending on their particular aims and missions. Applicants must therefore think carefully about the objectives of each funder that they apply to and check that they meet the criteria set by them. Thorough research of funder priorities is essential for artists and their teams, a process which will save time and energy for both applicants and funders. A 'copy and paste' approach to writing funding bids rarely works well, so artists should ensure that each application is tailored to the specific funder they approach. Are there expectations regarding social, cultural or economic benefits for stakeholders? If so, how can the funding application and project demonstrate the potential to meet them? As part of this consideration, artists and their managers should be realistic about whether they can deliver the programme of work for which they are requesting funds, including the preparation of detailed budgets.

State funding bodies in the US include the National Endowment for the Arts, while in the UK key organisations are Arts Council England, Creative Scotland, and the Arts Councils of Wales and Northern Ireland. Government funds may also be channelled through organisations that aim to support artists' career development, such as Canada's FACTOR programme and the BPI Music Export Growth Scheme (MEGS) in the UK. The latter awards international touring grants that have benefited many artists, including Ghostpoet, Catfish and the Bottlemen, Georgia and Lucy Rose. In addition to these national funding bodies, local authorities and regional councils will also support cultural activity in their specific areas. Collection societies around the world also support artists and organisations via linked funding organisations, such as PRS Foundation (UK), ASCAP Foundation (US) and Fundación SGAE (Spain). There are also many private funding bodies, family-based trusts and organisations linked to the legacies of orchestral composers (such as the Finzi Trust, RVW Trust and Bliss Trust in the UK). Trade bodies such as the MMF have also set up funding opportunities, such as the Accelerator Programme for aspiring artist managers (run in partnership with YouTube). In most cases, these funders will wish their investment to be clearly acknowledged, so artists in receipt of funding will place the organisation's logo on their promotional materials and, where relevant, on their physical releases. An evaluation form will usually need to be completed in order to receive payment of the final part of a grant, and post-funding reports may also be required to show how the aims of the funded project were achieved.

As we discussed in relation to live music in Chapter 8, funders and trade bodies responded strongly to the disruptions of the 2020–21 coronavirus pandemic, with the Association of Independent Music, New Music USA, Musicians' Union, Help Musicians and PRS Foundation (in partnership with Spotify, Warp Records and others) all offering emergency support to musicians whose income and livelihoods were affected. Other major cultural events and issues have affected the decisions and policies of the funding bodies. For instance, the Black Lives Matter protests in the summer of 2020 led to many organisations releasing statements to say that they would reconsider their funding criteria. One round of PRS Foundation's Sustaining Creativity Fund was adapted to provide direct support for Black music creators whose livelihoods had been affected by the coronavirus pandemic, with the funder partnering with Black-led organisations such as MOBO Trust and Tomorrow's Warriors to distribute support. It is therefore important for artists and their teams, and for venue/festival promoters, to keep up to date with developments in the music funding sector.

Direct-to-fan (D2F) opportunities may also be an important source of funding. We have previously discussed crowdfunding and micro-patronage (see Chapter 7), but an extension of this is the creation of online 'tip jars' or virtual gifting, through which fans can contribute directly to the artist. Examples include Spotify's Artist Fundraising Pick and, via Bandcamp, the ability to pay a greater than suggested purchase price for music downloads, or to set a pay-what-you-want option. Online tipping is a common practice in China, especially in relation to live performances, where a small percentage of each micro-payment is paid to the platform. Music industry journalist Cherie Hu (2018) suggests that this has led to companies such as Tencent becoming profitable in a way that Spotify has yet to achieve in Western markets. However, as Hu suggests, online tipping is much less common outside China because of cultural, bureaucratic and technical factors. Perhaps more common, especially in the Western classical music field, is philanthropic support, where individual donors contribute significant amounts to orchestras, opera houses, concert halls and festivals. Such donations are made either directly through bequests and donations, or through membership schemes. It is an especially common practice in the US, where there is less government support for the arts in comparison to Europe. Furthermore, many artists, such as Rob Swift, Amanda Palmer and Pentatonix, have amassed thousands of regular monthly subscribers on the US-based Patreon platform (see also Chapter 7). Other musicians have benefited from paid subscription tiers on the Twitch gaming and streaming network, including vocalists Daniel Tomkins (of TesseracT) and Matt Heafy (of Trivium).

OTHER INCOME STREAMS

Financial diversification is key for musicians. By expanding the number of potential income sources, they will be better able to cope should one (or more) of their revenue streams disappear. These income streams may, of course, be subject to a manager's commission or be included as part of a multiple rights recording contract, so artists and their managers should explore all the options available to them in detail. We have already examined (in Chapter 9) how artists can seek funding support from brand sponsors, ranging from basic brand endorsement and product placement deals through to more complex arrangements including co-branded campaigns and artist ambassadorships. In this section we will focus on other potential income routes.

For songwriters, there are additional potential income streams related to their publishing. These include royalties from cover versions of their songs recorded by other artists, the use of their lyrics on merchandise (such as mugs or clothing), and the sale of tuition books, guitar tabs and sheet music. One of the most lucrative income streams – for both songwriters and recording artists – is synchronisation (also known as 'sync'), whereby music is used on the soundtrack of a television programme, video game, film or advertisement. Synchronisation licences are negotiable, so there is considerable variation in the fees that may be charged, depending on how the music will be used and the bargaining power of the artist involved. High-profile uses may attain fees reaching into the tens of thousands of dollars, while a song featured as the title theme of a major film could achieve six-figure sums (Passman, 2019: 242–250). Even relatively new artists may be able to achieve licence fees of a few thousand pounds, and given how long it might take for that artist to earn such a sum from online streaming, it is no surprise that record companies and publishers often focus on the sync potential of an artist when deciding to sign them. Artists may also be commissioned to compose original soundtracks for films, television shows, computer games or theatre productions, and these may be considered separately from their publishing contract. Indeed, some artists focus almost exclusively on such commissions, while others compose for production music libraries (catalogues of music that are not officially released to the public, but are instead marketed directly to music supervisors in media companies). Well-known musicians, including Prince, Thom Yorke and Daft Punk, have all written specifically for films, while artists such as 65daysofstatic and Steven Wilson have written for video games.

2020 and 2021 saw a significant increase in established songwriters (such as Shakira and Stevie Nicks) making deals with 'song funds' such as Hipgnosis and Round Hill Music. These companies pay an upfront lump sum to the songwriter in exchange for the artist's share of the royalty rights income from their publishing catalogues. In other words, the company will receive all future royalty payments related to the artists songs, but does not actually own the publishing copyrights themselves. In some cases, the artist may also sign a deal related to future royalty rights payments due under their recording contracts or revenue from exploitation of their brand name and image. The figures for such deals are rarely disclosed, although news agency Reuters (2021) suggests that the majority of Ryan Tedder's catalogue was sold to private equity firm KKR for nearly $200 million.

Other musicians have leveraged their public profile and celebrity status to produce podcasts or to present radio and television shows. Artists may also earn money from a variety of personal appearances – from switching on Christmas lights to offering meet and greets, guesting at nightclubs and hosting events. Some musicians stage exhibitions of their visual art, with Yoko Ono, John Squire (The Stone Roses) and Kim Gordon (Sonic Youth) all receiving acclaim for their work in this field. In the literary arena, artists may generate income from book sales of both fiction and non-fiction. Highly acclaimed autobiographies include those by Bob Dylan, Patti Smith and Charles Mingus, whereas Nick Cave has published a successful series of novels. The Beastie Boys released an audio version of their memoir in 2018, chronicling their career with contributions from Snoop Dogg, Talib Kweli, Bette Midler and a host of other celebrities. The artforms of music and fashion have also long influenced each other (Codrea-Rado, 2019), so it is natural that many musicians are comfortable working in both fields. Artists including Kanye West and Rihanna have partnered with leading clothing brands to create new ranges, whereas Jay-Z and Drake have successfully developed and marketed their own clothing businesses.

There are also opportunities for artists to generate ancillary income linked to concert appearances and tours. In addition to ticket sales, promoter fees, merchandise sales and any broadcast, DVD or pay-per-view concert films, artists may offer meet and greets or perform after show parties or DJ sets, either at the same venue or at a nearby club. Some musicians, such as TesseracT drummer Jay Postones, schedule instrumental 'clinics' to tie in with their tour dates. Beyond touring, artists may make one-off paid live appearances at corporate events, weddings, birthday parties, house shows, holiday events and ocean liner cruises, such as the progressive rock-focused 'Cruise to the Edge', Paramore's 'Parahoy!', Kiss's 'KISS Kruise' or Ke$ha's 'Weird & Wonderful Rainbow Ride'. Superstar artists may also undertake a highly profitable Las Vegas casino/hotel residency, which offers a consistently high number of tourists keen to access nightly entertainment. This makes it an appealing option over touring, due to the removal of the gruelling daily travel commitments of a standard itinerary. Those who have enjoyed success in Las Vegas include Celine Dion, Calvin Harris, Tiësto and Lady Gaga. Musical theatre also offers potential riches to musicians, with *The Economist* (2016a) noting that such productions can be even more profitable than movies in the long run. Commercial successes based on rock band catalogues have included *We Will Rock You* (Queen) and *American Idiot* (Green Day). Musicals may thrive in a West End or Broadway residency, but may also operate concurrent productions around the world, as in the case of hip-hop musical *Hamilton* running simultaneously in New York, Los Angeles and London. But despite these runaway successes, *The Economist* (2016a) notes that just 20 percent of musicals make a profit, though the artist or publisher will still have received their rights income.

CONCLUSION

This chapter has considered many aspects of both generating and managing income streams within the music industries. Copyright is a complex area, but one that is essential for artists, managers and their teams to understand if they are to maximise their earning potential. Many copyright-related challenges remain for the music industries, including issues around data accuracy, copyright terms and global cooperation. The ways in which gatekeepers (such as streaming platforms, collection societies, record companies and publishing companies), distribute royalties is also a source of strong debate, with songwriters and performers arguing that they do not receive fair remuneration for the work that they do. Clearly, more data collection and analysis of the current situation is required, although this is made difficult by the lack of transparency that pervades the music industries. We have also considered the many other income streams available to artists, from introductory options such as teaching and joining collection societies, to larger-scale projects such as film scores and Las Vegas residencies. It is common for artists to adopt portfolio careers, drawing income from a range of activities. Therefore, managers and artists are encouraged to think carefully about their wider interests, and how these may be translated into further opportunities beyond music performance.

Key discussion points

- What factors should policymakers consider when they revise copyright laws?
- What are the pressures that could be placed on artists and their teams by the need to add and diversify income streams?
- How can global collection societies adapt or change over the next decade to ensure that they maximise royalty income for artists?
- What are the potential benefits and drawbacks for established artists to consider before signing a deal with a 'song fund'? How may such negotiations impact the wider music industries in the longer term?

FURTHER READING

To learn more about the flow of royalties, we recommend Chris Cooke's *Dissecting the Digital Dollar* (2020). In addition, Alan Krueger's *Rockonomics* (2019) provides an insightful economic overview of music industry structures. To learn more about the many options for releasing music (and the potential income streams from each), please see David Byrne's *How Music Works* (2012).

11

BEYOND THE MUSIC: WELL-BEING AND EQUALITY

SUMMARY

In this chapter we consider two vital elements of the music industries: well-being and diversity. Both issues have been at the forefront of industry debate in recent years, with musicians and companies now speaking more openly about common challenges and potential solutions. We analyse the many recent reports and publications on both areas, and consider the next steps recommended by trade bodies and researchers to create a more welcoming, supportive and inclusive music sector.

Chapter objectives

- To analyse the key literature and statistics on mental health and diversity in the music industries.
- To explore the potential health impacts of common industry practices on artists and managers, as well as strategies for maintaining or enhancing personal well-being.
- To consider ways of working that reduce the administrative burden on both musicians and managers.
- To examine aspects of the music industries and society that contribute (either directly or indirectly) to a lack of diversity, and to consider how such problematic situations may be addressed.

Managers and their teams typically look after all aspects of an artist's career, focusing not only on artistic and financial decisions, but also the personal well-being of the musicians with whom they work. There are considerable pressures placed upon musicians by touring, fan expectations, social media updates, recording schedules and media interviews. All of these factors are exacerbated by the requirement to be creative in challenging and sometimes chaotic commercial circumstances. Artists, managers and their team members must therefore work together to ensure that they all remain healthy, resilient and adaptable in order to avoid 'burning out'. Thankfully, well-being is an area that is now receiving considerable attention from music industry organisations. Thus, in this chapter we consider some of the issues raised in the literature, such as the networks of support required to allow music professionals and artists to achieve a good work–life balance and/or longevity within the marketplace. We evaluate recent music industry diversity reports, political developments and other data from both UK and US studies, analysing signs of progress and areas for urgent improvement. The chapter includes an interview with Natalie Wade, CEO of Small Green Shoots, a development charity that provides young people with access to the creative industries. Additionally, she is the co-founder of the female-focused creative career development enterprise The Cat's Mother. Wade is also an advisor to PRS Foundation's (2021a) Power Up initiative, which aims to better support aspiring Black music executives. We conclude the chapter by considering the many recommendations arising from recent reports and campaigns that aim to enhance diversity and inclusion in the music industries.

HEALTH AND WELL-BEING

There are many health benefits to both performing and listening to music, which are well documented in the literature (McGilchrist, 2011; Gross and Musgrave, 2016; Krueger, 2019). Yet, the current structure of the music industries leads to a difficult balancing act between creativity and commerce, where the aim to maximise profits may conflict with individual artistic ambition (Hesmondhalgh, 2019; Krueger, 2019). Occasionally, these conflicting needs may combine positively, particularly when labels, managers and artists understand each other's perspectives and plan for mutual benefit. However, some artists may be uncomfortable with the profit-seeking motives and demands placed upon them (see Chapter 3). Krueger (2019: 52) comments that, from an economic standpoint, an artist's 'inner drive' to make music 'creates a ready supply of musicians who are willing to sacrifice higher income and steadier work in order to practice their art'. As a result, musician salaries are typically low (Gross and Musgrave, 2017; Krueger, 2019; Hayman and Jones, cited in Savage, 2021), partly because so many are willing to work for free. As with any over-supplied product or service, this creates considerable downward force on incomes (Krueger, 2019: 57). Many artists also feel obliged to work for free given the highly competitive nature of the industry, with the benefits of such work often transferred to others. Talking Heads' David Byrne wryly summarises this situation by stating that being a musician is 'a good job, but that doesn't mean it's OK to go broke doing it' (Byrne, 2012: 207). Sadly, musician bankruptcies are common for a variety of reasons, as highlighted in Chapter 10.

Many musicians work as independent contractors and can therefore be considered part of the wider 'gig economy': defined as a labour market of short-term, *ad hoc* or freelance jobs (Gleim et al., 2019: 142). Such working practices may result in the loss of benefits offered to full-time employees, such as health insurance, retirement benefits and a set wage (Wiessner, cited in Gleim et al., 2019: 142). The resulting financial pressures can also lead to poor working conditions (Umney, 2016; Gross and Musgrave, 2017), which may in turn lead to poor physical and mental health. Indeed, much cultural work is both tiring and unpaid, despite often requiring a significant amount of effort, thought and time. Following Tiziana Terranova (2000), we might think of such unpaid work as a form of 'free labour', whereby musicians undertake work that will provide the most financial benefit to others (such as promoters, record companies and so on). This is often accepted by musicians as part of gaining experience of live performance (free gigs, open mics, pay to play) or as a trade-off in which a record company invests funds that a musician may not themselves have available for the recording and release of their music. Such financial difficulties for musicians, venues and touring crew were of course exacerbated during the 2020–21 Covid-19 pandemic, when live performance opportunities were minimised.

Moreover, we might argue that musical practices are also a form of 'affective labour' (Hardt, 1999: 89), in which performers seek to influence or change the emotions of their listeners. This can be both physically and emotionally draining, particularly over the course of a concert tour, but also in relation to critical reviews of work that musicians have invested significant time in creating. Hence, we find that some report considerable anxiety regarding media or public validation (or otherwise) of their music and performances (Gross and Musgrave, 2016: 8).

Research also demonstrates that musicians face an increased risk of substance abuse, depression and anxiety, often placing a strain on their personal lives (Krueger, 2019: 71). The context for such heightened risk is that the music and entertainment industries differ from other sectors in several ways. Industry professionals report widespread informal working practices and unstable career paths, potentially leading to exhaustion, poor diet or blurred lines between work and personal life. Drugs and alcohol are also widely available (Gritter, 2017; MMF and Music Support, 2017), with three related issues arising within the creative industries: the widespread, but flawed notion that drug use can enhance creativity; the use of drugs and alcohol as coping mechanisms; and the peer pressure of 'fitting in' with particular cultural contexts and the expectations of others. Furthermore, wider cultural tropes of the 'tortured artist' (as well as journalists' historic romanticisation of irresponsible or risky behaviour) do little to help artists who may be emotionally vulnerable or struggling to balance the needs of their music with other pressures. Indeed, in some cases, it may tragically lead to membership of the so-called '27 club' of performers who have met untimely deaths due to suicide or reckless behaviour (Hearsum, 2012).

Gross and Musgrave's two-part study for Help Musicians UK includes a wide-ranging survey of over 2,200 artists and music professionals, and detailed interviews with 26 musicians about their experiences. The headline findings of the survey are stark, with 71 percent of respondents reporting symptoms of anxiety and 69 percent experiencing depression. The results suggest that musicians are three times more likely to suffer from such illnesses when compared to the general public (Gross and Musgrave, 2016: 5). Poor working conditions are cited as a key issue, with unusual working hours often resulting in exhaustion. Financial precarity is another key concern, alongside loneliness linked to self-employment or long periods of working alone. Musicians also express frustration at the role that luck and randomness play in their careers, with success sometimes dependent on timing or chance events (also see Chapter 3). Furthermore, the survey found that musicians' need to believe in their own work is negatively affected by the unpredictable nature of the music business.

Such unpredictability is driven by precarious employment and an 'environment of constant critical feedback' (Gross and Musgrave, 2017: 7), including inevitable knockbacks from both industry personnel and the public. Finally, some family members and friends may not consider music to be 'real work', leading to a lack of recognition for those working as musicians (Gross and Musgrave, 2016: 14). Despite the pressures, the research found that musicians may not want to admit to any difficulties due to the highly competitive nature of the business and a desire to look organised (Gross and Musgrave, 2017: 7).

Three key areas for change were recognised by the report: enhanced education, a code of best practice and a mental health support service (2017: 29–31). Education will help to provide clearer guidance for both music students and artists on the issues that they may face in pursuing a career in music, and strategies on how to deal with them. A Code of Best Practice will call on organisations to demonstrate awareness of mental health problems, to take account of them in their policies and expectations, and to encourage a kinder and more tolerant view on creative workers' challenges. Finally, a mental health support service can provide a safe space for musicians to gain help. Help Musicians UK has since launched the Music Minds Matter initiative in the UK, providing a dedicated telephone helpline open 24 hours a day, 365 days a year. In addition to counselling, the helpline provides other resources related to financial and legal advice. Support services are also available in other countries, such as the MusiCares charity in the US (founded by the Recording Academy), which provides recovery services related to mental health and addiction. The organisation also offers financial support and assistance for a range of health and hardship issues.

The Music Managers' Forum (MMF) has also led efforts to support both artists and managers, seeking to change the nature of the conversation around health issues. The organisation recommends that managers can support artists through challenging times by engaging in open-minded listening, regularly checking-in and avoiding overly critical feedback. The manager must, however, maintain their own good mental health too, by ensuring that they do not take on too many tasks themselves. To this end, they should consider signposting their artists to professional mental health support services if required (MMF and Music Support, 2017). In sum, artists and managers are recommended to prioritise their physical and mental health, adapting as best they can to the unique and sometimes chaotic surroundings of the music business. Health considerations include: monitoring and moderating the intake of alcohol; exercising regularly; eating healthily; maintaining a positive balance between work and personal life; getting enough sleep; and being aware of any potential challenges or disruptions ahead so that they can be planned for as well as possible (MMF and Music Support, 2017). Despite the challenges that may be faced by musicians in undertaking their work, and in dealing with the press, social media and fans, it is important to remember that 'a career in music can also be incredibly fulfilling' (Jones, cited in Savage, 2021). Researcher Lucy Heyman notes further that a common research approach has been to focus primarily on the problems faced by musicians, despite many musicians also experiencing 'high levels of well-being' (cited in Savage, 2021). Indeed, working in music is so strong a passion that, for many artists, it becomes difficult to focus on anything else. Research has found that even the thought of not being a musician causes considerable anxiety to many artists (Gross and Musgrave, 2017: 21). Thus, when considering the many challenges facing artists, we must balance the debate by acknowledging the happiness, friendships and skills that are gained through performing music.

Emotional intelligence and authentic leadership

Music managers can enhance their personal well-being (and, subsequently, that of others) by developing their emotional intelligence, a concept popularised by writer Daniel Goleman (1995). Goleman (2011: 3) explains that emotional intelligence 'distinguishes great leaders from merely good ones', listing its key aspects as self-awareness, self-regulation, motivation and empathy. Such traits can be enhanced through sustained practice and feedback (2011: 3). Related socio-emotional leadership behaviours include engagement, steadiness, trustworthiness and collaboration (HBR, 2017: 12). Good leadership can also encompass building trust through competence and consistency, in addition to demonstrating respect, asking questions, inviting feedback and supporting others (HBR, 2017: 25). A recurring theme also mentioned by music industry professionals (as noted above) is the difficulty they have in maintaining separation between work life and personal life. This is partly due to the seemingly natural combination of both aspects within the highly social nature of the business. However, some distance from one's work and colleagues is still required in order to avoid burnout.

Another ongoing challenge, as noted above, is that managers often become the 'go-to' person for artists or team members to discuss their worries and concerns. Managers should thus reflect on whether they may be developing into a 'toxic handler' (Robinson and Schabram, 2017: 147–148), whereby, through the best intentions, they become overly involved in the stressful situations of others around them. Signs of adopting such a role can include difficulty in saying 'no', mediating communications between other team members and regularly offering advice to colleagues (2017: 147–148). However, managers must accept that many situations will involve making tough decisions, when considering the wider benefits that may arise. A potential solution to the 'toxic handler' scenario is therefore for managers to consider the concept of 'tough empathy', which 'balances respect for the individual and for the task at hand', although addressing both of these aspects may be difficult (Goffee and Jones, 2018: 90–91).

Understandably, it is emotionally tiring to both listen to and advise work colleagues on a constant basis. Individuals in this position may not seek support for themselves, thus adding to the layers of ongoing stress that they personally feel (Robinson and Schabram, 2017: 147–148). It is thus important for managers to build their own support networks rather than try to handle everything on their own: to seek emotional and practical support and advice from partners, mentors, families, colleagues and friends. These relationships help to build confidence and trust during tough times, cementing a positivity which the leader can then pass on to those around them (George et al., 2018: 26–27). Despite the difficulties of the role, managers may also help in the professional development of the wider team around the artists they work with. Academic Richard E. Boyatzis's 'intentional change theory' (cited in McKee, 2017: 215) considers how leaders – such as music managers – can help others to develop emotional intelligence by helping them to develop a vision for their future, and by supporting them in assessing how their current working methods may need to be amended if that vision is to be achieved.

Resilience is an important personal trait for any sector, but particularly so within the creative industries, where there will be many subjective opinions on an artist's work. Both managers and artists will therefore benefit from developing tenacity and grit. Furthermore, adopting an objective and constructive approach may also help to deal with negative situations or feedback. Hence, resilience can be interpreted as the ability to be realistic and to face tough consequences, while seeking to learn from every situation (including where things have gone well). It can also refer to flexibility, improvisation and inventiveness in difficult scenarios: by considering new possibilities, combining resources in new ways (Coutu, 2017: 182–183) and developing creative paths forward. In music, such grey areas require a combination of lateral thinking and flexible, adaptive approaches (see also Chapter 2). This was exemplified well during the Covid-19 pandemic, where musicians and their teams generated many new ideas, such as developments in livestreaming (see also Chapter 8) and a proliferation of social media, podcasting and blogging initiatives. Such activities ensured that artists maintained contact with their fans while also creating new revenue streams. It is therefore important to foster a 'willingness to commit to long-term goals and to persist in the face of difficulty' (Grant Halvorson, 2012: 17). In turn, this provides the discipline to create good routines, improve decision-making and enhance self-control (Grant Halvorson, 2012; Coleman, 2017). Such discipline can be difficult to maintain over the long term, yet it is vital for those working in the music industries, as setbacks may be as common as successes.

Maintaining positive professional relationships

Working within a team presents challenges as well as opportunities, as summarised in Chapter 2. In any large-scale project involving multiple team members, there will be difficult, complicated and often emotional issues to contend with. Musical and professional relationships often have a natural lifespan, with partnerships rapidly forming and dissolving (Morrow, 2018a). Artistic partnerships can be relatively temporary and managers may be at risk of replacement at key stages of an artist's career (hence the inclusion of a 'sunset clause' in many management contracts – see also Chapter 2). For instance, a manager may be able to support a new artist to the stage of achieving a recording deal and of touring on a national level. But after this stage, they may lack the experience or contacts to help propel them to international success or to deal with other aspects of their career. Such variations in the artist–manager relationship are partly due to human nature, where all types of relationship have the potential to break down. Indeed, collaboration on creative work requires an understanding of 'power fluctuations', where each partner contributes to a burgeoning artistic relationship in ways that shift over time (Gilfillan, cited in Morrow, 2018a: 11). For example, while the artist may follow 'the manager's lead' in the early stages of their career, the power relationship may gradually shift in favour of the artist as their success builds (Morrow, 2018a: 10). It is best for any potential problems or issues to be dealt with quickly and professionally in order to achieve a positive resolution, whether that is to maintain the relationship or to change it (Passman, 2019: 30).

Increasing efficiency and productivity

Improving efficiency, productivity and organisational skills can lead to a clearer focus on important tasks (Treseder, 2017; Crenshaw, 2018), allowing both managers and artists to achieve more and, ultimately, to reduce their stress levels. Key steps to increased efficiency include prioritisation, effective delegation and avoidance of procrastination, while prioritising one's own well-being and energy levels. A key step to becoming more productive is by maintaining focus, which can be achieved by setting uninterrupted chunks of time aside for specific tasks (Bregman, 2012a; Schwartz, 2012). For example, some managers find it useful to employ the 'Pomodoro' technique (or similar), which encourages 25-minute bursts of work, followed by a few minutes of rest, reflection or exercise (Cirillo, 2021). During such continuous periods of focus, both managers and artists have the potential to enter a psychological state of 'flow' or 'optimal experience', resulting in greater enjoyment and enhanced creativity (Csikszentmihályi, 1990). Such periods of uninterrupted work are vital because multi-tasking is, quite simply, bad for human brains. It creates the illusion of achieving more, but has a significantly negative effect on concentration, creativity and productivity (Bregman, 2012b; Hammerness and Moore 2017; Crenshaw, 2018).

In addition to these intense periods of focus, it is also important for artists and managers to consider the shorter gaps that appear during the day, often before or after meetings, studio time or live shows. Such gaps may seem insignificant, but can add up to considerable amounts of time across a month or year. They can be ideal for quickly completing easy tasks or even completing sections of longer tasks. It is therefore beneficial to plan for some activities that can be undertaken during such short periods, in order to better manage one's workload (Croft, 2016). Such planning can be aided by a humble to-do list. Creating an overarching (and possibly lengthy) list can often be daunting at first, but can then be categorised into shorter tasks and more strategic ones (Bregman, 2012c; Croft, 2016). Without such a list, it is very difficult to plan or prioritise. As a result, numerous tasks can become urgent, or workloads can become dictated by external forces outside the manager's or artist's control (Croft, 2016). When creating a task list, it is vital to balance urgency with importance. Many people focus on urgent tasks above all else (sometimes known as 'firefighting') whereas more efficient workers will balance the urgent tasks with beneficial longer-term activities (Crenshaw, 2018). Examples of the latter include building relationships, developing the culture of a team, investigating new opportunities and planning for change (Covey, cited in Sloane, 2017: 30). Both artists and managers would also benefit from using a clear digital filing system for such a list, so that key information can be found quickly and easily by multiple team members. Data should also be regularly backed up, to avoid any loss of important information (Croft, 2016; Crenshaw, 2018). In addition, a 'to-don't list' could also be created, which ensures that common distractions, such as smartphones, websites or social media, are avoided for set periods of time (Bregman, 2012d). Indeed, academic Tim Wu (2017: 276) argues that the online experience is the 'greatest procrastination aide ever devised' and that 'how we spend the brutally limited resource of our attention' impacts greatly on one's overall life experiences (2017: 7). To further embed good mental health and the ability to focus, many businesspeople also engage with mindfulness meditation (*The Economist*, 2013).

DIVERSITY IN THE MUSIC INDUSTRIES

Diversity is such a wide-ranging and complex subject that a full discussion of all protected characteristics (and the intersectionality between them) is beyond the scope of this book.

Therefore, this chapter will focus primarily on two key areas of recent research within the music industries: gender and ethnicity.

The widespread diversity of artists and genres is one of the greatest strengths of the music industries. Researchers representing the Annenberg Inclusion Initiative found that of 173 artists featured in the US Billboard end-of-year chart in 2020, 59 percent were of underrepresented ethnicities. This marked the fourth consecutive year of growth (Smith et al., 2021a). Figures for the gender balance of performers in 2020 were less impressive: only 22.1 percent were female. Fluctuation in the gender balance data was seen across the previous five years, yet at no point did female performers exceed a third of all performers (Smith et al., 2021a). The research literature on gender imbalance in the music industries makes for unambiguous and uncomfortable reading (as discussed further below), while the growth in ethnic diversity seen in the Billboard chart is not typically reflected in leadership positions in the wider music industries (UK Music, 2020b: 9–11; Smith et al., 2021b).

Yet within the arts, diversity and equality are considered of paramount importance for creative and organisational success (Serota, cited in ACE, 2020; UK Music 2020b: 7). Similarly, the wider business case is strong, with diverse teams offering a wider range of perspectives and knowledge, leading to better decisions and superior innovation (West, 2012; UK Music, 2020b; Feldman Barrett, 2021). For the music industries specifically, researcher Vick Bain (2016) argues that a fairer working environment leads to business gains, greater innovation and heightened creativity. Natalie Wade (interview with authors) expands on this theme when describing her working environment at Small Green Shoots: 'I have the best working life. I have the best office, the best team … because all of us are so different.' She believes that working in a diverse team 'teaches you the best about life', due to the different approaches adopted by team members from differing backgrounds. Furthermore, she asserts that encouraging dialogue within a diverse team helps to develop the 'people skills' and 'common ground' that are so important for success in the creative industries. To achieve such a dynamic work environment, she argues that it is vital for a workplace to welcome and support a mix of personalities. She advocates a more caring approach by music companies, encouraging employers to make their office 'a nice place to work'.

Given the clear benefits available to companies, why may diversity and equality be so difficult to achieve in some sectors? During the early 2010s, centre-right European leaders spoke publicly about the challenges of building a multicultural society, several years before both immigration and anti-globalisation became key factors in support for Brexit and Donald Trump's presidential campaign. In recent years, there has also been more research into the impact of structural racism, both within the music industries (Hopkins, 2022) and in wider society (Bailey et al., 2017; Yearby, 2020; Olusoga; 2021), affecting many aspects of life from healthcare to career pathways. US President Joe Biden also acknowledged the impact of 'systemic racism' within America in a 2021 speech, describing it as 'a stain on our nation's soul' (Charter and Dawber, 2021). One explanation that has been suggested is that humans have implicit (or subconscious) biases (Edmonds, 2017; Feldman Barrett, 2021). From a music business perspective, Natalie Wade (interview with authors) comments that pre-conceptions and biases have a significant part in both hiring processes and career progression for ethnic minorities, arguing that 'other people put that baggage on you – and that stereotype is hard to break out of'. Work colleagues can therefore recognise that both they (and others) have pre-conceived assumptions, but also have the ability to challenge and question such beliefs (Sloane, 2017: 40).

In addition to age, race, colour, ethnic origin, nationality, sexual orientation, disability and gender, UK government organisation Companies House also considers marriage or partnership status, religion, part-time workers, political opinions, pregnancy and maternity in its diversity policy. With such a wide range of considerations, company diversity policies often factor in aims for improving representation, alongside taking pride in achievements to date. Most large companies consider diversity to be an essential part of their strategy, with the BBC's policy cementing its commitment to an inclusive culture, which it claims is 'hardwired into everything the BBC does' (BBC, 2021). Similarly, Google's diversity statement references inclusion both in terms of its products and workforce, adding that its significant scale and reach bring additional responsibilities in building a 'workforce that's more representative of our users' (Google, 2021a). *The Economist* (2016b) argues that, while an encouraging sign of progress, diversity programmes do not automatically produce superior results by default. Such policies work best when they are well managed and combined with significant effort and clear thinking.

What does the data tell us about diversity in the music industries?

Data is available from a series of recent evidence-based reports, focusing on both the UK (Bain, V., 2019; ACE, 2020; UK Music, 2020b) and the US (Smith et al., 2021a). UK Music's biennial *Diversity Report* offers wide-ranging data regarding ethnicity, gender, age, disability, sexual orientation, geographical location, income and career stage. The organisation's CEO Jamie Njoku-Goodwin argues that: 'If our music industry is to tell the story of modern-day Britain, then it needs to look like modern-day Britain too' (UK Music, 2020b: 4), with the report providing a benchmark and catalyst for change. Data from 2019 shows that 49.6 percent of survey respondents identify as female, 48.8 percent as male, and 0.5 percent 'did not identify with the gender binary' (UK Music, 2020b: 7). The survey found 'a significant increase in Black, Asian and ethnic minority representation at all ages' compared to previous research (UK Music, 2020b: 9). However, the survey reports a substantial drop in both ethnic minority and female representation in older age-brackets and higher salary bands, suggesting that more could be done to ensure inclusive company cultures, better maternity policies and wider provision of mentoring (UK Music, 2020b: 9–11). UK Music (2020b: 17) argues that increasing transparency on pay 'would help to highlight the issues facing women and people from ethnic minorities', thus providing a platform for enhancing diversity.

Natalie Wade (interview with authors) explains that many aspiring executives will understandably lack the connections required for the informal recruitment strategies found in the music industries, with many also lacking knowledge of career paths. She comments that 'you can't aim towards it because you don't even know it exists … how can you get your foot in the door if you don't have those connections?'. Furthermore, Wade argues that aspiring executives may also lack the personal budget for socialising or entertaining. The lack of such a financial security net, may result in a risk-averse approach that can also affect attempts to attract investment for new businesses. She notes that Black-led start-ups 'traditionally don't get investment', aligning with findings from the *State of European Tech* report, which found a 'systematic exclusion of talent' from ethnic minority groups (Atomico, 2020). Such findings have led some companies to address inequalities, with Google establishing a Black Founders Fund. The European version of the funding programme offers $2 million of investment for Black-founded start-ups across the continent, with the company also providing access to a mentor network (Google, 2021b).

Finding and working with a mentor is considered one of the most important aspects of career development, with mentoring opportunities offered and promoted by several music funders (The Ivors Academy, 2020; PRS Foundation, 2021a). Mentoring offers the chance to learn from a 'critical friend', who can provide supportive feedback on career progression or ideas, along with introducing the mentee to useful contacts. It is all the more important in the music industries where, as noted above, social connections are paramount and many jobs are offered outside formal processes such as job adverts (see Chapter 2). Wade (interview with authors) sees many benefits to mentoring, stating that 'having that connection is so important ... it can be absolutely brilliant', but that there 'has to be a real understanding of what the relationship is'. She explains that such a lack of clarification or effort can result in 'some real horror stories', where both the mentor and mentee face challenges. It is therefore important to note that mentoring success does not happen automatically – the relationship must be mutually beneficial. Wade argues that the most valuable role of a mentor is to both 'champion' and expand the network of the mentee. In terms of a recipe for a successful mentoring relationship, she advises that a 'short and sharp' approach of concise regular meetings tends to work best, with clear guidelines set out in advance for both the mentor and mentee. Many mentoring schemes have been established for women working in the music industries that encourage networking and career progression. These include shesaid.so, Women in Music, Change the Conversation, SoundGirls, Moving the Needle, Keychange and Spotify's EQUAL initiative. Furthermore, Vick Bain created the F-List Directory, to ensure that female musicians can enhance their professional profiles.

Thirteen percent of respondents to UK Music's 2020 *Diversity Report* survey 'identified their sexual orientation as something other than "Heterosexual"', which is significantly higher than the UK average of 7 percent (UK Music, 2020b: 17). Yet despite the long-running contribution and influence of LGBTQ+ artists and executives within the music industries, writer Andrew Barker (2015) suggests that 'Pop music has borrowed from the aesthetics of gay culture for decades without necessarily embracing the social responsibility that ought to have come with it'. Similarly, music industry executive Parris OH (2021) notes that, although the 'relationship between popular music and queer culture has stood strong through time', multiple challenges remain for contemporary queer artists. Expanding further on this issue, journalist Katie Bain (2018) describes how a marginalised community of black gay men performing at venues such as Chicago's Warehouse during the 1970s and 1980s established the building blocks for dance music's current success. Yet despite this significant contribution, both LGBTQ+ and ethnic minority artists are currently underrepresented in electronic dance music (EDM). She also notes their lack of representation in influential annual music business 'power lists', adding that although the 'mainstream EDM scene is, in theory, open to LGBTQ artists ... representation remains paltry' (Bain, K., 2018).

Furthermore, Rumens and Broomfield (2014: 366) found that the performing arts sector has 'long been stereotyped' as 'gay-friendly'. However, there is a lack of research in the sector and a 'poor track record in developing equality and diversity policies' (Dean, cited in Rumens and Broomfield, 2014: 367). There are, however, positive signs of development, with more events focusing on underrepresented artists (Bain, K., 2018) and homophobic lyrics reportedly reducing across many genres, leading to hopes of a 'sea-change' (Barker, 2015). Musicians including Rina Sawayama, Olly Alexander, Sam Smith, Kylie Minogue, Dotty, MNEK, Dan Reynolds (Imagine Dragons) and Big Freedia are all strong advocates for LGBTQ+ communities. There are also several initiatives providing support for LGBTQ+ identifying music industry personnel, such as the UK charity Pride in Music.

Gender

Kristin Lieb (2018: 111) notes that the 21 interviewees who participated in her music industries gender research all reported (to varying degrees) 'that the music industry treats women differently than men'. Similarly, Colette Henry has noted that 'the same gender-related barriers that exist within other industry sectors are just as prevalent, if not more so, within the creative sector' (cited in Morrow, 2018b: 43–44). Chart data research by Smith et al. (2021a) found that, of the 173 artists on the year-end Billboard Hot 100 chart in the US, 79.8 percent were men and 20.2 percent were women. Of the 449 songwriters credited in the 2020 year-end chart, 87.1 percent were men and just 12.9 percent were women. Regarding producers, the difference is even more stark: 198 producers were credited in the 2020 chart, with a split of 98 percent men and just 2 percent women (Smith et al., 2021a: 7–10). Furthermore, in a review of their National Portfolio Organisations, Arts Council England (ACE) found that music organisations within the portfolio had the lowest percentage of female staff, at 32 percent (ACE, 2020). Although these statistics are focused on a relatively small group of workers, it aligns with US workforce data cited by Krueger (2019: 52), which show that '... about two-thirds of musicians are men' whereas 'the gender balance in the overall workforce is much closer to parity'.

In the UK, the 2019 *Counting the Music Industry* report shows similar gender disparities: just 14 percent of writers signed to 106 music publishers were female, and of the artists signed to 219 UK music labels, only 19 percent were female (Bain, V., 2019). A lack of representation at the senior level of music companies was also found, as was a significant gender pay gap. As of April 2021, the average pay gap was 25.4 percent at Sony Music UK, 30 percent at Warner Music UK, 29.2 percent at Universal Music UK, 34.3 percent at Live Nation UK and 15.3 percent at Spotify UK (Stassen 2021b). Notably, the data reported by the three major record labels showed that an average of nearly two-thirds of the top-earning quartile of executives were male, and that bonuses were significantly higher for male executives in comparison to female executives. Such figures provide clear evidence that music companies still need to do more to address the gender pay gap. Vick Bain (2019: 20) argues that this disparity can be partly explained by multiple barriers to entry. Such barriers include historic exclusion of women from musical activities, deep-rooted societal sexism, unconscious bias, harassment, a lack of high-profile role models and a lack of confidence (2019: 20–27). Lieb (2018: 274) notes that 'sexism and certain forms of harassment are deeply entrenched occupational hazards' for many women working in the music business. However, she also notes that a major change in recent years is that allegations are now considered both seriously and promptly, with a stronger atmosphere of support (2018: 281).

Vick Bain's (2019: 21) report also refers to 'the motherhood penalty', especially for women with portfolio or freelance careers. Natalie Wade (interview with authors) argues that more should be done to protect and encourage mothers returning to work, stating that 'when I got pregnant, I was written off'. When returning to work as a new mother, Wade found that the 'industry wasn't really set up for maternity leave'. With music business networking often happening in the evenings, Wade explains that many parents cannot afford the level of childcare required. She suggests that women are often 'typecast' into certain roles at companies, such as 'organiser' or 'administrative' positions, arguing further that such issues are ingrained from a young age (aligning with the literature on implicit bias and stereotyping discussed earlier in the chapter). Wade states that she was offered such positions in her career and that 'if I showed talent in other areas, it was suppressed' (interview with authors).

Ethnicity

In addition to the many issues raised in the UK Music *Diversity Report* (2020b), Stahl (cited in Hesmondhalgh, 2020: 11) shows that underpayment (or even non-payment) of royalties has historically disproportionately affected non-white musicians. Such imbalances are gradually being addressed by some music companies, with BMG CEO Hartwig Masuch acknowledging the 'music industry's record of shameful treatment of black artists' and announcing a review of historic contracts to check for 'inequities or anomalies' (Masuch, cited in Ingham, 2020b). Masuch also pledged a stronger effort to diversify the label's executive team, noting that the company had not made 'sufficient progress' in this area. The first-stage results of the process uncovered that four of BMG's 'historic acquired catalogs' showed 'statistically significant differences between the royalties paid to Black and non-Black artists (BMG, cited in Stassen, 2020b). The company announced additional research to establish the reasons for such differences, promising to implement measures to benefit lower-paid artists. Co-Chairs of the Black Music Action Coalition, Binta Niambi Brown and Willie 'Prophet' Stiggers stated that they welcomed BMG's initiative and encouraged other labels to undertake a similar process. They described it as potentially transformative for Black recording artists and performers (cited in Stassen, 2020b).

As noted previously, senior management positions within the UK music industries are less reflective of the country's ethnic diversity than entry-level positions (UK Music, 2020b). Such a noticeable disparity at executive level led the PRS Foundation to create the Power Up initiative. The funding programme addresses multiple challenges for Black musicians and industry professionals, including workplace prejudice, underrepresentation, lack of visibility in senior roles and economic inequality (PRS Foundation, 2021b). Journalist Natalie Morris (2021) reflects that it 'seems there is an inherent disconnect between the talent we see on the stages and in the music videos and who actually holds the power within the industry'. Another challenge facing Black artists in the UK is related to the booking of live shows at some venues. These challenges were exacerbated in 2005, when the controversial Form 696 was introduced following shooting incidents at several London clubs. The form was used by the Metropolitan Police as a risk-assessment for live shows, and included controversial questions relating to ethnicity and genre. These questions were removed in 2009, and use of the entire form revoked in 2017, something that was widely welcomed by music organisations and performers (Cooke, 2017).

Academic and musician Mykaell Riley explains that Form 696 had been 'disproportionately negative' towards Black artists, removing 'opportunities for income and development' (cited in Cooke, 2017). Riley's remarks were echoed in a subsequent report by a UK parliamentary committee, which cited 'concerns about discrimination hindering success' of Black music genres. The committee also expressed dismay that 'grime artists are continuing to face prejudice', thus negatively affecting the success of a strong UK musical export (DCMS, 2019b). The committee's report also referenced evidence of persistent discrimination against some Black music genres (particularly grime artists), again referencing the legacy of Form 696. The committee called for government action in providing better guidance to the police, venues and licensing authorities to ensure that Black music genres are not 'unfairly targeted' in the future (DCMS, 2019b). However, despite the removal of Form 696, many artists and promoters have argued that related discriminatory practices continue. Journalist Jesse Bernard (2018) writes that 'black promoters are still discriminated against', with admission policies, dress codes, relatively low drink sales, a lack of Black club owners and the legacy of Form 696 all described as problematic factors.

Recommendations

Although the UK Music *Diversity Report* highlights many current challenges, there are already positive signs of change. Action points recommended in the report for member organisations include: organisational diversity training; greater transparency on pay; greater boardroom diversity; an aim to increase representation in higher-salaried positions; and ensuring that their recruitment programmes encompass a diverse pool of candidates (UK Music, 2020b: 20–21). Changes in terminology are also recommended, with UK Music's Diversity taskforce suggesting that the terms 'urban music' and 'BAME' are replaced with more specific and appropriate alternatives (UK Music, 2020c). A number of other organisations work alongside UK Music to further promote diversity and equality through targeted initiatives, including The Black Music Coalition (BMC), Women in CTRL, PRS Foundation and disability-led charity Attitude is Everything (UK Music, 2020b: 22–25). Member organisations have also pledged support to better encourage and embed inclusion in their ongoing work, such as Ditto Music's Industry Access and MOBO's Mobolise programmes. In 2021, the Black Lives in Music initiative was launched with support from ACE, aiming to collect data on Black musicians in the UK and work towards a more inclusive music community. Furthermore, there is now an increased awareness of corporate social responsibility in the music industries, whereby businesses support positive causes via charitable donations (Krueger, 2019: 47; Ingham, 2020b; PRS Foundation, 2021c).

In his foreword to the organisation's 2020 diversity report, ACE's chair Nicholas Serota noted that the state-supported funder is 'still not representative of this country as a whole', with a 'long-standing issue of under-representation' which must be both 'recognised and addressed' (cited in ACE, 2020: 3). The organisation has also enshrined diversification of the cultural sector as a core element of its strategy from 2020 to 2030, across leadership, governance, audiences, workforce and artists. It hopes that creativity and innovation from its grantees will accelerate progress towards building a more relevant and inclusive arts sector in the UK (Serota, cited in ACE, 2020: 3). Indeed, music journalist Eamonn Forde (2016) posits that, despite the lack of diversity in senior leadership positions within the music industries, younger executives 'will slowly ascend through the corporate ranks'. With this increased visibility, there will be more evidence that the industries are changing and more role models to help progress matters further.

In terms of improving gender equality, Lieb recommends that students considering a career in the music business should reflect on the influential positions that they will eventually adopt, reminding them of the powerful images and ideas that they present to audiences and the wider public. Furthermore, by creating supportive networks of mutually beneficial connections, the executives of tomorrow have an opportunity to 'change the future of music' (Lieb, 2018: 282). Vick Bain (2019: 35) also makes several recommendations, focusing on the role of government (to improve legislation and funding levels), music companies (which should offer more ongoing support) and researchers (to discover more about career pathways, the gender pay gap and different international perspectives).

CONCLUSION

This chapter has considered two major issues that have been given greater prominence within the music industries in recent years. However, there is still a significant amount of work required in both areas. Regarding mental health and well-being, it is still unclear whether a duty of care towards musicians should be the domain of their record company, publisher, manager or family. The intricacies and complexities of music contracts (Chapters 2 and 3) do not create employment agreements as such, so it is harder to assign such responsibility to any single individual or company. Nonetheless it is heartening to see both artists and music companies speaking more openly about health and well-being, with Universal Music recently publishing a report on the importance of neurodiversity in the workplace (Universal Music Group, 2020). Similarly, there are encouraging signs of increasing diversity in both ethnicity and gender, as noted by some encouraging data from UK Music (2020b), ACE (2020) and Smith et al. (2021a). However, all three reports, in addition to the findings from Kristin Lieb (2018) and Vick Bain (2019), point to ongoing systemic issues. The many well-targeted interventions and recommendations in recruitment, training and funding noted above are therefore a welcome step in addressing them. Increasing diversity to better reflect society is not only a moral obligation; the business case is also clear: if music companies wish to thrive, then they must continue their efforts to ensure that everyone is included, with an equal chance to contribute.

Key discussion points

- How can music managers most effectively manage the multiple demands of their role?
- How can companies better support the health and well-being of both the artists and staff that work within the music industries?
- What steps should music companies take to ensure that their artists and/or staff better reflect the demographics of the countries in which they operate?
- How can companies ensure equitable ethnic and gender representation at higher salary levels?

FURTHER READING

For data and analysis of mental health in the UK music industries, we recommend Gross and Musgrave's *Can Music Make You Sick?* (2016). In addition, the MMF and Music Support's *The Music Manager's Guide to Mental Health* (2017) provides an overview of the challenges facing music professionals, alongside practical advice for overcoming such hurdles. Detailed overviews of diversity within the music industries can be found in Vick Bain's *Counting the Music Industry* (2019), the *UK Music Diversity Report 2020* (UK Music, 2020b) and Smith et al.'s *Inclusion in the Recording Studio?* (2021a).

12

CONCLUSION

In Chapter 1 we introduced our relationship approach to the study of the music industries. We argued that it is important to examine the cultural dimensions of economic activity to better understand how meaning is conveyed and how businesses operate. Interpersonal relationships and shared cultural worlds are central to creative and business decision-making, with connectivity and conversation as underpinning elements. In Chapters 2 and 3 we examined how artist managers and their teams must work together to understand every aspect of the artists they work with in order that they may better construct artist development strategies and routes forward. These chapters also discussed the various players within an artist's team, and the possible business relationships that may be made with record companies and publishers. The following three chapters focused on marketing and public relations staff, and their connections with media personnel such as journalists, playlisters, photographers and videographers. Active audiences and social media platforms were also highlighted in these chapters to show how traditional and online media often work together to build stories, image and buzz in order for artists or specific releases to reach the 'tipping point' (Gladwell, 2000) of success. The role of the PR is especially important here, as they work with artists, managers and others to manage information and reputation through both business-to-consumer (B2C) and business-to-business (B2B) relationships. B2B relationships were also discussed in Chapter 7, which outlined how music streaming sites operate. We also demonstrated how pressure from both the music industries and technology firms is shaping the development of revenue routes and copyright-related legislation. Furthermore, music recommendation systems were examined to show how data, playlisting and audiences are managed in an attempt to avoid the 'filter bubble effect' (Pariser, 2011). In Chapter 8, we considered the relationships between artist managers, promoters and bookers and the emergent technologies of livestreaming and virtual reality, while Chapter 9 looked at the relationships between brand sponsors and artists, venues and festivals. In Chapter 10, we looked at the financial challenges facing music businesses and the roles of both copyright and funding, noting that non-disclosure agreements (NDAs) serve to reduce communication. As a result of such agreements, it can be difficult for artist managers to find information about revenue streams associated with their artists. Finally, Chapter 11 examined the interpersonal and organisational politics of the music industries by considering issues related to mental health, gender and ethnicity, and the various support networks that have been introduced to address the many challenges that still remain. Throughout these chapters, we argued that the cultural backgrounds of industry personnel affect how they operate in their roles, as do the shared beliefs and preferences that emerge in different workplaces and sectors. Diversity was shown to be vital across the industries, with personnel from different backgrounds able to generate new ways of thinking and to develop new opportunities. However, power differences inevitably appear within these relationships, whether between people or between organisations, so it is important for anyone working in music to be aware of those power relationships and how they may be managed.

The 2020–21 coronavirus pandemic brought many issues into sharp focus, but we suggest that the most important ones for the music industries are the relative precarity of the different sectors and the pace of technological change. While we do not wish to engage in predicting the future, it is possible to recognise a number of ongoing trends that have been accelerated by the response to the pandemic. The first is the continued rise of music streaming, including short-form video apps and other user-generated content (TikTok, Triller, YouTube and so on), and music-focused podcasts and documentaries. Digital radio has also grown as a sector, with Apple Music and TikTok both launching stations, and partnerships have emerged with fitness apps and equipment (such as Peloton). However, traditional broadcast radio is likely to face challenges to its long-standing popularity as more people adopt streaming platforms as their preferred method of music discovery and listening. As streaming platforms are typically organised around themed and global playlists, there will be more potential for international cross-over hits. The success of Burna Boy, Angelique Kidjo, Wizkid, Neha Kakkar, Badshah, Luis Miguel, J Balvin and Shakira, in addition to the rise of K-Pop, has clearly demonstrated this worldwide demand. However, artists and their teams need to capitalise on any short-term viral success in order to build longer-term sustainable careers.

While streaming will remain the predominant driver of recorded music industry revenues for some time to come, there are indications of subscription saturation in the US and Europe. In these territories, prices will likely rise, alongside added-value features such as high-definition audio streams and the introduction of more 'vertically-oriented' service providers that focus on specific genres or activities. At the same time, there will be intense competition for the smartspeaker and in-car entertainment sectors, as well as efforts to gain market share and dominance in growing music markets around the world, such as Africa, India and Central and South America. Social entertainment apps and gaming sites will continue to grow and integrate, with music increasingly licensed as background content for online gaming, together with the eventification of games, as we have seen with the online concerts of Marshmello, Travis Scott and others. There is significant potential for merchandise sales here, such as artist-centric skins and other digital products, in addition to bespoke and collectible non-fungible tokens (NFTs). The livestreaming sector will also grow, with platforms battling for dominance and pay-per-view becoming standard practice for many artists, even as the live sector re-opens and returns to normal. Again, there will be significant opportunities for the creation and sale of digital merchandise, as well as for the expansion of virtual reality concerts and festivals.

These developments are largely positive for artists and the recorded music industry, including audio-visual marketing and PR, which boomed during the lockdown as artist teams sought to take advantage of the growth in online opportunities. However, for many artists, live performance has historically been the principal driver of their income. The pandemic largely cut off this revenue source, so artists have been looking at other ways to simultaneously diversify their income and reduce their risk profile. For instance, we see musicians and artists launching or extending in areas such as online music tuition, podcast and channel subscriptions, and micro-patronage sites. These also have the benefit of refocusing conversations around the artists themselves, in contrast to the song-centric playlists of the music streaming services. However, artists and their teams need to find ways to drive potential fans to their artist-centric content, and to continue pressurising the streaming companies to integrate artist-centric features and links. Diversification is also important for promoters, venue owners, bookers and the many others who are reliant on the live music sector, in order to boost their income and to protect themselves against any future lockdowns or restrictions.

Two other areas that have seen significant investment and growth are Blockchain-based solutions and the integration of machine-learning or artificial intelligence (AI) systems. Blockchain solutions for managing large amounts of data in a secure fashion – especially copyright management and revenue collection – are already being introduced (see Chapter 7), but the initial excitement around Blockchain has faded somewhat. This is due to ongoing concerns regarding the stability of the cryptocurrencies that underpin them, and the multiple and competing systems that have emerged. The utopian dream of a singular Blockchain through which all music could pass, thus enhancing transparency in the system, has been replaced by bespoke systems managed by different companies. At the same time, collection agencies are beginning to merge their resources in order to enhance their functionality and speed, and to track and monetise online uses of music more effectively.

AI-driven solutions are emerging for all manner of music-based activities. For instance, there are AI-based companies such as Evoke Music and Jukedeck (bought by TikTok's parent company ByteDance in 2019) that provide AI-produced music compositions for use in low budget video games, podcasts and other applications in much the same way as 'library music' companies, but at a much lower cost. There are also AI composer tools such as Amper and AIVA that are designed to create full songs or to assist in the songwriting process: for instance, by inputting a range of musical parameters and moods to the AI system, then working with its output. AI-composed songs have yet to receive much success, yet there are now many examples of artists using AI systems to help create compositions, including Taryn Southern's *I Am AI* (2018), Holly Herndon's *Proto* (2019) and YACHT's *Chain Tripping* (2019). YACHT's album used an AI system that had been 'trained' on the band's own back catalogue of songs, while other systems are trained on the back catalogues of entire record labels. In both cases, the songs become the input for a system that then learns from them to understand how musical phrases and elements work together. The copyright implications of this form of music use are yet to be worked out. For instance, who owns the copyright in any songs produced by an AI? Is it solely the musician who used the program to create those songs, or is it shared with the person or team who input the back catalogue data to the system, or the person or team who created the algorithms that the AI program uses? What happens when an AI creates a piece of music that, by chance, turns out to be similar to music that is already copyrighted? Who would be legally liable in such an instance?

Less controversially, perhaps, AI applications are used by streaming services to personalise playlists and auto-tag tracks with metadata, while copyright infringement services such as

Pex use AI to monitor and identify tracks that may not have licensing in place, even if the tracks have been modified or are cover versions. This allows the copyright owners to request takedown of the track or to monetise its use in some way. AI is also being used as an A&R discovery tool for the industry, with companies such as Instrumental (part-owned by Warner Music UK and Tencent) monitoring social media and playlists to identify artists whose music is gaining traction with listeners but has yet to be signed by a label or publisher. AI can also be used in music mastering to help artists create professional-sounding tracks, and by music supervisors in the advertising and media sectors to help brand sponsors and media producers find music that can be synced to advertising campaigns, films and television shows.

It is crucial for artists and their teams to fully understand the potential routes to market that they may have available to them – whether in terms of production and distribution, or in marketing, promotion or live performance. Related to this, we argue that they require a strong understanding of the complexities of music industry contracts, copyright law and revenue collection, as these underpin business strategy and need to be considered carefully in order to promote the best interests of an artist or business. The music and media industries are fast-paced sectors where the emergence of new technologies, companies and ways of working may provide fruitful opportunities for artist development and promotion. Anyone seeking to work within the music industries should keep up to date with these developments, as it is common for music industry professionals to frequently change job roles or pursue portfolio careers that see them working concurrently in more than one role. Staying informed of such developments will not only help to build a broad knowledge of the business, but will also provide relevant talking points for conversations and networking. There are many free email bulletins available, such as those from Music Business Worldwide and Complete Music Update, which can provide a helpful daily overview of key events in the music industries.

Working in the music industries, whether as an artist or an executive, is not without its challenges. However, such a career offers a rewarding combination of creativity, innovation and passion that is rarely experienced elsewhere. We hope that this book has provided our readers with new ideas, fresh perspectives and a knowledge of the industries' essential elements. We also hope that it has inspired readers to engage in the connections and conversations that make the music industries thrive.

REFERENCES

ACE (2020) 'Equality, diversity and the creative case', *Arts Council England* (www. artscouncil.org.uk/sites/default/files/download-file/ACE_DiversityReport_ Final_03032020_0.pdf).

AIF (2018) *Ten Year Report 2008–2018*. London: Association of Independent Festivals.

AIM (n.d.) 'Join as a rightsholder', *Association of Independent Music* (www.aim.org.uk/#/ pages/join-rightsholder).

Allen, Paul (2018) *Artist Management for the Music Business*, 4th ed. London: Taylor and Francis.

Alleyne, Mike (2014) 'After the storm: hipgnosis, Storm Thorgerson, and the rock album cover', *Rock Music Studies*, 1(3): 251–267.

Anderson, Benedict (2006) *Imagined Communities: Reflections on the Origins and Spread of Nationalism*, revised ed. London: Verso.

Anderson, Chris (2009) *Free: The Future of a Radical Price*. London: Random House Business Books.

Anderton, Chris (2008) 'Commercializing the carnivalesque: the V Festival and image/risk management', *Event Management*, 12(1): 39–51.

Anderton, Chris (2011) 'Music festival sponsorship: between commerce and carnival', *Arts Marketing*, 1(2): 145–58.

Anderton, Chris (2015) 'Branding, sponsorship and the music festival.' In George McKay (ed.), *The Pop Festival: History, Music, Media, Culture*, pp. 199–212. New York and London: Bloomsbury Academic.

Anderton, Chris (2019a) *Music Festivals in the UK: Beyond the Carnivalesque*. London and New York: Routledge.

Anderton, Chris (2019b) 'Risky business: the volatility and failure of outdoor music festivals in the UK', *Live Music Exchange*, February 2019 (livemusicexchange.org/blog/ risky-business-the-volatility-and-failure-of-outdoor-music-festivals-in-the-uk-chris- anderton/).

Anderton, Chris (2019c) 'Just for the fun of it? Contemporary strategies for making, distributing and gifting music.' In Marija Dumnić Vilotijević and Ivana Medić (eds.), *Contemporary Popular Music Studies: Proceedings of the 19th Conference of the Association for the Study of Popular Music*, pp. 269–277. Berlin: Springer.

Anderton, Chris (2022) 'Disruption and continuity: Covid-19, live music, and cyclic sociality.' In Chris Anderton and Sergio Pisfil (eds.), *Researching Live Music: Gigs, Tours, Concerts and Festivals*, pp. 68–83. London and New York: Routledge.

Anderton, Chris, and Chris Atton (2020) 'The absent presence of progressive rock', *Rock Music Studies*, 7(1): 8–22.

Anderton, Chris, Andrew Dubber, and Martin James (2013) *Understanding the Music Industries*. Los Angeles, CA: SAGE.

Anderton, Chris, and Sergio Pisfil (eds.) (2022) *Researching Live Music: Gigs, Tours, Concerts and Festivals*. London and New York: Routledge.

Andjelkovic, Ivana, Denis Parra, and John O'Donovan (2019) 'Moodplay: interactive music recommendation based on artists' mood similarity', *International Journal of Human-Computer Studies*, 121: 142–159.

Andrejevic, Mark (2014) 'Alienation's returns.' In Christian Fuchs and Marisol Sandoval (eds.), *Critique, Social Media and the Information Society*, pp. 179–190. Abingdon, UK: Routledge.

Arnold, Gina (2018) *Half a Million Strong: Crowds and Power from Woodstock to Coachella*. Iowa City, IA: University of Iowa Press.

Atomico (2020) 'State of diversity and inclusion', *Atomico* (2020.stateofeuropeantech.com/chapter/diversity-inclusion/article/diversity-inclusion/).

Atton, Chris (2009) 'Alternative and citizen journalism.' In Karin Wahl-Jorgensen and Thomas Hanitzsch (eds.), *The Handbook of Journalism Studies*, pp. 265–278. New York and London: Routledge.

Auslander, Philip (2008) *Liveness: Performance in a Mediatized Culture*, 2nd ed. London and New York: Routledge.

AWAL (2017) 'How to find the perfect music manager for you', *AWAL*, 16 October 2017 (www.awal.com/blog/how-to-find-the-perfect-music-manager-for-you).

Azerrad, Michael (2001) *Our Band Could Be Your Life*. New York: Little Brown.

Bailey, Zinzi D., Nancy Krieger, Madina Agénor, Jasmine Graves, Natalia Linos, and Mary T. Bassett (2017) 'Structural racism and health inequities in the USA: evidence and interventions', *The Lancet (British Edition)*, 389(10077): 1453–1463.

Bain, Katie (2018) 'Gay Black men helped create EDM: Why do straight white men dominate it?', *Billboard*, 14 June 2018 (www.billboard.com/articles/news/pride/8460757/gay-black-men-edm-influence-history).

Bain, Vick (2016) 'Addressing equality and diversity in the music industry', *Canadian Music Week* [guest blog, May 2016] (cmw.net/guest-blog-vick-bain-addressing-equality-and-diversity-in-the-music-industry/).

Bain, Vick (2019) *Counting the Music Industry: The Gender Gap. A Study of Gender Inequality in the UK Music Industry*. Self-published (vbain.co.uk/research).

Ballico, Christina, and Allan Watson (eds.) (2020) *Music Cities: Evaluating a Global Cultural Policy Concept*. Cham, Switzerland: Palgrave Macmillan.

Barabási, Albert-László (2002) *Linked: The New Science of Networks*. New York: Basic Books.

Barker, Andrew (2015) 'Is the music industry purging its record of homophobia?', *Variety*, 30 June 2015 (variety.com/2015/music/news/music-industry-homophobia-1201530923/).

Barna, Emília (2018) 'Curators as taste entrepreneurs in the digital music industries.' In Ewa Mazierska, Leslie Gillon, and Tony Rigg (eds.), *Popular Music in the Post-digital Age: Politics, Economy, Culture and Technology*, pp. 253–267. New York and London: Bloomsbury Academic.

Bartmanski, Dominik, and Ian Woodward (2018) 'Vinyl record: a cultural icon', *Consumption Markets & Culture*, 21(2): 171–177.

Barton, Laura (2004) 'Risky, thrilling and free', *The Guardian*, 16 July 2004 (www. theguardian.com/music/2004/jul/16/1).

Baskerville, David, and Tim Baskerville (2019) *Music Business Handbook and Career Guide*. Thousand Oaks, CA: Sage.

Bates, Eliot (2020) 'Vinyl as event: Record Store Day and the value-vibrant matter nexus', *Journal of Cultural Economy*, 13(6): 690–708.

Bauman, Zygmunt (2005) *Liquid Life*. Cambridge: Polity Press.

Baym, Nancy (2018) *Playing to the Crowd: Musicians, Audiences, and the Intimate Work of Connection*. New York: New York University Press.

Baym, Nancy K., and Robert Burnett (2009) 'Amateur experts: international fan labor in Swedish independent music', *International Journal of Cultural Studies*, 12(5): 433–449.

BBC (2021) 'Workforce diversity and inclusion: creating an inclusive workforce', *BBC* [website] (www.bbc.co.uk/diversity). Accessed 29 May 2021.

Beard, T. Randolph, George S. Ford, and Michael Stern (2017) 'Safe harbors and the evolution of music retailing', *Phoenix Center Policy Bulletin*, 41 (www.phoenix-center. org/PolicyBulletin/PCPB41Final.pdf).

Becker, Howard S. (1974) 'Art as collective action', *American Sociological Review*, 39(6): 767–776.

Becker, Howard S. (1976) 'Art worlds and social types', *American Behavioral Scientist*, 19: 703–715.

Behr, Adam, Matt Brennan, and Martin Cloonan (2014) 'Cultural value and cultural policy: some evidence from the world of live music', *International Journal of Cultural Policy*, 22(3): 403–418.

Behr, Adam, Matt Brennan, Martin Cloonan, Simon Frith, and Emma Webster (2016) 'Live concert performance: an ecological approach', *Rock Music Studies*, 3(1): 5–23.

Behr, Adam, and Martin Cloonan (2018) 'Going spare? Concert tickets, touring and cultural value', *International Journal of Cultural Policy*, DOI: 10.1080/10286632.2018.1431224.

Bennett, Andy, and Paula Guerra (eds.) (2019) *DIY Cultures and Underground Music Scenes*. London and New York: Routledge.

Bennett, Andy, and Richard A. Peterson (eds.) (2004) *Music Scenes: Local, Translocal and Virtual*. Nashville, TN: Vanderbilt University Press.

Berger, John (1972) *Ways of Seeing*. Harmondsworth: Penguin/BBC.

Berger, Jonah (2013) *Contagious: Why Things Catch On*. New York: Simon & Schuster.

Bernard, Jesse (2018) 'Form 696 is gone – so why is clubland still hostile to black Londoners?', *The Guardian*, 31 January 2018 (www.theguardian.com/music/2018/ jan/31/form-696-is-gone-so-why-is-clubland-still-hostile-to-black-londoners).

Bey, Hakim (1991) *T.A.Z.: The Temporary Autonomous Zone*. New York: Autonomedia.

Blake, Andrew (1997) *The Land without Music: Music, Culture and Society in Twentieth-century Britain*. Manchester: Manchester University Press.

Bonini, Tiziano, and Alessandro Gandini (2019) '"First week is editorial, second week is algorithmic": platform gatekeepers and the platformization of music curation', *Social Media + Society*, October–December 2019: 1–11.

Booms, Bernard H., and Mary Jo Bitner (1981) 'Marketing strategies and organization structures for service firms.' In James H. Donnelly and William R. George (eds.), *Marketing of Services*, pp. 47–51. Chicago, IL: American Marketing Association.

Borg, Bobby (2014) *Music Marketing for the DIY Musician: Creating and Executing a Plan of Attack on a Low Budget*. Milwaukee, WI: Hal Leonard Corporation.

Borgatti, Stephen P., Martin G. Everett, and Jeffrey C. Johnson (2013) *Analyzing Social Networks*. Newbury Park, CA: SAGE.

Bottà, Giacomo (2018) 'L'Ososphère: popular music, temporary uses and planning in Strasbourg France', *Tafter Journal*, no. 98 (no pagination) (www.tafterjournal.it/2018/01/15/lososphere-popular-music-temporary-uses-and-planning-in-strasbourg-france/).

Bourdieu, Pierre (1984) *Distinction: A Social Critique of the Judgement of Taste*. London: Routledge.

BPI (2021) 'More artists reaping the rewards of streaming, BPI data shows', *British Phonographic Industry*, 19 January 2021 (www.bpi.co.uk/news-analysis/more-artists-reaping-the-rewards-of-streaming-bpi-data-shows/).

Bregman, Peter (2012a) 'A practical plan for when you feel overwhelmed.' In Harvard Business Review (eds.), *HBR Guide to Getting the Right Work Done*, pp. 49–52. Boston, MA: Harvard Business Review.

Bregman, Peter (2012b) 'Stop multitasking.' In Harvard Business Review (eds.), *HBR Guide to Getting the Right Work Done*, pp. 63–66. Boston, MA: Harvard Business Review.

Bregman, Peter (2012c) 'Don't let long-term projects become last-minute panic.' In Harvard Business Review (eds.), *HBR Guide to Getting the Right Work Done*, pp. 57–62. Boston, MA: Harvard Business Review.

Bregman, Peter (2012d) 'An 18-minute plan for managing your day.' In Harvard Business Review (eds.), *HBR Guide to Getting the Right Work Done*, pp. 121–124. Boston, MA: Harvard Business Review.

Brennan, Matt, and Emma Webster (2010) *The UK Festival Market Report*. London: UK Festival Awards.

Bridson, Kerrie, Jody Evans, Rohit Varman, Michael Volkov, and Sean McDonald (2017) 'Questioning worth: selling out in the music industry', *European Journal of Marketing*, 51(9/10): 1650–1668.

Brown, Schuyler (2006) 'Buzz marketing: the next chapter'. In Justin Kirby and Paul Marsden (eds.), *Connected Marketing: The Viral, Buzz and Word of Mouth Revolution*, pp. 208–231. Burlington, MA: Butterworth-Heinemann.

Bull, Michael (2007) *Sound Moves: iPod Culture and Urban Experience*. London: Routledge.

Bull, Stephen (2010) *Photography*. Abingdon, UK: Routledge.

Burgess, Jean (2006) 'Hearing ordinary voices: cultural studies, vernacular creativity and digital storytelling', *Continuum*, 20(2): 201–214.

Burns, James MacGregor (1978) *Leadership*. New York and London: Harper and Row.

Byrne, David (2012) *How Music Works*. Edinburgh: Canongate Books.

Callahan, Kevin R., Gary S. Stetz, and Lynne M. Brooks (2011) *Project Management Accounting*, 2nd ed. Hoboken, NJ: Wiley.

Carah, Nicholas (2010) *Pop Brands: Branding, Popular Music, and Young People*. New York: Peter Lang.

Carah, Nicholas, and Eric Louw (2015) *Media and Society: Production, Content, Participation*. London: SAGE.

Carl, Walter J. (2006) 'What's all the buzz about? Everyday communication and the relational basis of word-of-mouth and buzz marketing practices', *Management Communication Quarterly*, 19(4): 601–634.

Carlisle, Stephen (2014) 'Copyrights last too long! (say the pirates): they don't; and why it's not changing anytime soon', *Nova Southeastern University*, 14 July 2014 (copyright. nova.edu/copyright-duration/).

Carù, Antonella, and Bernard Cova (2007) 'Consumer immersion in an experiential context.' In Antonella Carù and Bernard Cova (eds.), *Consuming Experience*, pp. 34–47. London: Routledge.

Castells, Manuel (2010) *The Rise of the Network Society*, 2nd ed. Oxford: Wiley-Blackwell.

Castells, Manuel (2013) *Communication Power*, 2nd ed. Oxford: Oxford University Press.

CDPA (1988) *Copyright, Designs and Patents Act 1988*. Legislation.gov.uk (www.legislation. gov.uk/ukpga/1988/48/section/20).

Chapple, Jon (2019) 'CTS combines 26 promoters into London-based Eventim Live', *IQ-Mag*, 6 March 2019 (www.iq-mag.net/2019/03/cts-combines-26-promoters-into-london-based-eventim-live/#.YDvFuWj7Q2w).

Chapple, Steve, and Reebee Garofalo (1977) *Rock 'n' Roll is Here to Pay: The History and Politics of the Music Industry*. Chicago, IL: NelsonHall.

Charter, David, and Alistair Dawber (2021) 'Derek Chauvin trial: racism is a stain on our soul, says Biden after Floyd conviction', *The Times*, 21 April 2021 (www.thetimes.co.uk/ article/police-officer-found-guilty-over-death-ofgeorge-floyd-hdzrs2mpt).

Cheng, Zhiyong, and Jialie Shen (2016) 'On effective location-aware music recommendation', *ACM Transactions on Information Systems*, 34(2): Article 13, 32pp.

Cheng, Zhiyong, Jialie Shen, Lei Zhu, Mohan Kankanhalli, and Liqiang Nie (2017) 'Exploiting music play sequence for music recommendation', *Proceedings of the Twenty-Sixth International Joint Conference on Artificial Intelligence* (Melbourne, Australia, 19–25 August 2017), pp. 3654–3660 (www.ijcai.org/proceedings/2017/0511.pdf).

CIM (2009) *Marketing and the 7Ps*. Maidenhead: Chartered Institute of Marketing (www. thensmc.com/sites/default/files/CIM%207Ps%20Resource.PDF).

CIPR (n.d.) 'About PR', Chartered Institute of Public Relations (www.cipr.co.uk/CIPR/ About_Us/About_PR.aspx?WebsiteKey=0379ffac-bc76-433c-9a94-56a04331bf64).

Cirillo, Francesco (2021) 'The Pomodoro® technique'. *Francescocirillo.com* [website] (francescocirillo.com/pages/pomodoro-technique). Accessed 29 May 2021.

Clarke, Michael (1982) *The Politics of Pop Festivals*. London: Junction Books.

Cloonan, Martin (2012) 'Selling the experience: the world-views of British concert promoters', *Creative Industries Journal*, 5(1): 151–170.

Cluley, Robert (2009a) 'Chained to the grassroots: the music industries and DCMS', *Cultural Trends*, 18(3): 213–225.

Cluley, Robert (2009b) 'Engineering great moments: the production of live music', *Consumption Markets and Culture*, 12(4): 373–388.

Codrea-Rado, Anna (2019) 'Music, fashion and town planning: how nightclubs change the world', *The Guardian*, 18 March 2019 (www.theguardian.com/music/2019/mar/18/nightclubs-influence-on-culture-drugs-town-planning-architecture).

Coldrick, Annabella (2019) 'Where are the missing song royalties?', *Music Business Worldwide*, 16 July 2019 (www.musicbusinessworldwide.com/where-are-the-missing-song-royalties-2/).

Coleman, John (2017) 'Faced with distraction, we need willpower: strengthen your self-control'. In Harvard Business Review (eds.), *HBR Guide to Being More Productive* [chapter 17]. Boston, MA: Harvard Business School Press.

Cooke, Chris (2017) 'Nearly half of grime fans reckon form 696 is discriminatory', *Complete Music Update*, 11 October 2017 (www.completemusicupdate.com/article/nearly-half-of-grime-fans-reckon-form-696-is-discriminatory/).

Cooke, Chris (2019) *The Song Royalties Guide*. London: Music Managers Forum.

Cooke, Chris (2020) *Dissecting the Digital Dollar*, 3rd ed. London: Music Managers Forum.

Coombs, Timothy (2012) *Ongoing Crisis Communication: Planning, Managing and Responding*. London: SAGE.

Cormany, Diane L. (2015) 'Coachella fans, online and translocal', *Journal of Popular Music Studies*, 27(2): 184–198.

Cornelissen, Joep (2017) *Corporate Communication: A Guide to Theory and Practice*, 5th ed. London: SAGE.

Coutu, Diane (2017) 'Cultivate resilience in tough times.' In Harvard Business Review (eds.), *HBR Guide to Emotional Intelligence* [chapter 22]. Boston, MA: Harvard Business Review.

Crenshaw, Dave (2018) 'Time management fundamentals', *LinkedIn Learning*, 13 August 2018 (www.linkedin.com/learning/time-management-fundamentals).

Croft, Chris (2016) 'Efficient time management', *LinkedIn Learning*, 9 August 2016 (www.linkedin.com/learning/efficient-time-management).

Croft, Malcolm (2007) *The Little Red Riders Book*. London: Anova.

Crossley, Nick (2015) *Networks of Sound, Style and Subversion: The Punk and Post-punk Worlds of Liverpool, London, Manchester and Sheffield 1975–1980*. Manchester: Manchester University Press.

Csikszentmihályi, Mihaly (1990) *Flow*. New York: Harper Perennial.

Danielsen, Anne, and Inger Helseth (2016) 'Mediated immediacy: the relationship between auditory and visual dimensions of live performance in contemporary technology-based popular music', *Rock Music Studies*, 3(1): 24–40.

DCMS (2019a) *Live Music*. Report by the UK Department of Culture, Media and Sport, 19 March 2019 (publications.parliament.uk/pa/cm201719/cmselect/cmcumeds/733/73302.htm).

DCMS (2019b) 'Committee calls for action to safeguard the future of the UK's live music industry', *UK Parliament*, 19 June 2019 (committees.parliament.uk/committee/378/digital-culture-media-and-sport-committee/news/103569/committee-calls-for-action-to-safeguard-the-future-of-the-uks-live-music-industry/).

Deacon, David (2018) 'The affect of neo-conservative politics and the externalisation of threat in Trent Reznor's post 9/11 aesthetic', *Crosstown Traffic, IASPM UK Conference* (University of Huddersfield, 3–5 September 2018).

Dee, Arne (2018) *The Survey: Facts and Figures of Music Venues in Europe*. Nantes: LIVE DMA.

Deezer (2019) 'Deezer wants artists to be paid fairly by adopting a user-centric payment system (UCPS)', *Deezer*, September 2019 (www.deezer.com/ucps).

DeNora, Tia (2000) *Music in Everyday Life*. Cambridge: Cambridge University Press.

Diabolical (2015) 'Chvrches: Every Open Eye', *Build Hollywood [Diabolical]* (www.buildhollywood.co.uk/work/chvrches-every-open-eye/).

Diabolical (2018) 'Travis Scott: Astroworld', *Build Hollywood [Diabolical]* (www.buildhollywood.co.uk/work/travis-scott-astroworld/).

Dimont, Joseph (2018) 'Royalty inequity: why music streaming services should switch to a per-subscriber model', *Hastings Law Journal*, 69: 675–700.

DJ Mag (2015) 'Resident records to expand under vinyl demand', *DJ Mag*, 30 October 2015 (djmag.com/news/resident-records-expand-under-vinyl-demand).

Dredge, Stuart (2021) 'Sony Music launches "Legacy Unrecouped Balance Program"', *Musically.com*, 11 June 2021 (https://musically.com/2021/06/11/sony-music-legacy-unrecouped-balance/).

Drengner, Jan, Steffen Jahn, and Cornelia Zanger (2011) 'Measuring event-brand congruence', *Event Management*, 15(1): 25–36.

Duffett, Mark (2013) *Understanding Fandom: An Introduction to the Study of Media Fan Culture*. New York and London: Bloomsbury.

du Gay, Paul, and Keith Negus (1994) 'The changing sites of sound: music retailing and the composition of consumers', *Media, Culture & Society*, 16(3): 395–413.

Edgar, Robert, Kirsty Fairclough-Isaacs, and Benjamin Halligan (eds.) (2013) *The Music Documentary: Acid Rock to Electropop*. Abingdon: Routledge.

Edmonds, David (2017) 'Implicit bias: Is everyone racist?', *BBC*, 5 June 2017 (www.bbc.co.uk/news/magazine-40124781).

Edwards, Lee (2012) 'Exploring the role of public relations as a cultural intermediary occupation', *Cultural Sociology*, 6(4): 438–454.

Edwards, Lee (2018) *Understanding Public Relations: Theory, Culture and Society*. London: SAGE.

Edwards Lee, and Caroline E.M. Hodges (eds.) (2011) *Public Relations, Society and Culture. Theoretical and Empirical Explorations*. Abingdon, UK: Routledge.

Ehrenreich, Barbara (2006) *Dancing in the Streets: A History of Collective Joy*. New York: Henry Holt & Co LLC.

Elkington, John (1997) *Cannibals with Forks: The Triple Bottom Line of 21st Century Business*. Stoney Creek, CT: New Society Publishers.

Eriksson, Maria, Rasmus Fleischer, Anna Johansson, Pelle Snickars, and Patrick Vonderau (2019) *Spotify Teardown: Inside the Black Box of Streaming Music*. London and Cambridge, MA: MIT Press.

Fabbri, Franco (1981) 'A theory of musical genres: two applications.' In David Horn and Phillip Tagg (eds.), *Popular Music Perspectives*, pp. 52–81. Goteborg and Exeter: International Association for the Study of Popular Music.

Fairclough, Norman (2015) *Language and Power*, 3rd ed. Abingdon, UK: Routledge.

Falassi, Alessandro (1987) 'Festival: definition and morphology.' In Alessandro Falassi (ed.), *Time Out of Time: Essays on the Festival*, pp. 1–10. Albuquerque, NM: University of New Mexico Press.

Farmiloe, Izzy, and Rhianna Cohen (2020) *The Future of Youth Culture: The Era of Monomass*. London: Dazed Media.

FEAT (2021) *Stop Touting: A Guide to Personalised Tickets in Europe*. Europe: FEAT (www.feat-alliance.org/wp-content/uploads/2021/01/FEAT-Personalised-Ticket-Guide-First-Edition.pdf).

Feldman Barrett, Lisa (2021) 'Variation is the stuff of life. So why can it make us uncomfortable?', *The Guardian*, 4 March 2021 (www.theguardian.com/commentisfree/2021/mar/04/variation-uncomfortable-embracing-difference-success-species).

Festival Insights (2018) *Festival 250 – 2017*. UK: Festival Insights & CGA (www.festivalinsights.com/2018/02/festival-250-2017-2/).

Finnegan, Ruth (1989) *The Hidden Musicians*. Cambridge: Cambridge University Press.

Fisher, Mark (2007) 'Downcast angel', *The Wire*, Issue 286: 28–31.

Fiske, John (2016) *Power Plays Power Works*, 2nd ed. Abingdon, UK: Routledge.

Fitterman-Radbill, Catherine (2017) *Introduction to the Music Industry: An Entrepreneurial Approach*, 2nd ed. New York: Routledge.

Forde, Eamonn (2016) 'Who are the most powerful people in music? Jay Z? Kanye? Beyoncé? No, it's old white men', *The Guardian*, 15 February 2016 (www.theguardian.com/music/musicblog/2016/feb/15/old-white-men-dominate-billboard-power-100-list).

Fortenberry, John L., and Peter J. McGoldrick (2020) 'Do Billboard advertisements drive customer retention?', *Journal of Advertising Research*, 60(2): 135–147.

Frith, Simon (1996) *Performing Rites: On the Value of Popular Music*. Oxford: Oxford University Press.

Frith, Simon (2001) 'The popular music industry.' In Simon Frith, Will Straw, and John Street (eds.), *The Cambridge Companion to Pop and Rock*, pp. 26–52. Cambridge: Cambridge University Press.

Frith, Simon (2015) 'Live music.' In John Shepherd and Kyle Devine (eds.), *The Routledge Reader on the Sociology of Music*, pp. 269–276. New York and London: Routledge.

Frith, Simon, Matt Brennan, Martin Cloonan, and Emma Webster (2013) *The History of Live Music in Britain, Volume 1: 1950–1967. From Dance Hall to the 100 Club*. London and New York: Routledge.

Frith, Simon, Matt Brennan, Martin Cloonan, and Emma Webster (2019) *The History of Live Music in Britain, Volume 2: 1968–1984. From Hyde Park to the Hacienda*. London and New York: Routledge.

Frith, Simon, Matt Brennan, Martin Cloonan, and Emma Webster (2021) *The History of Live Music in Britain, Volume 3: 1985–2015. From Live Aid to Live Nation*. London and New York: Routledge.

Gable, Olivia (2019) *Public Funding for Popular Musicians: What is it Good For? The Case of Momentum*. PhD thesis. The Open University.

Gable, Olivia (2020) '"A drop in the ocean"? Funding and support for UK musicians in the COVID-19 crisis', *Hypotheses.org: Working in Music*, 29 June 2020 (wim.hypotheses.org/1383).

Galuszka, Patryk (2015) 'New economy of fandom', *Popular Music and Society*, 38(1): 25–43.

Galuszka, Patryk (in press) 'Showcase festival as a gateway to foreign markets.' In Chris Anderton and Sergio Pisfil (eds.), *Researching Live Music: Gigs, Tours, Concerts and Festivals*, pp. tba. London and New York: Routledge.

GAO (2018) *Event Ticket Sale: Market Characteristics and Consumer Protection Issues.* Washington, DC: United States Government Accountability Office, April 2018.

George, Bill, Peter Sims, Andrew N. McLean, and Diana Mayer (2018) 'Discovering your authentic leadership'. In Harvard Business Review (eds.), *Authentic Leadership* [chapter 1]. Boston, MA: Harvard Business Review Press.

Gilson, Lucy L. (2015) 'Creativity in teams: processes and outcomes in creative industries.' In Candace Jones, Mark Lorenzen and Jonathan Sapsed (eds.), *The Oxford Handbook of Creative Industries*, pp. 50–74. Oxford: Oxford University Press.

Gladwell, Malcolm (2000) *The Tipping Point: How Little Things Can Make a Big Difference.* London: Little, Brown.

Gleim, Mark R., Catherine M. Johnson, and Stephanie Lawson (2019) 'Sharers and sellers: a multi-group examination of gig economy workers' perceptions', *Journal of Business Research*, 98(C): 142–152.

Goffee, Rob, and Gareth Jones (2018) 'Practice tough empathy.' In Harvard Business Review (eds.), *Authentic Leadership* [chapter 4]. Boston, MA: Harvard Business Review Press.

Goleman, Daniel (1995) *Emotional Intelligence: Why It Can Matter More Than IQ.* London: Bantam Books.

Goleman, Daniel (2011) 'What makes a leader?' In Harvard Business Review (eds.), *HBR's 10 Must Reads on Leadership*, pp. 1–22. Boston, MA: Harvard Business Review Press.

Google (2021a) 'Diversity', *Google* [website] (https://diversity.google/). Accessed 29 May 2021.

Google (2021b) 'Black Founders Fund', *Google* [website] (www.campus.co/europe/black-founders-fund/). Accessed 29 May 2021.

Grant Halvorson, Heidi (2012) 'Nine things successful people do differently.' In Harvard Business Review (eds.), *HBR Guide to Getting the Right Work Done*, pp. 9–22. Boston, MA: Harvard Business Review.

Gration, David, Charles Arcodia, Maria Raciti, and Robyn Stokes (2011) 'The blended festivalscape and its sustainability at nonurban festivals', *Event Management*, 15: 343–359.

Gritter, Lisa (2017) 'Where do you turn when the music industry skews your mental health?', *Vice*, 30 July 2017 (noisey.vice.com/en_us/article/ywg9em/where-do-you-turn-when-the-music-industry-skews-your-mental-health).

Gross, Sally, and George Musgrave (2016) *Can Music Make You Sick? Music and Depression: A Study into the Incidence of Musicians' Mental Health. Part 1: Pilot Survey.* London: Help Musicians UK (www.helpmusicians.org.uk/assets/publications/files/can_music_make_you_sick_part_1-_pilot_survey_report_2019.pdf).

Gross, Sally, and George Musgrave (2017) *A Study into the Incidence of Musicians' Mental Health. Part 2: Qualitative Study and Recommendations*. London: Help Musicians UK (www.helpmusicians.org.uk/assets/publications/files/can-music-make-you-sick-part-2-qualitative-study-1.pdf).

Grow, Kory (2014) 'Public Enemy reveal origins of name, crosshairs logo', *Rolling Stone*, 18 August 2014 (www.rollingstone.com/music/music-news/public-enemy-reveal-origins-of-name-crosshairs-logo-241248/).

Hall, Stuart (1999) 'Introduction to Part III – looking and subjectivity.' In Jessica Evans and Stuart Hall (eds.), *Visual Culture: The Reader*, pp. 309–314. London: SAGE.

Hammerness, Paul, and Margaret Moore (2017) 'Train your brain to focus.' In Harvard Business Review (eds.), *HBR Guide to Being More Productive* [chapter 16]. Boston, MA: Harvard Business School Press.

Hancox, Dan (2007) 'Only five people know I make tunes', *The Guardian*, 26 October 2007 (www.theguardian.com/music/2007/oct/26/urban).

Hand, Martin (2012) *Ubiquitous Photography*. Cambridge: Polity Press.

Hardt, Michael (1999) 'Affective Labor', *Boundary 2*, 26(2): 89–100.

Harris, Paul (2012) 'Lana Del Rey: the strange story of the star who rewrote her past', *The Guardian*, 21 January 2012 (www.theguardian.com/music/2012/jan/21/lana-del-rey-pop).

Harrison, Ann (2021) *Music: The Business*, 8th ed. London: Virgin.

Haynes, Jo, and Lee Marshall (2017) 'Beats and tweets: social media in the careers of independent musicians', *New Media and Society*, 20(5): 1973–1993.

HBR (2017) *Harvard Business Review Manager's Handbook: The 17 Skills Leaders Need to Stand Out*. Boston, MA: Harvard Business Review.

Hearsum, Paula (2012) 'A musical matter of life and death: the morality of mortality and the coverage of Amy Winehouse's death in the UK press', *Mortality* 17(2): 182–199.

Heath, Chip, and Dan Heath (2008) *Made to Stick: Why Some Ideas Take Hold and Others Come Unstuck*. London: Arrow Books.

Hebdige, Dick (1979) *Subculture: The Meaning of Style*. London: Methuen.

Hesmondhalgh, David (1998) 'Post-Punk's attempt to democratize the music industry: the success and failure of Rough Trade', *Popular Music*, 16(3): 255–274.

Hesmondhalgh, David (1999) 'Indie: the institutional politics and aesthetics of a popular music genre', *Cultural Studies*, 13(1): 34–61.

Hesmondhalgh, David (2013) *Why Music Matters*. Chichester: Wiley-Blackwell.

Hesmondhalgh, David (2019) *The Cultural Industries*, 4th ed. Los Angeles, CA: SAGE.

Hesmondhalgh, David (2020) 'Is music streaming bad for musicians? Problems of evidence and argument', *New Media & Society*, September 2020 (23pp). DOI: 10.1177/1461444820953541.

Hesmondhalgh, David, Ellis Jones, and Andreas Rauh (2019) 'Soundcloud and Bandcamp as alternative music platforms', *Social Media + Society*, October–December: 1–13.

Hirsch, Paul, M. (1990) 'Processing fads and fashions: an organization-set analysis of cultural industry systems.' In Simon Frith and Andrew Goodwin (eds.), *On Record: Rock, Pop, and the Written Word*, pp. 127–139. London and New York: Routledge.

Holt, Fabian (2010) 'The economy of live music in the digital age', *European Journal of Cultural Studies*, 13(2): 243–261.

Holt, Fabian (2012) 'Live music clubs in New York: an explorative study of cultural & organisational change', *Live Music Exchange Blog*, 8 November (livemusicexchange.org/blog/live-music-clubs-in-new-york-an-explorative-study-of-cultural-and-organisational-change-fabian-holt/).

Hopkins, Johnny (2016) *'From guest list to guest lecture to full-time academia: creative practice and creative pedagogy'*, IASPM UK & Ireland Biennial Conference: Popular Music: Creativity, Practice & Praxis (Brighton, 8–10 September 2016).

Hopkins, Johnny (2022) '"There's a crack in the Union Jack." Questioning national identity in the 1990s: the Britpop counter-narrative.' In Chris Anderton and Martin James (eds.), *Media Narratives in Popular Music*, pp. 141–160. New York and London: Bloomsbury Academic.

Hracs, Brian (2012) 'A creative industry in transition: the rise of digitally driven independent music production', *Growth and Change*, 43(3): 442–461.

Hracs, Brian (2015) 'Cultural intermediaries in the digital age: the case of independent musicians and managers in Toronto', *Regional Studies*, 49(3): 461–475.

Hracs, Brian, and Johan Jansson (2017) 'Death by streaming or vinyl revival? Exploring the spatial dynamics and value-creating strategies of independent record shops in Stockholm', *Journal of Consumer Culture*, 20(4): 478–497.

Hu, Cherie (2018) 'Tencent Music uses "tipping" to rack up revenues. Why aren't Western music streaming platforms doing the same?', *Music Business Worldwide*, 3 October 2018 (www.musicbusinessworldwide.com/tencent-music-uses-tipping-to-rack-up-revenues-why-arent-western-music-streaming-platforms-doing-the-same/).

Hull, George P., Thomas Hutchison, and Richard Strasser (2011) *The Music Business and Recording Industry*, 3rd ed. New York and London: Routledge.

Hutchison, Tom, Amy Macy, and Paul Allen (2010) *Record Label Marketing*, 2nd ed. Oxford: Focal Press/Elsevier.

ICC (International Chamber of Commerce) (2003) *ICC International Code on Sponsorship* (https://web.archive.org/web/20140611213212/www.sponsorship.org/freePapers/fp01.pdf).

ICE Services (2019) 'ICE joins forces with customers to drive best practice "clean claiming" on digital royalties', *ICE Blog*, 22 July 2019 (www.iceservices.com/blog/online-processing/ice-joins-forces-with-customers-to-drive-best-practice-clean-claiming-on-digital-royalties/).

IEG (2000) 'Year one of IRL title builds traffic, awareness for Northern Light', *IEG Sponsorship Report*, 19(23): 1–3.

IEG (2019) *Music Sponsorship 2018* (www.sponsorship.com/Latest-Thinking/Sponsorship-Infographics/Music-Sponsorship-2018-$1-61-Billion.aspx).

IFPI (2021) *Global Music Report 2021*. London: International Federation of the Phonographic Industries (https://gmr2021.ifpi.org/assets/GMR2021_State%20of%20the%20Industry.pdf).

Ingham, Tim (2016) 'Darius Van Arman: Majors "too often abuse their scale advantage"', *Music Business Worldwide*, 15 February 2016 (www.musicbusinessworldwide.com/darius-van-arman-majors-too-often-abuse-their-scale-advantage).

Ingham, Tim (2018) 'Can Kobalt's AWAL rewrite the rules of A&R', *Music Business Worldwide*, 9 July 2018 (www.musicbusinessworldwide.com/can-kobalts-awal-rewrite-the-rules-of-ar/).

Ingham, Tim (2019) '"Masters are owned by [the] artist": Chance The Rapper manager Pat Corcoran inks "unprecedented" deal with Warner Records for 99 Neighbors', *Music Business Worldwide*, 1 August 2019 (www.musicbusinessworldwide.com/masters-are-owned-by-the-artist-chance-the-rapper-manager-pat-corcoran-inks-unprecedented-deal-with-warner-records-for-99-neighbors/).

Ingham, Tim (2020a) 'Spotify dreams of artists making a living. It probably won't come true', *Rolling Stone*, 3 August 2020 (www.rollingstone.com/pro/features/spotify-million-artists-royalties-1038408/).

Ingham, Tim (2020b) 'BMG pledges to review historical record contracts "mindful of the music industry's shameful treatment of black artists"', *Music Business Worldwide*, 11 June 2020 (www.musicbusinessworldwide.com/bmg-to-review-historic-record-contracts-mindful-of-the-music-industrys-shameful-treatment-of-black-artists/).

Ingham, Tim (2021a) 'TikTok users watch the app for an average of 89 minutes per day – and there's 732 million of them worldwide', *Music Business Worldwide*, 14 April 2021 (www.musicbusinessworldwide.com/tiktok-users-watch-the-app-for-an-average-of-89-minutes-per-day-and-theres-732m-of-them-worldwide/).

Ingham, Tim (2021b) 'Over 60,000 tracks are now uploaded to Spotify every day. That's nearly one per second', *Music Business Worldwide*, 24 February 2021 (www.musicbusinessworldwide.com/over-60000-tracks-are-now-uploaded-to-spotify-daily-thats-nearly-one-per-second/).

IQ-mag (2020) 'Live music down 64% this year – but will rebound in 2021', *IQ-Mag*, 10 September 2020 (www.iq-mag.net/2020/09/live-music-down-64-this-year-but-rebound-2021-pwc/#.YDt6m2j7Q2w).

ISM (2018) 'Save Music campaign asks', *Incorporated Society of Musicians* (www.ism.org/savemusic/campaign-asks).

Izundu, Chi Chi (2017) 'Is the threat of a copyright lawsuit stifling music?', *BBC News*, 12 July 2017 (www.bbc.co.uk/news/entertainment-arts-40560477).

James, Malcolm (2021) *Sonic Intimacy*. New York and London: Bloomsbury Academic.

Jenkins, Amanda (2019) 'Copyright breakdown: the Music Modernization Act', *Library of Congress* [blog], 5 February 2019 (blogs.loc.gov/now-see-hear/2019/02/copyright-breakdown-the-music-modernization-act/).

Jenkins, Henry (2006) *Convergence Culture: Where Old and New Media Collide*. New York: New York University Press.

Jenkins, Henry, Sam Ford, and Joshua Green (2013) *Spreadable Media: Creating Value and Meaning in a Networked Culture*. New York: New York University Press.

Jobber, David, and John Fahy (2009) *Foundations of Marketing*. London: McGraw-Hill Education.

Jones, Graham (2010) *Last Shop Standing: Whatever Happened to Record Shops?* London: Proper Music Publishing.

Jones, Michael L. (2012) *The Music Industries: From Conception to Consumption*. London: Palgrave Macmillan.

Jones, Rhian (2017) 'Tobe Onwuka: "It's easy to look at labels with rose-tinted glasses. That's not the reality"', *Music Business Worldwide*, 2 March 2017 (www.musicbusinessworldwide.com/easy-look-labels-rose-tinted-glasses-thats-not-reality/).

Jopling, Keith (2020) 'Radio is switched on again', *MIDiA Research*, 9 April 2020 (www.midiaresearch.com/blog/radio-is-switched-on-again).

Judkins, Rod (2015) *The Art of Creative Thinking*. London: Sceptre.

Julier, Guy (2006) 'From visual culture to design culture', *Design Issues*, 22(1): 64–76.

Kanaar, Nick (2007) 'Management Agreements.' In Richard Verow, Estelle Overs and Vincent Scheurer (eds.), *Entertainment Law Handbook*. London: The Law Society.

Karakayali, Nedim, Burc Kostem, and Idil Galip (2018) 'Recommendation systems as technologies of the self: algorithmic control and the formation of music taste', *Theory, Culture & Society*, 35(2): 3–24.

Kennell, James, and Rebekah Sitz (2010) 'Greening Bonnaroo: exploring the rhetoric and the reality of a sustainable festival through micro-ethnographic methods', in *Global Events Congress IV* (Leeds, UK, 14–16 July 2010).

Kielich, Gabrielle (2022) 'Fulfilling the hospitality rider: working practices and issues in a tour's supply chain.' In Chris Anderton and Sergio Pisfil (eds.), *Researching Live Music: Gigs, Tours, Concerts and Festivals*, pp. 115–126. London and New York: Routledge.

King Gizzard and the Lizard Wizard (2017) 'Polygondwanaland', *Artist's Facebook* page, 13 November 2017. (www.facebook.com/permalink.php?story_fbid=1778783645467864&id=168329496513295).

Klein, Bethany (2020) *Selling Out: Culture, Commerce and Popular Music*. New York and London: Bloomsbury.

Klein, Naomi (2010) *No Logo*, 10th anniversary edition. London: Flamingo.

Klein, Zachary H. (2010) 'Who's the boss? The need for regulation of the ticketing industry', *Brooklyn Journal of Corporate, Financial and Commercial Law*, 5(1): 185–214.

Krueger, Alan B. (2019) *Rockonomics: What the Music Industry Can Teach Us about Economics (and Our Future)*. London: John Murray.

Laing, Dave (2004) 'The three Woodstocks and the live music scene.' In Andy Bennett (ed.), *Remembering Woodstock*, pp. 1–17. Aldershot: Ashgate.

Laing, Dave (2006) 'Anglo-American music journalism: texts and contexts.' In Andy Bennett, Barry Shank, and Jason Toynbee (eds.), *The Popular Music Studies Reader*, pp. 333–340. Abingdon, UK: Routledge.

Laing, Dave (2015) *One Chord Wonders: Power and Meaning in Punk Rock*, 2nd ed. Oakland, CA: PM Press.

Langley, Paul, and Andrew Leyshon (2017) 'Platform capitalism: the intermediation and capitalisation of digital economic circulation', *Finance and Society*, 3(1): 11–31.

Lauterborn, Bob (1990) 'New marketing litany: four P's passe; C-words take over', *Advertising Age*, 61(41): 26.

Levine, Lawrence (1988) *Highbrow/Lowbrow: The Emergence of Cultural Hierarchy in America*. Cambridge, MA: Harvard University Press.

Liao, Shannon (2019) 'Fortnite has an exclusive K-pop skin for those who preorder any Galaxy S10 phone: K-pop meets gaming again', *The Verge*, 20 February 2019 (www.theverge.com/2019/2/20/18233766/fortnite-k-pop-skin-exclusive-galaxy-s10-plus-preorder).

Lie, John (2012) 'What is the K in K-pop? South Korean popular music, the culture industry, and national identity', *Korea Observer*, 43(3): 339–363.

Lieb, Kristin J. (2018) *Gender, Branding and the Modern Music Industry: The Social Construction of Female Popular Music Stars*. New York and London: Routledge.

Lizé, Wenceslas (2016) 'Artistic work intermediaries as value producers: agents, managers, tourneurs and the acquisition of symbolic capital in popular music', *Poetics*, 59: 35–49.

Lynn, Guy, and George Greenwood (2018) 'Musicians hit by "management scam"', *BBC News*, 29 March 2018 (www.bbc.com/news/uk-england-london-43540298).

Maasø, Arnt (2014) 'User-centric settlement for music streaming', *Clouds & Concerts research group*, University of Oslo, Norway (www.hf.uio.no/imv/forskning/prosjekter/skyogscene/publikasjoner/usercentric-cloudsandconcerts-report.pdf).

Machin, David (2010) *Analysing Popular Music: Image, Sound and Text*. London: SAGE.

Macmillan, Fiona (2015) 'Copyright, the creative industries and the public domain.' In Candace Jones, Mark Lorenzen and Jonathan Sapsed (eds.), *The Oxford Handbook of Creative Industries*, pp. 439–55. Oxford: Oxford University Press.

Makagon, Daniel (2015) *Underground: The Subterranean Culture of DIY Punk Shows*. Portland, OR: Microcosm Publishing.

Manovich, Lev (2018) '100 billion data rows per second: media analytics in the early 21st century', *International Journal of Communication*, 12: 473–488.

Marino, Gabriele (2017) 'The (un)masked bard: Burial's denied profile and the memory of English underground music.' In Lee Brooks, Mark Donnelly, and Richard Mills (eds.), *Mad Dogs and Englishness: Popular Music and English Identities*, pp. 174–192. New York and London: Bloomsbury Academic.

Marshall, Lee (2013) 'The structural functions of stardom in the recording industry', *Popular Music and Society*, 36(5): 578–596.

Mazierska, Ewa, Les Gillon and Tony Rigg (eds.) (2020) *The Future of Live Music*. New York and London: Bloomsbury Academic.

McCarthy, E. Jerome (1960/1975) *Basic Marketing: A Managerial Approach*, 5th ed. Homewood, IL: Richard D. Irwin.

McGilchrist, Sonya (2011) 'Music "releases mood-enhancing chemical in the brain"', *BBC*, 9 January 2011 (www.bbc.co.uk/news/health-12135590).

McKay, George (2000) *Glastonbury: A Very English Fair*. London: Victor Gollancz.

McKee, Annie (2017) 'How to help someone develop emotional intelligence.' In Harvard Business Review (eds.), *HBR Guide to Emotional Intelligence* [chapter 26]. Boston, MA: Harvard Business Review.

McKelvey, Fenwick, and Robert Hunt (2019) 'Discoverability: toward a definition of content discovery through platforms', *Social Media + Society*, January–March: 1–15.

McLaney, Eddie, and Peter Atrill (2020) *Accounting and Finance: An Introduction*, 10th ed. Harlow, UK: Pearson Education.

McNeir, Owen (2016) 'Not all bad news', *Arts Professional*, issue 293 (www.artsprofessional. co.uk/magazine/293/feature/not-all-bad-news).

Measham, Fiona (2016) 'Time to test: the festival drug report – Part II', *Volteface Magazine* (volteface.me/features/the-festival-drug-report-part-ii/).

Meier, Leslie M. (2017) *Popular Music as Promotion: Music and Branding in the Digital Age*. Cambridge: Polity Press.

Michault, Niko (2019) *Lecture at Solent University, Southampton*, 29 October 2019.

Minsker, Evan (2021) 'Pussy Riot share AR video for new song "Panic Attack"', *Pitchfork*, 11 March 2021 (pitchfork.com/news/pussy-riot-share-ar-video-for-new-song-panic-attack-watch/).

MLC (2021) 'The Mechanical Licensing Collective receives $424 million in historical unmatched royalties from digital service providers', *theMLC.com*, 16 February 2021 (www.themlc.com/press/mechanical-licensing-collective-receives-424-million-historical-unmatched-royalties-digital).

MMF (2017) *MMF Code of Practice and Training Framework*. London: Music Managers Forum (themmf.net/site/wp-content/uploads/2017/09/Code-of-Practice-and-Training-Framework-MMF-UK-2017.pdf).

MMF (2019a) *The Fan Data Guide*. London: Music Managers Forum (themmf.net/site/wp-content/uploads/2019/01/MMF-Fan-Data-Guide.pdf).

MMF (2019b) *Managing Expectations*. London: Music Managers Forum.

MMF (2019c) *The $ong Royalties Guide*. London: Music Managers Forum (themmf.net/site/wp-content/uploads/2019/05/mmf_songroyaltiesguide-1.pdf).

MMF (2020) *MMF Code of Practice*. London: Music Managers Forum (themmf.net/about/code-of-practice).

MMF and Music Support (2017) *The Music Managers Guide to Mental Health*. London: Music Managers Forum (themmf.net/site/wp-content/uploads/2017/07/Managers-Guide-to-Mental-Health-Online-New-v.pdf).

Mokoena, Tshepo (2015) 'Riches to rags: a brief history of bankruptcy in pop', *The Guardian*, 15 July 2015 (www.theguardian.com/music/musicblog/2015/jul/15/a-history-of-bankruptcy-in-pop-50-cent-marvin-gaye-willie-nelson-tlc-mc-hammer).

Mollerup, Per (1997) *Marks of Excellence: History and Taxonomy of Trademarks*. London: Phaidon.

Montgomery, James (2007) 'Weird web trail: conspiracy theory – or marketing for Nine Inch Nails LP?', *MTV.com*, 15 February 2007 (www.mtv.com/news/1552470/weird-web-trail-conspiracy-theory-or-marketing-for-nine-inch-nails-lp/).

Morris, Jeremy Wade (2014) 'Artists as entrepreneurs, fans as workers', *Popular Music and Society*, 37(3): 273–290.

Morris, Natalie (2021) '"Your Blackness is dictated": how anti-Black racism still impacts the music industry', *Metro*, 9 March 2021 (metro.co.uk/2021/03/09/the-problem-with-anti-black-racism-in-the-music-industry-14205952/).

Morrow, Guy (2009) 'Radiohead's managerial creativity', *Convergence*, 15(2): 161–176.

Morrow, Guy (2018a) *Artist Management: Agility in the Creative and Cultural Industries*. London: Routledge.

Morrow, Guy (2018b) 'Distributed agility: artist co-management in the music attention economy', *International Journal of Arts Management*, 20(3): 38–48.

Morrow, Guy (2020) *Designing for the Music Business*. Cham, Switzerland: Springer International.

Mortimer, Julie Holland, Chris Nosko, and Alan Sorensen (2012) 'Supply responses to digital distribution: recorded music and live performances', *Information Economics and Policy*, 24(1): 3–14.

Muikku, Jari (2017) *Pro Rata and User Centric Distribution Models: A Comparative Study*. Helsinki: Digital Media Finland (www.fim-musicians.org/wp-content/uploads/prorata-vs-user-centric-models-study-2018.pdf).

Mulligan, Mark (2018) *Awakening: The Music Industry in the Digital Age*. London: MIDiA Research.

Mulligan, Mark (2021a) *'Global music subscriber market shares Q1 2021'*, MIDiA Research blog, 9 July 2021 (www.midiaresearch.com/blog/global-music-subscriber-market-shares-q1-2021).

Mulligan, Mark (2021b) 'Connecting the music business dots in 2021', *Hypebot*, 8 March 2021 (www.hypebot.com/hypebot/2021/03/connecting-the-music-business-dots-in-2021-mark-mulligan.html).

Mulligan, Mark (2021c) 'Virtual concerts: a new video format', *Musicindustryblog.com*, 8 January 2021 (musicindustryblog.wordpress.com/2021/01/08/virtual-concerts-a-new-video-format/).

Mulligan, Mark, Karol Severin, and Keith Jopling (2021) *Music and Gaming: A New Way to Play*. London: MIDiA Research (midiaresearch.com/reports/music-and-gaming-a-new-way-to-play).

Music & Copyright (2021) 'UMG and SME put the market share squeeze on WMG and the independent sector', *Music & Copyright* [blog], 21 April 2021 (musicandcopyright.wordpress.com/tag/market-share/).

Music Business Worldwide (2018) 'When superstars land here, we can handle it', *Music Business Worldwide*, 18 May 2018 (www.musicbusinessworldwide.com/when-superstars-land-here-we-can-handle-it/).

Musicians' Union (2021) 'We welcome Spotify's drive for clarity in streaming finances', *Musicians' Union* [website], 18 March 2021 (musiciansunion.org.uk/all-news-and-features/we-welcome-spotify-s-drive-for-clarity-in-streaming-finances).

Negus, Keith (1992) *Producing Pop: Culture and Conflict in the Popular Music Industry*. London: Arnold.

Negus, Keith (1996) *Popular Music in Theory. An Introduction*. Cambridge: Polity Press.

Negus, Keith (1999) *Music Genres and Corporate Cultures*. London: Routledge.

Negus, Keith (2019) 'From creator to data: the post-record music industry and the digital conglomerates', *Media, Culture & Society*, 41(3): 367–384.

Nichols, Paul (2019) 'PRS in the Middle-East', *M Magazine*, 8 April 2019 (www.prsformusic.com/m-magazine/news/prs-in-the-middle-east/).

Nickels, William G., and Marvin A. Jolson (1976) 'Packaging – the fifth P in the marketing mix', *Advanced Management Journal, Winter*: 13–21.

Nieborg, David B., and Thomas Poell (2018) 'The platformization of cultural production: theorizing the contingent cultural commodity', *New Media & Society*, 20(11): 4275–4292.

Nita, Maria, and Sharif Gemie (2019) 'Counterculture, local authorities and British Christianity at the Windsor and Watchfield free festivals', *Twentieth Century British History*, DOI: 10.1093/tcbh/hwy053.

Ofcom (2019) *Media Nations: UK 2019*. OFCOM, 7 August 2019 (www.ofcom.org.uk/__data/assets/pdf_file/0019/160714/media-nations-2019-uk-report.pdf).

Ogden, James R., Denise T. Ogden, and Karl Long (2011) 'Music marketing: a history and landscape', *Journal of Retailing and Consumer Services*, 18(2): 120–125.

OH, Parris (2021) 'Identity beyond commodity: queerness in mainstream music', *M Magazine*, 17 June 2021 (www.prsformusic.com/m-magazine/features/identity-beyond-commodity-queerness-in-mainstream-music/).

Oliver, Paul G. (2010) 'The DIY artist: issues of sustainability within local music scenes', *Management Decision*, 48(9): 1422–1432.

Olusoga, David (2021) 'The poisonously patronising Sewell report is historically illiterate', *The Guardian*, 2 April 2021 (www.theguardian.com/commentisfree/2021/apr/02/sewell-race-report-historical-young-people-britain).

O'Reilly, Daragh, Gretchen Larsen, and Krzysztof Jubacki (2013) *Music, Markets and Consumption*. Oxford: Goodfellow Publishers.

Osborne, Richard (2012) *Vinyl: The History of the Analogue Record*. Farnham: Ashgate.

Osborne, Richard (2021) '"I am a one in ten": success ratios in the recording industry.' In Richard Osborne and Dave Laing (eds.), *Music by Numbers: The Use and Abuse of Statistics in the Music Industries*, pp. 56–72. Bristol and Chicago, IL: Intellect.

Page, Will, and Chris Carey (2009) 'Adding up the music industry for 2008', *Economic Insight*, Issue 15. London: PRS for Music.

Paine, Andre (2021a) 'DCMS inquiry: YouTube defends its record on royalties and says it can be No.1 for streaming revenue', *Music Week*, 10 February 2021 (www.musicweek.com/digital/read/dcms-inquiry-youtube-defends-its-record-on-royalties-and-says-it-can-be-no-1-for-streaming-revenue/082582).

Paine, Andre (2021b) 'Scruff Of The Neck teams with Twitch on livestream series from Manchester', *Music Week*, 18 January 2021 (www.musicweek.com/digital/read/scruff-of-the-neck-teams-with-twitch-on-livestream-series-from-manchester/082406).

Paine, Andre (2021c) 'Magic moments: MPs grill CEOs on the economics of streaming and artist royalties', *Music Week*, 19 January 2021 (www.musicweek.com/digital/read/magic-moments-mps-grill-ceos-on-the-economics-of-streaming-and-artist-royalties/082427).

Paine, Andre (2021d) 'Beggars' Rupert Skellett tells MPs that majors should double streaming royalty rates', *Music Week*, 4 February 2021 (www.musicweek.com/labels/read/beggars-rupert-skellett-tells-mps-that-majors-should-double-streaming-royalty-rates/082539).

Paine, Andre (2021e) 'MMF's Annabella Coldrick calls on music industry to tackle streaming "inequalities & dysfunctions"', *Music Week*, 22 March 2021 (www.musicweek.com/management/read/mmf-s-annabella-coldrick-calls-on-music-industry-to-tackle-streaming-inequalities-dysfunctions/082879).

Pariser, Eli (2011) *The Filter Bubble: How the New Personalized Web is Changing What We Read and How We Think*. New York: Penguin Press.

Partridge, Chris (2006) 'The spiritual and the revolutionary: alternative spirituality, British free festivals, and the emergence of rave culture', *Culture & Religion*, 7(1): 41–60.

Passman, Donald (2019) *All You Need to Know about the Music Business*, 10th ed. New York: Simon & Schuster.

Percival, J. Mark (2011) 'Music radio and the record industry: songs, sounds, and power', *Popular Music and Society*, 34(4): 455–473.

Peterson, Richard A. (ed.) (1976) *The Production of Culture*. Beverley Hills, CA and London: SAGE.

Peterson, Richard A., and Narasimhan Anand (2004) 'The production of culture perspective', *Annual Review of Sociology*, 30: 311–334.

Phillips, Simon (2014) *The Complete Guide to Professional Networking*. London: Kogan Page.

PIAS (2016) '"We need to believe what we're working on is making the world better"', *The Independent Echo Blog (PIAS)*, 9 November 2016 (www.piasgroup.net/blog/we-need-to-believe-what-were-working-on-is-making-the-world-better/).

Pine, Joseph II, and James H. Gilmore (2011) *The Experience Economy*, updated ed. Boston, MA: Harvard Business Review Press.

Pink, Daniel H. (2013) *To Sell is Human: The Surprising Truth about Persuading, Convincing, and Influencing Others*. New York and Edinburgh: Canongate Books.

Pollstar (2019) 'Worldwide ticket sales: top 100 promoters, year end 2019', *Pollstar.com*, December 2019 (www.pollstar.com/Chart/2019/12/2019WorldwideTicketSalesTop100Promoters_796.pdf).

Pollstar (2020) 'Worldwide ticket sales: top 100 promoters, year end 2020', *Pollstar.com*, December 2020 (www.pollstar.com/Chart/2020/12/YEtop100Promoters_920.pdf).

Powers, Ann (2007) 'Nine Inch Nails: reset to "Year Zero"', *Los Angeles Times*, 17 April 2007 (www.latimes.com/archives/la-xpm-2007-apr-17-et-nails17-story.html).

Prey, Robert (2016) 'Musica analytica: the datafication of listening.' In Raphael Nowak and Andrew Whelan (eds.), *Networked Music Cultures*, pp. 31–48. London: Palgrave.

Prey, Robert (2018) 'Nothing personal: algorithmic individuation on music streaming platforms', *Media, Culture & Society*, 40(7): 1086–1100.

PRS Foundation (n.d.) 'Momentum guidance and FAQs', *PRS for Music Foundation* [website] (prsfoundation.com/funding-support/funding-music-creators/next-steps/momentum-music-fund/guidance-and-faqs/). Accessed 29 May 2021.

PRS Foundation (2021a) 'Power Up Participant Programme', *PRS for Music Foundation* [website] (prsfoundation.com/power-up-participant-programme/). Accessed 29 May 2021.

PRS Foundation (2021b) 'Evidence of need', *PRS for Music Foundation* [website] (prsfoundation.com/power-up-evidence-of-need/). Accessed 29 May 2021.

PRS Foundation (2021c) 'Power Up partners', *PRS for Music Foundation* [website] (prsfoundation.com/power-up-partners/). Accessed 29 May 2021.

Rackham, Jason (2016) 'Why an independent label is nearly always the best choice for artists', *The Independent Echo Blog (PIAS)*, 8 November 2016 (www.piasgroup.net/blog/independent-label-nearly-always-best-choice-artists/).

Rambarran, Shara (2021) *Virtual Music: Sound, Music and Image in the Digital Era*. London: Bloomsbury Academic.

Ravenscroft Neil, and Paul Gilchrist (2009) 'Spaces of transgression: governance, discipline and reworking the carnivalesque', *Leisure Studies*, 28(1): 35–49.

Rennie, Steve (2015) *'A&R checklist with Nick Raphael Capitol Records UK president'*, 13 May 2015 (www.youtube.com/watch?v=JdMrN8unP0M).

Rennie, Steve (2016) *An Insider's Guide to Today's Music Biz 04: Building a Professional Team* (lynda.com/Music-Business-tutorials/Insiders-Guide-Todays-Music-Biz-04-Building-Professional-Team/450274-2.html).

Resnikoff, Paul (2014a) 'Global Repertoire Database declared a global failure...', *Digital Music News*, 10 July 2014 (www.digitalmusicnews.com/2014/07/10/global-repertoire-database-declared-global-failure/).

Resnikoff, Paul (2014b) 'How streaming services are screwing Lady Gaga (and every other artist)', *Digital Music News*, 10 June 2014 (www.digitalmusicnews.com/2014/06/10/streamingservices-screwing-lady-gaga-every-artist/).

Reuters (2021) 'KKR bets $200 million on OneRepublic frontman Ryan Tedder's catalog', *Reuters*, 11 January 2021 (www.reuters.com/article/us-kkr-ryan-tedder-idUSKBN29G1FI).

Reynolds, Simon (2017) 'Why Burial's Untrue is the most important electronic album of the century so far', *Pitchfork*, 26 October 2017 (pitchfork.com/features/article/why-burials-untrue-is-the-most-important-electronic-album-of-the-century-so-far/).

Ries, Al, and Laura Ries (2004) *The Fall of Advertising and the Rise of PR*. New York: Harper Collins.

Robehmed, Natalie (2013) 'Rapper Nipsey Hussle and the $100 mixtape', *Forbes.com*, 6 November 2013 (www.forbes.com/sites/natalierobehmed/2013/11/06/rapper-nipsey-hussle-and-the-100-mixtape/).

Roberts, Dave (2017) 'We've never disagreed over anything major. 99% of the time we think the same way', *Music Business Worldwide*, 6 September 2017 (www.musicbusinessworldwide.com/stuart-camp-ed-sheeran-weve-never-disagreed-over-anything-major-99-of-the-time-we-think-the-same-way/).

Robinson, Roxy (2015a) *Music Festivals and the Politics of Participation*. Farnham: Ashgate.

Robinson, Roxy (2015b) 'No spectators! The art of participation, from Burning Man to boutique festivals in Britain.' In George McKay (ed.), *The Pop Festival: History, Music, Media, Culture*, pp. 165–181. New York and London: Bloomsbury Academic.

Robinson, Sandra L., and Kira Schabram (2017) 'What to do if you're a toxic handler.' In Harvard Business Review (eds.), *HBR Guide to Emotional Intelligence* [chapter 18]. Boston, MA: Harvard Business Review.

Rock, Mick (1995) *A Photographic Record 1969–1980*. Iver Heath, UK: Century 22.

Rojek, Chris (2011) *Pop Music, Pop Culture*. Cambridge: Polity Press.

Rose, Don (2005) 'Indie labels are seeking their fair share', *Billboard*, 13 August 2005.

Rumens, Nick, and John Broomfield (2014) 'Gay men in the performing arts: performing sexualities within "gay-friendly" work contexts', *Organization*, 21(3): 365–382.

Ryan, Bill (1992) *Making Capital From Culture: The Corporate Form of Capitalist Cultural Production*. Berlin and New York: Walter de Gruyter.

Rys, Dan (2016) 'Why superstar artists like Beyoncé and Bruno Mars are replacing powerful managers with salaried staffers', *Billboard.com*, 14 July 2016 (www.billboard.com/biz/articles/news/legal-and-management/7438501/why-superstar-artists-like-beyonce-and-bruno-mars-are).

Sacks, Oliver (2008) *Musicophilia: Tales of Music and the Brain*. London: Picador.

Savage, Jon (1989) 'The age of plunder' [originally published in *The Face*, No. 23, January 1983]. In Angela McRobbie (ed.), *Zoot Suits and Second-Hand Dresses: An Anthology of Fashion and Music*, pp. 169–180. London: Macmillan Education.

Savage, Mark (2018) 'Katy Perry in "tough conversations" with her record label', *BBC News*, 16 January 2018 (www.bbc.co.uk/news/entertainment-arts-42705445).

Savage, Mark (2021) 'To make it in music, be prepared for the pitfalls', *BBC*, 3 March 2021 (www.bbc.co.uk/news/entertainment-arts-56242568).

Schwartz, Tony (2012) 'Power through your day in 90-minute cycles.' In Harvard Business Review (eds.), *HBR Guide to Getting the Right Work Done*, pp. 117–120. Boston, MA: Harvard Business Review.

Seabrook, John (2015) *The Song Machine: Inside the Hit Factory*. London: Jonathan Cape.

Serazio, Michael (2013) *Your Ad Here: The Cool Sell of Guerrilla Marketing*. New York: New York University Press.

Scoullar, Jessie (2015) 'How to…engage with fans online', *M Magazine*, 3 March 2015 (www.prsformusic.com/m-magazine/how-to/engage-fans-online/).

Shambala (n.d.) 'Our principles', *Shambala* [official website] (www.shambalafestival.org/essential-info/our-guiding-principles/). Accessed 11 December 2021.

Shanley, Patrick (2019) '"Fortnite" CEO isn't worried about competing with Netflix, touts Game Store plans', *Hollywood Reporter*, 20 March 2019 (www.hollywoodreporter.com/news/fortnite-ceo-isnt-worried-competing-netflix-touts-game-store-plans-1196050).

Shanley, Patrick (2020) 'Travis Scott's "Fortnite" in-game concert draws more than 12M concurrent viewers', *Billboard*, 27 April 2020 (www.billboard.com/articles/columns/hip-hop/9366303/travis-scott-fortnite-in-game-concert-draws-12-million-viewers).

Shuhong, Fan (2019) 'Idol hands: how China's super fan groups make and break stars via the multi-million dollar "fan economy"', *Radiichina.com*, 7 January 2019 (radiichina.com/idol-hands-how-chinas-super-fan-groups-make-and-break-stars-in-the-multi-million-dollar-fan-economy/).

Shuker, Roy (2016) *Understanding Popular Music Culture*, 5th ed. London and New York: Routledge.

Singleton, Micah (2015) 'This was Sony Music's contract with Spotify. The details the major labels don't want you to see', *The Verge*, 19 May 2015 (www.theverge.com/2015/5/19/8621581/sony-music-spotify-contract).

Sloane, Paul (2017) *The Leader's Guide to Lateral Thinking Skills*, 3rd ed. London: Kogan Page.

Smith, Andrew (2012) *Events and Urban Regeneration: The Strategic Use of Events to Revitalise Cities*. London: Routledge.

Smith, Stacy L., Carmen Lee, Marc Choueiti, Katherine Pieper, Zoe Moore, Dana Dinh, and Artur Tofan (2021a) 'Inclusion in the music business: gender & race/ethnicity across executives, artists & talent teams', *USC Annenberg Inclusion Initiative* (assets. uscannenberg.org/docs/aii-inclusion-music-industry-2021-06-14.pdf).

Smith, Stacy L., Katherine Pieper, Marc Choueiti, Karla Hernandez, and Kevin Yao (2021b) 'Inclusion in the recording studio?', *USC Annenberg Inclusion Initiative* (assets. uscannenberg.org/docs/aii-inclusion-recording-studio2021.pdf).

Songtrust (2019) *The Modern Guide to Music Publishing*. Songtrust.com (www.songtrust. com/the-modern-guide-to-music-publishing).

Stanley, Bob (2009) 'Will the indie chart rise again?', *The Guardian*, 31 July 2009 (www. theguardian.com/music/2009/jul/31/indie-chart-rise-again).

Stassen, Murray (2020a) 'Ingrooves has built its own AI music marketing technology – and been granted a patent for it', *Music Business Worldwide*, 24 September 2020 (www.musicbusinessworldwide.com/ingrooves-has-built-its-own-ai-music-marketing-technology-and-been-granted-a-patent-for-it/).

Stassen, Murray (2020b) 'BMG publishes results of historic royalties review, pledges action and invites other labels to probe for evidence of racial disadvantage', *Music Business Worldwide*, 18 December 2020 (www.musicbusinessworldwide.com/ bmg-pledges-action-on-results-of-historic-royalties-review/).

Stassen, Murray (2021a) 'YouTube says it paid the music industry over $4 bn in the last 12 months', *Music Business Worldwide*, 2 June 2021 (www.musicbusinessworldwide.com/ youtube-says-it-paid-the-music-industry-over-4bn-in-the-last-12-months/).

Stassen, Murray (2021b) 'Here's what women are earning (compared to men) in the UK music industry', *Music Business Worldwide*, 5 October 2021 (www.musicbusinessworldwide. com/heres-what-the-three-major-music-companies-pay-women-compared-to-men-in-the-uk/).

Statt, Nick (2019) 'Fortnite's Marshmello concert was a bizarre and exciting glimpse of the future: a live concert inside a video game feels like the future', *The Verge*, 2 February 2019 (www.theverge.com/2019/2/2/18208223/ fortnite-epic-games-marshmello-concert-exciting-bizarre-future-music).

Steyn, Eleanor (2020) 'Qatar Airways grounded by English court in PRS copyright claim', *Simkins*, 29 September 2020 (www.simkins.com/2020/09/qatar-airways-grounded-by-english-court-in-prs-copyright-claim/).

Strachan, Rob (2007) 'Micro-independent record labels in the UK: discourse, DIY cultural production and the music industry', *European Journal of Cultural Studies*, 10(2): 245–265.

StubHub (2019) 'Fastest growing festivals', *StubHub.com* (www.stubhub.co.uk/ fastest-growing-festivals/).

Tan, Joanna (2021) 'China orders Tencent to give up exclusive music licensing rights as crackdown continues', *CNBC*, 24 July 2021 (www.cnbc.com/2021/07/24/china-crackdown-antitrust-regulator-orders-tencent-music-to-give-up-music-label-rights.html).

Taylor, Timothy (1995) 'When we think about music and politics: the case of Kevin Volans', *Perspectives of New Music*, 33(1/2): 504–536.

Terranova, Tiziana (2000) 'Free labor: producing culture for the digital economy', *Social Text*, 18(2): 33–58.

The Economist (2013) 'The mindfulness business', *The Economist*, 16 November 2013 (www.economist.com/business/2013/11/16/the-mindfulness-business).

The Economist (2016a) 'The economics of Broadway: no business like show business', *The Economist*, 16 June 2016 (www.economist.com/news/business/ 21700674-our-analysis-art-and-science-creating-hit-show-no-business-show-business).

The Economist (2016b) 'Diversity fatigue', *The Economist*, 13 February 2016 (www.economist.com/news/business/21692865-making-most-workplace-diversity-requires-hard-work-well-good-intentions-diversity).

The Economist (2018) 'Banding together: in popular music, collaborations rock', *The Economist*, 3 February 2018 (www.economist.com/business/2018/02/03/ in-popular-music-collaborations-rock).

The Ivors Academy (2020) 'Music creators mentoring programme', *The Ivors Academy* [website], 15 July 2020 (ivorsacademy.com/news/music-creators-mentoring-programme/).

The Smoking Gun (2008) 'Van Halen's legendary M&M's rider', *The Smoking Gun*, 11 December 2008 (www.thesmokinggun.com/documents/crime/van-halens-legendary-mms-rider).

Thomas, Mark Daman (2020) 'Digital performances: live-streaming music and the documentation of the creative process.' In Ewa Mazierska, Les Gillon, and Tony Rigg (eds.), *The Future of Live Music*, pp. 83–96. London: Bloomsbury Academic.

Thompson, Andrew (2012) 'Management agreements.' In Nicola Riches (ed.), *The Music Management Bible*, pp. 12–36. London: Music Sales.

Thorne, Scott, and Gordon C. Bruner (2006) 'An exploratory investigation of the characteristics of consumer fanaticism', *Qualitative Market Research*, 9(1): 51–72.

Thornton, Sarah (1995) *Club Cultures: Music, Media and Subcultural Capital*. Cambridge: Polity Press.

Tjora, Aksel (2016) 'The social rhythm of the rock music festival', *Popular Music*, 35(1): 64–83.

Toffler, Alvin (1980) *The Third Wave: The Classic Study of Tomorrow*. New York: Bantam.

Torres, Eric (2021) 'The 7 best music videos of March 2021'. *Pitchfork*, 1 April 2021 (pitchfork.com/thepitch/the-7-best-music-videos-of-march-2021/).

Toynbee, Jason (2000) *Making Popular Music: Musicians, Creativity and Institutions*. London: Arnold.

Treseder, William (2017) 'The two things killing your ability to focus: devices and meetings.' In Harvard Business Review (eds.), *HBR Guide to Being More Productive* [chapter 17]. Boston, MA: Harvard Business School Press.

UK Music (2013) *Wish You Were Here 2013*. London: UK Music. [And subsequent years.]

UK Music (2015) *Measuring Music 2015*. London: UK Music.

UK Music (2018a) *Measuring Music 2018*. London: UK Music.

UK Music (2018b) 'Brexit: UK Music's key concerns', *UK Music*, December (www.ukmusic. org/policy/brexit-uk-musics-key-concerns/).

UK Music (2020a) *Music by Numbers 2019*. London: UK Music (www.ukmusic.org/ wp-content/uploads/2020/08/Music_By_Numbers_2019_Report.pdf).

UK Music (2020b) *Diversity Report 2020*. London: UK Music (www.ukmusic.org/ wp-content/uploads/2020/11/UK_Music_Diversity_Report_2020.pdf).

UK Music (2020c) 'UK Music Diversity Taskforce Ten-Point Plan', *UK Music*, October (www. ukmusic.org/equality-diversity/ten-point-plan/).

Umney, Charles (2016) 'Musicians are exploited on the London and Paris jazz scenes', *London School of Economics*, 23 March 2016 (blogs.lse.ac.uk/businessreview/ 2016/03/23/musicians-are-exploited-on-the-london-and-paris-jazz-scenes/).

Universal Music Group (2020) 'Creative differences', *Umusic.co.uk* [website], 17 January 2020 (www.umusic.co.uk/creative-differences).

Vernallis, Carol (2007) 'Strange people, weird objects: the nature of narrativity, character, and editing in music videos.' In Roger Beebe and Jason Middleton (eds.), *Medium Cool: Music Videos from Soundies to Cellphones*, pp. 111–151. Durham, NC: Duke University Press.

Vernallis, Carol (2013) *Unruly Media: YouTube, Music Video, and the New Digital Cinema*. Oxford: Oxford University Press.

Voelz, Johannes (2017) 'Looking hip on the square: jazz, cover art, and the rise of creativity', *European Journal of American Studies*, 12(4), DOI: 10.4000/ejas.12389.

Wakefield, Kirk L. (2012) 'How sponsorships work: the sponsorship engagement model', *Event Management*, 16(2): 143–155.

Waksman, Steve (2010) 'Live recollections: uses of the past in US concert life', *Journal of the International Association for the Study of Popular Music*, 1(1): 1–16.

Waldfogel, Joel (2017) 'How digitization has created a golden age of music, movies, books, and television', *Journal of Economic Perspectives*, 31(3): 195–214.

Wall, Tim (2013) *Studying Popular Music Culture*, 2nd ed. Los Angeles, CA: SAGE.

Wall, Tim (2016) 'Music radio goes online.' In Christina L. Baade and James Deaville (eds.), *Music and the Broadcast Experience: Performance, Production, and Audiences*, pp. 259–272. New York: Oxford University Press.

Wall, Tim, and Andrew Dubber (2009) 'Specialist music, public service and the BBC in the Internet age', *The Radio Journal – International Studies in Broadcast and Audio Media*, 7(1): 27–47.

Wardle, Ben (2016) 'What's the point of A&R?', *Music Business Worldwide*, 18 January 2016 (www.musicbusinessworldwide.com/whats-the-point-of-ar/).

Webster, Emma, Matt Brennan, Adam Behr, and Martin Cloonan, with Jake Ansell (2018) *Valuing Live Music: The UK Live Music Census 2017 Report*, v.11 (February 2018) (uklivemusiccensus.org/wp-content/uploads/2018/03/UK-Live-Music-Census-2017-full-report. pdf).

Webster, Emma, and George McKay (2016) *From Glyndebourne to Glastonbury: The Impact of British Music Festivals*. Norwich: Arts & Humanities Research Council/University of East Anglia.

West, Michael A. (2012) *Effective Teamwork*, 3rd ed. Malden, MA: BPS Blackwell.

Westgate, Christopher J. (2019) 'Popular music fans and the value of concert tickets', *Popular Music and Society*, DOI: 10.1080/03007766.2019.1601152.

White, Peter (2020) 'The Beatles, The Velvet Underground & Billie Eilish... Music documentaries to watch for in 2021', *Deadline*, 28 December 2020 (deadline.com/2020/12/best-music-documentries-2021-list-beatles-billie-eilish-velvet-underground-1234660872/).

Wikström, Patrik (2019) *The Music Industry*, 3rd ed. Cambridge: Polity Press.

Wilks, Linda (2011) 'Bridging and bonding: social capital at music festivals', *Journal of Policy Research in Tourism, Leisure and Events*, 3(3): 281–297.

Williamson, John, and Martin Cloonan (2007) 'Rethinking the music industry', *Popular Music*, 26(2): 305–322.

Willis, Paul (1990) *Common Culture*. Milton Keynes: Open University Press.

WIPO (2017) *How to Make a Living in the Creative Industries*. Geneva: World Intellectual Property Organization (www.wipo.int/edocs/pubdocs/en/wipo_pub_cr_2017_1.pdf).

Worthington, Andrew (2005) *The Battle of the Beanfield*. Teignmouth, UK: Enabler Publications.

Wu, Tim (2017) *The Attention Merchants: The Epic Struggle to Get Inside Our Heads*. London: Atlantic Books.

Yearby, Ruqaiijah (2020) 'Structural racism: the root cause of the social determinants of health', *Harvard Law* [blog], 22 September 2020 (blog.petrieflom.law.harvard.edu/2020/09/22/structural-racism-social-determinant-of-health/).

Yin, Yiyi (2020) 'An emergent algorithmic culture: the data-ization of online fandom in China', *International Journal of Cultural Studies*, 23(4): 475–492.

Zhang, Cat (2020) 'The mystery of Doja Cat's unimpeachable TikTok reign', *Pitchfork*, 18 May 2020 (pitchfork.com/thepitch/the-mystery-of-doja-cats-unimpeachable-tiktok-reign/).

Zhang, Qian, and Keith Negus (2020) 'East Asian pop music idol production and the emergence of data fandom in China', *International Journal of Cultural Studies*, 23(4): 493–511.

INDEX

A-Z DUR___M

Ind___
Vil___
se___

REFERENCE

A Road	A36	Car Park (selected)	⏚
		Church or Chapel	†
	B3111	Cycleway (selected)	🚲
___ ___eway		Fire Station	■
___ ___y Street		Hospital	Ⓗ
___ on A Roads is also indicated ___ y line on the driver's left.		House Numbers (selected roads)	13 8 3
___ Under Construction ___ g dates are correct at the time of publication.		Information Centre	🄸
___posed Road		National Grid Reference	⁵40
___estricted Access		Park & Ride	Sniperley P+R
Pedestrianized Road		Police Station	▲
Track / Footpath		Post Office	★
Residential Walkway		Toilet	
		without facilities for the Disabled	▽
		with facilities for the Disabled	▼
Railway	Station Tunnel Level Crossing	Viewpoint	⋇
Built-up Area	MILK ST.	Educational Establishment	▨
		Hospital or Hospice	▨
Posttown Boundary		Industrial Building	▨
Postcode Boundary (within Posttown)		Leisure or Recreational Facility	▨
		Place of Interest	▨
Map Continuation	16 Large Scale City Centre 32	Public Building	▨
		Shopping Centre or Market	▨
City Wall (Large Scale only)	⊓⊔⊓⊔⊓⊔	Other Selected Buildings	▢

SCALE

Map Pages 4-31	1:15,840		Large Scale Page 32	1:7,920	
0	¼	½ Mile	0	⅛	¼ Mile
0 250 500 750 Metres			0 100 200 300 400 Metres		
4 inches (10.16 cm) to 1 mile 6.31 cm to 1 km			8 inches (20.32 cm) to 1 mile 12.63 cm to 1 km		

EDITION 4 2015
Copyright © Geographers' A-Z Map Co. Ltd.
Telephone: 01732 781000 (Enquiries & Trade Sales)
          01732 783422 (Retail Sales)

© Crown copyright and database rights 2014 Ordnance Survey 100017302.

Safety camera information supplied by www.PocketGPSWorld.com.
Speed Camera Location Database Copyright 2014 © PocketGPSWorld.com

A-Z AZ AtoZ
registered trade marks of
Geographers' A-Z Map Company Ltd

www. az.co.uk

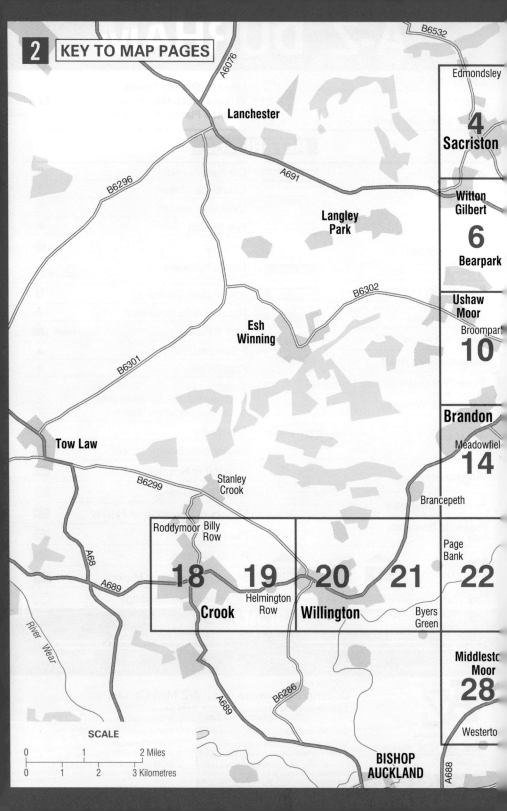

Edmondsley

Lanchester

4
Sacriston

Witton
Gilbert

6

Bearpark

A6076

B6296

A691

Langley
Park

B6302

Ushaw
Moor

Broompar

10

Esh
Winning

B6301

Brandon

Meadowfiel

14

Tow Law

Brancepeth

B6299

Stanley
Crook

Roddymoor Billy
Row

Page
Bank

A68

A689

18 **19** **20** **21** **22**

Helmington
Row

Crook **Willington**

Byers
Green

River Wear

**Middlesto
Moor**

28

A689

B6286

A689

SCALE

0   1   2 Miles

0   1   2   3 Kilometres

**BISHOP
AUCKLAND**

Westerto

A688

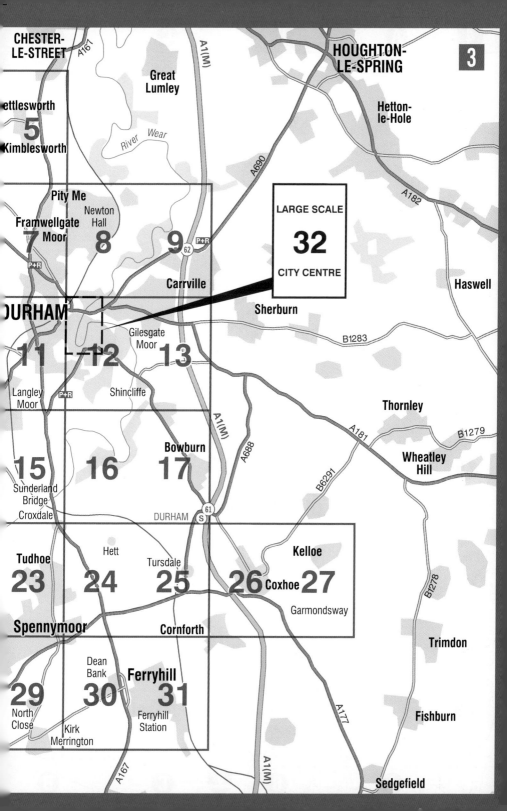

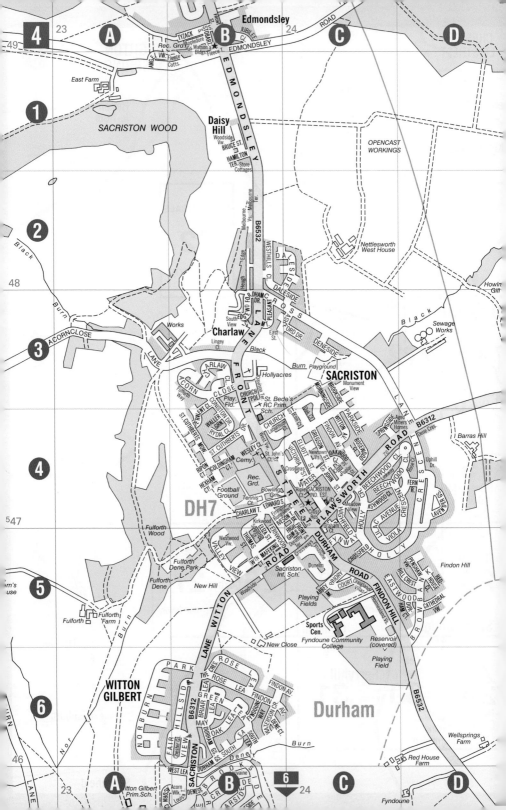

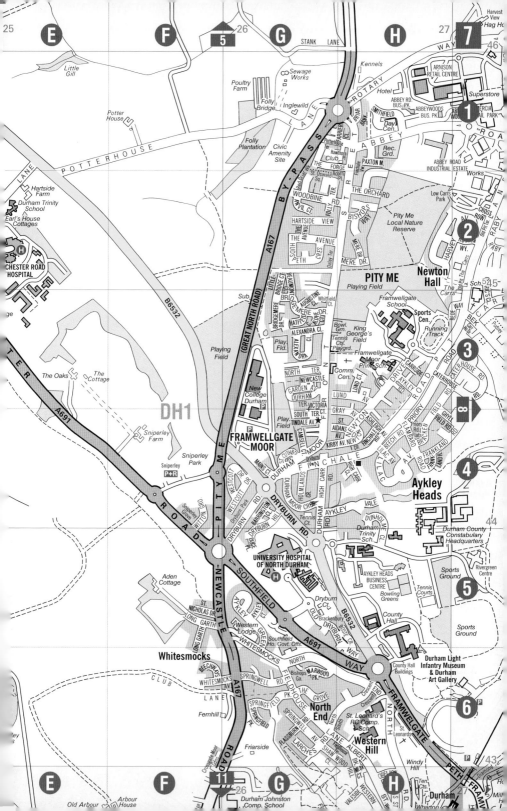

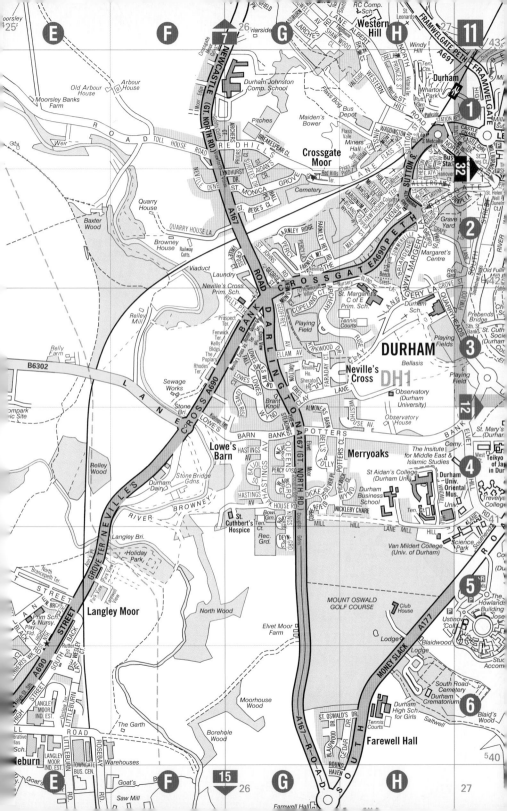

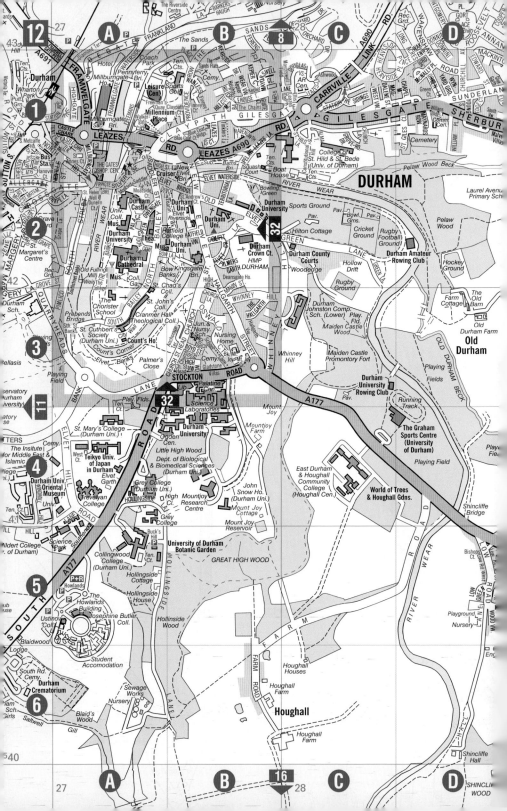

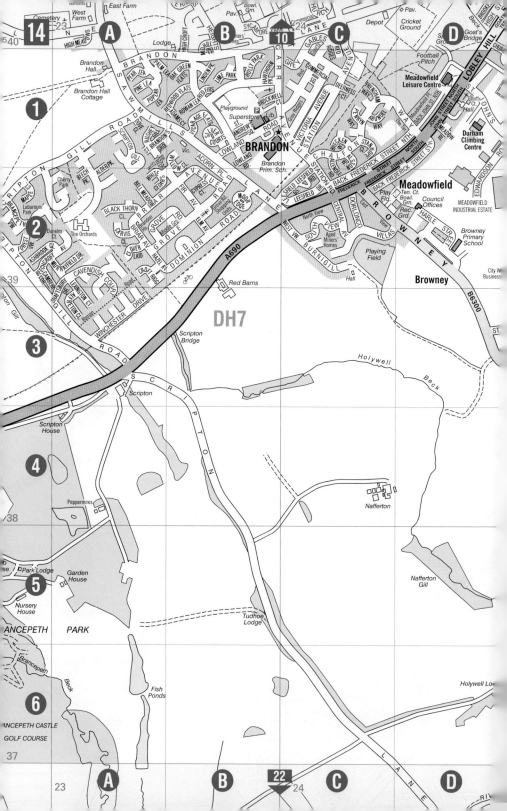

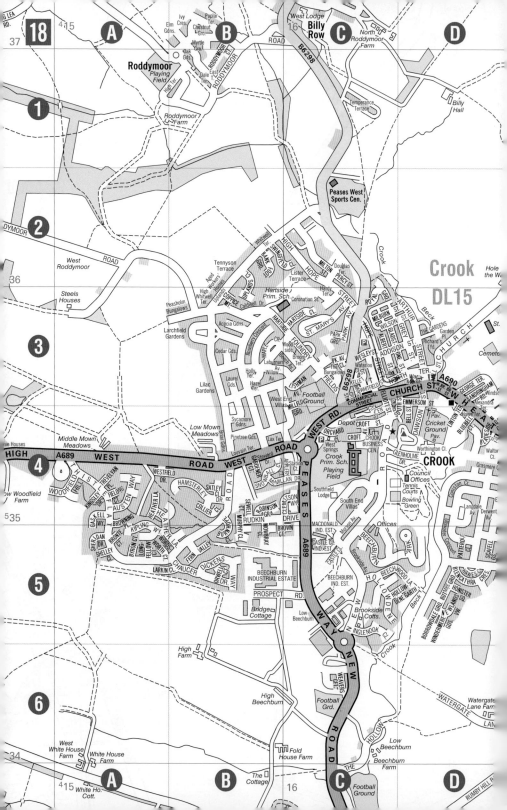

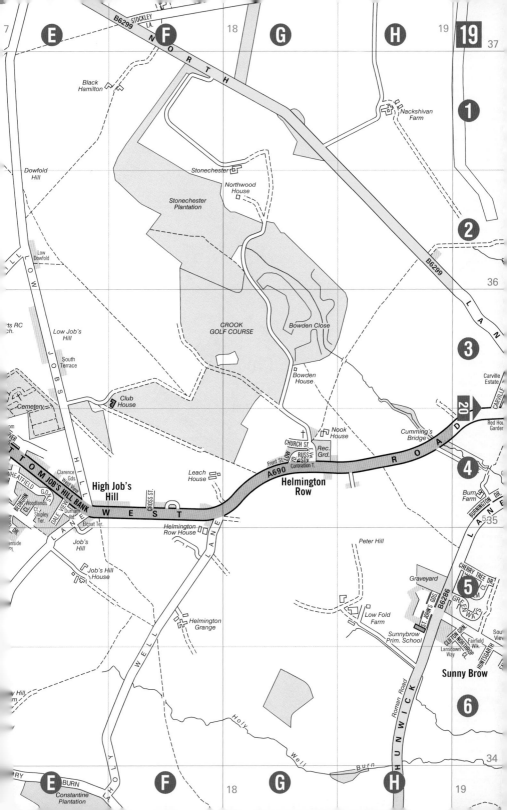

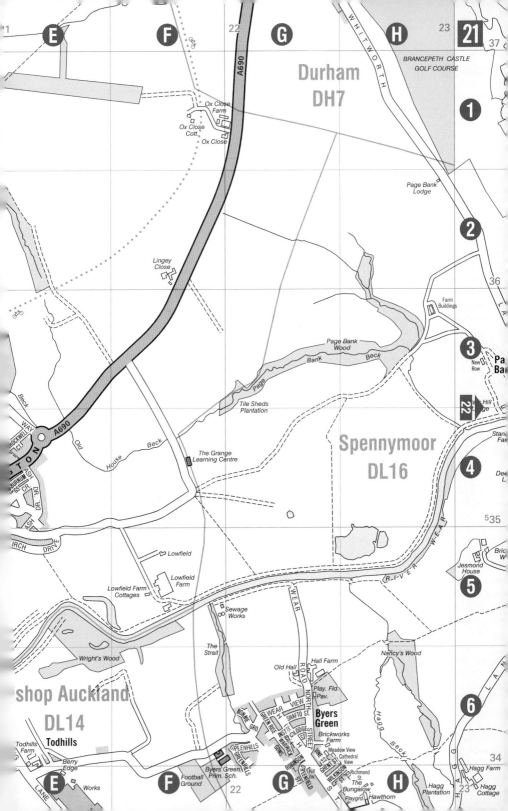

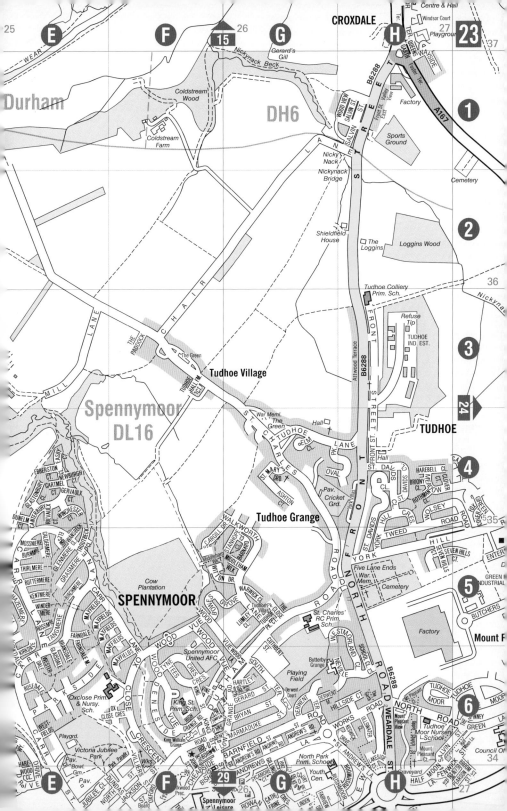

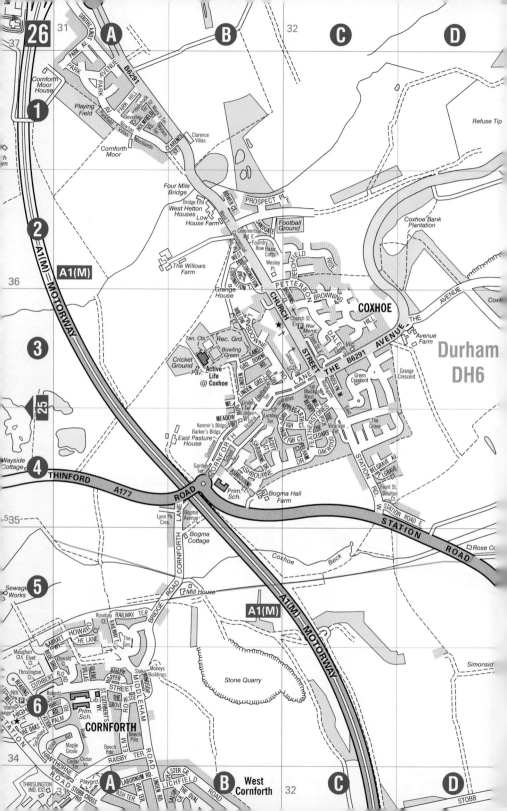

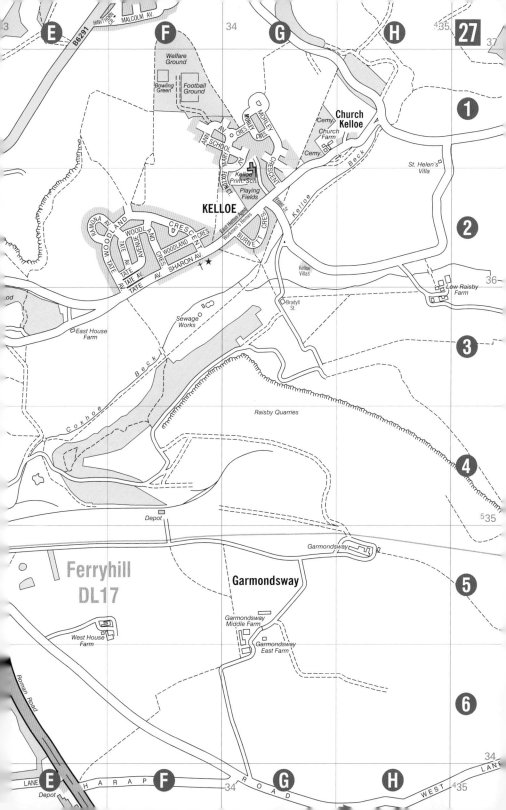

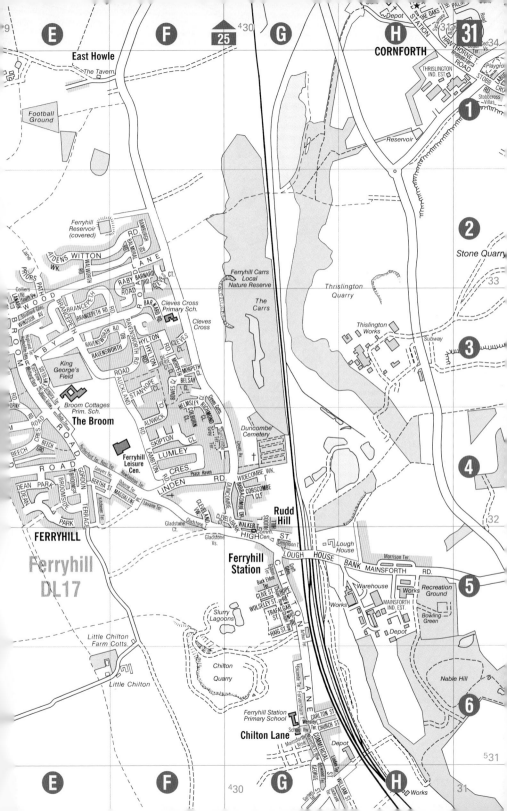

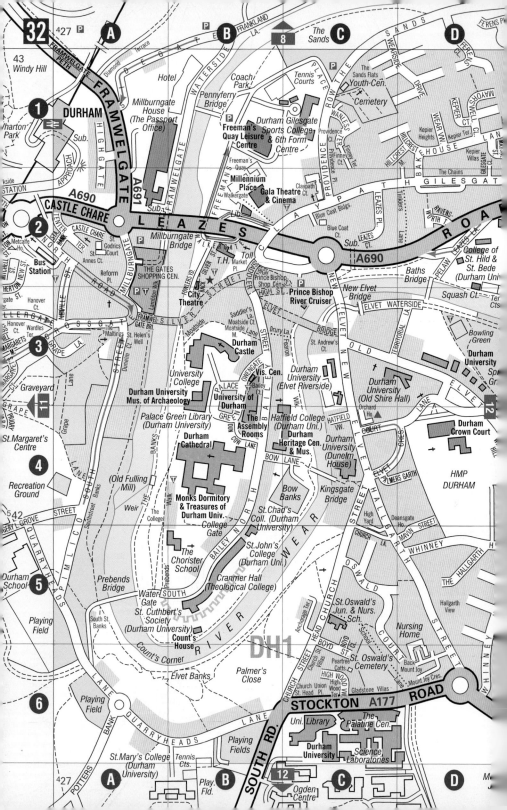

INDEX

Including Streets, Places & Areas, Hospitals etc, Industrial Estates, Selected Flats & Walkways, Service Areas, Stations and Selected Places of Interest.

HOW TO USE THIS INDEX

1. Each street name is followed by its Postcode District, then by its Locality abbreviation(s) and then by its map reference;
e.g. **Abbey Rd.** DH1: P Me . . . .1H **7** is in the DH1 Postcode District and the Pity Me Locality and is to be found in square 1H on page **7**. The page number is shown in bold type.

2. A strict alphabetical order is followed in which Av., Rd., St., etc. (though abbreviated) are read in full and as part of the street name; e.g. **Ash Dr.** appears after **Ashdown Av.** but before **Ashford Dr.**

3. Streets and a selection of flats and walkways too small to be shown on the mapping, appear in the index with the thoroughfare to which they are connected shown in brackets; e.g. **Alma Ter.** *DH1: Dur . . . .3G* **11** *(off Neville's Cross Bank)*

4. Addresses that are in more than one part are referred to as not continuous.

5. Places and areas are shown in the index in BLUE TYPE and the map reference is to the actual map square in which the town centre or area is located and not to the place name shown on the map; e.g. BEARPARK 6B 6

6. An example of a selected place of interest is **Durham Light Infantry Mus. & Durham Art Gallery** 6H 7

7. Example of stations are:
Durham Station (Rail) . . . .1A 32 (1H 11); **Durham Bus Station** . . . .2A 32 (1H 11); **Belmont (Park & Ride)** 3H 9

8. Service Areas are shown in the index in BOLD CAPITAL TYPE; e.g. **DURHAM SERVICE AREA** 6H 17

9. An example of a Hospital, Hospice or selected Healthcare facility is UNIVERSITY HOSPITAL OF NORTH DURHAM 5G 7

10. Map references for entries that appear on large scale page **32** are shown first, with small scale map references shown in brackets; e.g. **Leazes Rd.** DH1: Dur 2A **32** (1A **12**)

GENERAL ABBREVIATIONS

App. : Approach	**Flds.** : Fields	**Pk.** : Park
Av. : Avenue	**Gdns.** : Gardens	**Pl.** : Place
Bk. : Back	**Gth.** : Garth	**Pct.** : Precinct
Bri. : Bridge	**Ga.** : Gate	**Ri.** : Rise
Bldgs. : Buildings	**Grn.** : Green	**Rd.** : Road
Bungs. : Bungalows	**Gro.** : Grove	**Shop.** : Shopping
Bus. : Business	**Hgts.** : Heights	**Sth.** : South
Cen. : Centre	**Ho.** : House	**Sq.** : Square
Cl. : Close	**Ho's.** : Houses	**St.** : Street
Cotts. : Cottages	**Ind.** : Industrial	**Ter.** : Terrace
Ct. : Court	**La.** : Lane	**Up.** : Upper
Cres. : Crescent	**Mdw.** : Meadow	**Va.** : Vale
Cft. : Croft	**Mdws.** : Meadows	**Vw.** : View
Dr. : Drive	**M.** : Mews	**Vs.** : Villas
E. : East	**Mt.** : Mount	**Vis.** : Visitors
Ent. : Enterprise	**Mus.** : Museum	**Wlk.** : Walk
Est. : Estate	**Nth.** : North	**W.** : West
Fld. : Field	**Pde.** : Parade	**Yd.** : Yard

LOCALITY ABBREVIATIONS

Bearp : **Bearpark**	Garm : **Garmondsway**	Plaw : **Plawsworth**
Bill R : **Billy Row**	Helm R : **Helmington Row**	Quar H : **Quarrington Hill**
Bin : **Binchester**	Hett : **Hett**	Rodd : **Roddymoor**
Bowb : **Bowburn**	H Shin : **High Shincliffe**	Sac : **Sacriston**
Bran : **Brancepeth**	How W : **Howden-le-Wear**	S Hou : **Sherburn House**
B'don : **Brandon**	Hun : **Hunwick**	Shin : **Shincliffe**
Bras : **Brasside**	Kel : **Kelloe**	Spen : **Spennymoor**
Bro : **Broompark**	Kim : **Kimblesworth**	Sun B : **Sunderland Bridge**
Byer G : **Byers Green**	Kirk M : **Kirk Merrington**	Sunnb : **Sunnybrow**
Carr : **Carrville**	Lang M : **Langley Moor**	Tod : **Todhills**
Ches M : **Chester Moor**	Mead : **Meadowfield**	Tudh : **Tudhoe**
Chil : **Chilton**	Midd : **Middlestone**	Turs : **Tursdale**
Coxh : **Coxhoe**	Nett : **Nettlesworth**	Ush M : **Ushaw Moor**
Crook : **Crook**	New B : **New Brancepeth**	Wald : **Waldridge**
Crox : **Croxdale**	Newf : **Newfield**	W Corn : **West Cornforth**
Dur : **Durham**	Oak : **Oakenshaw**	W'ton : **Westerton**
Edm : **Edmondsley**	Page B : **Page Bank**	Will : **Willington**
F'hll : **Ferryhill**	P Me : **Pity Me**	Wit G : **Witton Gilbert**

A

	Abbots Grn. DL15: Will 4C 20	**Aden Ct.** DH7: Bearp 5A 6
	Abbots Row DH1: Dur 6D 8	**Adolphus Pl.** DH1: Dur 1F 13
	Acacia Gdns. DL15: Crook 3B 18	**Adventure Valley** .1F 9
Abbey Gdns. DL15: Will 4C 20	**Acorn Cl.** DH7: Sac 3B 4	**Aged Miners' Homes** DH2: Ches M 1H 5
Abbey Grn. DL16: Spen 5A 24	**Acornclose La.** DH7: Sac 3A 4	DH2: Nett 3F 5
Abbey Leisure Cen.	**Acorn Cft.** DH7: Wit G 1A 6	DH7: B'don 6B 10
Pity Me 1A 8	**Acorn Dr.** DL15: Oak 1C 20	DH7: Bearp 6A 6
Abbey M. DH7: Sac 5C 4	**Acorn Pl.** DH1: P Me 2G 7	DH7: Mead 2C 14
Abbey Rd. DH7: B'don 1H 7		DH7: Sac 4C 4
Abbey Rd. DH1: P Me 1H 7	**Acorn Wlk.** DH7: Wit G 1B 6	DL15: Will 5C 20
Abbey Rd. Bus. Pk. DH1: P Me 1H 7	**Acorn Way** DH2: Nett 3F 5	**Aged Mine Workers Memorial Homes**
Abbey Rd. Ind. Est. DH1: P Me 1H 7	**Active Life @ Coxhoe** 3B 26	DH6: Turs 4G 25
Abbeywoods DH1: P Me 1A 8	**Addison St.** DL15: Crook 3C 18	**Aged Workers' Homes** DL15: Crook 2B 18
Abbeywoods Bus. Pk. DH1: P Me 1H 7		

Aidens Wlk.—Borrowdale Dr.

Aidens Wlk. DL17: F'hll 2E **31**
Ainsley St. DH1: Dur 1H **11**
Albert Ct. DH6: Bowb 4H **17**
Albert St. DH1: Dur 6H **7**
DL15: Crook 3C **18**
Albion Pl. DL15: Will 4B **20**
(not continuous)
Albion St. DL16: Spen 3C **28**
Alderdene Cl. DH7: Ush M 2C **10**
Alderlea Cl. DH1: Dur 6E **9**
Alder Pk. DH7: B'don 2A **14**
Aldhome Ct. DH1: Dur 3G **7**
Aldin Grange Hall DH7: Bearp 1D **10**
Aldin Grange Ter. DH7: Bearp 6C **6**
Aldin Ri. DH7: Bearp 1C **10**
Aldridge Ct. DH7: Ush M 1A **10**
Alexandra Cl. DH1: Dur 3G **7**
Alexandra Ter. DL15: Crook 3D **18**
Alexandria Cres. DH1: Dur 2H **11**
Alfreton Cl. DH7: B'don 3A **14**
Alington Pl. DH1: Dur 1E **13**
Allendale Rd. DH7: Mead 1C **14**
Allergate DH1: Dur 2H **11**
Allergate Ter. DH1: Dur 3A **32**
Alma Pl. DH1: Dur 6F **9**
Alma Ter. *DH1: Dur 3G* ***11***
(off Neville's Cross Bank)
DH1: Dur 1C **12**
(Gilesgate)
Almond Cl. DL16: Spen 2D **28**
Almoners Barn DH1: Dur 4G **11**
Alnwick Cl. DL17: F'hll 4F **31**
Alnwick Dr. DL16: Spen 1D **28**
Alnwick Rd. DH1: Dur 2A **8**
Alston Way DH7: Mead 1C **14**
ALUM WATERS **3A 10**
Anchorage Ter. DH1: Dur 5C **32** (3B **12**)
Ancroft Gth. DH1: H Shin 1F **17**
Angel Vw. DH7: Edm 1A **4**
Angerstein Ct. DH1: Carr 5G **9**
Angus Sq. DH7: Lang M 6D **10**
Angus St. DH7: Lang M 5E **11**
Annand Rd. DH1: Dur 6D **8**
Ann Av. DH6: Kel 1F **27**
Ann's Pl. DH7: Lang M 5E **11**
Anvil Ct. DH1: P Me 2G **7**
Apperley Av. DH1: H Shin 1G **17**
Appleby Ct. DL15: Crook 4C **18**
Appledore Gdns. DH7: Edm 1B **4**
Applegarth DH6: Coxh 3C **26**
Archers Ct. DH1: Dur 1G **11**
Archery Ri. DH1: Dur 3G **11**
Arlington Way DL16: Spen 5B **24**
Armoury St. DL16: Spen 6F **23**
Armstrong Dr. DL15: Will 4B **20**
Arnison Retail Cen. DH1: P Me 1H **7**
Artemis Ct. DH7: Mead 1D **14**
Arthur St. DH7: Ush M 1A **10**
DL15: Crook 3D **18**
Arthur Ter. DL17: F'hll 5G **31**
Arundel Way DH7: Mead 1C **14**
Ash Av. DH1: Dur 2E **13**
DH7: Ush M 1A **10**
Ashbourne Ct. DH6: Coxh 4B **26**
Ashbourne Dr. DH6: Coxh 4B **26**
Ashbrook Cl. DH7: B'don 2A **14**
Ashdown Av. DH1: Dur 6F **9**
Ash Dr. DL15: Will 4E **21**
Ashford Dr. DH7: Sac 3C **4**
Ash Gro. DL16: Spen 2E **29**
Ashleigh Av. DH1: Dur 4H **7**
Ash Ter. DH6: Bowb 5H **17**
DL17: W Corn 6A **26**
Ashton Ct. DL16: Tudh 4G **23**
Ashwood DH1: Dur 1C **12**
Ashwood Cl. DH7: Sac 4C **4**
Aspen Cl. DH1: Dur 6E **9**
DL16: Spen 2D **28**
Assembly Rooms-Durham Student Theatre, The **4B 32 (2A 12)**
Atherton Cl. DL16: Spen 2F **29**
Atherton St. DH1: Dur 2A **32** (2H **11**)
Attwood Ter. DL16: Tudh 3H **23**
Auckland Ct. DL15: Will 5B **20**
Auckland Rd. DH1: Dur 2B **8**
DL17: F'hll 3F **31**
Augustine Cl. DH1: Dur 3G **7**
Austen Way DL15: Crook 4A **18**
Auton Cl. DH7: Bearp 6B **6**
Auton Ct. DH7: Bearp 6C **6**
Auton Fld. DH7: Bearp 6C **6**
Auton Fld. Ter. DH7: Bearp 6C **6**
Auton Stile DH7: Bearp 6B **6**
Avenue, The DH1: Dur 2G **11**
DH1: P Me 2G **7**
DH6: Coxh 3C **26**
Avenue St. DH1: H Shin 1F **17**
Ayden Gro. DH1: Dur 3A **8**
Aykley Ct. DH1: Dur 5G **7**
Aykley Grn. DH1: Dur 5G **7**
AYKLEY HEADS **5H 7**
Aykley Heads Bus. Cen. DH1: Dur 5H **7**
Aykley Rd. DH1: Dur 3H **7**
Aykley Va. DH1: Dur 4G **7**

B

Babbacombe Dr. DL17: F'hll 4G **31**
Bk. Coronation Ter. DH6: Coxh 2B **26**
Bk. Eldon Ter. DL17: F'hll 5G **31**
Bk. Frederick St. Nth. DH7: B'don 1A **14**
DH7: Mead 2C **14**
Bk. Frederick St. Sth. DH7: Mead 2C **14**
Bk. Front St. DH7: Sac 4C **4**
Bk. John St. Nth. DH7: Mead 1D **14**
Bk. Mount Joy DH1: Dur 6D **32** (3B **12**)
Bk. Silver St. DH1: Dur 2B **32**
Bk. Western Hill DH1: Dur 6H **7**
Baff St. DL16: Spen 2F **29**
Bailey Ct. DH1: Dur 3B **32**
Bainbridge Av. DL15: Will 4C **20**
Bainbridge St. DH1: Carr 4H **9**
Bakehouse La. DH1: Dur 1D **32** (1B **12**)
Baliol Sq. DH1: Dur 4G **11**
Balmoral Rd. DL17: F'hll 2F **31**
Bamburgh Pde. DL16: Spen 1G **29**
Bamburgh Rd. DH1: Dur 2A **8**
DL17: F'hll 2F **31**
Bank Foot DH1: H Shin, Shin 5E **13**
Bank Foot Gro. DL15: Crook 2B **18**
Banks, The DH1: Dur 4A **32** (2A **12**)
Bannatyne Health Club Durham **6F 9**
Bannerman Ter. DH7: Ush M 1A **10**
Barker's Bldgs. DH6: Coxh 4B **26**
Barkers Haugh DH1: Dur 6B **8**
Barnard Cl. DH1: Dur 2B **8**
DL16: Spen 5G **23**
Barnard Rd. DL17: F'hll 2F **31**
(not continuous)
Barnfield Rd. DL16: Spen 6G **23**
Barnfield Way DL15: Will 3D **20**
Barnsett Grange DH6: Sun B 5H **15**
Barnstones DH2: Plaw 3G **5**
Barrasford Rd. DH1: Dur 3B **8**
Barratt Way DL17: W Corn 5H **25**
Barrington Cl. DH1: Dur 4G **7**
Barrington Ter. DL17: F'hll 3C **30**
Barrington Way DH6: Bowb 4H **17**
Basic Cotts. DH6: Coxh 2B **26**
Bay Ct. DH7: Ush M 2B **10**
Beal Wlk. DH1: H Shin 6F **13**
Beaney La. DH2: Ches M, Plaw 1F **5**
BEARPARK **6B 6**
Beaumont Cl. DH1: Dur 2G **7**
DH6: Bowb 4H **17**
Beaumont St. DL17: F'hll 3C **30**
Beaurepaire DH7: Bearp 6A **6**
Beaver Cl. DH1: P Me 1A **8**
Beckwith Cl. DL16: Kirk M 6G **29**
Beckwith's La. DL16: Kirk M 6G **29**
Bedale Cl. DH1: Carr 5H **9**
Bedburn Cl. DL15: Crook 4E **19**
Bede Av. DH1: Dur 2E **13**
Bede Gro. DL17: W Corn 6H **25**
Bede Pl. DL16: Kirk M 6G **29**
Bede Ter. DH6: Bowb 3H **17**
DL17: F'hll 4E **31**
Bede Way DH1: Dur 3A **8**
Bedford Pl. DL15: Will 4C **20**
Bedfordshire Dr. DH1: Carr 6H **9**
Beech Av. DL15: Crook 3C **18**
DL16: Spen 2E **29**
Beechburn Ind. Est. DL15: Crook 5B **18**
(not continuous)
Beechburn Pk. DL15: Crook 5C **18**
Beech Cl. DH1: Bras 1C **8**
Beech Cres. DL17: F'hll 4E **31**
Beech Crest DH1: Dur 2H **11**
Beechcroft Av. DH7: B'don 2A **14**
Beechcroft Cl. DH1: Dur 6E **9**
Beechdale Rd. DH1: Carr 5H **9**
Beechfield Ri. DH6: Coxh 2C **26**
Beech Gro. DH7: Ush M 2B **10**
DL17: F'hll 4E **31**
Beech Pde. DL17: W Corn 6A **26**
(not continuous)
Beech Pk. DH7: B'don 2A **14**
Beech Rd. DH1: Dur 4H **7**
Beech Vw. DH1: S Hou 4H **13**
Beechways DH1: Dur 6F **7**
Beechwood Cl. DH7: Sac 4C **4**
Beechwood La. DL15: Crook 5C **18**
Beehive Workshops DH1: Dur 1F **13**
Bek Rd. DH1: Dur 3A **8**
Belgrave Av. DH6: Coxh 4C **26**
Belgrave Ct. DH6: Coxh 4C **26**
Bell Av. DH6: Bowb 3G **17**
Bellburn Way DL16: Spen 3C **28**
Belle Vue *DL15: Crook 4D* ***18***
(off Wheatbottom)
Belle Vue Ct. DH1: Dur 6F **9**
Belle Vue St. DL16: Spen 2E **29**
Belle Vue Ter. DH1: Dur 6F **9**
DL15: Will 4B **20**
Belle Vue Vs. *DL16: Spen 2E* ***29***
(off Belle Vue St.)
Bell Mdw. DH7: B'don 2A **14**
Bells Bldgs. DH2: Nett 3E **5**
Bell's Folly DH1: Dur 4G **11**
Bell St. DL15: Crook 4D **18**
DL17: W Corn 6H **25**
Bell's Ville DH1: Dur 1E **13**
BELMONT **6H 9**
Belmont (Park & Ride) **3H 9**
Belmont Bus. Pk. DH1: Dur 5F **9**
Belmont Ct. DH1: Carr 6G **9**
Belmont Ind. Est. DH1: Dur 4F **9**
Belmont Rd. DH1: Carr, Dur 5E **9**
Belsay Cl. DL17: F'hll 3F **31**
Beningborough Ct. DL16: Spen 1D **28**
Bent Ho. La. DH1: Dur 2F **13**
Berkshire Cl. DH1: Carr 6G **9**
Bertha St. DL17: F'hll 4E **31**
Bessemer St. DL17: F'hll 4C **30**
Bests Yd. DH7: Wit G 1A **6**
Bevan Gro. DH1: Dur 1F **13**
Beverley Cl. DH6: Coxh 1A **26**
BILLY ROW **1C 18**
BINCHESTER **5A 28**
BINCHESTER MOOR **3C 28**
Birch Dr. DL15: Will 5E **21**
Birchgrove Av. DH1: Dur 6F **9**
Birchmere DL16: Spen 5E **23**
Birch Pk. Av. DL16: Spen 5B **24**
Birch Rd. DL17: W Corn 6H **25**
Birkdale Gdns. DH1: Carr 6H **9**
Bishops Cl. DH1: Carr 5H **9**
DL16: Spen 1F **29**
Bishops Ct. DH1: Shin 5D **12**
Bishops Ga. DH1: Dur 6G **7**
Bishops Way DH1: P Me 2H **7**
Blackburn Cl. DH7: Bearp 5A **6**
Blackcliffe Way DH7: Bearp 5A **6**
Blackgate E. DH6: Coxh 3C **26**
Blackgate W. DH6: Coxh 3C **26**
Black Plantation (Nature Reserve) **5D 22**
Black Rd. DH7: Lang M 5E **11**
Black Thorn Cl. DH7: B'don 2A **14**
Bladeside DL15: Crook 4D **18**
Blaidwood Dr. DH1: Dur 6G **11**
Blair Av. DL16: Spen 1G **29**
Blair Ct. DH7: Lang M 6E **11**
Blanchland Av. DH1: Dur 3C **8**
Blandford St. DL17: F'hll 4C **30**
Blencathra Cres. DL15: Crook 5D **18**
Blind La. DH1: Dur 2H **11**
Bluebell Ct. DL15: Crook 4D **18**
Bluebell Dr. DL16: Spen 2D **28**
Blue Coat Bldgs. DH1: Dur 2C **32** (1B **12**)
Blue Coat Ct. DH1: Dur 2C **32** (1B **12**)
Blue Ho. Bldgs. DH1: Carr 5G **9**
Blue Ho. Est. DL16: Kirk M 6G **29**
Board St. DL16: Spen 1F **29**
Bogma Av. DH6: Coxh 4B **26**
Boldon Ho. DH1: P Me 6H **5**
Bolton Cl. DH1: Dur 2A **8**
Bonnie Gro. DL16: Byer G 6G **21**
Borrowdale Dr. DH1: Carr 5G **9**

34 A-Z Durham

Durham Light Infantry Mus. & Durham Art Gallery—Gardener Ct.

Durham Light Infantry Mus.
& Durham Art Gallery 6H **7**
Durham Moor DH1: Dur 4G **7**
Durham Moor Cres. DH1: Dur 4G **7**
Durham Rd. DH1: Dur 4G **7**
(Aykley Va.)
DH1: Dur 6C **6**
(Toll Ho. Rd.)
DH6: Bowb 4G **17**
DH7: Bearp 6C **6**
DH7: Sac 5C **4**
DH7: Ush M 1A **10**
DL15: Crook 4E **19**
DL16: Byer G, Spen 4B **28**
DL16: Spen 6F **23**
DL17: F'hll 3D **30**
Durham Rd. Nth. *DH6: Bowb* *4H* ***17***
(off Durham Rd.)
Durham Rd. W. DH6: Bowb 5H **17**
DURHAM SERVICE AREA **6H 17**
Durham Station (Rail) ....**1A 32 (1H 11)**
Durham St. DL16: Spen 3C **28**
Durham Ter. DH1: Dur 3G **7**
Durham University
Hatfield College **2B 12**
New Elvet **2B 12**
Old Elvet ....**3D 32 (2B 12)**
Palace Green ....**3B 32 (2A 12)**
Stockton Road ....**6C 32 (4B 12)**
Durham University Mus. of Archaeology
....**3B 32 (2A 12)**
Durham University Oriental Mus. **4H 11**
Durham University Rowing Club **3C 12**
Durham World Heritage Site Vis. Cen. **3B 32**

E

Eamont Rd. DL17: F'hll 3D **30**
Easby Ct. DL16: Spen 4E **23**
E. Atherton St. DH1: Dur 3A **32** (2H **11**)
East Block DH7: Wit G 1A **6**
East Bri. St. DL15: Crook 3D **18**
E. Hetton Aged Workmen's Homes
DH6: Kel 2G **27**
East Pde. DH2: Kim 4F **5**
E. Side Av. DH7: Bearp 6A **6**
East St. DH6: Hett 1C **24**
DH7: Sac 3B **4**
East Ter. DL15: Rodd 1B **18**
East Vw. DH2: Kim 5F **5**
DH7: Mead 2C **14**
DL15: Helm R 4G **19**
DL17: F'hll 3E **31**
Eastwood DH7: Sac 5C **4**
Ebberston Ct. DL16: Spen 4E **23**
Eden Rd. DH1: Dur 3A **8**
DL16: Spen 2F **29**
Eden St. DL16: Spen 2E **29**
Eden Ter. DH1: Dur 6G **9**
DL15: Will 4C **20**
DL16: Kirk M 6F **29**
Eden Vw. DL14: Midd 6E **29**
Edge Ct. DH1: Dur 1D **12**
(not continuous)
Edgewood Ct. DH7: Sac 3B **4**
Edison Dr. DL16: Spen 1H **29**
Edlingham Rd. DH1: Dur 4A **8**
EDMONDSLEY 1B **4**
Edmondsley La. DH7: Sac 1B **4**
Edmondsley Rd. DH7: Edm 1B **4**
Edmund Ct. DH7: Bearp 5A **6**
Edna St. DH6: Bowb 5H **17**
Edward Av. DH6: Bowb 4H **17**
Edwardson Rd. DH7: Mead 2D **14**
Edward St. DH1: Dur 1D **12**
DH7: Sac 4B **4**
DL16: Spen 1E **29**
Eggleston Cl. DH1: Dur 3C **8**
Elcoat Ter. DL15: Crook 4E **19**
Elder Cl. DH7: Ush M 2B **10**
Eldon Ter. DL17: F'hll 5G **31**
Eliza St. DH7: Sac 5B **4**
Ellam Av. DH1: Dur 3G **11**
Ellesmere DL16: Spen 5E **23**
Elliott Ct. DH7: Mead 1D **14**
Elliott St. DH7: Sac 4C **4**
DL15: Crook 3C **18**
Ellis Leazes DH1: Dur 1C **12**
Elm Av. DH7: B'don 2B **14**
Elm Cl. DL15: Sunnb 5A **20**
DL16: Tudh 4G **23**
Elm Ct. DH7: Sac 4C **4**
Elm Cres. DH2: Kim 4F **5**
Elmfield Av. DH1: Dur 6F **9**
Elm Gdns. DL15: Rodd 1A **18**
Elm Gro. DH7: Ush M 2B **10**
Elm Rd. DL17: F'hll 4E **31**
DL17: W Corn 6A **26**
Elsdon Rd. DH1: Dur 3B **8**
Elvet Bri. DH1: Dur 3B **32** (2A **12**)
Elvet Cl. DL17: W Corn 6H **25**
Elvet Cres. DH1: Dur 4C **32** (2B **12**)
Elvet Hill Rd. DH1: Dur 4A **12**
Elvet Moor DH1: Dur 4G **11**
Elvet Waterside DH1: Dur 3C **32** (2B **12**)
Ely Rd. DH1: Dur 1B **8**
Embleton Cl. DH1: Dur 3B **8**
Emmerson St. DL15: Crook 3D **18**
Empire Bldgs. DH1: Dur 1E **13**
Encombe Ter. DL17: F'hll 6G **31**
Ennerdale Cl. DH1: Carr 5H **9**
Ennerdale Dr. DL15: Crook 4D **18**
Enterprise City DL16: Spen 4B **24**
Enterprise Way DL16: Spen 5A **24**
Ernest Pl. DH1: Dur 1F **13**
Errington Bungs. DH7: Sac 4B **4**
Esh Wood Vw. DH7: Ush M 1A **10**
Eskdale Cl. DH1: Carr 5H **9**
Esk Gdns. DL15: Crook 5D **18**
Essex Pl. DL15: Will 4C **20**
Etherley Cl. DH1: Dur 2B **8**
Eureka M. DH2: Nett 3F **5**
Evans Bus. Cen. DH1: Dur 4F **9**
Eve La. DL16: Spen 6B **24**

F

Fairfield Wlk. DL15: Sunnb 5A **20**
Fair Vw. DH7: Wit G 6A **4**
Fairview Dr. DL16: Spen 1G **29**
Falkous Ter. DH7: Wit G 1A **6**
Fallsway DH1: Carr 4H **9**
Faraday Cl. DL16: Spen 1H **29**
Faraday Ct. DH1: Dur 3G **11**
Faraday St. DL17: F'hll 4B **30**
(not continuous)
FAREWELL HALL **6H 11**
Farewell Vw. DH7: Lang M 5E **11**
Farm Bldgs. DL16: Page B 3H **21**
Farm Rd. DH1: Dur 5B **12**
Farndale DL16: Spen 5E **23**
Farnham Cl. DH1: Dur 4A **8**
Farnham Rd. DH1: Dur 3A **8**
Farnley Hey Rd. DH1: Dur 2G **11**
Farnley Mt. DH1: Dur 2G **11**
Farnley Ridge DH1: Dur 2G **11**
Farrier Cl. DH1: P Me 1H **7**
Fearon Wlk. DH1: Dur 3C **32** (2B **12**)
Featherstone Rd. DH1: Dur 4B **8**
Featherstones DH6: Coxh 4C **26**
Fellside Gdns. DH1: Carr 5G **9**
Fenwick St. DL16: Spen 1H **29**
Fenwick Ter. DH1: Dur 3F **11**
Ferens Cl. DH1: Dur 1D **32** (6B **8**)
Ferens Pk. DH1: Dur 1D **32** (6B **8**)
Ferndale DH1: Carr 6H **9**
Fern Gro. DL16: Spen 3D **28**
Fern Rd. DH7: Sac 4D **4**
Fern Valley DL15: Crook 5B **18**
Fernwood DH7: Sac 5B **4**
FERRYHILL **3D 30**
Ferryhill Carrs Local Nature Reserve **2G 31**
Ferryhill Ct. DL17: F'hll 3D **30**
Ferryhill Leisure Cen. **4F 31**
FERRYHILL STATION **5G 31**
Feversham Ter. DL17: F'hll 6G **31**
Festival Wlk. DL16: Spen 1F **29**
Fieldhouse La. DH1: Dur 6G **7**
Fieldhouse Ter. DH1: Dur 6H **7**
Fielding Ct. DL15: Crook 4A **18**
Field Vw. DH7: Bearp 6B **6**
Filby Dr. DH1: Carr 4H **9**
Finchale Av. DH1: Bras 1C **8**
Finchale Rd. DH1: Dur 1B **8**
(Canterbury Rd.)
DH1: Dur 4G **7**
(Durham Moor)
Finchale Vw. DH1: P Me 1H **7**
Findon Av. DH7: Sac 4C **4**
DH7: Wit G 6B **4**
Findon Hill DH7: Sac 5C **4**
Finney Ct. DH1: Dur 1C **32** (1B **12**)
Finney Ter. DH1: Dur 1C **32** (1B **12**)
Fir Av. DH1: Dur 2E **13**
DH7: B'don 2B **14**
Fir Pk. DH7: Ush M 1B **10**
Firs, The DH2: Kim 4F **5**
Fir Tree Cl. DH1: Dur 5E **9**
Firwood Ter. DL17: F'hll 6G **31**
Five Ho's. DL15: Crook 4A **18**
Flambard Rd. DH1: Dur 4H **7**
Flanders Way *DL15: Crook* *3C* ***18***
(off Kellet Sq.)
Flass Av. DH7: Ush M 1A **10**
Flassburn Rd. DH1: Dur 6G **7**
Flass St. DH1: Dur 1H **11**
Flass Ter. DH7: Ush M 1A **10**
Flass Va. DH1: Dur 1H **11**
Fleece Cotts. DH7: Edm 1B **4**
Fleece Ter. DH7: Edm 1B **4**
Fleming Way DL15: Will 4D **20**
Flora St. DL16: Spen 1E **29**
Folly Ter. DH1: P Me 2G **7**
Fordham Dr. DH7: Sac 3B **4**
Fordham Rd. DH1: Dur 3A **8**
Ford Rd. DH1: Dur 2B **8**
Forest Vw. DH7: B'don 2A **14**
Forge, The DH1: P Me 1G **7**
Foster Ter. DH6: Crox 1H **23**
Foundry Flds. DL15: Crook 3C **18**
Foundry Row DH6: Coxh 2B **26**
Fowlers Yd. DH1: Dur 2B **32**
Fox Covert DL16: Tudh 4A **24**
Foxton Ct. DH6: Kel 2G **27**
Foxton Way DH1: H Shin 6F **13**
Framwelgate DH1: Dur 1A **32** (1A **12**)
Framwelgate Bri. DH1: Dur 3A **32** (2A **12**)
Framwelgate Peth DH1: Dur 1A **32** (6H **7**)
Framwelgate Waterside
DH1: Dur 2B **32** (1A **12**)
FRAMWELLGATE MOOR 4G **7**
Framwellgate School Sports Cen. **3H 7**
Frankland La. DH1: Bras, Dur 1B **32** (6A **8**)
Frankland Rd. DH1: Dur 4H **7**
Frank St. DH1: Dur 1E **13**
Frederick St. Nth. DH7: Mead 2C **14**
Frederick St. Sth. DH7: Mead 2C **14**
Freemans Pl. DH1: Dur 2B **32** (1A **12**)
Freeman's Quay DH1: Dur 1B **32** (1A **12**)
Freeman's Quay Leisure Cen.
....**1B 32 (1A 12)**
Frensham Way DH7: Mead 1C **14**
Friarside DH7: Wit G 1B **6**
Friars Row DH1: Dur 6D **8**
Front St. DH1: Dur, P Me 3G **7**
DH1: Dur, S Hou 2E **13**
DH2: Plaw 3G **5**
DH6: Coxh 4C **26**
DH6: Crox 5H **23**
DH6: Kel 2G **27**
DH7: Edm 1B **4**
DH7: Lang M 5E **11**
DH7: Sac 3B **4**
DH7: Wit G 1A **6**
DL15: Helm R 4G **19**
DL15: Sunnb 6B **20**
DL16: Kirk M 6G **29**
DL16: Spen 1G **29**
DL16: Tudh 3H **23**
Front St. E. DH6: Coxh 3C **26**
DH6: Crox 1H **23**
Frosterley Cl. DH1: Dur 3B **8**
Fulforth Cl. DH7: Bearp 5A **6**
Fulforth Way DH7: Sac 3B **4**
Fyndoune DH7: Sac 5C **4**
Fyndoune Community College Sports Cen.
....**5C 4**
Fyndoune Way DH7: Wit G 6B **4**
Fynway DH7: Sac 5C **4**

G

Gair Ct. DH2: Nett 3F **5**
Gala Theatre & Cinema **2B 32**
Garden Av. DH1: Dur 3G **7**
Gardener Ct.
DL15: Crook 4B **18**

A-Z Durham 37

Rear Festival Wlk.—Snowdrop Cl.

Rear Festival Wlk. *DL16: Spen* 1F 29
(off Festival Wlk.)
Rectory Gdns. DL15: Will 4D 20
Rectory Ter. *DH1: Shin* 5E 13
(off High St.)
Red Briar Wlk. DH1: P Me 2G 7
Red Courts DH7: B'don 1C 14
Red Firs DH7: B'don 1B 14
Redhills La. DH1: Dur 1G 11
Red Hills Ter. DH1: Dur 2G 11
Red Hill Vs. DH1: Dur 1H 11
Redhouse Cl. DH7: Sac 5D 4
Red Ho. Gdns. DL15: Will 4A 20
Red Ridges DH7: B'don 6C 10
Redwood Flats DH7: B'don 1B 14
Reed Av. DL15: Oak 1C 20
Reform Pl. DH1: Dur 2A 32
Regents Ct. DH1: Dur 2F 13
Relley Gth. DH7: Lang M 6D 10
Relly Cl. DH7: Ush M 2B 10
Relly Path DH1: Dur 3G 11
Rennie St. DL17: F'hll 3C 30
Renny's La. DH1: Carr, Dur 1E 13
Renny St. DH1: Dur 1C 12
Rhodes Ter. DH1: Dur 3F 11
Richardson Ct. DL15: Will 4B 20
Richardson Pl. DL16: Kirk M 6F 29
Richard's Yd. DL15: Crook 3D 18
Richmond Cl. DL17: F'hll 4F 31
Richmond Ct. DH1: Dur 2B 8
Richmond Rd. DH1: Dur 2B 8
Richmond St. DL16: Byer G 6H 21
Ridgeside DL16: Kirk M 4G 29
Rievaulx Ct. DL16: Spen 4E 23
Riggs, The DH7: B'don 6C 10
Ripley Cl. DL16: Spen 6D 22
Ripley Ct. DH7: Sac 4C 4
Ripon Ct. DH7: Sac 4B 4
Ripon Dr. DL15: Will 6B 20
Ripon Rd. DH1: Dur 1B 8
Ripon Ter. DH2: Plaw 4G 5
Ritson Av. DH7: Bearp 6A 6
Rivergreen Cen. DH1: Dur 5A 8
Riverside Cen., The DH1: Dur 6B 8
River Vw. DL15: Will 5D 20
Robert Moore Cl. DH6: Bowb 3G 17
Roberts Sq. DL17: W Corn 6H 25
Robert St. DL16: Spen 2E 29
Robert Ter. DH6: Bowb 3H 17
Robinson Cl. DL15: Will 5B 20
Robinson Gro. DL15: Crook 4B 18
Robinson Ter. DL16: Byer G 6G 21
Robson Cres. DH6: Bowb 3H 17
Robson Ter. DH1: Shin 5D 12
Rochester Rd. DH1: Dur 2B 8
Rockcliffe Ter. DL16: Kirk M 6G 29
Rockingham Rd. DL15: Sunnb 6B 20
Rock Rd. DL16: Spen 2E 29
RODDYMOOR 1B 18
Roddymoor Ct. DL15: Rodd 1B 18
Roddymoor Rd. DL15: Rodd 2A 18
(Crook)
DL15: Rodd 1B 18
(Roddymoor)
Rogerson Cl. DH6: Crox 6H 15
Rogerson Ter. DH6: Crox 6H 15
Rokeby Sq. DH1: Dur 4G 11
Romaine Sq. *DH6: Bowb* 4H 17
(off Bede Ter.)
Roman Rd. DH7: B'don 3A 14
Romney Dr. DH1: Carr 4H 9
Roosevelt Rd. DH1: Dur 6D 8
Rosa St. DL16: Spen 1E 29
Rose Acre DH1: Shin 5E 13
Rosebay Ct. DL17: W Corn 5A 26
Rosebay Rd. DH7: Lang M 6E 11
Roseberry Cres. DL15: Crook 3B 18
Rose Cres. DH7: Sac 4D 4
Rosedale DL16: Spen 6E 23
Rosedale Gdns. *DH7: Edm* 1B 4
(off Tyzack St.)
Rosedale Rd. DH1: Carr 5H 9
Rosedale Ter. DL15: Will 4C 20
Rose Lea DH7: Wit G 6B 4
Rosemead Av. DL15: Will 4C 20
Rosemount DH1: P Me 1B 8
Rosemount Ter. *DL15: Crook* 3C 18
(off Albert St.)
Rosewood Cl. DH7: Sac 4C 4
Rosewood Wlk. DH7: Ush M 1A 10
Roslyn M. DH6: Coxh 3C 26
Rossmere DL16: Spen 5E 23
Ross Ter. DL17: F'hll 4E 31
Rotary Way DH1: P Me 1H 7
Rothbury Rd. DH1: Dur 2A 8
Rothery Wlk. DL16: Spen 1D 28
Rothman Cl. DL16: Tudh 4H 23
Roundhaven DH1: Dur 6G 11
Roundhill Way DL15: Will 3D 20
Rowan Ct. DL16: Spen 1G 29
Rowan Dr. DH1: Bras 1C 8
Rowan Lea DH7: B'don 1B 14
Rowan Tree Av. DH1: Dur 5E 9
Rowlandson Ter. DL17: F'hll 4F 31
Rowley Dr. DH7: Ush M 2B 10
Royal Cnr., The *DL15: Crook* 3C 18
(off North Ter.)
Royal Gro. DL15: Crook 3C 18
RUDD HILL 4G 31
Rudds Hill DL17: F'hll 4G 31
Rudkin Dr. DL15: Crook 4B 18
Rumby Hill Bank DL15: How W 6D 18
Rumby Hill La. DL15: Crook 6D 18
Runcie Rd. DH6: Bowb 5H 17
Rushey Gill DH7: B'don 1A 14
Rushmoor DL16: Spen 1G 29
Russell Pl. DL15: Will 3C 20
Russell's Yd. DL15: Will 4B 20
Russ St. DL15: Helm R 4G 19
Rutherford Ct. DL15: Will 5B 20
Rutherford Ter. DL17: F'hll 4E 31
Rutland Dr. DL15: Will 4C 20
Rutter St. DH7: Lang M 5E 11
Rydal Cl. DH7: Sac 4B 4
Rydal Dr. DL15: Crook 4E 19
Rydal Rd. DL17: F'hll 4D 30
Ryedale DH1: Carr 6H 9
Ryelands Way DH1: P Me 1A 8

S

SACRISTON 4C 4
Sacriston Ind. Est. DH7: Sac 4C 4
Sacriston La. DH7: Wit G 1A 6
Saddler's La. DH1: Dur 3B 32 (2A 12)
Saddler St. DH1: Dur 2B 32 (1A 12)
DL17: F'hll 3C 30
St Agathas Cl. DH7: B'don 6C 10
St Aidans Av. DH1: Dur 4H 7
St Aidan's Cres. DH1: Dur 1G 11
St Andrew's Ct. DH1: Dur 3C 32 (2B 12)
St Andrew's La. DL16: Spen 1G 29
St Andrew's Rd. DL16: Spen 6G 23
(not continuous)
St Andrew's Sq. DH7: B'don 1B 14
St Annes Ct. DH1: Dur 2A 32 (1A 12)
St Bede's Cl. DH1: Dur 2G 11
St Bedes Way DH7: Lang M 6E 11
St Brandon's Gro. DH7: B'don 1A 14
St Charles Rd. DL16: Tudh 4G 23
St Cuthberts Av. DH1: Dur 4G 7
St Cuthberts Dr. DH7: Sac 4B 4
ST CUTHBERT'S HOSPICE 4G 11
St Cuthberts Mdw. DH7: Sac 4B 4
St Cuthbert's Ter. DL17: F'hll 3C 30
St Cuthberts Wlk. DH7: Lang M 6E 11
St Cuthbert's Way DL17: W Corn 6A 26
St Davids Cl. DL16: Tudh 4H 23
St Giles Cl. DH1: Dur 1D 12
St Godric's Cl. DH1: Dur 2A 8
St Godrics Ct. DH1: Dur 2A 32
St Helen's Well DH1: Dur 3A 32 (2A 12)
St Hilds Ct. DH1: Dur 1E 13
St Hild's La. DH1: Dur 1C 12
St Johns Ct. DH7: Mead 1E 15
DH7: Sac 4B 4
DL16: Kirk M 6G 29
St John's Cres. DH6: Bowb 4H 17
St John's Gdns. DL15: Sunnb 5H 19
St Johns Rd. DH1: Dur 2G 11
DH7: Mead 1D 14
St Josephs Cl. DH1: Dur 1E 13
St Leonards DH1: Dur 6H 7
St Lukes Pl. DL17: F'hll 3D 30
St Margaret's Ct. DH1: Dur 3A 32 (2H 11)
St Margarets Gth. DH1: Dur 2H 11
St Margarets M. DH1: Dur 3A 32 (2H 11)
St Mary's Av. DL15: Crook 3C 18
St Mary's Cl. DH1: Shin 5D 12
St Mary's Gro. DL16: Tudh 4G 23
St Mary's Rd. DH1: Carr 5G 9
St Mary's Ter. DH6: Coxh 1A 26
St Monica Gro. DH1: Dur 2G 11
St Nicholas Dr. DH1: Dur 5F 7
St Oswald's Dr. DH1: Dur 6G 11
St Oswald Sq. DH1: P Me 2G 7
St Paul's Cl. DL16: Spen 1E 29
St Pauls Ct. DL16: Spen 2E 29
St Pauls Gdns. DL16: Spen 1E 29
St Pauls St. DL16: Spen 1E 29
St Stephen's Cl. DL15: Will 4C 20
St Stephens Ct. DL15: Will 3D 20
St Thomas' Cl. DL15: Will 4B 20
Salisbury Cres. DL17: W Corn 6B 26
Salisbury Rd. DH1: Dur 1C 8
Salisbury St. DL15: Will 5C 20
Salvin St. DH6: Crox 1H 23
(not continuous)
DL16: Spen 6H 23
Sanderson St. DH6: Coxh 3C 26
Sandgate DH6: Coxh 2B 26
Sandringham Rd. DL15: Crook 3D 18
Sands, The DH1: Dur 1C 32 (1B 12)
Sands Flats, The DH1: Dur 1C 32 (1B 12)
Satley Cl. DL15: Crook 4B 18
Sawmills La. DH7: B'don 1A 14
Saxby Dr. DL15: Sunnb 6A 20
Scafell Gdns. DL15: Crook 5D 18
Scardale Way DH1: Carr 5H 9
Scargill Dr. DL16: Spen 5F 23
School Av. DH6: Coxh 4B 26
DH6: Kel 1F 27
School Cl. DL16: Spen 6H 23
School Ct. DH7: Bro 3C 10
School La. DH1: Dur 5C 32 (3B 12)
School Row DL15: Oak 1C 20
School St. DH6: Turs 3G 25
School Vw. DL17: F'hll 6G 31
School Way DH1: Dur 6E 9
Scotts Cotts. DH1: Dur 1F 11
Scripton Gill DH7: B'don 1A 14
Scripton Gill Rd. DH7: B'don 2A 14
Scripton La. DH7: Bran 3A 14
Sedgefield Ent. Cen. DL16: Spen 5B 24
Seven Hills Ct. DL16: Spen 5H 23
Sewell Ct. DL15: Crook 4B 18
Shafto St. DL16: Byer G 6G 21
DL16: Spen 2E 29
Shaftsbury Dr. DH7: B'don 3A 14
Sharon Av. DH6: Kel 2F 27
Sharp Cres. DH1: Dur 6E 9
(not continuous)
Shaw St. DL16: Spen 1F 29
Shaw Wood Cl. DH1: Dur 6G 7
Shelley Cl. DL15: Crook 5A 18
Shepherds Ct. DH1: Dur 1E 13
Sheraton Ho. DH1: Dur 3G 11
SHERBURN HOUSE 4H 13
Sherburn Rd. DH1: Dur 1D 12
Sherburn Rd. Est. DH1: Dur 2E 13
Sherburn Rd. Flats *DH1: Dur* 1D 12
(off Sherburn Rd.)
Sheridan Dr. DL15: Crook 5A 18
SHINCLIFFE 5E 13
Shincliffe La. DH1: S Hou, Shin 4F 13
Shipley Ter. DL15: Crook 4E 19
Shire Chase DH1: P Me 1B 8
Shropshire Dr. DH1: Carr 1G 13
Sidegate DH1: Dur 1A 32 (1A 12)
Sidings, The DH1: Dur 1C 12
Siemens St. DL17: F'hll 3C 30
Silver Courts DH7: B'don 1B 14
Silver St. DH1: Dur 3A 32 (2A 12)
DL16: Spen 1F 29
Sir Bobby Robson Sports Cen., The 1A 10
Skippers Mdw. DH7: Ush M 2B 10
(not continuous)
Skipton Cl. DL17: F'hll 4F 31
Skylark Way DL16: Spen 2C 28
Slake Ter. DL17: W Corn 6A 26
Slater Pl. DH6: Bowb 5H 17
Sledmore Dr. DL16: Spen 6D 22
Sleetburn La. DH7: Lang M 5D 10
Smithfield DH1: P Me 1H 7
Sniperley (Park & Ride) 4F 7
Sniperley Gro. DH1: Dur 4F 7
Snowball Cl. DL15: Crook 4B 18
Snowden Ter. DL15: Will 5C 20
Snowdrop Cl. DL16: Spen 3D 28

South Acre—Wareham Way

South Acre DL15: Oak 1C 20
South Bailey DH1: Dur 5B 32 (3A 12)
South Ct. DL16: Spen 4D 28
South Cres. DH1: Dur 6H 7
South Durham Gymnastics Club *1F 29*
(off Merrington Vw.)
South End Vs. DL15: Crook 4C 18
Southfield Lodge DL15: Crook 4C 18
Southfield Way DH1: Dur 5G 7
South Grn. DH6: Hett 2C 24
Southlands DH6: Coxh 6H 17
South Lea DH7: Wit G 6B 4
South Rd. DH1: Dur 6B 32 (1H 15)
Southside DL17: F'hll 4D 30
South St. DH1: Dur 4A 32 (2A 12)
DL15: Crook 4D 18
DL15: Sunnb 6B 20
DL15: Will 4B 20
DL16: Spen 2F 29
South St. Banks DH1: Dur 5A 32 (3A 12)
Southstreet Banks DH1: Dur 4A 32 (3A 12)
South Ter. DH1: Dur 4G 7
DL15: Crook 3E 19
DL16: Spen 6G 23
South Vw. DH1: Dur 1D 12
DH2: Kim 4F 5
DH6: Hett 1C 24
DH7: Bearp 6B 6
DH7: Mead 2C 14
DH7: Sac 3B 4
DH7: Ush M 1A 10
DL15: Sunnb 5A 20
DL16: Kirk M 6G 29
DL16: Spen 4C 28
DL17: F'hll 3E 31
South Vw. Ter. DH7: Bearp 6B 6
Sowerby St. DH7: Sac 5B 4
Spectrum Leisure Cen. 4A 20
SPENNYMOOR 1F 29
Spennymoor Leisure Cen. 1F 29
Spinney, The DL16: Spen 6A 24
Springfield Pk. DH1: Dur 6G 7
Springfield Ter. DL15: Will 4A 20
Springside DH7: Sac 4C 4
Springwell Av. DH1: Dur 6G 7
Springwell Rd. DH1: Dur 6G 7
Spring Wood (Nature Reserve) 4D 22
Spruce Ct. DL16: Spen 2F 29
Stack Gth. DH7: B'don 6C 10
Staffordshire Dr. DH1: Carr 6H 9
Staindrop Rd. DH1: Dur 3B 8
Stanhope Cl. DH1: Dur 2B 8
DH7: Mead 1C 14
DL16: Spen 5G 23
DL17: F'hll 3F 31
Stanhope Ter. *DL15: Crook* *3D 18*
(off Wheatbottom)
Stank La. DH1: P Me 6G 5
Stanner's La. DL16: Spen 4A 22
Station App. DH1: Dur 2A 32 (1H 11)
Station Av. DH7: B'don 6C 10
Station Bank DH1: Dur 2A 32 (1A 12)
Station Ct. DL15: Crook 4C 18
Station La. DH1: Dur 1C 12
Station Rd. DH6: Coxh 4C 26
DH7: Mead 1C 14
DH7: Ush M 2A 10
DL17: W Corn 6H 25
Station Rd. E. DH6: Coxh 4C 26
Station Rd. W. DH6: Coxh 4C 26
Steadings, The DH1: Dur 4G 11
Steavenson St. DH6: Bowb 5H 17
Stephenson St. DL17: F'hll 4B 30
(not continuous)
Steward Dr. DL15: Crook 4B 18
Stobart St. DH7: Edm 1B 4
Stobb Cross La. DL17: Garm, W Corn 6D 26
Stobb Cross Rd. DL17: W Corn 6A 26
Stobbcross Vs. DL17: W Corn 1H 31
Stobb Ho. Vw. DH7: B'don 6A 10
Stockley Ct. DH7: Ush M 2C 10
Stockley La. DL15: Crook, Oak 1F 19
Stockton Rd. DH1: Dur 6C 32 (3B 12)
Stony Bank DL15: Will 5D 20
Store Cotts. DH7: Sac 1B 4
Stratford Gdns. DL17: F'hll 3E 31
Stratton St. DL16: Spen 2E 29
Strawberry La. DH1: H Shin 1E 17
DL17: F'hll 1D 30
Studley Dr. DL16: Spen 6D 22
Suffolk Way DH1: P Me 1B 8
Summerville DH1: Dur 2H 11
SUNDERLAND BRIDGE 5H 15
Sunderland Rd. DH1: Dur 1D 12
SUNNYBROW 5H 19
Surrey Pl. DL15: Will 4C 20
Surtees Av. DH6: Bowb 4H 17
Surtees Dr. DH1: Dur 1G 11
DL15: Will 4D 20
Surtees Ter. DL17: F'hll 6G 31
Sutherland Pl. DH1: Dur 2E 13
Sutton St. DH1: Dur 2A 32 (2H 11)
Swale Ct. DH7: Lang M 6D 10
Swingfield Cl. DL15: Crook 2B 18
Swinside Dr. DH1: Carr 5G 9
Sycamore Ct. DL16: Spen 1G 29
Sycamore Gdns. DL15: Crook 4B 18
Sycamore Gro. DL15: Will 4D 20
Sycamore Pk. DH7: B'don 6B 10
Sycamore Rd. DH2: Kim 4F 5
DL17: W Corn 6H 25

T

Tail-upon-End La. DH6: Bowb 3G 17
Tangmere DL16: Spen 5E 23
TAN HILLS 3G 5
Tanmeads DH2: Nett 3F 5
Tate Av. DH6: Kel 2F 27
Taylor Av. DH7: Bearp 6B 6
Taylor Ct. DH1: Carr 4H 9
DL15: Will 4B 20
Teasdale Ter. DH1: Dur 1F 13
Tees Cres. DL16: Spen 6F 23
Teikyo University of Japan in Durham 4A 12
Telford Cl. DH1: H Shin 1F 17
Temperance Ter. DL15: Bill R 1C 18
Tennyson Ter. DL15: Crook 2B 18
Tenter Ter. DH1: Dur 2A 32 (1A 12)
Terrace, The DH7: Mead 1D 14
Territorial La. DH1: Dur 3C 32 (2B 12)
The . . . . . .
Names prefixed with 'The' for example 'The Avenue' are indexed under the main name such as 'Avenue, The'
THINFORD 5C 24
Thinford La. DH6: Hett 5C 24
Thinford Rd. DH6: Turs 4G 25
Thinford St. DH6: Hett 5F 25
Thirlmere DL16: Spen 5E 23
Thirlmere Rd. DL17: F'hll 4D 30
Thistle Cl. DL16: Spen 2D 28
Thistleflat Rd. DL15: Crook 4A 18
Thistle Rd. DH7: Lang M 1F 15
Thomas St. DH7: Sac 5B 4
DL16: Spen 1F 29
Thompson St. DL16: Spen 6F 23
Thorn Cl. DL16: Spen 3D 28
Thorndale Rd. DH1: Carr 5H 9
Thornley Cl. DH7: Ush M 2B 10
Thrislington Cl. DL17: W Corn 6H 25
Thrislington Ind. Est. DL17: W Corn 1H 31
Thropton Cl. DH1: H Shin 6F 13
Thrush Cross Pl. DH1: Dur 6F 9
Thurstan Grange DL17: W Corn 6H 25
Timothy Ter. DL16: Spen 2E 29
Tindale Av. DH1: Dur 4G 7
Tinklers La. DH1: Dur 2D 32 (1B 12)
Tiree Cl. DH7: B'don 6C 10
Todd St. DL16: Spen 1E 29
TODHILLS 6E 21
Toll Ho. Rd. DH1: Dur 1F 11
Top Gear Indoor Karting 1G 13
Towngate Bus. Cen. DH7: Lang M 6E 11
Trafalgar St. DL17: F'hll 5G 31
Trevelyan Pl. DL15: Crook 4A 18
Trinity Gdns. DL15: Will 4C 20
Troutbeck Cl. DL16: Spen 5E 23
Trout's La. DH1: Dur 2D 6
TUDHOE 4H 23
TUDHOE GRANGE 5G 23
Tudhoe Hall Farm Ct. DL16: Tudh 3F 23
Tudhoe Ind. Est. DL16: Tudh 3H 23
Tudhoe La. DL16: Tudh 4G 23
Tudhoe Moor DL16: Spen 6H 23
Tudhoe Pk. Ct. DL16: Spen 5G 23
Tudhoe Pk. Vs. DL16: Spen 5G 23
TUDHOE VILLAGE 3F 23
Tunstall Av. DH6: Bowb 4H 17
Turnbull Cl. DH1: Dur 1E 13
Turners Bldgs. DH7: Wit G 1A 6
TURSDALE 3G 25
Tursdale Bus. Pk. DH6: Turs 3G 25
Tursdale Rd. DH6: Bowb 6H 17
Tursdale Works DH6: Turs 3G 25
Tweddle Ter. DH6: Bowb 4G 17
Tweed Rd. DL16: Tudh 5H 23
Tyne Cres. DL16: Spen 6F 23
Tyzack St. DH7: Edm 1B 4

U

Ugly La. DH2: Nett 3F 5
Ullerdale Cl. DH1: Carr 5H 9
Ullswater Cl. DL16: Spen 6H 23
Ullswater Cres. DL15: Crook 4D 18
Ullswater Rd. DL17: F'hll 4D 30
Union Pl. DH1: Dur 6C 32
UNIVERSITY HOSPITAL OF NORTH DURHAM 5G 7
University of Durham Botanic Garden 5B 12
Uphill Dr. DH7: Sac 4D 4
Uplands DL15: Crook 3B 18
Uplands Cl. DL15: Crook 3B 18
Up. Church St. DL16: Spen 6H 23
USHAW MOOR 1A 10
Ushaw Ter. DH7: Ush M 1A 10
Ushaw Vs. DH7: Ush M 1A 10
(not continuous)

V

Valeside DH1: Dur 1H 11
Valley Vw. DH6: Crox 1H 23
DH7: Sac 5B 4
DH7: Ush M 2B 10
Verdun Ter. DL17: W Corn 6H 25
Vicarage Flats DH7: B'don 1B 14
Vicarage Gdns. DL15: Will 5C 20
Vicarage Rd. *DL17: W Corn* *6A 26*
(off High St.)
Vicarage Ter. DH6: Coxh 4C 26
Victoria Av. DH7: B'don 1C 14
DL15: Crook *3D 18*
(off Osborne Gdns.)
Victoria Cl. DH6: Bowb 3H 17
Victoria Ct. DH1: Dur 3G 7
DH7: Ush M 1A 10
Victoria Gdns. DL16: Spen 2E 29
Victoria St. DH7: Sac 4C 4
DL15: Crook *3C 18*
(off Whitfield St.)
DL15: Will 3C 20
DL16: Spen 2E 29
Victoria Ter. DH1: Dur 1H 11
DH6: Coxh 4B 26
Victor Ter. DH7: Bearp 6B 6
Viewforth Vs. DH1: Dur 1F 11
Village Farm DL17: F'hll 3D 30
Villas, The DL17: F'hll 4B 30
Villa St. DL16: Spen 2E 29
Villiers St. DL16: Spen 6F 23
Vine St. DL16: Byer G 6G 21
DL16: Spen 6F 23
Viola Cres. DH7: Sac 5C 4
Vyners Cl. DL16: Kirk M, Spen 4G 29
Vyner St. DL16: Spen 1E 29

W

Waddington St. DH1: Dur 1H 11
Wakenshaw Rd. DH1: Dur 6D 8
Waldridge La. DH2: Ches M, Wald 1F 5
Walkergate DH1: Dur 2B 32 (1A 12)
Walker St. DH6: Bowb 5H 17
Walker Ter. DL17: F'hll 4G 31
Walkworth La. DL16: Spen 4G 23
Wallington Ct. DL16: Spen 1E 29
Walton Ct. DL15: Crook 4D 18
Walton's Ter. DH7: New B 3A 10
Walworth Rd. DL17: F'hll 2E 31
Wanless Ter. DH1: Dur 1C 32 (1B 12)
Wansbeck Cl. DL16: Spen 5E 23
Wantage Rd. DH1: Carr 4H 9
Wardles Ter. DH1: Dur 3A 32
Wareham Way DL15: Sunnb 6A 20

A-Z Durham 43